THE
WEXFORD
WAR DEAD

THE
WEXFORD
WAR DEAD

Tom Burnell
& Margaret Gilbert

N

First published 2009

Nonsuch Publishing
119 Lower Baggot Street
Dublin 2
Ireland
www.nonsuchireland.com

British Library Cataloguing in Publication Data.
A catalogue record for this book is available from the British Library.

ISBN 978 1 8458 8964 7

Typesetting and origination by The History Press
Printed in Great Britain

Contents

Foreword

The only axe being ground in the pages which follow is that of the steel of truth, tempered as it has been by decades of falsehood and neglect about the Irish involvement in the Great War. The 874 names for Wexford's dead alone considerably exceed the total death-toll for all sides, and for none, in the Easter Rising in 1916. Yet for decades the people of Wexford were denied the simple truth about the fate that had consumed so many of the men from the county, from Allen to Zander: about what had happened to the fourteen Wexford Byrnes who were killed in the Great War, say, or the thirty-six Wexford Doyles.

One of those Doyles was Father Denis Doyle, of the many gallant Irish chaplains of the Great War who gave his life while tending to his men. He has vanished from memory, as have his many namesakes – such as the Doyle brothers, of Kilmore. One, Patrick Doyle of the Royal Irish Regiment was wounded three times in action, and spent eight months recuperating in Salonika. He died of his fourth and final wounds in September 1918, and is buried in Palestine. His brother John was already dead, lost when HN HMS *Laurentic* was torpedoed and lost with all hands the year before.

Another Doyle from Kilmore, also called Patrick, died when SS *Formby* was torpedoed in 1917, and was lost with all hands. One of his shipmates was Edward Hennessey, and he too was from Kilmore. The only body to float ashore was that of stewardess Annie O'Callaghan, aged 52, of Waterford. And two Wexford Doyles were to perish on SS *Ugyemi*, sunk in November 1917, Patrick from Campile, who was drowned outright, and P.J., who died later of his injuries. And when HMS *Goliath* was sunk in the Dardanelles in May 1915, she took five Wexford men with her: M.J. Allen, W Barron, Patrick Kavanagh, William Dempsey and Michael Meyler.

The vast majority of the Wexford dead, as with all Irish counties, lost their lives fighting as soldiers – with the British army, but also with the armies of Canada, Australia, New Zealand and the USA. All those lives were of unrealised potential – yet some stories reach out from the pages of the dead, and touch your heart with what Ireland lost through these terrible years. Take this, for example.

CANAVAN, Michael: Rank: Lance Corporal. Regiment or Service: Irish Guards Unit: 1st Bn. Date of death: 8 August 1915. Service No: 5872. Killed in action. From an article in the *People,* 'Although born in Irishtown, Dublin about 24 years ago, Lance Corporal Michael Canavan lived since his childhood with his uncle Mr James Canavan, Kilcavan, Tara Hill, Gorey. A young man of fine physique, he was of a cheerful and unassuming manner and deservedly popular.

He was an ardent and sincere Gaelic Leaguer, and as a musician and Irish step dancer, he was known all over Ireland, having won the all Ireland hornpipe competition at the Wexford Feis in the year of 1906, and a similar distinction at the Wicklow Feis the following year. He answered his coutries call towards the end of last year joining the Irish Guards (2nd Battalion) and on St Patricks day last he was awarded first place in the Regimental Irish Step dancing competition by the Earl of Kerry (Colonel).'

An Irish Irishman, in other words, with so much to give; and all lost by August 1915, even before the great slaughters of '16 and '17 were to begin. Another touching story is of Albert Buttle, the son of a Wexford bacon-curer and merchant. In addition to his skills with rashers, young Albert was also a musician; one can imagine him, a studious, earnest, Protestant shopkeeper's boy, who was already frail of health before he participated in the terrible battles of 1916. Commissioned from the ranks, he was invalided out of the front line, and spent a year in barracks in Tipperary, from where he wangled his way back to front line duties. He was fatally wounded with the Royal Irish Rifles a few days before war's end, and is buried in Belgium.

One man foreshadowed the fate of so many Irish dead, and not just those of Wexford. William Charles Barton was a pro-Carsonite unionist who rather imprudently before the war – according to the later death notices – had committed himself 'to the fiction of Catholic intolerance,' prompting great demonstrations against him in Wexford. Perhaps out of merely prudential motives, he then enlisted in the pro-Home Rule Irish National Volunteers, before joining the British army with the outbreak of war. Commissioned into the Royal Irish Rifles, he was gassed in 1915, and again – fatally – in 1918. 'The fiction of Catholic intolerance' proved to be not such a fiction after all. Wexford was one of half a dozen southern Irish counties which after the war was to introduce an employment-ban on all ex-servicemen, even disqualifying their children from county educational-scholarships.

The many-layered complexity of these things 'Irishness' and 'identity' may possibly be glimpsed in the fate of Wexfordman Michael Goodwin, whose brief entry records that he was recruited for the army in Dublin and was killed on the first day of the Somme, 1 July 1916, with the 9th Inniskilling Fusiliers. Which suggests (although without proving) that he was a southern Irish Unionist, who had pre-war enlisted in the Loyal Dublin Volunteers, which, with the Loyal Wicklow Volunteers, was to give the 9th Inniskillings of the 36th 'Ulster' Division such a pronounced 'southern' feeling.

But for all I know, Michael Goodwin was not a Unionist in any sense, and the strange tides of war had simply brought him into rather unexpected company for the last days of his life. Certainly the vast majority of the Wexford men who died in the Great War would have been of nationalist stock, whether they were professional soldiers or sailors, or were war-time volunteers. Nonetheless, it would be rash to rush to judgment as to why any single individual enlisted: all the reasons that you might possibly imagine, and others you never could, underwrite most human conduct.

So what comes overwhelmingly from these pages is not any sense of a binding 'identity' (whatever that negotiable commodity might mean), but rather of an enormous sense of loss: a loss of life, a loss of human love and a loss of cultural potential. Turn, please, if you will, to the entry for young Michael Keenan, serving with the Leinster Regiment, and read his superb accounts of battle, written in letters to a neighbour, and which by chance were published in the local newspaper.

And then wonder at the writer who was taken from us, and wonder also at what happened to the rest of his letters, those which were not vouchsafed to us by the accidents of journalism. For they almost certainly suffered that fate which nearly consumed all public memory of our Irish dead of this war, our own war: indeed, our very war of wars.

So, lest we forget – *again*.

Kevin Myers

Terminology

Killed in action: The soldier was killed during engagement with the enemy.

Died of wounds: The soldier was not killed outright and may have made it back to the Regiments Aid post or Casualty Clearing Station before he eventually died of his wounds.

Died at home: Death by drowning, suicide, accident or illness in the UK or Ireland. Home in these cases means back in the UK or Ireland and not necessarily where he lived. Many times I have come across this and it turned out to be that the soldier died in a hospital.

Died of wounds at home: The soldier was not killed outright and may have made it back to the Regiments Aid post or Casualty Clearing Station before he eventually died of his wounds back in the UK or Ireland.

Died: Can mean death by drowning, suicide, accident or illness.

Sources: The Commonwealth War Graves Commission, Soldiers Died in the Great War. Soldiers of the Great War, The New Library and Archives Canada. The National Archives of Australia. Nominal Rolls of the New Zealand Expeditionary Force, De Ruvigny's Roll of Honour, Wexford and Wicklow newspapers of the period, The War Graves of the British Empire, Commonwealth War Graves Commission registers for the Irish Free State and Ireland's Memorial Records.

A

ALLAN, Bernard: Rank: Private. Regiment or Service: Royal Irish Regiment. Unit: 2nd Bn. Formerly he was with the Royal Dublin Fusiliers where his number was 30643. Date of death: 23 August 1918. Service No: 6527. Born in St Augustine's, Birmingham. Enlisted in Waterford while living in Newbawn, Co. Wexford. Died of wounds. Age at death: 20.

Supplementary information: Son of James and Christina Allen. Born at Liverpool. Grave or Memorial Reference: V.A.8. Cemetery: Bagneux British Cemetery, Gezauncourt in France.

ALLEN, James: Rank: Private. Regiment or Service: Royal Irish Regiment. Unit: 1st Bn. Age at death: 23. Date of death: 23 February 1915. Service No: 4467. Born in New Ross, Co. Wexford. Enlisted in New Ross. Killed in action.

Supplementary information: Son of John (a Shoemaker in Mary Street) and Bridget Allen of Upper Mary Street, New Ross, Co. Wexford. Listed in the *Enniscorthy Guardian* as **John ALLEN**. From an article in the *Enniscorthy Guardian*:

ROSS MEN KILLED AT THE FRONT.

On Saturday last, Mr John Allen, shoemaker, of Mary Street, New Ross, received the melancholy intelligence from the War Office that his son, John, belonging to the 18th Royal Irish Regiment, was killed in the recent fighting in France. The young man was well known and popular in the town and was home on leave some months ago. Great sympathy is felt with his father who enjoys a wide popularity amongst his fellow townsmen.

Grave or Memorial Reference: Panel 33. Memorial: Ypres (Menin Gate) Memorial in Belgium.

ALLEN, James: Rank: Private. Regiment or Service: Royal Munster Fusiliers. Unit: 9th Bn. Age at death: 34. Date of death: 22 April 1916. Service No: 1325. Born in Murrintown, Co. Wexford. Enlisted in Penrhiwceiber, Wales while living in Wexford. Died of wounds.

Supplementary information: Son of John and Margaret Allen of Murrintown, Co. Wexford. Grave or Memorial Reference: III.H.21. Cemetery: Bethune Town Cemetery in France.

ALLEN, James: Rank: Private. Regiment or Service: The King's (Liverpool Regiment). Unit: 1st Bn. Age at death: 26. Date of death: 16 May 1915. Service No: 9615. Born in Birkenhead. Enlisted in Birkenhead while living in Birkenhead in Cheshire. Killed in action.

Supplementary information: Son of John Mary Allen of Irishtown, New Ross, Co. Wexford. Grave or Memorial Reference: Panels 6 to 8. Memorial: Le Touret Memorial in France.

ALLEN, Lawrence: Rank: Gunner. Regiment or Service: Royal Field Artillery. Unit: 'D' Bty. 3rd Bde. Age at death: 38. Date of death: 28 September 1918. Service

No: 202011. Born in Wexford. Enlisted in Birkinhead. Died in Mesopotamia.

Supplementary information: Son of James and Mary Allen of Harry Street, New Ross, Co. Wexford. Husband of E. Allen of 58 Back, St Anne Street, Birkinhead. From an article in the *Echo*, 'Another New Ross soldier to meet his death on the battlefield was Private J Allen, aged about 25 years, a native of Irishtown, who went to reside at Birkinhead six or seven years ago, and volunteered his services from there.' Grave or Memorial Reference: 149. Cemetery: Kirechkoi-Hortakoi Military Cemetery in Greece.

ALLEN, Michael Joseph: Rank: Seaman. Regiment or Service: Royal Naval Reserve. Unit: HMS *Goliath*. Age at death: 32. Date of death: 13 May 1915. Service No: 3623B.

Supplementary information: Son of Michael and Catherine Allen of New Ross, Co. Wexford. Husband of Marianne Allen of 8 Derby Road, Weaste, Manchester. From an article in the *Enniscorthy Guardian*, 'Michael Allen whose mother lives at Cross Lane, New Ross was killed at the Dardanelles last week. HMS *Goliath* was sunk by three torpedoes from German destroyer 'Muvanet-I-Milet', she blew up and capsized immediately taking 570 of her 750 crew including the Captain to a watery grave.' Grave or Memorial Reference: 8. Memorial: Plymouth Naval Memorial UK.

ANDERSON, Hans: Rank: Private. Regiment or Service: Manchester Regiment. Unit: 20th Bn. Formerly he was with the Lancashire Fusiliers where

James Anderson.

his number was 4320. Date of death: 12 October 1916. Service No: 40273. Born in New Ross, Co. Wexford. Enlisted in Bury, Lancs while living in Waterford. Died of wounds. Age at death: 30. Grave or Memorial Reference: II.F.255. Cemetery: Bailleul Communal Cemetery Extension (Nord) in France.

ANDERSON, James: Rank: Private. Regiment or Service: Leinster Regiment. Unit: 2nd Bn. Age at death: 37. Date of death: 20 October 1914. Service No: 5624. Born in New Ross, Co. Wexford. Enlisted in Dublin. Killed in action.

Supplementary information: Son of William and Ellen Anderson of 3 Trinity Place, Wexford. Also served in the South African War. From an article in the *Enniscorthy Guardian*:

> Private James Anderson, Leinster Regiment has been missing since the Battle of the Rivers on October 18 1914, and though his parents, who reside at Trinity Place, Wexford, have made anxious enquiries about him, no trace of his whereabouts have been discovered. He had fifteen years service and was all through the second South African campaign with the 2nd Battalion, Leinster Regiment. He was drafted out with the first Expeditionary Force to Flanders and participated in the famous retreats in the earlier stages of the war.

Grave or Memorial Reference: 2.F.17. Cemetery: Canadian Cemetery No. 2, Neuville-St. Vaast in France.

ARMSTRONG, Joseph: Rank: Private. Regiment or Service: Royal Dublin Fusiliers. Unit: 10th Bn. Age at death: 40. Date of death: 15 December 1916. Service No: 25465. Born in Dublin. Enlisted in Dublin. Died of wounds.

Supplementary information: Husband of Mary Armstrong of Fethard, Co. Wexford. Grave or Memorial Reference: VIII.B.1. Cemetery: Contay British Cemetery, Contay in France.

ASKEW, John Amos: Rank: Able Seaman. Regiment or Service: Mercantile Marine. Unit: SS *Dalewood*. Age at death: 34. Date of death: 26 February 1918. Grave or Memorial Reference: Near the north-east corner. Cemetery: Kilmore (Grange) Graveyard, Wexford.

ATKINS, Samuel: Rank: Private. Regiment or Service: Royal Irish Regiment. Unit: 2nd Bn. Age at death: 40. Date of death: 24 May 1915. Service No: 6885. Born in Wexford. Enlisted in Longford while living in Wexford. Killed in action.

Supplementary information: Son of Samuel Atkins of South Main Street, Wexford. Grave or Memorial Reference: Panel 33. Memorial: Ypres (Menin Gate) Memorial in Belgium.

AUSTIN, John: Rank: Private. Regiment or Service: Royal Irish Regiment. Unit: 2nd Bn. Date of death: 25 September 1914. Service No: 5898. Born in Ballycarreal, Co. Wexford. Enlisted in Wexford while living in Ballycarreal. Killed in action. He has no known grave but is commemorated on the La Ferte-Sous-Jouarre-Memorial in France.

J. A. ASKEW
ABLE SEAMAN
S.S. "DALEWOOD"
26TH FEBRUARY 1918 AGE 34

AN ABSENT FACE
A MEMORY DEAR

John Amos
Askew.

B

BARBER, Thomas: Rank: Private. Regiment or Service: Royal Irish Regiment. Unit: 2nd Bn. Date of death: 27 September 1918. Service No: 3637. Born in Gorey, Co. Wexford. Enlisted in Dublin while living in Gorey. Died. He has no known grave but is commemorated on Panel 5. Vis-En-Artois Memorial in France.

BARKER, Philip: Rank: Private. Regiment or Service: Royal Irish Regiment. Unit: 'B' Company, 2nd Bn. Date of death: 21 August 1918. Service No: 11493. Born in Rowe Street, Wexford. Enlisted in Wexford. Died of wounds. Age at death: 22.

Supplementary information: Son of Mrs Elizabeth Barker of Duke Street, Wexford. Grave or Memorial Reference: A.14. Cemetery: Railway Cutting Cemetery, Courcelles-Le-Comte in France.

BARLOW, T. J.: Rank: Airman 1st Class. Regiment or Service: Royal Flying Corps. Unit: 57th Sqdn. Age at death: 24. Date of death: 2 October 1917. Service No: 402818.

Supplementary information: Son of Mrs A. Canning of Broadway, Lady's Island, Co. Wexford. Grave or Memorial Reference: XII.B.15. Cemetery: Harlebeke New British Cemetery in Belgium.

BARNWELL, Sylvester: Rank: Private. Regiment or Service: Canadian Infantry (Manitoba Regiment). Unit: 8th Bn. Age at death: 30. Date of death: 28 April 1917. Service No: 187231.

Supplementary information: Son of Thomas and Mary Barnwell of Mayglass, Wexford. Information from his enlistment documents: Eyes: grey. Complexion: ruddy. Hair: dark brown. Address on enlistment: none. Date of birth: 1 August 1887. Place of birth: Co. Wexford. Marital status: single. Name and address of next of kin: Mother, Mary Barnwell, Mayglass, Ballycoglay, Co. Wexford. Date of attestation: 4 November. Location of attestation: Winnipeg. Occupation on enlistment: farmer. From an article in a Wexford newspaper:

Private Sylvester Barnwell, Rain Street, Wexford, has been reported missing since April 28th, and though diligent inquiries have been instituted by the authorities as to his whereabouts, no clue as to his fate has been forthcoming.

The only information available on the subject is contained in a report submitted by Private R Cobben, a wounded Canadian, who stated "Barnwell went over with me in the advance on Arleux and was still by me when we had gone half a mile. Then we suddenly missed him, and I was about the last to see him. He had only got about half way, then so that he can't be a prisoner, since we took our objective. Whether he got turned up by a shell or got wounded and went back we could not find out. We were keeping very close to our own barrage, and we missed him badly, for he was carrying two buckets of ammunition."

Private Barnwell, who was well and popularly known in Wexford prior to his emigration to Canada, had been serving with the Canadian Contingent for some time. The news that he has been so long missing will be learned with regret by his many friends in his native town.

Grave or Memorial Reference: V.E.18. Cemetery: Orchard Dump Cemetery, Arleux-En-Gohelle in France.

BARRON, William: Rank: Seaman. Regiment or Service: Royal Naval Reserve. Unit: HMS *Goliath*. Age at death: 22. Date of death: 13 May 1915. Service No: 2842A.

Supplementary information: Son of William and Mary Barron of Ballyhack, Arthurstown. Co. Wexford. From an article in the *Enniscorthy Guardian*:

William Barron.

Amongst those who lost their lives on HMS *Goliath* at the Dardanelles naval engagement recently was a young man named Barron from Ballyhack. He is the son of Mr William Barron, of Ballyhack and there are two other brothers of his in the navy who at with their ships at other places. The deceased was on the naval reserve, and was called up at the outbreak of the war. He went through several engagements in German East Africa, and was returning home when his ship was ordered to the Dardanelles. So severe was the damage done to the ship in which he served that it went down in four or five minutes of being struck. There are several other young men from Ballyhack and district in the navy. In the same ship in which young Barron lost his life several men from Passage went down with it also.

A Passage man who was serving in the same ship was transferred to another the very day before the disaster. HMS *Goliath* was sunk by three torpedoes from German destroyer 'Muvanet-I-Milet', she blew up and capsized immediately taking 570 of her 750 crew including the Captain to a watery grave.

From an article in the *People*, 1915:

Many who cross the ferry from Ballyhack Co. Wexford to Passage East in Co Waterford, with the strong-armed ferryman, Patsey Barron, are not aware that Patsey comes of a brave fighting family whose members are in the thick of the great world conflict now raging. Patsey, quiet, unobtrusive, and unassuming, is one of those brave fearless men who without boast or braggart face danger and death unflinchingly. Three of his nephews, Tom, Jim and Bill, joined the navy. Tom and Jim are at present keeping that ceaseless vigil in the North Sea which is holding in a grip of blood and steel one of the mighty war arms of the German foe. Bill, is a brave lad, with all the traditional valour of the Celt, went down with his ship the 'Goliath'. He has given all that a brave man can give in the mighty combat. Patsey, who today quietly crosses and re-crosses the silver streak of water between the two counties saw 21 year's service as did also his brother William.

Grave or Memorial Reference: 8. Memorial: Plymouth Naval Memorial UK.

BARRY, John: Rank: Private. Regiment or Service: Royal Dublin Fusiliers. Unit: 7th Bn. Age at death: 26. Date of death: 7 December 1915. Service No: 17986. Born in Kilmore Quay, Co. Wexford. Enlisted in Maesteg while living in Hereford. Killed in action in the Balkans.

Supplementary information: Son of John and Bridget Barry of Neamstown,

Michael Barry.

Kilmore Quay, Wexford. Memorial: Doiran Memorial in Greece.

BARRY, Michael: Rank: Private. Regiment or Service: Welsh Regiment. Unit: 2nd Bn. Age at death: 28. Date of death: 23 July 1918. Service No: 52569. Born in Kilmore, Co. Wexford. Enlisted in Cardiff while living in Kilmore. Killed in action.

Supplementary information: Son of John and Bridget Barry of Neamstown, Kilmore Quay. Grave or Memorial Reference: P.26. Cemetery: Cambrin Military Cemetery in France.

BARRY, Patrick Joseph: Rank: Private. Regiment or Service: The King's (Liverpool Regiment). Unit: 1st/7th Bn. Age at death: 35. Date of death: 3 October 1917. Service No: 203019.

Supplementary information: Son of John

John Barry.

and Ellen Barry of 'Fort' Rosslare, Co. Wexford. Grave or Memorial Reference: III.C.20. Cemetery: Abbeville Communal Cemetery Extension in France.

BARTON, Charles Erskine: Rank: Captain. Regiment or Service: Royal Irish Rifles. Unit: 4th Bn. Attached to the 2nd Bn. Age at death: 35. Date of death: 23 August 1918.

Supplementary information: Son of the late C.W. Barton, D.L. of Glendalough House, Annamoe, Co. Wicklow. Husband of Norah Deane Barton, of 4 Mount Pleasant Villas, Bray, Co. Wicklow. Died of wounds. From an article in the *Enniscorthy Guardian* in 1918:

> Captain C Erskine Barton, RIR, formerly of Ruane Cottage, New Ross, died of the 23rd inst, at the age of 36 at an hospital at the Base, in France, from gas poisoning. He had been resident at Ruane Cottage since about 1910, volunteered for the war in August 1914, and went to France in May 1915, being subsequently invalided home from gas poisoning. He had only returned to the front a few weeks when he was again severely gassed on the 14th of the present month. He had been through several engagements, including the battle of Hill 60. He was the second son of the late Mr Charles W Barton of Glendalough House, Annamoe, Co. Wicklow, and his younger brother; Lieut Thos E Barton, fell in action in 1916.
>
> Captain Barton, who was a Magistrate for the Co. Wexford, used to sit at the Arthurstown petty sessions when residing at Ruane Cottage. He was a former member of the New Ross Agricultural Show Society, and took a practical interest in fowl, having

exhibited some fine specimens at the shows. In politics he was a follower of Sir Edward Carson, and was for some time secretary of the Wexford Unionist Association, and his experience with the ways of political life was shown in the storm which surrounded his name in 1914, when he incautiously committed himself to the fiction of Catholic intolerance in South Wexford. This pronouncement produced an indignant protest, and a public meeting of repudiation was held at Ballykelly in the district where he was residing at the time when the matter was exposed and evidence of the privilege enjoyed by him was given by his Catholic neighbours referred to. He joined the New Ross Corps of the National Volunteers a short time previous to volunteering for the war.

Grave or Memorial Reference: II.D.41. Cemetery: Terlincthun British Cemetery, Wimille in France.

BARTON, John: Rank: Private. Regiment or Service: Leinster Regiment. Unit: 1st Bn. Date of death: 19 April 1915. Service No: 9062. Born in New Ross, Co. Wexford. Enlisted in Dublin. Killed in action. Grave or Memorial Reference: III.A.7. Cemetery: Ypres Town Cemetery in Belgium.

BASS, Joseph: (Also listed as **BASS, J.W.**) Rank: Private. Regiment or Service: Irish Guards. Unit: 1st Bn. Date of death: 2 December 1915. Service No: 6401. Born in Ballyoughter, Co. Wexford. Enlisted in Gorey, Co. Wexford. Killed in action. There is a picture of Joseph Warren Bass in the *Enniscorthy Guardian* around this time but it is too dark to add.

The article states:

Widespread regret was felt in Gorey when the news became known of the death of Private Joseph W Bass. 1st Irish Guards, eldest son of Mr Thos A Bass of Carrigbeg House, Gorey. He was killed in action near the village of Les Mesnil in France, on December 2nd. He joined the colours early in the war and had seen much active service on the Western Front. Just before being killed, his company were in a very hot engagement, and were about being relieved when he was struck down by a piece of shrapnel. Before going to the front, Mr Bass was engaged in business in Gorey for a number of years in connection with the firm of Mr E. W. Reynolds and Mr Percy Hutchinson. He was of a most amiable disposition and popular everywhere.

He was cousin to Mr George W Warren, auctioneer, with whom and his family, the deepest sympathy is felt as well as with their bereaved parents of this gallant soldier who gave up a promising career in the business world to do his duty at the front. He fought through neary ten months of a rigorous campaign and finally laid down his life like a hero.

From an article in the *People*, 1915:

Word has just reached Gorey that Private Joseph Warren Bass of the 1st Irish Guards, and eldest son of Mr Thos, A, Bass, Carrickbeg, near Gorey, had been killed in action at le-Mesnel in northern France, on the 2nd inst.

Very shortly after the outbreak of hostilities he volunteered for active service, joining the above distinguished regiment. In Gorey, where he had been in business in the establishment of Messrs W, Reynolds, and subsequently at Mr Percy, S, Hutchinson, he was extremely popular and when the sad news of his death reached Gorey the greatest sorrow was felt on all sides. The deceased was a nephew of Mrs Warren, Gorey Avenue, to whose family the deepest sympathy is tendered on this sad occasion.

Grave or Memorial Reference: I.E.11. Cemetery: Rue-Du-Bacquerot No 1 Military Cemetery, Laventie in France.

BATTERTON, William: Rank: Private. Regiment or Service: Royal Inniskilling Fusiliers. Unit: 7th/8th Bn. Age at death: 27. Date of death: 16 September 1918. Service No: 48624. Formerly he was with the Royal Irish Regiment where his number was 5290. Enlisted in Enniscorthy. Killed in action.

Supplementary information: Son of William Batterton of 57 Irish Street, Enniscorthy, Co. Wexford. Grave or Memorial Reference: III. A.19. Cemetery: Dranoutre Military Cemetery in Belgium.

BEATTY, Charles Harold Longfield: Rank: Major. Regiment or Service: Special Lists, New Armies. Date of death: 17 May 1917. Died of wounds. Awards. D.S.O. From an article in the *Enniscorthy Guardian*:

The news of the death which occurred in an hospital in England on Thursday of last week, of Major C.H. Beatty, D.S.O., of Borodale, Enniscorthy will be heard of with much regret in County Wexford.

The eldest son of the late Captain David Beatty, Commander of the Grand Fleet, he came of a family long and popularly connected with the county Wexford. Born in 1870 he received his education in England, and having passed through a successful course of military instruction at Sandhurst he joined the army being gazetted to the Royal Warwickshire Regiment. He served in that Regiment through the South African War, being an A.D.C. to the Brigadier General Mounted Infantry Brigade. During that campaign he was twice mentioned in dispatches and was awarded the Queens medal with six clasps and the D. S. O. On the outbreak of the present war he again offered his services and was accepted, being appointed A.D.C. to General Sir Edwin A. H. Alderson, while commanding the Canadian Expeditionary Force. On April 2nd, 1916, in an engagement on the Western Front he was badly wounded, and as a result had to have his right arm amputated. Last summer he returned to his native home, Borodale, and his numerous friends in the county were glad to see him back amongst them again, though looking in poor health.

The fighting he had gone through told on his health, and he always complained of illness. He returned to England at the end of last year and underwent two operations in the hope of regaining his former health, but his strength not proving equal to the demand made on it, he died shortly after the second operation at an hospital in Atherstone, England. The deceased was well known in the County Wexford as a breeder of horses. He owned the famous sire, Poussin, which won for him two first prizes at the Dublin Show.

Charles Harold Longfield Beatty.

He refused several tempting offers for the sire, preferring that the farmers of his native county would get the services of such a good animal, and by that means continued to maintain for itself the high name it has earned as a good horse breeding centre.

In England as well as Ireland he was well know as a steeplechase rider and trainer of racers. Some years back he partnered the mastership of the Island Hounds with Mr Hall-Dare. In 1892 he won his first steeplechase on Radical at Rugby and subsequently he won the Hunt Cup at Warwick and Rugby three times, and at the Worcester Meeting in 1894 he won four steeplechases on the same afternoon, and was only beaten a neck in the fifth. The following year he won the Grand International Steeplechase at Sandown on Kestrel, and on Nun, the property of his father, he took many races, and the Atherstone Point-to-Point on a horse of his own named Jarnac in 1897 and 1898. he had the mount on Filbert in the Liverpool Grand National in the following year getting second, and in 1898 fourth… Deceased leaves a wife and child, a boy six years old, to succeed him.

His wife, whose second husband, the late Major Beatty was, has suffered heavily by the war. She lost one son by her first marriage in the early stage of the war and another son has been rendered incapable through wounds received. With the loss now of her husband there will be much sympathy for her in the great penalty that the appalling war has enacted from her.

Grave or Memorial Reference: Old Ground, 1952. Cemetery: Atherstone Old Cemetery, UK.

BEATTY, Richard George: Rank: Captain. Regiment or Service: 1st Duke of York's Lancers (Skinner's Horse). Age at death: 34. Born 2 November 1881. Date of death: 9 June 1915.

Supplementary information: Son of Mr and Mrs David Longfield Beatty of Wexford. Husband of Florence Mary Beatty of Hove, E. Sussex. Served in the South African War. Youngest brother of Admiral of the Fleet Earl Beatty, P.C, G.C.B. His youngest son, David Lion Beatty is buried at the foot of his father's grave. Memorial: Karachi 1914-1918 War Memorial in Pakistan. He is also listed on the Haleybury register.

BEER, William: Rank: Leading Stoker. Regiment or Service: Royal Navy. Unit: HMS *Collingwood*. Age at death: 26. Date of death: 30 December 1917. Service No: K/20771.

Supplementary information: Son of John and Mary Beer of Wexford. Grave or Memorial Reference: XR.RC.2507. Cemetery: Widnes Cemetery UK.

BELL, Edward John: Rank: Acting Sergeant. Regiment or Service: South Lancashire Regiment. Unit: 9th Bn. Date of death: 8 September 1918. Service No: 13628. Born in Wexford. Enlisted in Liverpool. Killed in action in Salonika.

Supplementary information: Husband of Mary Catherine Bell of 9 Castor Place, Belmont Road, Liverpool. Died of wounds. He has no known grave but is listed on the Doiran Memorial in Greece.

BERNEY, Patrick: Rank: Acting Corporal. Regiment or Service: Royal Welsh Fusiliers. Unit: 8th Bn. Date of death: 7 January 1916. Service No: 12418. Born in Wexford. Enlisted in Bala. Killed in action in Gallipoli. He has no known grave but is listed on Panel 77 to 80 on the Helles Memorial in Turkey.

BERRY, J.: Rank: Private. Regiment or Service: Royal Irish Regiment. Unit: 2nd Bn. Age at death: 37. Date of death: 9 July 1918. Service No: 7567.

Supplementary information: Husband of Katie Berry of Mary's Lane, Gibson Street, Wexford. C.128. Cemetery: Wexford (St Ibar's) Cemetery.

BERRY, John: Rank: Rifleman. Regiment or Service: Royal Irish Rifles. Unit: 1st Bn. Date of death: 25 September 1915. Service No: 1868. Born

J. Berry.

in New Ross, Co. Wexford. Enlisted in Inverkeithing, Fife. Killed in action. Has no known grave but is commemorated on Panel 9 Memorial: Ploegsteert Memorial in Belgium.

BERRY, Patrick: Rank: Private. Regiment or Service: Royal Irish Regiment. Unit: 1st Bn. Date of death: 8 December 1917. Service No: 7638. Born in Bride Street, Wexford. Enlisted in Wexford. Died of wounds in Palestine. From an article in the *People*, 1917:

> News has reached Wexford during the week that Private Patrick Berry, Back Street, Wexford. Who was serving in the Royal Irish Regiment has been killed in action.
>
> He had been at the front for the past three years. He served in the Boer War, and in 1915, he volunteered again, and went through several big engagements. He leaves a wife and four children to mourn his loss. Another brother, Private Richard Berry, was killed four months ago.

See Richard below. Grave or Memorial Reference: G. 21. Cemetery: Ramleh War Cemetery in Israel.

BERRY, Richard: Rank: Private. Regiment or Service: Royal Dublin Fusiliers. Unit: 1st Bn. Date of death: 20 August 1917. Service No: 16990. Born in Wexford. Enlisted in Wexford. Killed in action. Age at death: 23.

Supplementary information: Son of John and Mary Berry. Husband of Ellen Donohoe (formerly Berry) of 10 Summer Hill, Sandy Cove, Kingstown, Co. Dublin.

Thomas Berry.

See Patrick Berry above. He has no known grave but is commemorated on Panel 144 to 145 on the Memorial; Tyne Cot Memorial in Belgium.

BERRY, Thomas: Rank: Private. Regiment or Service: Royal Irish Regiment. Unit: 2nd Bn. Date of death: 19 October 1914. Service No: 7253. Born in St Mary's, Wexford. Enlisted in Enniscorthy while living in Tullow, Co Carlow. Killed in action. Age at death: 38.

Supplementary information: Husband of Margaret Jordan (formerly Berry) of 18, Married Quarters, 8th Hussars, Cavalry Barracks, York. From an article in a Wexford newspaper,

> Private Thomas Berry, Royal Irish Regiment is a native of Newtownbarry district. He had eleven years' service with the colours and had been stationed in India. At the outbreak of the war his regiment was drafted out to Flanders, and in the terrible combats in the earlier stages of the war Private Berry took part. After

the second Battle of Mons Private Berry was reported missing. His brother, Patrick, who has had twelve years service with the 11th Hussars, is also in the firing line, where on two occasions he was wounded.

He has no known grave but is commemorated on Panel 11 and 12. Memorial: Le Touret Memorial in France.

William Bishop.

BIRNEY, John: Rank: Private. Regiment or Service: Irish Guards. Unit: 1st Bn. Age at death: 28. Date of death: 6 December 1914. Service No: 2942. Born in ferns, Co. Wexford. Enlisted in Enniscorthy. Killed in action.

Supplementary information: Son of Patrick and Ellen Birney of Strahart, Ferns, Co. Wexford. Grave or Memorial Reference: Panel 11. Memorial: Ypres (Menin Gate) Memorial in Belgium.

BISHOP, Walter: Rank: Private. Regiment or Service: Household Cavalry and Cavalry of the line including the Yeomanry and Imperial Camel Corps. Unit: 2nd Dragoon Guards (Queen's Bays). Date of death: 13 May 1915. Service No: 3577. Born in Enniscorthy, Co. Wexford. Enlisted in Kilkenny. Killed in action. Age at death: 33.

Supplementary information: Son of Thomas Bishop of Shee Institute, Manor Street, Waterford. The Life Guards are a unit of the Household Cavalry. He has no known grave but is listed on Panel 3 on the Ypres (Menin Gate) Memorial in Belgium.

BISHOP, William: Rank: Private. Regiment or Service: Royal Irish Regiment. Unit: 1st Bn. Date of death: 24 April 1915. Service No: 4498. Born in Castlebridge, Co. Wexford. Enlisted in Wexford. Killed in action.

Supplementary information: Son of John and Kate Bishop of Hayestown, Co. Wexford. From an article in a Wexford newspaper, 'Private William Bishop, 1st Battalion, Royal Irish Regiment, son of Mr and Mrs John Bishop of Hayestown, Wexford. Private Bishop was wounded on 24 April, 1915, and since then was reported missing.' Grave or Memorial Reference: Panel 33. Memorial: Ypres (Menin Gate) Memorial in Belgium.

BLAKE, Thomas: Rank: Bombardier. Regiment or Service: Royal Field Artillery. Unit: 11th Div. Ammunition Col. Age at death: 32. Date of death: 14 April 1917. Service No: 105125. Born in Coddstown, Co. Wexford. Enlisted in Bridgend, Glam. Died at home.

Supplementary information: Son of Francis and Ellen Blake of Coddstown. Husband of Mary Blake of Coddstown,

Killinick, Co. Wexford. From an article in a Wexford newspaper:

> Killinick soldiers fate; It was officially reported during the week that Bombardier Thomas Blake, whose relatives reside at Coddstown, Killinick, had died on active service in France. The deceased had volunteered for active service at the outbreak of the war, enlisting in the Royal Field Artillery, with which he had been serving with in France since July, 1916. Much sympathy is felt with his relatives.

Grave or Memorial Reference: V.E. 54. Cemetery: Doullens Communal Cemetery Extension No. 1 in France.

BLANCH/BLANCHE, Patrick: Rank: Private. Regiment or Service: Machine Gun Corps. Unit: 82nd Coy. Age at death: 36. Date of death: 3 October 1916. Service No: 49033. Born in St Mary's, Wexford. Enlisted in Wexford. Died in Salonika.

Supplementary information: Son of John and Catherine Blanche. Husband of Mary Ann Blanche of 32, Bewely Street, New Ross, Co. Wexford. Grave or Memorial Reference: III.A.15. Cemetery: Struma Military Cemetery in Greece.

BOLAND, Edward: Rank: Private. Regiment or Service: Princess Patricia's Canadian Light Infantry. Unit: Eastern Ontario Regiment. Date of death: 4 June 1916. Age at death: 24. Service No: 475780. Born in Crossabeg, Co. Wexford. Enlisted in Regina, Sask. Occupation on enlistment: clerk. Next of Kin: Mother, Mrs Mary A. Boland, Mill Park Road Enniscorthy. From an article in the *People*,

Mr E Boland Enniscorthy. Amongst the Irish soldiers who recently died in the trenches at the front was Mr Edward Boland, formerly of Enniscorthy. He was serving with the Canadian forces when killed. He was brother to Mr Thomas Boland, Millpark Road, Enniscorthy; to Mrs P. E. Kelly, Slaney Place; Miss Minnie Boland, Enniscorthy, and to Sisters of Charity, Carlisle, London. Much sympathy is felt with his mother, Mrs Boland, Millpark Road and the members of his family.

Grave or Memorial Reference: Panel 10. Memorial: Ypres (Menin Gate) Memorial in Belgium.

BOLAND, James: Rank: Private. Regiment or Service: Welsh Regiment. Unit: 13th Bn. Date of death: 10 July 1916. Service No: 34767. Born in Kiltealy, Co. Wexford. Enlisted in Pontypridd while living in Treforest, Glam. Killed in action. Age at death: 32. Has no known grave but is commemorated on Pier and Face 7A and 10A. Memorial: Thiepval Memorial in France.

BOLGER, James: Rank: Private. Regiment or Service: Royal Irish Regiment. Unit: 1st Bn. Age at death: 26. Date of death: 3 March 1915. Service No: 8816. Born in Enniscorthy, Co. Wexford. Enlisted in Wexford while living in Enniscorthy. Killed in action.

Supplementary information: Son of James and Catherine Bolger of 7 Mernagh Street, Enniscorthy. Grave or Memorial Reference: Panel 33. Memorial: Ypres (Menin Gate) Memorial in Belgium.

BOLGER, John: Rank: Private. Regiment or Service: Royal Irish Regiment. Unit: 2nd Bn. Date of death: 27 May 1915. Service No: 5667. Born in Kilmuckridge, Co. Wexford. Enlisted in Wexford. Died of wounds. From an article in the *People*:

Sergeant [*sic*] John Bolger, Royal Irish Regiment, who belonged to Kilmuckridge, and was well know in Gaelic and athletic circles, met his death on May 24th in France being a victim of gas poisoning. Rejoining his Regiment at the outbreak of hostilities he fought in some of the fiercest battles in France and Flanders and the sincerest sympathy is extended to his young wife in the loss of a devoted husband and brave soldier.

Grave or Memorial Reference: A. 10. 46. Cemetery: St Sever Cemetery Extension, Rouen in France.

Private John Bolger.

BOLGER, John: Rank: Seaman. Regiment or Service: Royal Naval Reserve. Unit: HMS *Grafton*. Age at death: 50. Date of death: 12 August 1915. Service No: 2320D. From an article in the *Echo*:

His wife received news on Wednesday that John Bolger of Byrnes Lane, had been killed in action on the 10th inst. The deceased was on the naval reserve, and was called up for service at the outbreak of the war, being subsequently appointed to serve on HMS *Grafton*. He has two sons serving with the colours.

Son of John and Mary Bolger of Wexford. Husband of Mary Bolger of Byrnes Lane, Wexford. His son Corporal P Bolger (49878) below is his son. Grave or Memorial Reference: 8. Memorial: Plymouth Naval Memorial UK.

BOLGER, Patrick: Rank: Private. Regiment or Service: Worcestershire Regiment. Unit: 15th Bn. Age at death: 21. Date of death: 25 October 1918. Service No: 49878. Born in Wexford. Enlisted in Wexford. Died at home.

Sergeant John Bolger.

Supplementary information: Son of Mrs Mary Bolger of Byrne's Lane, Wexford. John Bolger (2320D) listed above is his father. From an article in a Wexford newspaper:

Patrick Bolger.

Corporal P, Bolger, of Byrnes Lane, Wexford, who while serving with the Irish Guards at Guinchy, in the capture of which the Irish troops played such a conspicuous part, was wounded, his thumb being blown off by shrapnel. Prior to volunteering for active service Corporal Bolger was on the staff of a local printing works. In September, 1915, he went on active service, and has since been in the front line with the Irish Guards. His father was killed in August, 1915, while serving on board HMS Gratton [*sic*] in the Dardanelles.

His eldest brother, John, is also with the colours, being at present engaged at Salonika with the Royal Irish. Corporal Bolger, who is at present undergoing treatment at a military hospital in Brigton, gave an interesting description in the course of a letter to his mother, last weekend, of the capture of Guinchy, at which he said, a heavy toll was exacted from the Irish Guards and the Royal Irish Regiment.

Grave or Memorial Reference: About middle of East part. Cemetery: Kilmacree Old Graveyard.

BOLGER, Patrick: Rank: Private. Regiment or Service: Royal Irish Regiment. Unit: 1st Bn. Age at death: 24. Date of death: 10 March 1918. Service No: 3/8670 and 8670. Born in Enniscorthy. Enlisted in Enniscorthy. Killed in action.

Supplementary information: Husband of Annie Bolger of 17 Palatine Square, Burnley. Native of Enniscorthy, Co. Wexford. Born in Enniscorthy. Enlisted in Enniscorthy. Killed in action in Palestine. Grave or Memorial Reference: J.o. Cemetery: Jerusalem War Cemetery, Israel.

BOWLES, Robert: Rank: Private. Regiment or Service: Hampshire Regiment. Unit: 14th Service Battalion. Date of death: 27 March 1918. Service No: 18662. Born in New Ross, Co. Wexford. Enlisted in Portsmouth while living in New Ross. Died of wounds. Grave or Memorial Reference: III.B.7 Bellicourt British Cemetery in France.

BOYCE, Joseph: Rank: Corporal. Regiment or Service: Royal Irish Regiment. Unit: 2nd Bn. Age at death: 28. Date of death: 21 August 1918. Service No: 12060 and 12069. Born in Rowe Street, Wexford. Enlisted in Wexford. Killed in action.

From an article in the *Enniscorthy Guardian* in 1917, 'Corporal Joseph Boyce, Abbey Street, Wexford has been wounded in the present fighting at the front line while serving with the R.D.F. He had been previously wounded at the Dardanelles and is at present in an hospital in Birmingham.'

Supplementary information: Son of Joseph and Mary Boyce of 16 Abbey Street, Wexford. From another article in a Wexford newspaper,

Much regret was felt in Wexford during the week at the official announcement od the deaths of several young soldiers hailing from the town, who had been serving with the Irish Brigade in France, and who were killed in action during the recent fierce engagements, in which the Irish Regiments played such a prominent part.

Amongst those deaths reported are Private Nicholas Redmond (Irish Guards), Wygram Place; Private Thomas Byrne (Royal Irish) John Street; Private J Boyce (do), Abbey Street; Private John Murphy (do), The Faythe, Wexford; and Private Breen (do), Whitemill Road. All the above mentioned lads are well and popularly known in the town and much sympathy is felt with their relatives in their sad bereavements.

Grave or Memorial Reference: Panel 5. Memorial: Vis-En-Artois Memorial in France.

BOYLE, J.: Rank: Bandsman. Regiment or Service: Royal Irish Regiment. Unit: 2nd Bn. Age at death: 46. Date of death: 9 May 1920. Service

No: 4469. Husband of Catherine Boyle of 10 Green Street, Wexford. Grave or Memorial Reference: Q.25. Cemetery: Wexford (St Ibar's) Cemetery.

BOYLE, Peter: Rank: Private. Regiment or Service: Royal Irish Regiment. Date of death: 9 May 1916. Service No: 1883. Born in Bride Street, Wexford. Enlisted in Wexford. while living in Curracloe, Co. Wexford. Killed in action. From an article in a Wexford newspaper:

During the week, Mrs Phillips, of School Street, Wexford, was notified that her nephew, Private Peter Boyle had been killed in action on May 9th, while serving with the 6th Batt, Royal Irish Regiment in France. He volunteered for active service shortly after the outbreak of war and was drafted out with the Irish Brigade lase December. He has two brothers serving with the colours-Richard, who was gassed in France, while serving with the 1st batt, Royal Irish, and who is now on service in Salonika; and James, who joined the 4th Batt, Royal Irish towards the close of last year, and is at present at training in Fermoy.

Grave or Memorial Reference: II.F.16. Cemetery: Dud Corner Cemetery, Loos in France.

BRADLEY, Richard: Rank: Private. Regiment or Service: Royal Irish Regiment. Unit: 2nd Bn. Date of death: 16 September 1918. Service No: 6941. Born in Newbawn, Co. Wexford. Enlisted in Waterford while living in Newbawn. Killed in action. He has no

J. Boyle.

known grave but is commemorated on Panel 5. Vis-En-Artois Memorial in France.

BRADY, John: Rank: Private. Regiment or Service: Royal Dublin Fusiliers. Unit: 8th Bn. Age at death: 26. Date of death: 14 February 1916. Service No: 16881. Born in Reedstown, Co. Wexford. Enlisted in Bridgend. Died of wounds.

Supplementary information: Son of James and Ellen Brady of Churchtown, Kilrane, Wexford. Husband of Ellen Brady of Butlerstown, Broadway, Wexford. From an article in the *Enniscorthy Guardian*:

> News has been received at Broadway of the death of Private J Brady, Royal Irish, who was killed a few days ago in action in France. The greatest sympathy is felt with his wife who resides at Trane, Broadway, was who received the distressing news by wire on Sunday morning. Private Brady was a fine type of fellow, and previous to joining the army had been working at Fishguard Harbour. He had also been employed with the G. S. and W. R. Company at Rosslare Harbour where the news of his death was received with genuine feelings of regret.
>
> He was a native of Tacumshane, and joined the colours just after the outbreak of the war. He was only married a short time before the war broke out, and much sympathy is felt for his wife and child.

Grave or Memorial Reference: IV.E.22. Cemetery: Lillers Communal Cemetery in France.

BRADY, Michael: Rank: Private. Regiment or Service: Royal Army Service Corps. Unit, 4th Coy, 74th Div, Train. Date of death: 14 September 1918. Service No: TS/8966. Born in Dublin. Enlisted in Gorey, Co. Wexford while living in Gorey. Died of wounds. Grave or Memorial Reference: II.E.38. Cemetery: Bronfay Farm Military Cemetery, Bray-Sur-Somme in France.

BREEN, James: Rank: Private. Regiment or Service: Royal Irish Fusiliers. Unit: 2nd Bn. Date of death: 25 May 1916. Service No: 11148. Born in Ballindaggin, Co. Wexford. Enlisted in Longford. Died in Malta. Grave or Memorial Reference: E. EA. A. 688. Cemetery: Addolorata Cemetery in Malta.

BREEN, James: Named **James BRIEN** in the *People* newspaper and also in the *Enniscorthy Guardian*. In another article in the *Enniscorthy Guardian* he is called James Breen. Rank: Private. Regiment or Service: Irish Guards. Unit: 1st Bn. Age at death: 35. Date of death: 18 May 1915. Service No: 5387. Born in Enniscorthy. Enlisted in Wexford. Killed in action.

Supplementary information: Son of Mrs Margaret Breen of 66 Ross Road, Enniscorthy, Co. Wexford. Born in Enniscorthy. Enlisted in Wexford. Killed in action. From an article in the *Enniscorthy Guardian*:

> On Saturday morning, Mrs Breen, Ross Road, Enniscorthy, received a notice from the War Office that her son, James, had been killed in action on 18th may last. There were details sent as to how the

James Breen.

deceased came by his death; whether he had been killed by shell fire or as a result of a bullet wound. His mother and sister had in a sense, been prepared for the sad news. An Enniscorthy man also at the front wrote last week saying that he heard that Jim had been killed. Inquiries were made, and then, as announced in ours columns last week, the report he had been wounded.

Now, however, the official message, which confirms the earlier report, has been received. The deceased, who was quite a young fellow had, prior to enlisting on the 18th September last, been employed as shop assistant at Mr W. K. Stamp's, the Market Square, where he enjoyed the confidence of his employer, and the very cordial esteem of the may who had business relations with him. A quiet and unassuming young man, attentive and painstaking at his work and courteous with his customers, he was alike trusted and respected and those who knew him deeply regret his death. He had been a member of the White Boy's dramatic class, and took part in a number of their public performances with much credit. His brother, Thomas Breen, who was married in town, joined the Royal Irish on the 1st September last. The deceased, influenced evidently by his brothers example, enlisted in the Irish Guards eighteen days later.

He was sent to England and remained in training there until about the middle of March last, when he sent with his Regiment to the front. From the seat of war he sent some letters to his mother which were always of a most optimistic nature. Very much local sympathy is felt for her and with his sister in their sorrow. At the meeting of the Men's Holy Family Confraternity – of which the deceased was a member – on Tuesday evening, the Rosary was offered for the happy repose of his soul, while prayers were also offered for him at all Masses on Sunday. Last week his brother left with his Regiment for service in Egypt.

Note: see **BREEN, Thomas,** his brother listed below. Grave or Memorial Reference: Panel 4. Memorial: Le Touret Memorial in France.

BREEN, John: Rank: Private. Regiment or Service: Royal Dublin Fusiliers. Unit: 1st Bn. Age at death: 25. Date of death: 3 March 1917. Service No: 43105. Born in Wexford. Enlisted in Liverpool while living in Wexford. Killed in action.

Supplementary information: Son of Patrick and Mary Breen of Clonamona, Craanford, Gorey, Co. Wexford. Grave or Memorial Reference: III.C.20. Cemetery: Grove Town Cemetery, Meulte in France.

BREEN, John Joseph: Rank: Private. Regiment or Service: Royal Irish Regiment. Unit: 2ⁿᵈ Bn. Date of death: 13 March 1915. Age at death: 23. Service No: 7288. Born in Wexford. Enlisted in Liverpool while living in Wexford. Killed in action. From an article in the *Echo*:

> During the week his parents in King Street have been notified that Private John Breen of the Royal Irish Regiment has been killed at the front on 15 March. His brother was within

John Joseph Breen.

a couple of yards of him when he fell fatally wounded and another Wexford soldier named Dalton from Barrack Street was in close proximity. The deceased had been a Naval reservist and volunteered for service in the Royal Irish Regiment at the beginning of the war.

Supplementary information: Grave Son of Moses and Annie Breen of 7 Ruskin Avenue, Rock Ferry, Birkenhead. He has no known grave but is listed on Panel 33 on the Ypres (Menin Gate) Memorial in Belgium.

BREEN, Joseph: Rank: Private. Regiment or Service: Royal Irish Regiment. Unit: 1ˢᵗ Bn. Date of death: 24 April 1915. Service No: 4660. Born in Bride Street, Wexford. Enlisted in Wexford while living in Tullow, Co Carlow. Killed in action. Age at death: 18.

Supplementary information: Son of Moses and Annie Breen of 7 Ruskin Avenue, Rock Ferry, Birkenhead. From a newspaper article:

> Mr Moses Breen of King Street has been notified by the War Office that his son Joseph, a Private in the Royal Irish Regiment, was killed in action.
>
> Only a short time previously another son of Mr Breen's, John who was also with the Royal Irish, was killed on active service. Both young men were exceedingly popular in Wexford and the greatest sympathy is felt with Mr Breen on his double bereavement.

Grave or Memorial Reference: Has no known grave but is commemorated on Panel 33. Memorial; Ypres (Menin Gate) Memorial in Belgium.

BREEN, Matthew: Rank: Lance Corporal. Regiment or Service: Machine Gun Regiment. Unit: 4th Bn. Formerly with the Irish Guards where his number was 9529. Date of death: 11 October 1918. Service No: 1844. Born in Templetown, Co. Wexford. Enlisted in Ayr, Ayrshire while living in Fethard, Co Tipperary. Died of wounds. Age at death: 23.

Supplementary information: Son of Mrs Margaret Breen of Herrylock, Fethard, Waterford. Grave or Memorial Reference: I.D.5. Cemetery: Masnieres British Cemetery, Marcoing in France.

BREEN, Thomas: Rank: Private. Regiment or Service: Royal Dublin Fusiliers. Unit: 1st Bn. Date of death: 4 March 1917. Service No: 27570. Born in Ferns, Co. Wexford. Enlisted in Gorey while living in Ferns. Died of wounds. Grave or Memorial Reference: III.C.22. Cemetery: Grove Town Cemetery, Meaulte, France.

BREEN, Thomas: Rank: Lance Corporal. Regiment or Service: Manchester Regiment. Unit: 11th Bn. Age at death: 33. Date of death: 9 September 1915. Service No: 4370.

Supplementary information: Son of James Breen of 66 Ross Road, Enniscorthy. Husband of Margaret Breen of 4 Patrick's Place, Enniscorthy, Co. Wexford. Born in Enniscorthy. Enlisted in Wexford. Died of wounds at sea. From an article in the *Enniscorthy Guardian*:

Volunteered for active service, September 1st, 1914. Wounded at the Dardanelles Sept 7th 1915, died September 9th 1915. He was attended by and Irish Chaplain-Father Wallace

Thomas Breen.

who administered the last rites of the Catholic Church.

From another article in a Wexford newspaper:

During the week Mrs Margaret Breen, Patricks Place, Enniscorthy, received a letter from a Priest serving with the forces, that her husband, Private Thomas Breen, of the Manchester Regiment, who was wounded at the Dardanelles, and who was being conveyed on an hospital ship to Malta, died when some days at sea. The letter which Mrs Breen received was of a most consoling character. The Priest informed her that he was on the vessel with her husband, who made a most exemplary preparation for death and received the last Sacraments and all the consolation of the Catholic

Church. His death was most edifying.

The deceased leaves a wife and two children to mourn his loss, and for both much sympathy is felt. His aged mother resides with her daughter on the Ross Road, and to them also sympathy will go out. A brother of the deceased, James Breen, who has been a shop assistant in Enniscorthy, joined the army also last year and was killed in May in some part of France.

Grave or Memorial Reference: Panel 158 to 170. Memorial: Helles Memorial in Turkey.

BRENNAN, James: Rank: Guardsman. Regiment or Service: Grenadier Guards. Unit: 2nd Bn. Date of death: 4 February 1915. Service No: 8310. Born in New Ross, Co. Wexford. Enlisted in Pontypridd. Killed in action. From an article in the *Enniscorthy Guardian:*

News has also reached a distant relative of his in the town that James Brennan, belonging to the Royal Field Artillery, and a native of New Ross, has also been killed in the trenches. The young man's family left New Ross some years ago and he himself settled in Pontypridd, where on the outbreak of War, he joined the colours. Four Ross men have now lost their lives in the war.

Grave or Memorial Reference: II.D.20. Cemetery: Cuinchy Communal Cemetery in France.

BRENNAN, James: Rank: Private. Regiment or Service: Royal Irish Regiment. Unit: 6th Bn. Age at death: 21.

Date of death: 12 August 1916. Service No: 8029.

Supplementary information: Son of John Brennan of The Faythe, Wexford and Mary Brennan (stepmother). Grave or Memorial Reference: Screen Wall. 3378. Cemetery: Nottingham General Cemetery UK.

BRENNAN, Myles: Rank: Rifleman. Regiment or Service: Royal Irish Rifles. Unit: 1st Bn. Date of death: 18 April 1917. Service No: 10314. Born in Wexford. Enlisted in Wexford. Died of wounds. From an article in a Wexford newspaper,

Rifleman Myles Brennan, Well Lane, Wexford, who has served in the Royal Irish Rifles on the Western Front since the outbreak of war, was killed in action on the 18th April, 1917, notification of his death has just been received in Wexford by his widow, Mrs Alice Brennan, with whom much sympathy is felt.

Grave or Memorial Reference: A.4. Cemetery: Heudicourt Communal Cemetery Extension in France.

BRESLIN, Edward: Rank: Private. Regiment or Service: Royal Irish Regiment. Unit: 2nd Bn. Date of death: 3 September 1916. Service No: 1884. Born in Bride Street, Wexford. Enlisted in Wexford while living in Broadway, Co. Wexford. Killed in action. Grave or Memorial Reference: Pier and Face 3A. Memorial: Thiepval Memorial in France.

BRESTLAUN, Owen: Rank: Private. Regiment or Service: Royal Dublin

Fusiliers. Unit: 1st Bn. Age at death: 28. Date of death: 29 June 1915. Service No: 10053. Born in Carnew, Wexford. Enlisted in Carlow while living in Taney, Co. Wexford. Killed in action in Gallipoli.

Supplementary information: Son of the late Daniel Brestlaun of Ballyellis, Gorey, Co. Wexford and of Bessie McGuinness (formerly Brestlaun) of Ardoyne, Tullow, Co. Carlow. Grave or Memorial Reference: Panel 190 to 196. Memorial: Helles Memorial in Turkey.

BRIEN, Andrew: Rank: Sergeant. Regiment or Service: Royal Irish Regiment. Unit: 2nd Bn. Date of death: 19 October 1914. Service No: 5493. Born in Kilmore, Co. Wexford. Enlisted in Longford while living in Lightwater, Co. Wexford. Killed in action.

From an article in the *Enniscorthy Guardian*, January 1915, 'Mrs O'Brien, Byrnes-Lane, Wexford, has received a communication from the War Office stating that her husband, John Brien, who has been missing since the engagement in which he was in from the 19th to the 21st of October. The man is probably a prisoner of the Germans.' He has no known grave but is commemorated on Panel 11 and 12 of the Touret Memorial in France.

BRIEN, James: See **James BREEN**.

BRIEN, John: Rank: Private. Regiment or Service: Royal Irish Regiment. Unit: 2nd Bn. Age at death: 26. Date of death: 11 May 1915. Service No: 5458. Born in Enniscorthy, Co. Wexford. Enlisted in Wexford while living in Enniscorthy. Died of wounds.

Supplementary information: Son of Martin and Mary Brien of Chapel Lane, Enniscorthy. From a snippet in the *Echo*:

During the week the wife of John Brien, Drumgoold, Enniscorthy, received word from the War Office authorities in France that her husband had died in an hospital there as the result of wounds received some weeks ago. The deceased belonged to the Royal Irish, and was called up at the outbreak of the war. He was sent to France in October, where he was wounded and invalided home, but as soon as he had recovered he was again sent to the front.

Grave or Memorial Reference: I.G.16A. Cemetery: Wimereux Communal Cemetery in France.

BRIEN, John: Rank: Private/ Lance Corporal. Regiment or Service: Royal Irish Regiment. Unit: 2nd Bn. Date of death: 19 October 1914. Service No: 6952. Born in St Mary's, Wexford. Enlisted in Wexford. Killed in action. From an article in the *Enniscorthy Guardian*:

Private John Brien of the Royal Irish Regiment, was reported missing on the 21st of October last. Since then nothing has been heard of him and it is concluded that he was killed. Private Brien had been all through the Boer war and escaped without a scratch.

He had been attached to the special reserve and when the present conflict broke out he was called to the colours. He came safely through the engagment at Mons and it was subsequent to that battle that he lost his life as is presumed. His wife, Mrs

Nellie Brien, who lives in Byrne's Lane, Wexford, was informed by the War Office at the time that he was missing and men who fought with him, including his brother, believed he was killed. This week Mrs Brien received a communication from the War Office, which leaves no doubt, as to his being dead. Private Brien served for some years in India. His three brothers and four nephews are in the firing line at the front for months past.

He has no known grave but is commemorated on Panel 11 and 12. Memorial: Le Touret Memorial in France.

BRIEN, John: Rank: Private. Regiment or Service: Royal Scots Fusiliers. Unit: 1st Bn. Date of death: 16 June 1915. Age at death: 35. Service No: 13545. Born in Wexford. Enlisted in Kilwinning, Ayrshire while living in Belfast. Died.

Supplementary information: Husband of Mary C. Doherty (formerly Brien) of 46 Colinward Street, Springfield Road, Belfast. He has no known grave but is listed on Panel 19 and 33 on the Ypres (Menin Gate) Memorial in Belgium.

BRIEN, William: Rank: Private. Regiment or Service: Royal Irish Regiment. Unit: 1st Bn. Date of death: 16 April 1915. Age at death: 23. Service No: 9972. Born in Rowe Street, Wexford. Enlisted in Wexford. Killed in action.

Supplementary information: Son of William and Mary Brien. Grave or Memorial Reference: Has no known grave but is commemorated on Panel 33. Memorial; Ypres (Menin Gate) Memorial in Belgium.

BROADERS, William: Rank: Private. Regiment or Service: Royal Dublin Fusiliers. Unit: 8th Bn. Age at death: 25. Date of death: 28 June 1916. Service No: 21718. Born in Wexford. Enlisted in New Ross, Co. Wexford. Killed in action.

Supplementary information: Son of E. and Bridget Broaders of 10 William Street, New Ross. Grave or Memorial Reference: Panel 127 to 129. Memorial: Loos Memorial in France.

BROOKE, George: Rank: Lt. Regiment or Service: Irish Guards. Unit: 1st Bn. Age at death: 37. Date of death: 7 October 1914. Service No: 6599. Died of wounds.

Supplementary information: Son of Sir George F. Brooke, 1st Bart., and Lady Brooke (*née* Shakerley). Husband of Nina Brooke, of 21 Southwick Street, Oxford Square, London. From an article in a Wexford newspaper:

Death of Lieut, Brooke, Ballyfad; Lieutenant George Brooke, Ballyfad House, Coolgreany, one of the finest types of young Irish gentlemen to be found has died in France from wounds received in action near Soissons. About Coolgreany the greatest sorrow was felt when the sad news was published, for young Mr Brooke was a universal favourite. He was a splendid type of Irish manhood, 35 years of age, and standing 6 feet 3 inches in height. He was one of the tallest and best developed officers in the British Army. The late Mr Brooke, who was the owner of the beautiful manor and demesne at Ballyfad, had previously spent a short period in the Army before his marriage. On the outbreak of the present war he volunteered for active service, his letter been written while prostrated with a bad attack of influenza.

He was advised by many not to go abroad, on account of his state of health at the time, and even when leaving Inch station he had not quite recovered, having to be muffled up in wraps. He immediately got a Commission from the War Office as Lieutenant of the Irish Guards, and crossed over to France about the last week in August. From that onwards he was in the very thick of the fighting, and throughout displayed the greatest bravery. After a successful charge by the Irish Guards he was unfortunately struck by a piece of shell, which inflicted frightful wounds. This occurred just north of the village of Soissons, a fortnight ago. He was taken to a field hospital, but never rallied, and his death was officially announced at the early part of this week.

Amongst the people of Coolgreany, Ballyfad, and Johnstown, Both Mr and Mrs Brooke of Ballyfad House, were held in the highest esteem, and every year it was their custom to give an entertainment in their own grounds to all the schoolchildren of the neighbourhood. School sports were also held, and prizes distributed by Mr and Mrs Brooke. His death will be keenly felt by in that locality for many a day, as he was universally looked upon as one of the best. He was the son of Sir G. F. Brooke Bart., Celbridge, and leaves his young widow and one daughter to mourn his sad fate, but they have the greatest consolation in knowing that he died most nobly, and also that they have the sympathy of the whole countryside.

From De Ruvigny's Roll of Honour:

BROOKE, GEORGE, Lieut., Reserve of Officers, attd. 1st Battn. Irish Guards, eldest s. of Sir George Brooke, 1st Bart., J.P., D.L., by his wife, Anna Maris. Dau. Of Geoffgrey Joseph Shakerley, of Belmont Hall, co. Chester; b. Summerton, co. Dublin, 10 June, 1877; educ. Eton; obtained a Lieutenancy in the 3rd Hamshire Regt. 4 Sept. 1897; served in the South African War, 1899-1902 (Medal with three clasps); subsequently joined the Reserve of Officers; was posted to the Irish Guard 8 Aug. 1914, after the outbreak of the European War; served with the Expeditionary Force in France and Flanders, and died 9 Oct. following, from wounds received in action on the Aisne 7 Oct. He m. in 1907. Nina, dau. Of the Right Hon. Lord Arthur Hill, P. C., and had a dau., Nancy Myra.

Grave or Memorial Reference: A.7. Cemetery, Soupir Communal Cemetery in France.

BROOKS, John: Rank: Private. Regiment or Service: Royal Irish Regiment. Unit: 2nd Bn. Age at death: 38. Date of death: 19 October 1914. Service No: 6599. Born in St Mary's, Enniscorthy, Co. Wexford. Enlisted in Enniscorthy. Killed in action.

Supplementary information: Son of John and Ellen Brooks of Enniscorthy. Husband of Margaret Brooks of 18 Duffy Gate, Enniscorthy. From an article in the *Enniscorthy Guardian* in 1916, 'Mrs Margaret Brooks, Duffrey-Gate, Enniscorthy, has received official intelligence of the death at the front of her husband, Private John Brooks, C Company, Royal Irish Regiment. She had not heard from him for some time, and was quite prepared for the worst when the sad news arrived.'Grave or Memorial Reference: Panel 11 and 12. Memorial: Le Touret Memorial in France.

BROOKS, Patrick: Rank: Rifleman. Regiment or Service: Royal Irish Rifles. Unit: 14th Bn. Date of death: 7 June 1917. Service No: 9130 and 3/9130. Born in Enniscorthy, Co. Wexford. Enlisted in Enniscorthy. Killed in action.

Supplementary information: Son of Mrs M. Brooks. From an article in a Wexford newspaper:

Enniscorthy National Volunteer Joins the Colours. Patrick Brooks, employee of Enniscorthy Urban Council and Armoury Sergeant in the local Corps of the National Volunteers, has enlisted in the Royal Irish Rifles. He was an ex-soldier, and served with the Royal Irish Regiment throughout practically the whole of the South African War.

From another article in a Wexford newspaper:

Enniscorthy Soldier Killed. During the recent heavy fighting in Flanders one of the Irish soldiers, who figure in the casualty lists, was Patrick Brooks, of Patrick Street, Enniscorthy, who is reported killed in action. The deceased, who had been in the employment of the Urban Council, re-joined the army after the outbreak of the rebellion in 1916, and almost from that date to the time of his death he had been in one or the other of the different theatres of war. He had previously served through the South African War.

When the Volunteer movement was started in Enniscorthy, his military experience was availed of, and he became one of the instructors. His death is deeply regretted in Enniscorthy, and for his relatives the greatest sympathy is felt. At the meeting of the Men's Confraternity on Tuesday night, of which the deceased had been a member, prayers were offered for the happy repose of his soul. RIP.

Grave or Memorial Reference: II.A.3. Cemetery: Lone Tree Cemetery in Belgium.

BROPHY, Andrew: Rank: Private. Regiment or Service: Royal Irish Regiment. Unit: 2nd Bn. Date of death: 14 July 1916. Service No: 5037. Born in New Ross, Co. Wexford. Enlisted in Kilkenny while living in Graiguenamanagh, Co. Kilkenny. Killed in action. Age at death: 24.

Supplementary information: Son of Andrew and Mary Brophy of High Street, Graiguenamanagh. He has no known grave but is listed on Pier and Face 3.A. on the Thiepval Memorial in France.

BROWN, Charles H.S.: Rank: Lance Corporal. Regiment or Service: Leinster Regiment. Unit: 1st Bn. Date of death: 6 April 1916. Age at death, 15 (from Ireland's Memorial Records). Service No: 8996. Born in Ferns, Co. Wexford. Enlisted in Navan. Killed in action. He has no known grave but is listed on Panel 44 on the Ypres (Menin Gate) Memorial in Belgium.

James Browne.

BROWNE, James: Rank: Private. Regiment or Service: Leinster Regiment. Unit: 2nd Bn. Date of death: 1 May 1915. Service No: 9663. Born in Wexford. Enlisted in Wexford. Died of wounds.

Supplementary information: Son of Mr J. Browne of Green Street, Wexford. From an article in the *Enniscorthy Guardian:*

The parents of Gunner James Browne, Green Street, Wexford, recently received intelligence of his death at the front. Captain Macartnee, machine gun officer, writes as follows – On active service – I expect by now you have been informed of the death of your son in machine gun section. Please accept the heartfelt sympathy of all his comrades amongst whom he was so popular. He was a brave boy and was chosen to look after a machine gun in a very important place when he was killed. It is a great loss to me and I will not be able to fill his place easily. It will, I know, console you a little in your great loss to know that he died a soldiers death and passed away quite peacefully.

Grave or Memorial Reference: C.4. Cemetery: Ferme Buterne Military Cemetery, Houplines in France.

BROWNE, Martin: Rank: Mate. Regiment or Service: Mercantile Marine. Unit: S.V. *Mary Fanny* (Bideford). Age at death: 40. Date of death: 15 September 1918.

Supplementary information: Son of Patrick and Mary Browne. Born at New

Ross, Co. Wexford. Memorial: Tower Hill Memorial UK.

BROWNE, Michael: Rank: Rifleman. Regiment or Service: Rifle Brigade. Unit: 9th Bn. Date of death: 15 September 1916. Service No: S/341. Born in Gorey, Co. Wexford. Enlisted in London while living in Gorey. Killed in action. Grave or Memorial Reference: I.L.4. Cemetery: A.I.F Burial Ground, Flers in France. He is also commemorated on the Cahir War Memorial.

BROWN/BROWNE, Nicholas: Rank: Private. Regiment or Service: Royal Irish Regiment. Unit: 1st Bn. Date of death: 24 June 1915. Service No: 9653. Born in Tagoat, Co. Wexford. Enlisted in Wexford. Died. From and article in the *People* newspaper and the Enniscorthy *Echo*:

Nicholas Brown.

Amongst the list of killed on Monday last appears the name of Nicholas Browne. He was born in Milltown, Tagoat, and was aged twenty-four. He joined the 1st Batt, Royal Irish Rangers seven years ago and served in India from which country he went staright to France at the end of last year, when the Royal Irish were drafted to the firing line, but he was sent back to Cork owing to illness. He then came on a short visit to Mr Murphy, King Street Wexford, with whom he lived for many years befoe he joined the army. He went to the front again in May, and now his name goes to swell the list of Irishmen who have died in France.

Grave or Memorial Reference: X.L.4. Cemetery: Strand Military Cemetery in Belgium.

BROWNE, Robert Patrick: Rank: Private. Regiment or Service: Royal Dublin Fusiliers. Unit: 10th Bn. Age at death: 21. Date of death: 13 December 1916. Service No: 25343. Born in Wexford. Enlisted in Londonderry. Killed in action.

Supplementary information: Son of John and Mary E. Browne of 7 Upper George Street, Wexford. From an article in the *People*, 1916:

The sad news has been received by Nurse Browne, George Street, of the death in action of her only son. Patrick Robert [*sic*], who joined the 10th Battalion, Royal Dublin Fusiliers in November, 1915. Private Browne, who was about 21 years of age, was a former pupil of the Christian Brother's School's, Wexford, and for some years prior to joining the colours he was attached to the teaching profession, and held appointments in Waterford, Maryborough and Drogheda. He served through the recent Dublin Insurrection, and was commended by his commanding officer for his great bravery on that occasion. He met his death when requisitioning for his comrades in distress.

The sad announcement of his demise is rendered all the more poignant by the fact that his mother and sisters were anxiously awaiting his arrival home for the Christmas holidays, as he had written them only a short time ago that he had been promised leave at Christmas.

Grave or Memorial Reference: C.14. Cemetery: Y Ravine Cemetery, Beaumont-Hamel in France.

Edward Busher.

BUSHER, Edward: Rank: Private. Regiment or Service: Royal Irish Regiment. Unit: 2nd Bn. Age at death: 20. Date of death: 7 June 1916. Service No: 4525. Born in St Bridget's, Co. Wexford. Enlisted in Wexford. Died of wounds.

Supplementary information: Son of Edward and Margaret Busher of Bride Street, Wexford. From an article in a Wexford newspaper,

Private Edward Busher, 2nd Battalion, Royal Irish Regiment, son of Mr Edward Busher Bride Street, Wexford. During the week his parents were notified that he had died of wounds. Prior to the war he was a reservist and on the outbreak of hostilities he rejoined the army. He had been fourteen months on active service in France and came home for a brief holiday at the end of May. In an engagement shortly after his return to the firing line he was seriously wounded, and on the 7th inst, succumbed to his injuries.

Grave or Memorial Reference: Plot 1. Row A. Grave 13. Cemetery: Corbie Communal Cemetery Extension in France.

BUSHER, James: Rank: Private. Regiment or Service: Royal Munster Fusiliers. Unit: 6th Bn. Age at death: 28. Date of death: 28 December 1917. Service No: 2786. Born in Ballyseskin, Co. Wexford. Enlisted in Maesteg in

Glamorgan while living in Kilmore, Co. Wexford. Died of wounds in Palestine.

Supplementary information: Son of Joseph and Annie Busher of Ballyseskin, Kilmore. From an article in a Wexford newspaper:

> News has been received by Mr Joseph Busher, Ballyseskin, Kilmore that his eldest son, Private James Busher, has died from wounds received in action on December 28th while serving with the Eastern Expeditionary Force. Private Busher joined the 6th Royal Munster Fusiliers over three years ago. Mr Busher has another son with the colours, Peter, who has been serving with the R.A.M.C., in France for over two years.

Grave or Memorial Reference: F.39. Cemetery: Jerusalem War Cemetery, Israel.

BUTLER, Edward: Rank: Seaman. Regiment or Service: Royal Naval Reserve. Unit: HMS *Lady Cory Wright*. Age at death: 38. Date of death: 26 March 1918. Service No: 1991D.

Supplementary information: Son of Nicholas and Martha Butler of 24 Parnell Street, Wexford. Husband of Annie Butler of 24, Parnell Street, Wexford. From an article in the *Enniscorthy Guardian*, 'Lost at Sea; Official intimation reached Mrs Butler, Parnell Street, Wexford, on Saturday that her husband, Edward Butler, was lost at sea, being one of a crew whose vessel was torpedoed, he was attached to the Irish Lights before volunteering.' Grave or Memorial Reference: 29. Memorial: Plymouth Naval Memorial UK.

BUTLER, Philip: Rank: Private. Regiment or Service: Royal Irish Regiment. Unit: 2nd Bn. Date of death: 19 October 1914. Service No: 4391. Born in Newtownbarry, Co Kilkenny. Enlisted in Graiguenamanagh, Co. Kilkenny while living in Tinahely, Co. Wicklow. Killed in action. He has no known grave but is listed on Panels 11 and 12 on the Le Touret Memorial in France.

BUTTLE, Albert Edward: Rank: Second Lieutenant. Regiment or Service: Royal Irish Rifles. Unit: 17th Bn attached to the 2nd Bn. Age at death: 23. Date of death: 2 October 1918. Died of wounds.

Supplementary information: Son of John and Annie Buttle of Templeshannon, Enniscorthy, Co. Wexford. From an article in the *Enniscorthy Guardian*:

> On Thursday afternoon, 3rd inst, the death was officially announced of Lieut, E. A. Buttle [*sic*], youngest son of Mr and Mrs John Buttle, Enniscorthy. The family of the deceased were not altogether unprepared for the sad announcement, as they had received intimation on the previous day that he had been seriously wounded. The announcement of the young officers death, when it became generally known, aroused a feeling of deep regret in the town, where deceased and members of the family enjoyed a high degree of popularity. One of the first of his class in the town to join the army, the late Lieut Buttle, not wishing to avail of the advantages which his education, training and position gave him, and which might have easily secured for him a commission in the army, enlisted as a private in the

Inniskilling Fusiliers.

His abilities being early recognised, he was transferred to the Officers Training Corps attached to the Queens University, Belfast, and at the conclusion of his course of instruction was gazetted as a Second Lieutenant in the Royal Irish Rifles. He left early in 1916 with his regiment for France, where he took part in several severe engagements. His constitution, never very robust, failed to withstand the hardships of the battlefield, and he was obliged to leave for England, where he remained on service for some months. His next removal was to Tipperary, where he was promoted to the rank of Lieutenant, and remained for almost 12 months.

Feeling that the object for which he had joined the army was not being achieved while he remained on home service, he made application to be allowed to proceed to the front. His application was refused on medical grounds, but so keenly was he to be with those engaged in the gigantic struggle on the western front, now happily moving to a desired point of success, he renewed his application, and after repeated refusals it was acceded to. He again took his place in the firing line and early in September was slightly wounded but quickly recovered. On Tuesday, 1st inst, he received the wounds to which he succumbed on the following day.

No detail have yet come to hand as to how he met his injuries, but all who knew the deceased and had come to admire the manly, generous principles which guided his life, feel assured that the manner of his death was but a fitting compliment to the high purpose which influenced him to give up all that life holds dear so that he might be free to join with those banded together for the purpose of repelling a ruthless tyranny. His early demise is deeply deplored, and the greatest sympathy is felt for his highly esteemed Parents, Brothers, Sisters, Uncle and other relatives in their sad bereavement. Prior to joining the army he had been actively associated with his Father and Uncle (Messrs Buttle Brothers) in the management of their extensive business. In social circles he was extremely popular.

He was an accomplished musician and assisted frequently at public and other classes of entertainments.

From De Ruvigny's Roll of Honour:

youngest son of John Buttle of Templeshannon, Enniscorthy, Director of Messrs Buttle, Brothers and Co., Ltd., Bacon Curers and Merchants; b, 6 Jan 1895; educ, Newtown School, Waterford, and Model School, Enniscorthy; volunteered for active service, and enlisted in the Inniskilling Fusiliers, 1 April, 1915; received a commission, and was gazetted 2nd Lieut, 2nd Royal Irish Rifles, 23rd Aug, following; promoted Lieut, 1 July, 1917; served with the Expeditionary Force in France and Flanders from, 16th June 1916, taking part in the Battles of the Somme in July; was invalided home, 9 Jan, 1917; was subsequent offered his discharge as being medically fit, but again volunteered for active service, and rejoined his regiment in France, 29 May, 1918, and died at No 3 Australian Casualty Clearing Station, 2 Oct following, of wounds received in action the previous day. Buried in Haringhe (Bandaghem) Military Cemetery.

Grave or Memorial Reference: III.B.24. Cemetery: Haringhe (Bandaghem) Military Cemetery in Belgium.

BYRNE, Francis: (Soldiers died in the Great War),**BYRNE, Thomas Francis:** (Commonwealth War Graves Commission). Rank: Private. Regiment or Service: Royal Inniskilling Fusiliers. Unit: 7ᵗʰ Bn. Date of death: 4 October 1916. Age at death, 19. Service No: 29537 (Soldiers died in the Great War), 29539 (Commonwealth War Graves Commission). Born in Whitefoot, Wexford. Enlisted in Belfast. Died of wounds at home.

Supplementary information: Son of Richard and Bridget Byrne, of 36 Roe Street, Belfast. Born in Co. Wexford. Grave or Memorial Reference: St Patrick's DA14. Cemetery: Sheffield (St Michael's) Roman Catholice Cemetery, Yorkshire, UK.

BYRNE, Garret: Rank: Private. Regiment or Service: Royal Dublin Fusiliers. Unit: 1ˢᵗ Bn. Age at death: 30. Date of death: 27 April 1915. Service No: 10096. Born in Gorey. Enlisted in Naas while living in Ballyfadd. Killed in action in Gallipoli.

Supplementary information: Son of Peter and Mary Byrne of Rathpierce Cottage, Ballyfad, Gorey, Co. Wexford. Grave or Memorial Reference: Special Memorial A.14. Cemetery: V Beach Cemetery in Turkey.

BYRNE, James: Rank: Private. Regiment or Service: Welsh Regiment. Unit: 15ᵗʰ Bn. Date of death: 28 July 1917. Service No: 53948. Born in Ballinatray. Enlisted in Cardiff while living in Gorseinon, Glamorganshire. Killed in action. Grave or Memorial Reference; XXVII. F. 20. Cemetery: New Irish Farm Cemetery in Belgium.

BYRNE, James: (Also listed as **JOHN**). Rank: Private. Regiment or Service: Irish Guards. Unit: 1ˢᵗ Bn. Age at death: 38. Date of death: 30 October 1914. Service No: 1462. Born in Hook, Co. Wexford. Enlisted in New Ross, Co. Wexford. Died of wounds.

Supplementary information: Son of Michael and Bridget Byrne of Hook. Husband of Mary Byrne of Arthurstown, Co. Wexford. From an article in the *Enniscorthy Guardian*:

Amongst those killed in Flanders, was Private James Doyle from Ballysop, Campile. He was on the army reserve and his time was within a week of being expired when the war broke out, and he was called up. Shortly after arriving in Flanders he took part in several desperate engagements and received a severe wound. He died in hospital of its effect. He was active of the Hook, and was a young man of great physique.

Grave or Memorial Reference: III.B.13. Cemetery: Boulogne Eastern Cemetery in France.

BYRNE, James: Rank: Private. Regiment or Service: Royal Irish Regiment. Unit: 1ˢᵗ Bn. Age at death: 22. Date of death: 16 March 1915. Service No: 4204. Born in Ballyoughter, Camolin, Co. Wexford. Enlisted in Gorey, Co. Wexford while living in

Camolin. Killed in action.

Supplementary information: Son of John Byrne of Ballyhast, Leakinfere, Gorey. Grave or Memorial Reference: Panel 33. Memorial: Ypres (Menin Gate) Memorial in Belgium.

BYRNE, John: Rank: Private. Regiment or Service: Black Watch (Royal Highlanders). Unit: 1st Bn. Age at death: 25. Date of death: 10 March 1916. Service No: S/10203 and 10203. Born in Gorey, Co. Wexford. Enlisted in Edinburgh. Killed in action.

Supplementary information: Son of Joseph Byrne of Ballycanew, Gorey, Co. Wexford. From an article in the *Free Press*, 1916:

> The sad news reached his relatives at the end of last week that Private John Byrne, of Ballycanew (who's photo we published in this column some time ago) has been killed in action in La Boiselle. He belonged to the 3rd Battalion, Royal Irish Regiment, and had been the front for the past twelve months. He wrote home regularly to his relatives, and strange to say he complained in his last letter of the dullness and inactivity they were experiencing in the trenches, which he said, was far more trying on ones nerves than actual fighting. He had two brothers also at the front.
>
> He was a shoemaker by trade prior to the war, and was well know in Ballycanew, and Monamolin. His last residence before joining the Colours was Bray. He was a brother to My Myles Byrne, Upper William Street Gorey, and to Mr Joseph Byrne of Ballycanew. The exact manner in which he met his death, whether in

a charge or by shell fire has not yet transpired.

Grave or Memorial Reference: III.E.8. Cemetery: St Patrick's Cemetery, Loos in France.

BYRNE, M.: Rank: Private. Regiment or Service: Royal Defence Corps. Unit: 1st Bn. Age at death: 23. Date of death: 26 December 1918. Service No: 83711.

Supplementary information: Son of Mrs Rosanna Byrne, of 39 Irish Street, Enniscorthy. Grave or Memorial Reference: C.253. Cemetery: Enniscorthy New Catholic Cemetery, Wexford.

BYRNE, Patrick: Rank: Rifleman. Regiment or Service: Royal Irish Rifles. Unit: 2nd Bn. Date of death: 24 November 1916. Service No: 6699. Born in New Ross, Co. Wexford. Enlisted in New Ross. Killed in action. Grave or Memorial Reference: C.8. Cemetery: Hyde Park Corner (Royal Berks) Cemetery in Belgium.

BYRNE, Patrick: (Alias, true name is **CARTON, Patrick**) Rank: Private. (listed in De Ruvigny's Roll of honour as a Lance Corporal) Regiment or Service: Leinster Regiment. Unit: 2nd Bn. Date of death: 20 October 1914. Service No: 6731. Born in Enniscorthy, Co. Wexford. Enlisted in Enniscorthy. Killed in action. Age at death: 39. He has no known grave but is listed on Panel 10 on the Ploegsteert Memorial in Belgium.

83711 PRIVATE
M. BYRNE
ROYAL DEFENCE CORPS
26TH DECEMBER 1918 AGE 23

IN LOVING MEMORY
OF MY DEAR SON
R.I.P.

M. Byrne.

BYRNE, Peter: Rank: Lance Corporal. Regiment or Service: Irish Guards. Unit: 2nd Bn. Date of death: 20 June 1916. Age at death: 20. Service No: 6723. Born in Wexford. Enlisted in Dublin while living in Ballinacarrig, Co. Wicklow. Killed in action.

Supplementary information: Son of Peter and Mary Byrne of Ballinacarrig. He has no known grave but is listed on Panel 11 on the Ypres (Menin Gate) Memorial in Belgium.

William Byrne.

BYRNE, Samuel: Rank: Private. Regiment or Service: Royal Irish Regiment. Unit: 1st Bn. Age at death: 27. Date of death: 4 May 1915. Service No: 8995. Born in Ballymitty, Co. Wexford. Killed in action.

Supplementary information: Son of John and Lucy Byrne of Ballinglee, Ballymitty, Co. Wexford. Grave or Memorial Reference: Panel 33. Memorial: Ypres (Menin Gate) Memorial in Belgium.

BYRNE, Thomas: Rank: Private. Regiment or Service: Royal Irish Regiment. Unit: 6th Bn. Date of death: 5 August 1917. Service No: 1900. Born in Rowe Street, Wexford. Enlisted in Wexford while living in John Street Hook. Killed in action. Has no known grave but is commemorated on Panel 33. Memorial; Ypres (Menin Gate) Memorial in Belgium.

BYRNE, Thomas Francis: Rank: Private. Regiment or Service: Royal Inniskilling Fusiliers. Unit: 7th Bn. Age at death: 19. Date of death: 4 October 1916. Service No: 29539.

Supplementary information: Son of Richard and Bridget Byrne of 36 Roe Street, Belfast. Born in Co. Wexford. Grave or Memorial Reference: St Patrick's. DA14. Cemetery: Sheffield (St Michael's) Roman Catholic Cemetery UK.

BYRNE, William: Rank: Private. Regiment or Service: Irish Guards. Unit: 1st Bn. Date of death: 1 December 1914. Service No: 2894. Born in Killivaney, Co. Wexford. Enlisted in Gorey, Co. Wexford. Killed in action.

Supplementary information: Son of Tobias and Mary Byrne of Ballythomas, Tinahely, Co. Wicklow. He has no known grave but is listed on Panel 11 on the Ypres (Menin Gate) Memorial in Belgium.

C

CAHILL, Patrick: Rank: Leading Stoker. Regiment or Service: Royal Naval Reserve. Unit: HMS *Indefatigable.* Age at death: 23. Date of death: 31 May 1916. Service No: 2172S.

Supplementary information: Son of Patrick and Mary Cahill of William Street, Wexford. Grave or Memorial Reference: 19. Memorial: Plymouth Naval Memorial United Kingdom.

CAIRNS, Richard Frederick: (Alias, real name was **ZIMBER, Richard Frederick**). Rank: Rifleman. Regiment or Service: King's Royal Rifle Corps. Unit: 4th Bn. Age at death: 28. Date of death: 8 May 1915. Service No: R/10201. Born in New Ross, Co. Wexford. Enlisted in Liverpool while living in Wexford. Killed in action.

Supplementary information: Son of Aaron and Elizabeth Zimber of New Ross, Co. Wexford. Grave or Memorial Reference: Panel 51 and 53. Memorial: Ypres (Menin Gate) Memorial in Belgium.

CALLAGHAN, Thomas: Rank: Gunner. Regiment or Service: Royal Field Artillery. Unit: 'C' Bty. 91st Bde. Age at death: 31. Date of death: 9 January 1916. Service No: 29327. Born in New Ross, Co. Wexford. Enlisted in Maesteg, Glam. Killed in action.

Supplementary information: Son of Michael and Bridget Callaghan of Irishtown, New Ross, Co. Wexford. From an article in the *Enniscorthy Guardian*:

New Ross man Killed at the Front; On Saturday official intimation reached his parents and sister that Private Thos Callaghan, son of Mr Michael Callaghan, accountant, Irishtown, New Ross, was recently killed in France. He was killed by a German sniper, the bullet passing through his head killing him instantly. He was about 28 years of age and volunteered from Wales where he had a good job. He joined soon after the outbreak of the war in the Royal Field Artillery and proceeded to the front on the beginning of July. He went through nearly all the big engagements in France since he went out and escaped unhurt until he met his death at the hands of the sniper.

In his letters home to his parents and sister he used to speak very highly of the courage of the boys at the front and writing since Christmas he said that on Christmas Day the Germans commenced banging at them from sunrise and they returned the fire and thus the battle continued until sunset and he thanked God that he came through it safe. He was held in great esteem by his commanding officer and the regiment as the following extract from a letter of the commanding officer and signallers to his sister, Miss Cissie Callaghan shows – "Myself and the boys of the regiment wish to tender our deepest sympathy to the family, friends and relatives of poor Tom. He was shot through the head by an enemy's sniper, death being instantaneous. He was a real sport and I assure you he will be missed by us." There is another brother of his, Private James Callaghan, who volunteered in January of last year.

He is in the training quarters in Salisbury Plain and was at home recently on furlough. Through the kindness of his officer he was allowed home again on furlough to see his parents and the members of the family during the week on the occasion of the death of his brother at the front. He was well known in football and hurling circles before he volunteered.

Grave or Memorial Reference: I.D.3. Cemetery: Rue-David Military Cemetery, Fleurbaix in France.

CAMPBELL, Thomas: Rank: Private. Regiment or Service: Connaught Rangers. Unit: 3rd Bn. Date of death: 13 June 1915. Service No: 3/6021 and 6021. Born in Wexford. Enlisted in Enniscorthy while living in Wexford. Died at home. From an article in the *People*, 1915:

Lance Corporal, Thomas Campbell, son of the late Mr Thomas Campbell, Shanbogh, New Ross, was wounded in the recent fighting at France. He had a miraculous escape on the occasion.

Shrapnel burst around him and he was hit in the back and leg and is in the convalescent hospital in Southampton at present. His wounds were not serious in themselves, but the poisonous gas emitted from the enemy's trenches tended to intensify them. He had some exciting experiences, having gone through several heavy charges, and on the occasion that he received the wounds at the famous Battle of Hooge his Battalion charged with desperate vigour trench by trench of the Germans midst firing line from the enemy accompanied by clouds of gas.

The Battalion suffered heavily, and he was one of the survivors that returned after capturing an important stronghold of the enemy. He was a land steward in Ballina, and in July last he volunteered joining the Irish Guards. He went through the South African War and had some miraculous escapes, his horse being shot from under on a number of occasions. His bravery attracted the attention of the superior officer and he was accorded distinction medals.

Grave or Memorial Reference: Special Memorial. Cemetery: Kinsale (Old Abbey) Graveyard Co Cork.

CANAVAN, Mathew/Matthew: Rank: Private. Regiment or Service: Royal Irish Regiment. Unit: 2nd Bn. Date of death: 19 October 1914. Service No: 7667. Born in Clonegal, Co. Wexford. Enlisted in Carlow while living in Ballon, Co Carlow. Killed in action. He has no known grave but is listed on Panels 11 and 12 on the Le Touret Memorial in France.

CANAVAN, Michael: Rank: Lance Corporal. Regiment or Service: Irish Guards Unit: 1st Bn. Date of death: 8 August 1915. Service No: 5872. Born in Sandymount. Enlisted in Dublin. Killed in action. From an article in the *People* newspaper:

Although born in Irishtown, Dublin about twenty-four years ago, Lance Corporal Michael Canavan lived since his childhood with his uncle Mr James Canavan, Kilcavan, Tara Hill, Gorey. A young man of fine physique, he was of a cheerful and unassuming manner and deservedly popular.

He was an ardent and sincere Gaelic Leaguer, and as a musician and Irish step dancer, he was known all over Ireland, having won the all Ireland hornpipe competition at the Wexford Feis in the year of 1906, and a similar distinction at the Wicklow Feis the following year. He answered his coutry's call towards the end of last year joining the Irish Guards (2nd Battalion) and on St Patrick's day last he was awarded first place in the Regimental Irish step dancing competition by the Earl of Kerry (Colonel). He went with a draft of his Regiment to France in June, but remained at the base before going to the firing line until the middle of July.

During a terrific artillery engagement on the 8th of August, he was struck by a German shell and a noble, kindly Irish heart was stilled forever, and a career, full of hope and promise brought to a tragic end but glorious close. The news of his death caused a profound feeling of regret amongst a large circle of friends in the Gorey District and in his native City of Dublin.

Grave or Memorial Reference: I.B.13. Cemetery: Guards Cemetery, Windy Corner, Cuinchy in France.

CANE, Michael: Rank: Private. Regiment or Service: Royal Irish Regiment. Unit: 2nd Bn. Age at death: 24. Date of death: 5 July 1916. Service No: 10656. Born in Marshalstown, Co. Wexford. Enlisted in Wexford while living in Enniscorthy, Co. Wexford. Killed in action.

Supplementary information: Son of Mrs Margaret Cane of Milehouse, Enniscorthy. Grave or Memorial Reference: VII.C.2. Cemetery: Flatiron Copse Cemetery, Mametz in France.

CANHAM, Herbert: Rank: Private. Regiment or Service: Royal Irish Regiment. Unit: 2nd Bn. Date of death: 21 March 1918. Service No: 1691. Born in Killurin, Co. Wexford. Enlisted in Wexford. Killed in action. He has no known grave but is listed on Panels 30 and 31 on the Pozieres Memorial in France.

CANTY, Daniel: Rank: Private. Regiment or Service: Royal Irish Regiment. Unit: 1st Bn. Age at death: 28. Date of death: 8 May 1916. Service No: 7562. Born in Exchange Street, Dublin. Enlisted in Waterford. Died at home.

Michael Canavan.

Daniel Canty.

Supplementary information: Husband of Margaret T. Shiel (formerly Canty) of Ardanoon, Rosslare Harbour. From an article in the *Enniscorthy Guardian*:

Private D Canty; Ex-Station Master, Kilrane, Royal Irish Regiment, gassed at Loos, recovered and was subsequently sent to Salonika, where he contracted enteric fever, from which he succumbed at Welsh Metropolital Hospital, Whitechurch, Cardiff, on the 7th inst. On Wednesday the 10th inst, the remains arrived at Rosslare Harbout by cross channel boat and during the day internment took place at Kilrane Cemetery.

Grave or Memorial Reference: In north-east part. Cemetery: Kilrane Catholic Churchyard, Co. Wexford.

CARDIFF, Patrick: Rank: Private. Regiment or Service: Royal Irish Regiment. Unit: 2nd Bn. Age at death: 22. Date of death: 19 October 1914. Service No: 4380. Born in Taghmon, Co. Wexford. Enlisted in Wexford while living in Taghmon. Killed in action. *Supplementary information*: Son of Mrs Elizabeth Kinsella of Taghmon, Co. Wexford. From an article in the *Enniscorthy Guardian*:

Private Patrick Cardiff, Trinity, has been reported killed in action in Flanders. He belonged to the 4th Royal Irish and was reported missing on the 19th Oct, 1914. Lately the War Office have given him up as killed. He was only 24 years of age and was on the special reserve. When the war broke out he was in the employment of Mr Thomas Kendrick, Coolaw,

and was drafted out to Flanders in October 1914. There is a photograph of his brother John Cardiff who also served in this newspaper above the article. When war broke out John was in the employment of Mr J Winters, Ballyturtin. He was in the 4th Battalion, Leinster Regiment.

Grave or Memorial Reference: Panel 11 and 12. Memorial: Le Touret Memorial in France.

CARLEY, Joseph: Rank: Private. Regiment or Service: Irish Guards. Unit: 2nd Bn. Date of death: 3 October 1916. Age at death, 23. Service No: 6380. Born in Wexford, Co. Wexford. Enlisted in Wexford. Died at home. From an article in the *Enniscorthy Guardian*:

Of the many Wexford soldiers who have fallen in battle in the present European conflict the first as far as we are aware whose remains have been interred in his native soil is Private Joseph Carley, The Faythe, Wexford. This young soldier, who volunteered shortly after the outbreak of the war, was attached to the Irish Guards and had been in the firing line for over eighteen months. He received shrapnel wounds to the cheek and right arm at Ypres early in April last and was granted a short holiday in May. On recovery he returned to the fighting line and took part in many of the recent battles. On Monday of last week his parents were notified that he had been severely wounded at Guillemot on the 15th September.

A shell struck him in the left leg inflicting such injuries that it was found necessary to amputate the leg. For

Joseph Carley.

some days he lay in a critical condition in Millroad Infirmary, Liverpool, where he was brought shortly after receiving his injuries, but from the outset little hope was entertained for his recovery and he passed away on Tuesday fortified by all the consolations of the Catholic Church and with his parents and some relatives at his bedside. The remains were conveyed to Wexford for internment and arrived at the North Station on Thursday afternoon. The sympathy felt for his parents and friends was illustrated in the great concourse of people who waited the arrival of the train and which subsequently followed the hearse to Crosstown Cemetery.

On the route to the cemetery a detachment of the Munster Fusiliers in charge of Lieutenant Slattery marched with arms reversed and on the grave being closed the 'Last Post' was sounded and three volleys discharged by the firing party. Wreaths from the Military and a number of friends were placed on his grave. Rev Martin Ryan, B.D., C.C., officiated at the graveside, R.I.P.

Joseph Carley.

Grave or Memorial Reference: Q. 80. Cemetery: Wexford (St Ibar's) Cemetery.

CARROLL, Joseph: Rank: Sapper. Regiment or Service: Corps of Royal Engineers. Unit: 327th Quarrying Company, R.E. Date of death: 3 September 1917. Service No: 270922. Born in New Ross, Co. Wexford. Enlisted in Wexford while living in New Ross. Died. Grave or Memorial Reference: Plot D, Row 1A, Grave 11. Cemetery: Calais Southern Cemetery in France.

CARROLL, John Joseph: Rank: Boatswain (Bosun). Regiment or Service: Mercantile Marine. Unit: SS *Southborough* (Sydney, N.S.W.). Age at death: 28. Date of death: 16 July 1918. Sunk by German Submarine U-110. There were no survivors.

Supplementary information: Son of William and Mary Carroll (*née* Cullen) of 26 Upper Distillery Road, Wexford. Memorial: Tower Hill Memorial UK.

CARROLL, Michael Joseph: Rank: Private. Regiment or Service: Canadian Infantry (Central Ontario Regiment). Unit: 58th Bn. Age at death: 32. Date of death: 12 April 1917. Service No: 850727.

Supplementary information: Son of Tom and Ellen Carroll of New Ross. Information from his enlistment documents: Eyes: blue. Hair: dark brown. Complexion: fair. Height: 5 foot 8 inches. Date of birth: 3 July 1883. Age on enlistment: 33 years 11 months. Place of birth: New Ross, Co. Wexford. Marital status: single. Name and address of next of kin: Mother, Ellen Carroll, New Ross. Date of attestation: 2 June 1916.

Location of attestation: Bridgeburg. Occupation on enlistment: Seaman. Grave or Memorial Reference: VII. D. 4. Cemetery: La Chaudiere Military Cemetery, Vimy in France.

CARROLL, Richard: Rank: Private. Regiment or Service: Royal Irish Regiment. Unit: 2ⁿᵈ Bn. Date of death: 19 October 1914. Service No: 10641. Born in Ferns, Co. Wexford. Enlisted in Enniscorthy, Co. Wexford. Killed in action. He has no known grave but is listed on Panels 11 and 12 on the Le Touret Memorial in France.

CARTHY, J.: Rank: Private. Regiment or Service: Royal Irish Regiment. Unit: Depot. Date of death: 26 March 1919. Age at death, 26. Service No: 4449.

Supplementary information: Son of James Carthy, of 12 Shannon Hill, Enniscorthy. Grave or Memorial Reference: C. 657. Cemetery, Enniscorthy New Catholic Cemetery, Wexford.

J. Carthy.

CARTHY, John: Rank: Private. Regiment or Service: Royal Dublin Fusiliers. Unit: 1ˢᵗ Bn. Date of death: 7 August 1915. Service No: 18047. Born in Wexford. Enlisted in Wexford. Killed in action in Gallipoli. An article from the *Enniscorthy Guardian*:

> Official information has been received that Private John Carty [*sic*], Green Street Wexford, belonging to the Dublin Fusiliers, was killed in action at the Dardanelles on the 7th of August last-the same date on which a comrade in action, Private John Sinnott of cornmarket met his death.

John Carty.

[Note : I have not found John Sinnott from Cornmarket in any war-dead databases.]

Grave or Memorial Reference: Special memorial A.1. Cemetery: Twelve Tree Copse Cemetery in Turkey.

CARTON, Patrick: (served under the Alias **BYRNE, PATRICK**) Rank: Private. Regiment or Service: Leinster Regiment. Unit: 2nd Bn. Date of death: 20 October 1914. Service No: 6731. Born in Enniscorthy, Co. Wexford. Enlisted in Enniscorthy, Co. Wexford. Killed in action. Age at death: 39. He has no known grave but is listed on Panel 10 on the Ploegsteert Memorial in Belgium.

CARTY, John: (RDF) See **CARTHY John:**

CARTY, John: Rank: Stoker. Regiment or Service: Royal Naval Reserve. Unit: HMS *Monmouth*. Date of death: 1 November 1914. Service No: 1656S.

Supplementary information: Son of Mr Philip Carty, Trinity Street, Wexford. Born March, 1890. Joined ther Royal Naval Reserve 8 April 1910 while he was living at William Street and renewed it 23 April 1912. Height: 5' 3 ½. Fair hair and blue eyes. He worked as a Fireman, (boiler man) at the Mill Road Ironworks in 1911 and 1912. He also did a few trips at sea in the Merchant Navy as a Fireman. He was on the *Muretania* for a few trips between January 1913 and April 1913, amongst other ships. The casualty notice was sent to Wexford on 12 November 1914. From an article in the *Enniscorthy Guardian*:

John Carty.

The British cruiser *Monmouth* was sunk in a naval action in the Pacific Ocean, off the coast of Chile, South America.

The cruisers "Good Hope" and "Glasgow" were severely damaged, but apparently escaped with an auxiliary cruiser. A message from Otranto (Italy) says that three German warships are now in Valparaiso Bay, Chile. Five more warships and auxiliaries are outside the bay. The *Monmouth* was an armoured cruiser of 9,800 tons built at Glasgow at a cost of £979,000. She belonged to what is known as the County Class, and carried a crew of 537 men. Her armoured belt was 4.2 inches of Krupp steel and her 14.6 inch guns were protected by 5.4 inches of steel and her secondary guns by four inches. She was fitted with two torpedo tubes and had a speed of nearly 23 knots.

The "Good Hope" is also and armoured cruiser, but much more

heavily armoured and armed than that the *Monmouth*. Her belt is six inches of Krupp steel. And her 9.2 inch guns are protected by 6.5 inches. She also carries 16 6-inch guns and 15 quickfirers. Her speed is over 23 knots and she has a crew of 900 men. The *Monmouth* was commissioned in July, 1914, under the command of Captain Frank Brandt. The Good Hope was commissioned in 1912, and carried the flag of Sir Christopher Cradock, K.C.V.O.

The record states that "reported to have been serving on HMS *Monmouth* when that vessel was sunk in action on the 1st November 1914 and in the absence of evidence to the contrary must be regarded as having been lost."

Grave or Memorial Reference: 5. Memorial Plymouth Naval Memorial. UK.

CASEY, Nicholas: Rank: Gunner. Regiment or Service: Royal Garrison Artillery. Unit: 1st Mountail Battery. Date of death: 1 September 1914. Service No: 14535. Born in Wexford. Enlisted in London while living in Tramore, Co Waterford. Died in India. Grave or Memorial Reference: 4. A. 25. Cemetery: Rawalpindi War Cemetery in Pakistan.

CASH, Thomas: Rank: Private. Regiment or Service: Royal Fusiliers, City of London Regiment. Unit: 9th Bn. Date of death: 7 July 1916. Service No: 666 and G/666. Born in Ballyruane. Enlisted in Lambeth while living in Screen. Killed in action. From another article from the *Enniscorthy Guardian*:

News has been received of the death

of Private Thomas Cash, of the Royal Fusiliers, who was killed in action on July 7th 1916. Private Cash, who was 33 years of age, was third son of Mr John Cash, D. C. Ballyrouan, Screen.

He volunteered at the outbreak of the war, and was through several engagements. He was connected with the G.A.A. clubs of Wexford and Enniscorthy, and was a member of the Red Rapparees. He was also a proficient handballer. His death is regretted by his former comrades. At a meeting of the Wexford District Council on Saturday a vote of condolence was passed with Privates Cash's father.

Grave or Memorial Reference: VIII. G. 6. Cemetery: Ovillers Military Cemetery in France.

CASS, William: Rank: Pioneer. Regiment or Service: Corps of Royal Engineers. Unit: Roads and Quarries. Formerly he was with the Royal Irish Regiment (302nd Road Construction Company) where his number was 3/6740. Date of death: 9 October 1918. Service No: WR/42194. Born in New Ross, Co. Wexford. Enlisted in Clonmel, Co Tipperary. Killed in action. From an article in the *People*, 1915:

On Monday last Private James Furniss, of Neville Street, New Ross, who was a postman up to the time of volunteering, and who was recently invalided suffering from a dose of gas which he received in the trenches, left Ross for the front.

On the same day Private Peter Stafford, of Rosbercon, who was gassed in the trenches, came home recently, also returned to the front. Private William Cass, who got a slight dose of gas and was wounded also, left Ross at the end of last week. He had been home for about a month.

Grave or Memorial Reference: D20. Cemetery: Queant Communal Cemetery British Extension in France.

CAULFIELD, Patrick: Rank: Lance Corporal. Regiment or Service: Royal Scots Fusiliers. Unit: 7th Bn. Age at death: 35. Date of death: 26 September 1915. Service No: 12901. Born in Coolroe, Co. Wexford. Enlisted in Ayr while living in Largs, Ayrshire. Killed in action.

Supplementary information: Son of John and B. Caulfield of Coolroe, Co. Wexford. Husband of Mary Dougan Caulfield of 18 Wilson St, Largs, Ayrshire. From and article in the *Enniscorthy Guardian*:

News has reached Coolroe, Ballycullane, where his mother and family reside, that Lance Corporal Patrick Caulfield was killed in battle in France on September 26th. Lance Corporal Caulfield was in Scotland for a number of years and volunteered for service when the war began.

He had been two months in France when he fell fighting. He was in the drapery business in New Ross in his early years, and afterwards emigrated to Scotland where he secured a good position and married. He leaves a wife and five children. Many a happy day the writer of this notice spent in the class in the old schoolhouse in Ballycullane. He was a man of great ability possessing a wonderful power in the solution of mathematical problems. No truer heart ever beat in an Irish Breast than

his. Now that its beat is forever stilled beneath the soil of gentle, beautiful France, and the legions of war trample over it, we pray that his spirit enjoys the peace and happiness of the valiant, true and brave, who have dared everything in this awful war.

Mrs Caulfield has received the following letter; "Dear Madam. Your note to hand, and in reply to your inquiry, I must regret to inform you that your husband was killed at Hill 70 on the 25th September. He was killed by a rifle bullet, and it may be some consolation to you to know that death was instantaneous, he suffering no pain. From personal knowledge of him, I think that God may compensate you in the loss such a good husband, and his comrades, amongst whom he was held in the highest esteem, join with me in expressing our sincere regret at the loss of such a good comrade. I remain, Madam, yours in sorrow, Colour Sergeant, M Willestrop."

Grave or Memorial Reference: Panel 46 to 49. Memorial: Loos Memorial in France.

CAULFIELD, Robert: Rank: Lance Corporal. Regiment or Service: London Regiment (Post Office Rifles). Unit: 1st/8th Bn. Age at death: 23. Date of death: 9 July 1917. Service No: 371737. Enlisted in New Ross, Co. Wexford while living in New Ross, Co. Wexford. Killed in action.

Supplementary information: Son of Margaret Caulfield of Lady Lane, New Ross, Co. Wexford. Grave or Memorial Reference: H.4. Cemetery: Oak Dump Cemetery in Belgium.

CAVANAGH, Joseph: Rank: Lance Corporal. Regiment or Service: Royal Irish Regiment. Unit: 5th Bn. Age at death: 33. Date of death: 13 September 1917. Service No: 9634. Born in Ramsgrange, Co. Wexford. Enlisted in Brecon while living in Ebbw Vale, Monmouthshire. Died at Sea.

Supplementary information: Son of the late Charles Brian Cavanagh of Duncannon Fort, Co. Wexford. Memorial: Doiran Memorial in Greece.

CHAPMAN, Edward: Rank: Private. Regiment or Service: Royal Irish Regiment. Unit: 2nd Bn. Date of death: 5 July 1916. Service No: 9539. Born in Clongee, Co. Wexford. Enlisted in Maestig, Glam while living in Tagoat, Co. Wexford. Killed in action. From an article in the *Enniscorthy Guardian*:

> Mrs Chapman, Newtown, Tagoat, has recently received news of the death of her husband, Private Edward Chapman, 1 8th Royal Irish. He joined the colours in May, 1915, and shortly after was drafted out to the Western front. 'Somewhere in France' he received a bullet wound to the head, which proved fatal. He was only 22 years of age. Mrs Chapman received news of her husband's death from a companion of her late husband, who recounted in pathetic words the last hours of the young Private. He was only a couple of years married, and much sympathy is felt for his young widow and child in their bereavement.

He has no known grave but is listed on Pier and Face 3 A on the Thiepval Memorial in France.

CHEEVERS, Matthew: Rank: Private. Regiment or Service: The King's (Liverpool Regiment). Unit: 12th Bn. Age at death: 23. Date of death: 27 March 1917. Service No: 14211. Born in Carrigbyrne, Co. Wexford. Enlisted in Llanelly, Wales while living in Co Waterford. Died of wounds.

Supplementary information: Son of James and Catherine Cheevers (*née* Hanlon) of Horeswood, Campile, Co. Wexford. Grave or Memorial Reference: II. B. 40. Cemetery: Hermies Hill British Cemetery in France.

CHEEVERS, Patrick: Rank: Sergeant. Regiment or Service: Kings Liverpool Regiment. Unit: 13th Bn. Date of death: 3 May 1917. Service No: 14122. Born in Carrigbyrne, Co. Wexford. Enlisted in Llanelly, North Wales while living in Waterford. Killed in action. Age at death: 26.

Supplementary information: Son of James and Catherine Cheevers of Horeswood, Campile, Waterford. He has no known grave but is listed in Bay 3 on the Arras Memorial in France.

CLEARY, John: Rank: Sergeant. Regiment or Service: Kings Own (Royal Lancashire Regiment). Unit: 8th Bn. Date of death: 2 March 1916. Service No: 14090. Born in Liverpool, Birmingham. Enlisted in Manchester. Killed in action. Age at death, 28.

Supplementary information: Son of John and Lavinia Cleary, of 21 Glen Helen Street, Salford, Manchester. From an article in the *People*:

> His relatives in the Co. Wexford have received the sad news of the death

in action of Sergeant John Cleary, Liverpool, son of Mr J. Cleary, formerly of Duncormack District. Prior to his joining the King's Own Royal Lancasters about 18 months ago.

Mr Cleary was headmaster of St Joseph's Catholic School, Pemblebury. His promotion was rapid and he had been for some time on active service in France when he received the fatal blow. Sergeant Cleary was a member of several Catholic societies at Pemblebury and Swinton, and was very popular with his numerous friends. He was well known and esteemed amongst a large circle of relatives and acquaintances in South Wexford, where he had occasionally spent his holidays, and the announcement of his death has caused a painful shock to them all. He was a nephew of Mr Richard Cleary, D. C., Rath, Duncormack, and a cousin of Mr Stephen Cleary, Merchant, Taghmon.

Grave or Memorial Reference: Panel 12. Memorial: Ypres (Menin Gate) Memorial in Belgium.

CLEARY, Patrick: Rank: Private. Regiment or Service: Royal Welsh Fusiliers. Unit: 17th Bn. Age at death: 38. Date of death: 9 July 1916. Service No: 25457. Born in Co. Wexford. Enlisted in Co. Wexford while living in Co. Wexford. Killed in action.

Supplementary information: Husband of Johanna Roche (formerly Cleary) of Kingsford, Barntown, Wexford. Grave or Memorial Reference: Pier and Face 4A. Memorial: Thiepval Memorial in France.

CLINCH, James: Rank: Private. Regiment or Service: Australian Infantry,

A.I.F. Unit: 15th Bn. Age at death: 37. Date of death: 15 July 1919. Service No: 6955.

Supplementary information: Son of Patrick and Anastasia Clinch. Age on Enlistment: 34 years, 6 Months. 'Brought in dead Endell Street Military Hospital London at 10 40pm, 15 July 1919'. Height: 5 Feet 3½ inches. Hair: light brown. Eyes: brown. Complexion: medium. Born in Wexford. Occupation in Ireland: Mixed farming with C. Clinch, Templeshindo, Ferris, Co. Wexford. Occupation on enlistment: labourer. Next of kin: brother, Mr John Clinch, 619 Main Street, Kangaroo Point, Brisbane, Queensland. Also listed is his eldest brother, Christopher Clinch. Bally Busk, Templeshambo, Ferns. Date of enlistment: 30 September 1916. Place of enlistment: Brisbane, Queensland. Illnesses suffered while in service: Trench Fever, 20 October 1917. Admitted to Bath War Hospital, England. Wounded in Action: Shotgun wound to the leg, 26 February 1918. Grave or Memorial Reference: IV.K.20. Cemetery: Brookwood Military Cemetery.

CLOWREY/CLOWERY, Murtha: Rank: Private. Regiment or Service: Royal Dublin Fusiliers. Unit: 1st Bn. Date of death: 5 October 1917. Service No: 18217. Born in Wexford. Killed in action. From an article in the *People*, 1917, 'News has also been received of the death in action of Private Murtha Clowry (R.I.R.) Green Street, Wexford. He leaves a widowed mother to mourn his loss.' He has no known grave but is listed on Panels 144 and 145 on the Tyne Cot Memorial in Belgium.

COADY, John: Rank: Private. Regiment or Service: Highland Light

Infantry. Unit: 1ˢᵗ Bn. Date of death: 25
October 1918. Service No: 20181. Born
in Wexford. Enlisted in Glasgow. Killed
in action in Mesopotamia. He has no
known grave but is listed on Panel 35
and 64 on the Basra Memorial in Iraq.

COADY, James. Rank: Fireman.
Regiment or Service: Mercantile
Marine. Unit: SS *Lusitania* (Liverpool).
The *Lusitania* was sunk by German
Submarine U-20. Age at death: 53. Date
of death: 7 May 1915.

Supplementary information: Born
in Wexford. Grave or Memorial
Reference: Screen Wall. Cemetery:
Cobh Old Church Cemetery, County
Cork.

COADY/CODY, John: Rank: 2
Lt. Regiment or Service: Connaught
Rangers. Unit: Attached to the 2ⁿᵈ Bn
Royal Irish Regiment. Age at death: 37.
Date of death: 21 August 1918.

Supplementary information: Croix de
Geurre (Belgium). Son of James and
Margaret Coady. Husband of Florence
Mary Dounes (formerly Coady) of
Duncannon, Waterford. Killed in action.
From an article in a Wexford newspaper:

> Lieut Cody Killed; regret was felt in
> Duncannon when the sad news arrived
> to Mrs Cody that her husband, Lieut
> Cody, had been killed in action.
>
> The deceased Officer was pro-
> moted only a few months ago from
> the ranks for conspicuous bravery on
> the field. Besides his service on the
> Western Front he had also seen serv-
> ice formerly in South Africa where he
> also won distinction for bravery. While
> gallantly leading his platoon on 22nd

of August last on the Lys sector he fell.
Lieut. Cody belonged to a Kilkenny
family, but had recently married a
Duncannon Lady.

He has no known grave but is listed on
the Vis-En-Artois Memorial in France.

CODD, Michael: Rank: Private.
Regiment or Service: Royal Munster
Fusiliers. Unit: 2ⁿᵈ Bn. Age at death: 39.
Date of death: 10 December 1917. Service
No: 6621. Born in Ballymore, Co. Wexford.
Enlisted in Llanelley, Carmarthen while
living in Enniscorthy. Killed in action.

Supplementary information: Son of
Nicholas Codd of Milehouse, Enniscorthy,
Co. Wexford. Grave or Memorial
Reference: Panel 143 to 144. Memorial:
Tyne Cot Memorial in Belgium.

COLFER, James Richard: Rank:
Lieutenant. Regiment or Service: Royal
Munster Fusiliers. Unit: 9ᵗʰ Bn. Age at
death: 25. Date of death: 26 February
1917. Died.

Supplementary information: Son of John
Redmond Colfer and Martha Colfer of
New Ross, Co. Wexford. From an arti-
cle in the *Enniscorthy Guardian*:

> Mr John R Colfer, solicitor, New Ross,
> has received the following letter con-
> cerning the death of his son, Lieut, James
> R Colfer, R.M.F., from Major L, Roche,
> R.M.F., "Dear Mr Colfer, I have learned
> with the greatest possible regret of the
> death of your dear son in action. I knew
> him well, and stood side by side with
> him in the trenches in France for nine
> months in the Loos and Helloch sectors
> and at the Somme in September, 1916,
> and a more gallant fellow I never met.

We of the old 9th Munsters shall sorely miss genial presence. His bravery at the taking of Guillemont and Ginchy will never be forgotton by his old comrades, Sincerely Yours, L Roche, Major 8th, R.M.F. "Mr Colfer also received the following wire from Buckingham Palace" The King and Queen deeply regret the loss you and the army have sustained by the death of your son in the service of his country. Their majesties truly sympathise with you in your sorrow-Keeper of the Privvy Purse!" Vow of Condolence; At the New Ross Harbour Board on Wednesday, on the proposition of Mr John O'Sullivan, J.P. chairman seconded by Mr James Power, a vote of condolence was passed with Mr Colfer, solicitor to the board, on the death of his son Lieut James R Colfer, in France, and adjourned the meeting as a mark of respect.

Grave or Memorial Reference: III.F.1. Cemetery: Wimereux Communal Cemetery in France.

COLFER, Patrick: Rank: Private. Regiment or Service: Royal Irish Regiment. Unit: 2nd Bn. Date of death: 15 October 1914. Service No: 8166. Born in Rathangan, Co. Wexford. Enlisted in Wexford while living in Duncormick, Co. Wexford. Killed in action. From and article in the *Echo* newspaper, 'Mrs. Colfer, of Rathangan parish, recently received the sad news that her only son, Patrick, has been killed at the front. The news is doubly sad by reason of the fact that the poor woman has no one to share her bitter sorrow but her daughter, who is an invalid.' Grave or Memorial Reference: V.A.13. Cemetery: Vieille-Chapelle New British Cemetery, Lacouture in France.

COLLINS, Francis John: Rank: Lt Commander. Regiment or Service: Royal Indian Marines, Attached to the Inland Transport. Killed by accident in Discharge of his duty on the river Tigris. Date of death: 25 March 1917. Age at death, 35 also listed as 37. Born in Carnew.

Supplementary information: Son of Bernard J. and Teresa M. Collins of 6 Beresford Terrace, Ferrybank, Arklow, Co. Wicklow. Grave or Memorial Reference: IV.J.3. Cemetery: Basra War Cemetery in Iraq.

COLLINS, Patrick: Rank: Gunner. Regiment or Service: Royal Garrison Artillery. Unit: 122nd Siege Battery. Date of death: 2 October 1917. Service No: 43735. Born in Wexford. Enlisted in Plymouth while living in Wexford. Died of wounds. Grave or Memorial Reference: VIII.D.6. Cemetery: Ramscappelle Road Military Cemetery in Belgium.

COMERFORD, Laurence: Rank: Able Seaman. Regiment or Service: Mercantile Marine. Unit: SS *Coningbeg* (Glasgow). Torpedoed by German Submarine U-62. There were no survivors. Age at death: 39. Date of death: 18 December 1917.

Supplementary information: Born in Fethard-on-Sea in 1878. Son of Catherine Comerford and the late Patrick Comerford. Husband of Anastasia Comerford (*née* Hawkins) of 5 Presentation Row, Waterford. Laurence's brother Patrick is also mentioned on the Tower Memorial. Able Seaman Patrick Comerford drowned on the SS *Clune Park* in 1941, aged 52. Patrick's death in the Second World War brought an end to the male line of the Comerfords of Dungulph. Submarine U-62 which sunk the Connigbeg surrendered in November 1918 and was broken up on Bo'ness in 1920 for scrap. SS *Clune Park* was one of the nineteen ships in the unescorted convoy SLS64 when it was attacked by the German Crusier *Admiral Hipper* on the 12 February 1941. The *Admiral Hipper* was scuttled in dock in Germany in May 1945. Memorial: Laurence is listed on the Tower Hill Memorial UK and also on the War Memorial to the SS *Coningbeg*, Adelphi Quay, Waterford City.

COMERTO, James: Rank: Fireman. Regiment or Service: Mercantile Marine. Unit: SS *Antinoe* (London). She was torpedoed by a German Submarine about 150 miles off Bishop Rock. Age at death: 42. Date of death: 28 May 1917. From an article in the *Enniscorthy Guardian*, 1917:

FEARED LOSS OF WEXFORD SAILOR.
It is feared that Stoker James Comerford, of the Mercantile Marine, whose ship was recently sunk, is amongst those drowned. The most exhaustive inquiries by the family have failed in getting information as to his safety. He was son of Mr Martin Comerford, John Street, Wexford, and was, for a number of years in the Mercantile Marine Service.

Supplementary information: Son of Martin and Mary Comerton. Husband of Julia Comerton (*née* O'Connol) of Wygram Place, Wexford. Born at Wexford. Memorial: Tower Hill Memorial, UK.

CONBY, Henry Brodie: Rank: Lieutenant. Regiment or Service: Royal Naval Reserve. Unit: HM Drifter *George V.* Age at death: 30 (his family headstone in Avoca old Graveyard gives his age at death as 28 and gives his name as Brodie Henry Conby). Date of death: 3 June 1917. Awards: D S C, Mentioned in Despatches and listed in the *London Gazette* 19 January 1915.

Supplementary information: Son of Henry Brodie Conby (Master Mariner) and Sophia Louisa Conby. Husband of Eleanor Hutchinson Conby of 3 St John's Terrace, Enniscorthy, Co. Wexford. From an article in the *Enniscorthy Guardian*, 1917,

Much regret was felt in Enniscorthy on receipt of the news of the death of Lieut H. Brodie Conby of the Royal Naval reserve. The deceased, was son of Captain Conby, Ballymoney, Arklow, was married some two years ago to Miss N Armstrong, youngest daughter of the late Mr Wm Armstrong, and sister of Messrs Wm and John Armstrong, merchants, Enniscorthy. The late Lieut Conby was Lieutenant in the mercantlile marine, and having taken out his captains ticket volunteered for the naval reserve, and 12 months ago was appointed full Lieutenant.

He was in charge of a patrol of mine sweepers when his boat struck a mine and all hands were lost. Mrs Conby will have many sympathesers in the great loss she has sustained.

From another article in a Wexford newspaper:

The death is announced of Lieut H. Brodie Conby, R. N. R., who was killed by a mine explosion while on patrol duty on June 3rd. The deceased officer, who was a native of Arklow, was brother-in-law of Messrs William and John Armstrong, merchants, Enniscorthy, and for them and Mrs Conby much sympathy is felt in their bereavement.

Grave or Memorial Reference: 25. Memorial: Chatham Naval Memorial, UK.

CONDON, Patrick: Rank: Private. Regiment or Service: Royal Irish Regiment. Unit: 2nd Bn. Date of death: 29 March 1918. Service No: 2281. Born in Taghmon, Co. Wexford. Enlisted in Maryborough, Queens County while living in Taghmon. Died of wounds. From an article in a Wexford newspaper:

> Taghmon soldier's death. Mrs Alice Condon, Taghmon, as been notified by the War Office that her son Private Patrick Condon, 18th R. I. Regiment, died in hospital in France on Good Friday from wounds received a few days previously. Private Condon, who was only 25 years of age, volunteered at the beginning of the war and was wounded three times.
>
> He received the parchment certificate for gallant conduct and devotion to duty from Major-General W. B. Hickie. His brother, Private John Condon, has been a prisoner of war since the battle of Mons.

Grave or Memorial Reference: VII. D.23. Cemetery: Wimereux Communal Cemetery, Pas de Calais, France.

CONNOLLY, Patrick: Rank: Stoker. Regiment or Service: Royal Naval Reserve. Unit: HMS *Pheasant*. Age at death321: 48. Date of death: 1 March 1917. Service No: 1394U.
Supplementary information: Husband of Eliza Connolly of The Faythe, Wexford. From an article in the *People*, 1917, 'The relatives of Stoker Patrick Connolly have been informed that he has lost his life at sea. Stoker Connolly who was a well known pugalist leaves a wife and five children.' Grave or Memorial Reference: 24. Memorial: Plymouth Naval Memorial, UK.

CONNOLLY, Thomas Augustin: Rank: Private. Regiment or Service: Royal Dublin Fusiliers. Unit: 9th Bn. Age at death: 36. Date of death: 27 May 1917. Service No: 13982. Born in New Ross, Co. Wexford. Enlisted in Cardiff. Killed in action.
Supplementary information: Son of Thomas and Ellen Connolly (*née* Kehoe) of New Ross, Co. Wexford. From an article in a Wexford newspaper:

> NEW ROSS SOLDIER KILLED
> The news was learned with regret in New Ross of the death of Private Thos Augustine Connolly, R. E. [*sic*] who was killed by shellfire on the 27th of May.
>
> The deceased joined the army in September 1914 and was at the front since December 1915. He was a young man in his prime and a great favourite with his comrades in arms. The deceased was a brother of Mr William Connolly, formerly of Messrs, Colfer and Son's office, and nephew of Mr James Connolly, builder, Priory Street, New

Ross. He was interred in the Cemetery Noeux-Les-Mines on 28th of May with all honour and respect in the presence of officers and men of his unit.

Grave or Memorial Reference: I.T.2. Cemetery: Noeux-Les-Mines Communal Cemetery in France.

CONNORS/CONNERS/O'CONNOR, Denis: Rank: Rifleman. Regiment or Service: Royal Irish Rifles. Unit: 1st Bn. Age at death: 19. Date of death: 16 August 1917. Service No: 3/5926 and 5926. Born in Enniscorthy, Co. Wexford. Enlisted in Enniscorthy. Died of wounds.

Supplementary information: Son of William Thomas and Bridget Connors of 24 Ross Road, Enniscorthy. From an article in the *Enniscorthy Guardian* in 1917:

> News was received in Enniscorthy during the week of the death of Private Denis O'Connor, Royal Irish Rifles. Private O'Connor had been in the army for the past two years and had been through several engagements escaping without injury. He was the eldest son of Mr Wm, O'Connor, foreman in Messrs Buttle Bros' victualling establishment, with whom much sympathy will be felt in his bereavement.

Grave or Memorial Reference: XVII. AA.10A. Cemetery: Lijssenthoek Military Cemetery in Belgium.

CONNORS, Michael: Rank: Private. Regiment or Service: Royal Irish Regiment. Unit: 2nd Bn. Date of death: 21 August 1918. Service No: 6807. Born in Wexford. Enlisted in Clonmel, Co Tipperary while living in Wexford. Killed in action. Has no known grave but is commemorated on Panel 5. Memorial: Vis-En-Artois Memorial in France.

CONNORS, Michael J.: Rank: Private. Regiment or Service: Royal Dublin Fusiliers. Unit: 8th Bn. Age at death: 20. Date of death: 9 September 1916. Service No: 22338. Born in Gorey. Enlisted in Hertford while living in Gorey. Killed in action.

Supplementary information: Son of Mr Annie Connors of 35 William Street, Gorey, Co. Wexford. From an article from the *Enniscorthy Guardian*:

> Private Michael Connors, William Street, Gorey, aged 20, who was attached to the Royal Dublin Fusiliers, was killed in action at the front. Previous to joining he had been in London, where he had been in the employment of Miss Doyne, formerly of Webb's, Gorey, and having volunteered in June, 1915, he was sent with his company in February of the present year to France.
>
> A letter received by his mother from Lieutenant Colonel Bellingham, of his regiment, stated that he was killed at the taking of Ginchy, on the 9th of September last, and was buried at Guillemont, by a Pioneer Battalion, and conveying to her, the deepest sympathy of all in her irreparable loss. Her brother, William, who was aged just 23 years was killed on the 7th August, 1915, during the Dardanelles operations, and this coming so close to the death of William, makes the sorrow all the

more intense. Both young men when in Gorey were much respected, and the greatest sympathy is expressed with their widowed mother in the loss of her two brave boys, at such a young age.

Grave or Memorial Reference: II.F.6. Cemetery: Delville Wood Cemetery, Longueval in France.

CONNORS, Patrick: (also listed as **O'CONNOR, Patrick**) Rank: Private. Regiment or Service: Royal Irish Regiment. Unit: 2nd Bn. Date of death: 26 August 1914. Service No: 8281. Born in Rathangan, Co. Wexford. Enlisted in Clonmel while living in Duncormick, Co. Wexford. Killed in action. Age at death: 28.

Supplementary information: Son of Michael O'Connor of Johnstown, Duncormick, Wexford. Grave or Memorial Reference: I.D.3. Cemetery: Belgrade Cemetery in Belgium.

CONNORS, Philip: Rank: Private. Regiment or Service: Leinster Regiment. Unit: 3rd Bn. Date of death: 2 April 1915. Service No: 3985. Born in Enniscorthy, Co. Wexford. Enlisted in Enniscorthy. Died at home. Grave or Memorial Reference: Buried in Cork Military Cemetery and commemorated on the special memorial in Grangegorman Cemetery in Dublin.

CONNORS, William: Rank: Private. Regiment or Service: Royal Dublin Fusiliers. Unit: 1st Bn. Age at death: 23. Date of death: 7 August 1915. Service No: 17934. Born in Gorey. Enlisted in Gorey. Killed in action in Gallipoli.

Supplementary information: Son of Mrs Annie Connors of 35 William Street Gorey, Co. Wexford. From an article in the *People* and the *Enniscorthy Guardian*:

William Connors of William Street, Gorey, aged about 33 years, who was attached to the 3rd Battalion of the Royal Dublin Fusiliers, was killed in action in the Dardanelles on the 7th of August last.

Previous to volunteering for the front, shortly after the outbreak of the war, he had been in the employment of Mr Hutchinson, Merchant, Gorey, and was a hard working, industrious young man, temperate and most upright in every way. He leaves behind his widowed mother and three sisters, and a brother to mourn their loss and much sympathy in tendered on this sad occasion. His brother, Michael, who is only ninetten years of age, is attached to the same Battalion, is at present in Cork and expects to be shortly sent to the front.

Note: see Private Michael Connors, No 22338. Grave or Memorial Reference: Panel 190 to 196. Memorial: Helles Memorial, in Turkey.

CONNORS, William: Rank: Private. Regiment or Service: Royal Irish Regiment. Unit: 'C' Coy. 2nd Bn. Age at death: 23. Date of death: 12 July 1916. Service No: 8689. Born in Monageer, Co. Wexford. Enlisted in Enniscorthy.

Supplementary information: Son of Willaim and Annie of Mile House, Enniscorthy, Co. Wexford. From an article in the *Enniscorthy Guardian*:

AN ENNISCORTHY SOLDIER'S DEATH

We have been asked to publish the following letter, addressed to a Mrs Connors, Enniscorthy, which owing to an insufficient address, it has been found impossible by the postal officials to deliver. The letter is evidently intended for an inquirer in Enniscorthy district, and is from Rev Wilfred Pickering, Roman Catholic Chaplain to the British Forces in France. It is in the following terms – "Dear Mrs Connors – The Officer commanding No 2 Stationary Hospital has handed me today (Jusy 31st last) your letter of inquiry in regard to your son. I am sorry to have to inform you that he died here on July 12th.

You asked if he suffered much. Of that I cannot tell you, as he died on the day he came into hospital, not however, before he received the last sacraments. This at least will be a source of great consolation to you. Be assured of my sincerest sympathy with you in your great sorrow, and be assured too, that I shall not forget him and you in my prayers and in the holy sacrifice of the Mass. Your son is buried in the Catholic Cemetery in Abbeville. R.I.P.

Grave or Memorial Reference: V.E.4. Cemetery: Abbeville Communal Cemetery in France.

CONROY, James: Rank: Private. Regiment or Service: Royal Irish Regiment. Unit: 2nd Bn. Date of death: 14 July 1916. Service No: 7790. Born in Marshalstown, Co. Wexford. Enlisted in Kilkenny. Killed in action. Age at death: 20.

Supplementary information: Son of Michael and Annie Conroy of New Street, Kilkenny. Has no known grave but is commemorated on Pier and Face 16C. Memorial: Thiepval Memorial in France.

CONROY, Thomas: Rank: Sapper. Regiment or Service: Corps of Royal Engineers. Unit: 97th Field Company, Royal Engineers. Date of death: 4 May 1917. Service No: 23045. Born in Enniscorthy, Co. Wexford. Enlisted in Carlow while living in Paddington in Middlesex. Killed in action. Age at death: 26.

Supplementary information: Husband of M. Scales (formerly Conroy) of 8 City Road, Lakenham, Norwich, Norfolk. He has no known grave but is listed on the Special Memorial 67. Cemetery: Wancourt British Cemetery in France.

CONVERY, Thomas: Rank: Private. Regiment or Service: Northumberland Fusiliers. Unit: 8th Bn. Date of death: 19 August 1915. Service No: 4088. Born in Wexford. Enlisted in Newcastle-On-Tyne. Killed in action in the Mediterranean. He has no known grave but is listed on Panel 33 to 35 on the Helles Memorial in Turkey.

CONWAY, John: Rank: Stoker 1st Class. Regiment or Service: Royal Naval Reserve. Unit: Anson Battalion, Royal Naval Division. Date of death: 6 May 1915. Service No: 2471T. Born in John Street, Wexford. From an article in the *Enniscorthy Guardian:*

WEXFORDMAN KILLED IN ACTION.
John Conway (Green Street, Wexford) of the Naval Brigade, has been killed

John Conway.

in action at the Dardanelles. The rumour circulated last week concerning his death has been confirmed by a telegram received by his wife from the Admiralty. John Conway, who son of the late Owen Conway, John Street, Wexford was a great favourite among his associates.

He was engaged for some time as an engineer, but he afterwards joined the navy and his name adds to the long list of brave Irishmen who have gone down in the struggle. The deepest sympathy is felt for his young widow and two children and also for his mother, brothers and sisters who deeply mourn their loss.

Note: The offensive words of following article have been omitted. From the *Free Press*, 1915:

Peter Nolan, Distillery Road Wexford, who is serving in the Naval Brigade at the Dardanelles, writes a very interesting letter to his parents in the course of which he says "You wont know me when I get home, as I am as black as a --------. My chum Hayden and myself were thinking of running a -------- show when we get o this business. We have not had such a bad time since we landed but it was very rough at first. I am very sorry to tell you that poor Jack Conway got killed when we advanced on May 6th. Hayden, Hagan and all the boys of Wexford in our lot laid the poor lad to rest.

Father Finn [see *The Tipperary War Dead*], of Dublin, who was killed by the Turks since, said the prayers at poor Jack's graveside. All our boys were lucky, but poor Jack, but our lads paid him the last tribute. When we were burying poor Conway we nearly got hit ourselves. Snipers sent bullets hissing round us, but we did not mind them. We have the Turks on the run now, and they go like hares when we get near them. The band plays every day with the big guns playing ' The West's Awake. ' In conclusion he returns thanks for some gifts, and desires to be remembered to all his friends, Nolan, it is stated, but not officially, has since been wounded.

He has no known grave but is listed on Panel 7 on the Helles Memorial in Turkey.

COONEY, Patrick: Rank: Private. Regiment or Service: Royal Irish Regiment. Unit: 5th Bn. Age at death: 30. Date of death: 4 May 1918. Service No: 3/8759 and 8759. Born in New Bawn Co. Wexford. Enlisted in New Bawn while living in Enniscorthy. Died in Egypt.

Supplementary information: Husband of Catherine Cooney of Bree, Macmine, Co. Wexford. Grave or Memorial Reference: C.74. Cemetery: Alexandria (Hadra) War Memorial Cemetery in Egypt.

COOPER, John: Rank: Sergeant. Regiment or Service: Royal Irish Regiment. Unit: 2nd Bn. Age at death: 32. Date of death: 14 May 1915. Service No: 7571. Born in Clongeen, Co. Wexford. Enlisted in Wexford while living in Taghmon, Co. Wexford. Killed in action.

Supplementary information: Son of John and Mary Cooper of Taghmon, Co. Wexford. From another article in the *Enniscorthy Guardian*:

Taghmon N. C. O killed in action. Much sympathy was felt in Taghmon on Monday when it made know that Sergeant John Cooper, 2nd Battalion, Royal Irish Regiment, was killed in action 'somewhere in France' on the 14th May. Sergeant Cooper was most popular with his comrades in the army. As a lad of 17 years he volunteered for service in the South African war and went through that tedious campaign. Since then he was stationed at different parts of the British Empire. Up till last Christmas he was a drill instructor in a depot in Dublin, and on three occasions offered himself for service at the front, but was not accepted, as the authorities informed him that he was needed as badly at home training recruits.

However, he again applied and was sent out. His last letter home was written three days before he was killed, in which he stated they were on the march to the firing line, and that he obtained his stationary in a farmhouse, and had only left, when a shell burst beside the building, and six of his comrades were killed. The greatest sympathy is expended to his sorrowing parents, brothers and sisters. He was only 31 years of age. He has a younger brother in training in the Irish Brigade.

Grave or Memorial Reference: Panel 33. Memorial: Ypres (Menin Gate) Memorial in Belgium.

John Cooper.

COOPER, Michael: Rank: Private. Regiment or Service: Royal Irish Regiment. Unit: 6th Bn. Date of death: 14 August 1917. Service No: 2273. Born in Clongeen, Co. Wexford. Enlisted in Maryborough, Queens County while living in Taghmon Co. Wexford. Died of wounds. He won the Military Medal and is listed in the *London Gazette*. From an article in the *People*, 1916:

Taghmon man wins the Military Cross. For gallantry displayed in the advance on the western front, Private Michael Cooper, Taghmon, has been awarded the Military Cross.

He was attached to the Headquarters staff and brought dispatches to the firing line under terrific fire. He is warmly congratulated by his many friends and amongst the first to extend their congratulations to him were Private M. J. Martin, Taghmon, Privates P. Fox, P. Condon, and E. Walsh, who fought in the big push and came through the struggle without a scratch. Private Cooper was one of the best known athletes in Taghmon district, especially as a footballer.

Grave or Memorial Reference: V.D.1. Cemetery: Brandhoek New Military Cemetery in Belgium.

COPELAND, James: Rank: Private. Regiment or Service: Royal Irish Regiment. Unit: 2nd Bn. Date of death: 19 October 1914. Service No: 5432. Born in St Mary's, Enniscorthy, Co. Wexford. Enlisted in Wexford while living in Enniscorthy. Killed in action. He has no known grave but is listed on Panels 11 and 12 on the Le Touret Memorial in France.

CORISH, Patrick Joseph: Rank: Private. Regiment or Service: London Regiment. Unit: 15th (County of London) Battalion (P.W.O Civil Service Rifles), also listed as 1/15th Battalion. Date of death: 15 October 1916. Service No: 4824. Age at death, 24. Enlisted in London. Killed in action. From an article in the *Enniscorthy Guardian*:

His friends in Wexford are sorry to learn of the death in action of Patrick Joseph Corish, son of Patrick and Mrs Corish, Ballinacourty, Dungarvan, and grandson of Mr Patrick Walsh, Johns Street, Wexford. Mr Corish, who was only 24 years of age, joined the colours

since the outbreak of the war and was attached to the London Regiment.

Supplementary information: Son of Patrick and Mary Corish, of 19 Hollybank Avenue, Sandford Road., Ranelagh, Dublin. A Civil Servant at the Board of Education, Whitehall, London. Grave or Memorial Reference: Pier and Face 13 C. MemoriaL; Thiepval Memorial in France.

CORNICK, Percy James: Rank: Leading Boatman. Regiment or Service: H.M. Coastguard. Unit: 2nd Bn. Date of death: 26 November 1918. Service No: 202822. Born on the Island of Jersey. Grave or Memorial Reference: 597. Cemetery, Gorey (Christ Church) Church of Ireland Churchyard.

COSGRAVE, Daniel Joseph: Rank: Acting Corporal. Regiment or Service: South Lancashire Regiment. Unit: 2nd Bn. Date of death: 3 July 1916. Age at death, 28. Service No: 12993. Born in Enniscorthy Co. Wexford. Enlisted in Birkenhead Cheshire while living in Dublin. Killed in action.

Supplementary information: Son of John and Annastalia Cosgrave. Husband of Mary E. Cosgrave of 7 Newgrove Avenue, Sandymount, Dublin. From an article in the *Enniscorthy Guardian*:

His many friends and numerous comrades will regret to hear of the death at the front on July 4th of Sergeant Daniel J Cosgrave, of the South Lancashire Regiment, a native of Oylgate, and second son of Mr John Cosgrave, Oylgate. He was a splendid specimen of young Irish manhood,

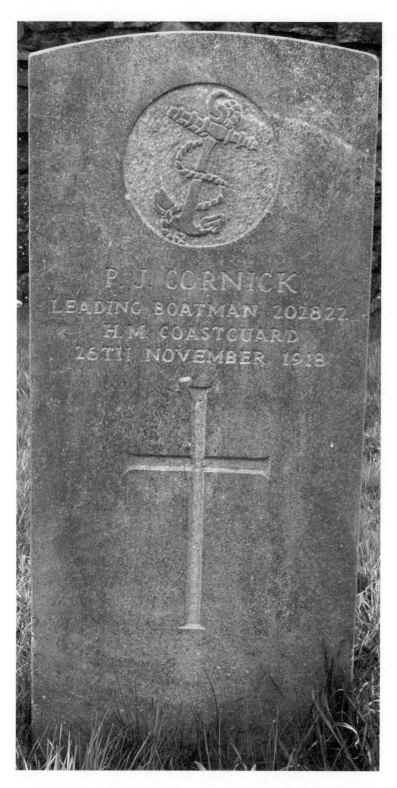

P. J. CORNICK
LEADING BOATMAN 202822
H.M. COASTGUARD
26TH NOVEMBER 1918

Percy James
Cornick.

standing six feet one inch in height, a finely proportioned. He served some years in the Dublin Metropolitan Police before going to England, where he joined the Lancashires shortly after the outbreak of the war. He won the D. C. M. twice, and was promoted full Sergeant on the battlefield. He also received the Order of St George of Russia. During the year 1915 he was in seven bayonet charges, and received three wounds, two in the leg and shrapnel wound in the shoulder.

He was in the fighting on the 9th October, 1914, when the Prussian Guards were routed at Ypres. Sergt Cosgrave was home last December, when some thrilling accounts of his prowess and daring were published in these columns. A comrade, writing to Sergt Cosgrave's brother, Mr P Cosgrave, in Dublin, says the Sergeant fell whilst bravely leading on his platoon, and was killed instantly by a bullet through the head. Much sympathy is felt with Mr John Cosgrave, the sorrowing father of the deceased soldier, and all the members of the family who are most popular in Oylgate. R.I.P.

From another article in the *People*:

Sergeant D J Cosgrave, son of Mr. J Cosgrave, arrived home on Friday last for a brief furlough. Sergeant Cosgrave is a splendid specimen of Irish manhood, standing six feet one inch in height, finely proportionate and weighing a little over 15 stone. He was the centre of all eyes when he stepped lightly onto the platform at Enniscorthy on Friday morning last with his rifle and knapsack, just as he left the trenches, the soil of France or Belgium adhering in large quantities to his boots, puttees and clothing. Sergeant Cosgrave belongs an English regiment, having enlisted in England. He served some years in the Dublin Metropolitan Police before going to England.

He was promoted full sergeant on the battlefield, three times, and received the DCM. Twice and also the order of St. George of Russia. In a chat with some fiends, Sergeant Cosgrove said he has been in the trenches since the 14th of August, 1914, just fifteen months. He was in seven bayonet charges and received three wounds, two in the leg and a shrapnel wound in the left shoulder. He retains the piece of shrapnel. "In one bayonet charge," he said, we lost 650 men, that was not at La Basse, the charge lasted half an hour. 350 of a reinforcement came to our aid, but only seven of us were left, six and myself. On the 9th October, 1914, at Ypres we routed the Prussian Guards, they were the finest body of men I ever saw together. I thought I should never see home again when we met them. I am fairly big myself, but I was as a child compared with some of those fellows, though I stand six feet one inch."

Grave or Memorial Reference: Pier and Face 7A and 7B. Memorial; Thiepval Memorial in France.

COSGRAVE, Jeremiah: Rank: Private. Regiment or Service: Royal Dublin Fusiliers. Unit: 2nd Bn. Age at death: 32. Date of death: 16 August 1917. Service No: 17962. Born in Galbally, Co. Wexford. Enlisted in Maesteg. Killed in action.

Supplementary information: Son of

John and Mary Cosgrave of Galbally, Bree, Enniscorthy, Co. Wexford. Grave or Memorial Reference: Panel 144 to 145. Memorial: Tyne Cot Memorial in Belgium.

COSGRAVE/COSGROVE, Michael:

Rank: Sergeant. Regiment or Service: East Lancashire Regiment. Unit: 11th Bn. Date of death: 13 April 1918. Service No: 31438. Born in Wexford. Enlisted in Birkinhead, Cheshire while living in Wexford. Killed in action. From an article in a Wexford newspaper:

His many friends in Wexford will learn with regret of the death in action of Sergt, Michael W Cosgrave, East Lancashire Regiment.

The late Mr Cosgrave, who was aged 38, was educated at St Peters College, Liverpool. Prior to going on active service he had been representative of an extensive English grocery firm. With the members of his family in Wexford, much sympathy is felt.

From an article in the *People*, 1918:

Sergeant Michael Cosgrave Killed. His many friends in Wexford will learn with regret of the death in action on the 12th April, of Sergeant Michael Cosgrave, East Lancashire Regiment. The late Mr Cosgrave, who was aged 38, was traveller for an extensive grocery firm in England when he volunteered.

He was educated at St Peter's College, Wexford, and later at St Edward's College, Liverpool. Sergeant was son of the late Mr Francis Cosgrave, Wexford, and nephew of

Very Rev. Canon Cosgrave P. P. Preston.

From an article in the *People*, 1918:

The relatives of Sergt Michael Cosgrave have received official notification from the war office of his death in action on April 13. He was brother of Mr N. J. Cosgrave, Wexford, nephew of Very Rev Canon Cosgrave, P. P. Preston; brother in law of Messrs John J Kehoe, J.P., M.C.C., and Hugh McGuire, Wexford. Although Sergt Cosgrave left home when very young, the news of his death came as a great shock to relatives and numerous Wexford friends.

His parents laid the foundation for his future career by seeing that he was provided with a thorough education, which he received in Liverpool, finishing up at St Edward's College of that city. He commenced his commercial life about 19 years ago with the famous firm of Messrs Lever Brothers, Port Sunlight, when he resided in New Ferry and Bebington district. In the course of a few years he became a successful commercial traveller, and at the time he joined up he was acting in this capacity for Messrs Bancroft, the well-known firm of lard refiners in Liverpool, who have lost a trusted servant. Sergt Cosgrave's genial disposition soon finds its counterpart in his social life, and there are few, if any, better known or more enthusiastic workers in the Irish and Catholic circles of New Ferry.

When the late Sergeant went to reside in New Ferry it was necessary to walk a distance of over two miles to Rock Ferry for Mass, but later on a Catholic Mission was opened in the former township, and for a time all services were held in a small hall attached to some cocoa rooms. This was the commencement of the organisation of the Catholic community in the neighbourhood. In the course of two or three years building operations commenced in connection with the school chapel of St John's, New Ferry, and from that day to this there has been no-one more closely associated with the Catholic and Irish propaganda than was Michael Cosgrove. Whenever an Irish concert or picnic was organised, he was always the moving and organising spirit.

He was one of the first members of the New Ferry Young Men's Catholic Society, which began in a very humble way in the upper rooms of a private house, but it was the enthusiastic work done by Mr Cosgrave and others under great disadvantages that made possible the furnishing of the present clubroom, with its two magnificent full-sized billiard tables. The Gaelic League could not have had a more energetic promoter, and Michael Cosgrave did much in the endeavour to establish the League permanently in the district. How many hours and weeks has he not spent in the interests of the revival of the Irish language? Under his fatherly care and tuition the youngsters used to look forward to the classes with considerable pleasure and became much attached to their teacher.

He was universally loved by the juvenile population of New Ferry that came in contact with him. Sergt Cosgrave was a member of the United Kingdom Commercial Traveller's Association, and always prominent in connection with the social side of the Birkinhead and Wirral Branch. When the announcement was made on Sunday week last in St John's Catholic Church, New Ferry, Birkinhead, that Mass was being offered for "Michael Cosgrave" those who have known him for so many years felt as if part of their self had been cut off- there was something missing, a blank. His death was the one topic of discussion after service. The Irish and Catholics of New Ferry have lost one of their most unselfish, large-hearted, and genial of God's creatures, and for them to have to think that "Cossy", (as he was familiarly called) is no more, seems impossible to realise.

When 'Irelands Own' was first published Sergt Cosgrave rendered great assistance in securing a high place for it in the districts through which he travelled.

He has no known grave but is listed on Panel 5 and 6 on the Ploegsteert Memorial in Belgium.

COSGROVE/COSGRAVE, James.

Rank: Private. Regiment or Service: Royal Dublin Fusiliers. Unit: 2nd Bn. Age at death: 36. Date of death: 2 May 1915 also listed as 1 May 1915. Service No: 9598. Formerly he was with the Leinster Regiment where his number was 4619. Born in Oulart/Owlart, Co. Wexford. Enlisted in Carlow while living in Wexford. Died of wounds.

Supplementary information: Son of Robert and Johanna Cosgrove of Killisk, Ballagh, Enniscorthy, Co. Wexford. From an article in a Wexford newspaper:

Ballaghkeene Man dies of Wounds. Intelligence was conveyed to his relatives at Killisk, Ballaghkeene, during the week, that Private James Cosgrave, of the Royal Dublin Fusiliers, had died from wounds on May 1st, somewhere in France. The deceased, who was for some years on foreign service, had returned home sometime previous to the war, from whence he was called up at the outbreak of hostilities. He was through most of the big battles of the great war, but he visited his native home some months ago on a short furlough, from whence he again returned to the firing line.

Grave or Memorial Reference: II.A.198. Cemetery: Bailleul Communal Cemetery Extension (Nord) in France.

COTTON, Edward: Rank: Able Seaman. Regiment or Service: Mercantile Marine. Unit: SS *Mary Fanny* (Bideford). Age at death: 22. Date of death: 15 September 1918.

Supplementary information: Son of Edward and Elizabeth Cotton (*née* Druhan) of 31 Cross Lane, New Ross, Co. Wexford. Memorial: Tower Hill Memorial, UK.

COTTON, Laurence: Rank: Private. Regiment or Service: Royal Irish Rifles. Unit: 2nd Bn. Date of death: 26 April 1916. Service No: 7829. Born in Wexford. Enlisted in New Ross, Co. Wexford. Killed in action. From an article in the *Enniscorthy Guardian*:

New Ross Man Killed; Private Laurence Cotton, Maiden Lane, New Ross, was recently killed at the war.

He was about 20 years of age and son of Thomas Cotton, chimney cleaner.

He volunteered last July, and was at the front since last November. He used to write very interesting letters home to his parents, and the last one contained an account of how himself and his comrades received Holy Communion on Palm Sunday.

Grave or Memorial Reference: I.G.9. Cemetery: Ecoivres Military Cemetery Mont-St. Eloi in France.

COTTON, Phillip/Philip: Rank: Private. Regiment or Service: Royal Irish Regiment. Unit: 2nd Bn. Age at death: 42. Date of death: 23 May 1915. Service No: 6746. Born in St Mary's, New Ross, Co. Wexford. Enlisted in Enniscorthy while living in New Ross. Died.

Supplementary information: Son of Thomas and Maria Cotton. Husband of Katie Cotton of 15 Wind Mill Lane, New Ross. From another article in the *Enniscorthy Guardian*:

Information received New Ross during the week that Philip Cotton, Barrack Street, New Ross, was killed at the front recently by lightening. He was in the trenches when a thunderstorm occurred and was struck by a flash and was killed.

He had been on a visit to Ross some months ago wounded and leaves a wife and three or four children. His death has been officially confirmed. He was through the Boer war and escaped harm during the campaign.

From De Ruvigny's Roll of Honour:

Son of Thomas Cotton, Chimney Sweep; b, New Ross, Co, Hereford [*sic*], 1885; educ, there; served 13 years in the Royal Irish Regt. (India Medal, 1895); re-enlisted after the outbreak of war, 21 Sept, 1914; served with the Expeditionary force in France, and was killed in the trenches by a flash of lightening, 22nd May, 1915. He married at New Ross, 20 May, 1907, Kate (2, Michael Street, New Ross) day, of James Hennebury, of New Ross, and had three daus. ; Anastatia, b. 1 Jan, 1908; Elizabeth, b. 1 feb, 1912; and May, b. 27 Feb, 1915.

Grave or Memorial Reference: Panel 33. Memorial: Ypres (Menin Gate) Memorial in Belgium.

COURTNEY, Mathew Joseph: Rank: Corporal and Lance Corporal. Regiment or Service: Leinster Regiment. Unit: 1st Bn. Age at death: 23. Date of death: 4 October 1916. Service No: 9267. Born in Wexford. Enlisted in Wexford. Died of wounds in Salonika.

Supplementary information: Son of Patrick J. and Ellen Courtney of Coolgarrow, Enniscorthy, Co. Wexford. Grave or Memorial Reference: II.J.8. Cemetery: Struma Military Cemetery in Greece.

COUSINS, Ernest Joseph: Rank: Private. Regiment or Service: Kings Liverpool Regiment. Unit: 7th Bn. Date of death: 28 August 1916. Service No: 1533. Born in Kilmore, Co. Wexford. Enlisted in Bootle, Liverpool while living in Kirkdale in Liverpool. Killed in action. Age at death: 22.

Supplementary information: Son of Herbert and Hebe Cousins of Nettlecombe, Melplash, Dorset. He has no known grave but is commemorated on Pier and Face 7B. Memorial: Thiepval Memorial in France.

COUSINS, Patrick: Rank: Private. Regiment or Service: 5th Dragoon Guards (Princess Charlotte of Wales's). Date of death: 4 January 1916. Service No: D/10056. Born in Dublin. Enlisted in Aberdare, Penriwceiber. Died of wounds.

Supplementary information: Brother of Katie Rossiter of 7 Dempsey's Terrace, Wexford. Native of Wexford. From an article in the *People* 1915:

A TROOPER'S LETTER.

Trooper Patrick Cousins, 5th Dragoon Guards, writing to his sister, Mrs T Rossiter, Dempsey's Terrace, Wexford, under date of 22nd inst, gratefully acknowledges receipt of parcel and describes some of the recent fighting.

In a recent encounter he points out that they were twelve hours in action. "We were called out" he says, "at 4a.m., and went into the firing line. We got into the trenches at 9p.m. on the same day. The Germans were 400 yards in front of us. Everything went all right until four a. m. on the following morning, and then it was 'hell on earth'. The Germans must have had 109 guns on us. They bursted in the trench on top of us by 12 o'clock. There were dead and wounded in the trench. I cannot explain the noise and roar of their guns, and our trench was rocking. Our officers and men expected we would be killed at any moment. This bombardment was kept up all day, and at four p.m. we had to retire. When leaving the trench they fired and shelled us. We lost about 110 men of the regiment during the day." In conclusion he states he is in perfect health and spirits. Trooper Cousins has been in the fighting line since November last. He was slightly wounded about two months ago.

Grave or Memorial Reference: VI.B.13. Cemetery: Etaples Military Cemetery in France.

COY, Charles: Rank: Guardsman. Regiment or Service: Grenadier Guards. Unit: 3rd Bn. Date of death: 11 March 1916. Service No: 20343. Born in Wexford. Enlisted in Galway. Died of wounds. Age at death: 24.

Supplementary information: Son of Hugh and Mary Coy of 27 Douglas Road, Derby Road, Nottingham. Grave or Memorial Reference: Plot B, Row 4, Grave 7. Cemetery: Calais Southern Cemetery in France.

COX, Luke: Rank: Private. Regiment or Service: Royal Army Medical Corps. Age at death: 27. Date of death: 27 December 1919. Service No: 62842.

Supplementary information: Son of Mrs. Mary Cox of Rathduff, Killanne, Enniscorthy, Co. Wexford. From an article in the *Enniscorthy Guardian*, December 1915,

Gone to Egypt. Luke Cox, Kiltealy, formerly in charge of Kiltealy National Volunteers, who volunteered some time ago spent a few days at home recently. He is now on his way to Egypt.

From an article in the *People*, 1915:

Corporal Cox, Enniscorthy. Corporal Cox, R.I.R. Enniscorthy, is at present home on sick leave suffering from a bullet wound in the knee. He is progressing favourably, and hopes to rejoin his company at Clonmel about the end of the week.

Grave or Memorial Reference: III.C.9. Cemetery: Mazargues War Cemetery, in France.

CROMBIE, Francis Newton Allen: Rank: Captain. Regiment or Service: Royal Navy. Naval Attache, Petrograd. Awards, C.B., D.S.O. Age at death: 36. Date of death: 31 August 1918.

Supplementary information: Chevalier, Legion of Honour; Order of St Vladimir with Swords (Russia); Cross of St George (Russia). Son of the late Capt. F. C. Cromie, Hampshire Regt. (Consul General, Dakar), and of Mrs Lennard (formerly Cromie). Husband of Mrs Cromie, of 9 Old Park Road, Clapham Common, London. Awarded Royal Humane Society's Medal (1906). Served in Boxer Rebellion, 1900 (Mentioned in Despatches). From an article in the *People*, 1918,

Captain Crombie of Duncannon. -Daring exploits. Captain Crombie of the British Embassy who was murdered at Petrograd, Russia last week by the Bolshevist soldiers, was 36 years of age, a son of the late Captain F Crombie, and was born at Duncannon Fort, South Wexford. He offered heroic resistance to the intruding miscreants on their attack on the British Embassy, and killed three of the intruders. He was afterwards murdered, and his corpse outraged, and an

English clergyman was forbidden to say prayers over the body. He was the British Naval Attache. "As commander of the British submarine flotilla in the Baltic, Captain Crombie, D.S.O., did" says the Daily Mail "Sterling work for Russia and the Allies, and the Germans have reason to remember his daring exploits. Commanding E18 he forced a passage into the Baltic in September, 1915, and sank the German cruiser 'Undine', 22 miles from the Swedish Coast in November, 1915. She was convoying the German steam ferry, 'Prussia'. E18 also sank, or drove ashore a large number of German merchant ships, and entirely suspended German traffic for a period. In May, 1916, he was awarded the D.S.O. for his services, and in October last was promoted acting Captain.

The late Czar when paying a visit of inspection to the submarines decorated him with the Cross of St George, and he also received several other Russian honours. In April last when the submarines were destroyed and their crews dispersed he was responsible for the arrangements. Owing to his knowledge of Russian and familiarity with the conditions prevailing in Russia, he remained at the Embassy as Assistant Naval Attaché, and shortly after was made British Naval Attaché. He joined the submarine service, and when the war broke out he was in command of the Hong Kong Flotilla. Dr Harold Williams, describing the late Captain Crombie in the 'Daily Chronicle' says "Crombie was a pale, slight, quiet man, very reserved about his exploits, with eyes intent and strained, as though from excess of responsibility.

It is bitter to think that a man who risked innumerable dangers to protect the Russian seaboard against Germany should be killed by a Russian mob, brutalised by Bolshevik rule."

He has no known grave but is listed on the Archangel Memorial in the Russian Federation.

CROWE, Michael: Rank: Private. Regiment or Service: Irish Guards. Unit: 1st Bn. Date of death: 12 October 1915. Service No: 7753. Born in Gorey, Co. Wexford. Enlisted in Coatbridge, Lanarkshire while living in Darkley, Co Armagh. Killed in action. Age at death: 36.

Supplementary information: Son of James and Mary Crowe. Husband of Bridget Crowe of 29 Darkley Keady, Co. Armagh. He has no known grave but is listed on Panel 9 and 10 on the Loos Memorial in France.

CROWTHER, William: Rank: Corporal. Regiment or Service: Royal Irish Fusiliers. Unit: A Company, 1st Bn. Date of death: 22 October 1914. Service No: 10767. Born in Wexford. Enlisted in Dublin. Killed in action. Age at death: 19.

Supplementary information: Son of William and Julia Crowther of 5 Graham's Cottages, Ballybough Road, Dublin. Born at Wexford. Grave or Memorial Reference: II.C.33. Cemetery: Houplines Communal Cemetery Extension in France.

CULLEN, Archibald Patrick: Rank: Private. Regiment or Service: South Wales Borderers. Unit: 2nd Bn. Date

John Joseph Cullen.

of death: 21 August 1915. Service No: 18627. Born in Clogheen, Co. Wexford. Enlisted in Birkinhead. Killed in action in Gallipoli. Age at death: 24.

Supplementary information: Son of the late Patrick Cullen. He has no known grave but is commemorated on Panel 80 to 84 and 219 to 220. Memorial: Helles Memorial in Turkey.

CULLEN, John Joseph: Rank: Private. Regiment or Service: Grenadier Guards. Unit: No.3 Coy. 4th Bn. Age at death: 25. Date of death: 2 October 1915. Service No: 20453. Born in Ballysop, Co. Wexford. Enlisted in Cardiff. Died of wounds.

Supplementary information: Son of Edward and Margaret Cullen of Ballybrize Cottage, Campile, Co. Wexford. From an article in the *People*:

Private John Cullen who was recently killed in the fighting in Flanders after delivering a brilliant attack along with his Regiment on the enemy, was a son of Mr Edward Cullen, steward, and Mrs Cullen, Ballysop, Aclare. He was

about 21 years of age and volunteered from England. He was at home on a visit some three months ago. He has another brother who volunteered some months ago.

Grave or Memorial Reference: I.D.19. Cemetery: Lapugnoy Military Cemetery in France.

CULLEN, John: Rank: Private. Regiment or Service: Irish Guards. Unit: 2nd Bn. Age at death: 20. Date of death: 11 October 1917. Service No: 10711. Born in New Ross, Co. Wexford. Enlisted in New Ross. Died of wounds.

Supplementary information: Son of Andrew Cullen of 2 Abbeyview Terrace, New Ross. From an article in the *People*:

The Cullen family, New Ross, between

Thomas Cullen.

its members, sons and relations, has twenty with the colours. There are four brothers of the family who before joining were well known in the building trade that is Messrs, Andrew, John, Martin and Richard. Andrew whose family reside at Abbey Terrace, volunteered last July in the Irish Guards and is stationed in England.

He has a son, Seaman Andrew Cullen, aged 20, who volunteered in the Navy in April of last year, and his second son, Private John Cullen, aged 18, joined in December last in the same regiment as his father and is still in training. Andrew's second brother, John, of Church Lane, formerly belonged to the Royal Garrison Artillery and served in India and his time has expired. He rejoined a few months after the outbreak of the war and was wounded and taken prisoner and is at present in Germany. He was rather severely wounded at the battle of Mons and was unconscious when taken by the Germans. The third brother, Gunner Richard Cullen, who is married in Carrick on Suir, rejoined in February, 1916, got wounded and is at the front again.

The fourth brother, Martin, is a native of the Bullawn, a Lance Corporal, rejoined some few months after the war and is at the front. He was in the Boer War. Private James Cullen and Private Michael Cullen, sons of Mr James Cullen, Mary Street, who are also with the colours, are cousins of the above mentioned brothers, and nephews of them with the colours are Sergeant Kenny, Chapel Lane, who has been through several of the big engagements and his brother, Michael Kenny, who was at the front and got frostbitten, and Andrew Cullen, who volunteered after his father from Carrick on Suir. Some

of the other relatives are at the front and more in training quarters.

Grave or Memorial Reference: V.I.14. Cemetery: Dozinghem Military Cemetery in Belgium.

CULLEN, Matthew: Rank: Private. Regiment or Service: Royal Scots (Lothian Regiment). Unit: 12th Bn. Date of death: 27 October 1915. Service No: 3515 Born in Wexford. Enlisted in Glencorse while living in Methil, Fifeshire. Died of wounds. Grave or Memorial Reference: I.B.32A. Cemetery: Lijssenthoek Military Cemetary in Belgium.

CULLEN, Maurice: Rank: Private. Regiment or Service: Royal Irish Regiment. Unit: 2nd Bn. Date of death: 24 April 1915. Service No: 10614. Born in St Mary's, Enniscorthy. Enlisted in Wexford while living in Enniscorthy. Killed in action. From an article in the *Enniscorthy Guardian*:

> During the past week, Mr and Mrs Robert Cullen, Irish Street, Enniscorthy, received the sad news from official sources of the death of their two sons at the front. On Friday the news arrived of the death of Private Thomas Cullen and on Wednesday came the news of the death of Private Maurice Cullen R. I. R., their second youngest son.
>
> Mr and Mrs Cullen had six sons serving with the colours, and much sympathy is felt with the parents on the death of their boys. Maurice, the last boy killed, was buried on the battlefield by another of his brothers, Myles Cullen assisted by a neighbour named

O'Neill from irish Street, Enniscorthy, who is serving in the same Regiment.

Another article in a Wexford newspaper continues:

Information has been received by Mr Robert Cullen, tailor, Irish Street, Enniscorthy, of the death while serving with their Regiments in France of his two sons Thomas and Maurice Cullen who were in the Royal Irish Regiment.

Mr Cullen has six sons serving in the army. Intimation was first received of the death of Private Thomas Cullen, and three days later news came of the death of Private Maurice Cullen of the same Regiment. The latter was interred by his brother Myles Cullen of the same Regiment, and by a neighbour, Private O'Neill, whose people live in Irish Street.

He has no known grave but is listed on Panel on the Ploegsteert Memorial in Belgium.

CULLEN, Michael: Rank: Stoker. Regiment or Service: Royal Naval Reserve. Unit: SS *Transylvania*. Date of death: 4 May 1917. Service No: 2847S. From an article in the *People*, 1917:

Official information has been received of the death of Stoker Michael Cullen, R.N.R., who was lost when his ship, the Transylvania was sunk on the 4 May in the Mediterranean. He was the son of Mr Thomas Cullen, High Street, Wexford, who is serving in the Royal Irish Regiment. Deceased, who was about 23 years of age, joined the navy on the 4 August, 1914.

He fought with the naval division

at Antwerp, and subsequently at the Dardanelles where he was wounded about two years ago. SS *Transylvania* was commissioned troopship in 1915 with accommodation for 200 officers and 2860 men. She was sent to the bottom by a German torpedo from submarie U63 off Cape Noli, 40 miles from Genoa. 402 lives were lost in the sinking. The submarine surrendered in 1919 and was broken up for scrap.

Grave or Memorial Reference: 24. Memorial: Plymouth Naval Memorial.

CULLEN, Myles: Rank: Private. Regiment or Service: Royal Irish Regiment. Unit: 6th Bn. Age at death: 25. Date of death: 22 July 1916. Service No: 8112. Born in St Mary's, Enniscorthy, Co. Wexford.

Supplementary information: Son of Robert and Mary Cullen of 20 Irish Street, Enniscorthy, Co. Wexford. From an article in the *Enniscorthy Guardian* in 1916:

Mr and Mrs Cullen, Irish Street, Enniscorthy, have received the sad news that their youngest son, Christopher Cullen, a Private in the Royal Irish Fusiliers, has been severely wounded.

He lost his arm in the recent fighting, also receiving a shrapnel wound to the back. He is at present in a military hospital, and is doing as well a can be expected. Private Christy Cullen is the fourth of six sons in the army to fall a victim of the Germans. Three of the brothers are already killed; only two weeks ago an account of the death of Private Myles Cullen, with photo, was published in this column. Another son is at present home discharged from the army, part of one hand being blown away. Much sympathy is felt with Mr and Mrs Cullen in their many troubles.

Grave or Memorial Reference: V.G.20. Cemetery: Bethune Town Cemetery in France.

CULLEN, Patrick: Rank: Private. Regiment or Service: Leinster Regiment. Unit: 2nd Bn. Date of death: 18 August 1915. Service No: 3642. Born in Cranford, Co. Wexford. Enlisted in Maryborough, Queen County. Died of wounds. Grave or Memorial Reference: II.D.37. Cemetery; Lijssenthoek Military Cemetary in Belgium.

CULLEN, Thomas: Rank: Private. Regiment or Service: Kings Liverpool Regiment. Unit: 7th Bn. Date of death: 10 August 1916. Service No: 2164 and 3164. Born in Wexford. Enlisted in Bootle, Liverpool while living in Bootle. Died of wounds. Age at death: 22.
Supplementary information: Son of Michael and Mary Cullen of 39 Tennyson Street, Bootle, Liverpool. Grave or Memorial Reference: I.F.9. Cemetery: La-Neuville British Cemetery, Corbie in France.

CULLEN Thomas: (Served as **MURPHY, Thomas**). Rank: Private. Regiment or Service: Royal Irish Regiment. Unit: 6th Bn. Age at death: 25. Date of death: 6 June 1916. Service No: 8926. Born in Enniscorthy and enlisted in London while living in Enniscorthy, Co. Wexford.
Supplementary information: Killed in action. Son of Robert and Mary Cullen

of 20 Irish Street, Enniscorthy. From an article in the *Enniscorthy Guardian*:

TWO BROTHERS KILLED.
During the past week, Mr and Mrs Robert Cullen, Irish Street, Enniscorthy, received the sad news from official sources of the death of their two sons at the front. On Friday the news arrived of the death of Private Thomas Cullen, R.I.R., third son of Mr and Mrs Cullen, and on Wednesday came the news of the death of Private of Private Maurice Cullen, R. I. R., their second youngest son. Mr and Mrs Cullen had six sons serving with the colours, and much sympathy is felt with the parents on the death of their boys. Maurice, the last boy killed, was buried on the battlefield by another of his brothers, Myles Cullen, assisted by a neighbour named O'Neill from Irish Street, Enniscorthy, who is serving in the same Regiment. R.I.P.

Grave or Memorial Reference: I.J.20. Cemetery: Dud Corner Cemetery, Loos in France.

CULLIMORE, George Henry: Rank: Private. Regiment or Service: Connaught Rangers. Unit: 1st Bn. Formerly he was with the 18th London Regiment where his number was 5101. Date of death: 16 November 1918. Service No: 20505. Born in Wexford. Enlisted in London while living in London. Died in Egypt. Grave or Memorial Reference: C. 125. Cemetery: Alexandria (Hadra) War Memorial Cemetery in Egypt.

Joseph Albert Cullimore.

CULLIMORE, Joseph Albert: Rank: Second Lieutenant. Regiment or Service: Royal Irish Fusiliers. Unit: 8th Bn. Age at death: 22. Date of death: 23 May 1916. Killed in action.

Supplementary information: Son of Elizabeth and Joseph Albert Cullimore of Wexford. From an article in the *Enniscorthy Guardian* in 1915,

BRAVE WEXFORD BROTHERS.

Recommended for Military Crosses. Irish Brigade Officer's Gallantry. As Wexford has given so generously of its sons to uphold the great for which the Allies are battling, it is not surprising to find that amongst the those whose names are singled out for special mention for bravery on the battlefield those of Wexfordmen figure rather frequently. Wexford has its V.C., its D.S.O., its D.C.M, and other distinctions and the latest decoration to be merited by Wexfordmen in the Military Cross. The coveted distinction was earned by two youths

scarcely out of their teens, and their bravery on the occasion evoked well-merited tributes from both officers and men. The young heroes are Lieut, Joseph A Cullimore, Royal Irish Fusiliers, who has since been reported killed in action, and his younger brother, Lieut, Aiden Cullimore, Royal Irish Fusiliers, who is at present in Wexford on a brief holiday recuperating from the effects of gas poisoning.

They are the sons of the late Mr Joseph Cullimore, Clarence House, Wexford, and grandsons of Mr Moses Harpur, 57 South Main Street, Wexford. The two young gentlemen and their younger brother, Lieut, George Cullimore, Royal Inniskilling Fusiliers, were educated at St Savoiur's College, Bruges, Belgium, and having completed their scholastic studies they went to business at Waterford. Shortly after the Irish Leader issued its manifesto as to Ireland's attitude in the war, the three brave boys volunteered for active service. They were attached to the Cadet Corps of the 7th Leinsters at Fermoy, and their qualifications speedily secured them commissions. They were gazetted to regiments in the 16th Division and went out to France with the Irish Brigade.

Grave or Memorial Reference: IV.C.13. Cemetery: British Cemetery in France.

CUNNINGHAM, Arthur Joseph: Rank: Second Lieutenant. Regiment or Service: London Regiment (London Irish Rifles). Unit: 18th Bn. Age at death: 25. Date of death: 15 September 1916. Killed in action. Awards: DCM. He is listed in the *London Gazette* dated 11 March 1916. His citation reads, '1694 Sgt. (now 2nd Lt) A.J. Cunningham, 18th (County of London) London Irish Rifles, London Regt., TF. For conspicuous gallantry. During the attack he assumed command of his company when the officers became wounded, and led it with conspicuous bravery and skill until wounded himself.'

Supplementary information: Son of Patrick Tuhan Cunningham and Margaret Cunningham, of 43 Tavistock Road, Westbourne Park, London. Born at Clonmel, Co. Tipperary. From an article in the *Enniscorthy Guardian*, 1916;

WEXFORD LIEUTENANT KILLED.

Lieutenant A.J. Cunningham, London Regiment, killed in action, was a native of Wexford, and served in the ranks for some time before getting his commission. As a Sergeant he took part in the Battle of Loos, and there won the Distinguished Conduct Medal and his commission, and was severely wounded. He was afterwards gazetted to his own regiment.

A brother of his was killed at Ypres whilst serving with the Irish Guards in the early part of the war. This may be his brother as listed in *The Tipperary War Dead*.

CUNNINGHAM, James F. Rank: Lance Corporal. Regiment or Service: Irish Guards. Unit: 1st Bn. Date of death: 20 November 1914. Service No: 2114. Born in Clonmel. Enlisted in Dublin while living in Pimlico in Middlesex. Died of wounds at home. Grave or Memorial Reference: R. 291. Cemetery: Aldershot Military Cemetery, UK.

Michael Curran.

CURRAN, Michael: Rank: Private. Regiment or Service: Royal Irish Regiment. Unit: 2nd Bn. Date of death: 25 May 1915. Service No: 4001. Born in Bride Street, Wexford. Enlisted in Wexford. Died of wounds. From an article in the *People* newspaper:

The roll of honour is increased by the death of another young Wexford man, Private Michael Curran, aged 19, son of Mr P Curran, R. N. R. William Street, Wexford. He was in the fighting line in Flanders for some months, and his dath on May 27th, is due to gas poisoning.

Grave or Memorial Reference: I.F.72. Cemetery: Bailleul Communal Cemetery Extension (Nord) in France.

CUSACK, William Patrick: Rank: Fireman and Trimmer. Regiment or Service: Mercantile Marine. Unit: SS *Luis* (West Hartlepool). The Steam

Ship was carrying a cargo of shells when she was torpedoed 3 miles off St Catherine's. Four of the crew were killed in the explosion. Age at death: 40. Date of death: 13 April 1918.

Supplementary information: Son of the late Thomas and Mary Cusack. Husband of Catherine Cusack (*née* Starkey) of 36 Alice Street, South Shields. Born at Wexford. Memorial: Tower Hill Memorial, UK.

CUSH, Michael: Rank: Private. Regiment or Service: Royal Irish Regiment. Unit: 7th (South Irish Horse) Bn. Age at death: 17. Date of death: 17 August 1918. Service No: 6587. Formerly he was with the Connaught Rangers where his number was 6785. Born in Cranford, Co. Wexford. Enlisted in Gorey, Co. Wexford. Killed in action.

Supplementary information: Son of James and Mary Cush of Boley, Cranford, Co. Wexford. Grave or Memorial Reference: M.1. Cemetery: Westoutre British Cemetery in Belgium.

CUSH, Peter: Rank: Private. Regiment or Service: Royal Irish Regiment. Unit: 1st Bn. Age at death: 29. Date of death: 22 March 1915. Service No: 8799. Born in Cranford, Co. Wexford. Enlisted in Gorey. Died of wounds.

Supplementary information: Son of James and Mary Cush of Boley, Upper Cranford. From an article in a Wexford newspaper:

During the past few days, the news of the death of Private Peter Cush, of the Irish Guards, a native of Hollyfort, Wexford, Gorey, has been received. He was engaged as a farm labourer in the Hollyfort and Kilanerin districts and lony enlisted in the Irish Guards short time ago. The place where he was killed is not stated in the dispatch received. His relatives were briefly informed that he was killed in action.

Grave or Memorial Reference: J. 41. Cemetery: Bailleul Communal Cemetery (Nord) in France.

D

DALY, James J.: Rank: Private. Regiment or Service: Royal Irish Regiment. Unit: 6th Bn. Age at death: 27. Date of death: 15 April 1916. Service No: 1986. Born in New Ross, Co. Wexford. Enlisted in Enniscorthy, Co. Wexford. Died of wounds.

Supplementary information: Son of Bridget Daly of New Ross. Grave or Memorial Reference: III.G.77. Cemetery: Bethune Town Cemetery in France.

DALY, John: Rank: Private(Lance Corporal). Regiment or Service: Royal Irish Regiment. Unit: 1st Bn. Date of death: 16 March 1915. Service No: 10160. Born in New Ross, Co. Wexford. Enlisted in Waterford while living in New Ross. Killed in action. From an article in the *Enniscorthy Guardian*:

A pathetic incident occurred in connection with the death of Private Daly, son of Denis Daly, summons-server, Mary Street, New Ross. He was at the front, and went through a number of engagements.

His parents had letters regularly from him up until March, when they ceased. He was subsequently reported, and as time wore on it was thought he was a prisoner of war. His parents had a letter stating that there was a man of that name taken prisoner, and the chaplain of the Regiment, Rev Father Crotty, put them in communication with this man, who in turn wrote to yong Daly's parents in Ross stating that he was not their son, and that he knew nothing about him. The parents were hoping however that he might still be alive until his mother received a letter from a soldier in France, named Private T. G. Rivett, on Friday of last week conveying the sad news that her son was killed, and that he identified him under circumstances that were pathetic. He stated that he came across his body, and that there was nothing left but the bones.

Beside the body he found a pay book, another small book, and a postcard containing the superscription, "To Mrs K Daly, Mary Street, New Ross". From this he was able to ascertain who it was, and he enclosed the partially defaced card in the letter to his mother, and gave the pay book and other small book to the Commandant. Continuing, he said in his letter that after discovering the skeleton he went out in the darkness of the night and buried him in a grave in Belgium soil. In conclusion he expressed his sympathy with his parents. He was 21 years of age.

He has no known grave but is commemorated on Panel 33. Memorial; Ypres (Menin Gate) Memorial in Belgium.

DALY, Joseph: Rank: Private. Regiment or Service: Royal Irish Regiment. Unit: 6th Bn. Date of death: 7 August 1915. Service No: 2130. Born in St Mary's, New Ross, Co. Wexford. Enlisted in Enniscorthy while living in New Ross. Died at home. Age at death: 23.

Supplementary information: Son of Mrs Bridget Daly of Irishtown, New Ross.

2130   PRIVATE
J. DALY
ROYAL IRISH REGIMENT
7TH AUGUST 1915 AGE 23

R.I.P.

Joseph Daly.

From an article in the *People* newspaper:

The remains of Private Joseph Daly, Irishtown, New Ross, who died at Fermoy military barracks from pneumonia were brought to New Ross on Monday evening and were met by a large number at the station.

The body was taken home and waked, and on Tuesday interred in St Stephens Cemetery. The deceased was about 22 years of age, and volunteered for the war some four or five months ago. He was at home about a month on a visit. His brother, James, who belongs to the same Regiment, accompanied the remains to Ross. Deceased father was a fireman on the SS Ida some years ago, and one of his brothers is a pilot under the New Ross Harbour board. On Monday evening the vessels on the harbour set their flags half mast. On Tuesday the New Ross Volunteers Corps honoured the memory of Private Daly, Irishtown, who died in Fermoy where he was training. He was a member of the National Volunteers in Ross before volunteering for the war.

The Volunteers Corps marched in full equipment to the house and took the coffin to the hearse, and marched to the St Stephen's Cemetery in the procession where they formed a guard of honour, and as the coffin was being lowered into the grave they fired a volley and when covered covered two volleys. They were in charge of Captain James Hutchinson, Lieutenant P. O'Gorman, H. C, U. C, and Mr J Halpin, drill instructor.

Grave or Memorial Reference: About the centre of the North Part. Cemetery: New Ross (St Stephen) Catholic Churchyard, Co. Wexford.

D'ARCY, Michael: Rank: Private. Regiment or Service: Royal Dublin Fusiliers. Unit: 10th Bn. Date of death: 13 November 1916. Service No: 26912. Born in Gorey, Co. Wexford. Enlisted in Dublin while living in Gorey, Co. Wexford. Killed in action. He has no known grave but is listed on Pier and Face 16C on the Thiepval Memorial in France.

DARLING, Claude Henry Whish: Rank: Second Lieutenant. Regiment or Service: Royal Irish Rifles. Unit: 3rd Bn. attd. 2nd Bn. Age at death: 20. Date of death: 12 December 1915.

Supplementary information: Son of the Revd Oliver Warner Darling and the late Edith Darling (*née* Dunn). Native of Duncannon, Co. Wexford. From an article in a Wexford newspaper:

Scarcely had the sorrow felt by Mrs Darling, Chelsea Lodge, Duncannon, for the loss of her eldest stepson began to wane when the sad news reached her that the second had fallen.

The gallant Lieutenant was serving with the Royal Irish Rifles in France, where he was killed on the 12th inst. He was second son of Rev Oliver W Darling, Rector of All Saints, Duncannon, and was most popular in the district.

From De Ruvigny's Roll of Honour:

att, 2nd (86th Foot), Battn, The Royal Irish Rifles, 2nd, s, of the late Rev, William Oliver Darling, Rector of Killesk, Duncannon, Co Waterford, by his wife, Edith, 2nd dau, of George Newman, Dunn, of Kinsale, Co Cork, M.D.; and brother to Lieut William Oliver Fortescue Darling (q. v.); b, Winkle, Co Chester, 13 April, 1895; educ, Braidlea, Stoke Bishop, Bristol; Monkton Coombe School, near Bath, where he was a member of the O.T.C., and on the Worcester, training ship for the Mercantile Marine; but while in training there his eyesight was found not to be sufficiently good, and he was obliged, to his great disappointment, to give up that life; subsequently he was destined for the Colonies, but found the preparation distasteful, and joined the 8th Hussars as a trooper, being sent to the 4th Hussars at the Curragh Camp; but on the outbreak of was applied for a commission, and was gazetted 2nd Lieut, 3rd Royal Irish Rifles 10 March, 1915; went to France at the end of Sept, and was killed in action 12 Dec, following; Buried in the Far Military Cemetery, Touquet des Mages, near Bols Grenier, south of Armentieres. His Commanding Officer wrote of his, when in training in Dublin; "Your boy has done exceedingly well, and I lose a good and promising officer."

Grave or Memorial Reference: I.G.10. Cemetery: Tancrez Farm Cemetery in Belgium.

DARLING, William Oliver Fortesque: Rank: Lieutenant. Regiment or Service: Royal Irish Rifles. Unit: 3rd Bn. attd. 1st Bn. Age at death: 23. Date of death: 16 October 1915. Killed in action.

Supplementary information: Son of

William Oliver Fortesque Darling.

the Revd Oliver Warner Darling and Edith Darling (*née* Dunn). Native of Duncannon, Co. Wexford. From an article in a Wexford newspaper:

Mrs O.W. Darling, Chelsea Lodge, Duncannon, Co. Wexford, has received a message of condolence from the King and Queen on the death of her stepson, Lieutenant W.O. Fortescue Darling, attached to the 1st Battalion, Royal Irish Rifles, who was killed in action in France. Lieutenant W. O. Fortescue Darling was the eldest son of the late Rev Oliver W Darling, Rector of Killesk Parish, Co. Wexford, and grandson of Dr George Newman Dunn, of Kinsale Co Cork. Born at Carham, Northumberland, September 11, 1892, was educated at Braidlea Stoke Bishop, and at Haileybury College, Herts, where he became a member of the O. T.C.

Subsequently he served as a cadet on the Medway, one of the mercantile marine trading vessels, under Lord Brassey's scheme. He returned home to volunteer at the outbreak of the war, and was gazetted to the 14th Battalion,

Royal Irish Rifles in September 1914. Transferred to the 3rd Battalion in April 1915, he was sent to France early in August, and was promoted Lieutenant during the same month. The General Commanding the Division in which he was serving (in his letter of condolence) says; "He had done excellent work whilst serving with this division, and was a most promising Officer. You have every reason to be proud of his gallantry and devotion to duty."

From another article in a Wexford newspaper:

Regret was felt by all classes in Duncannon and vicinity on receipt of the news of Lieut Farlings death at the front.

The deceased was the eldest son of the late Rev Oliver Darling, Rector of All Saints, Duncannon, and obtained his commission last October, in the 14th Rifles, Ulster Division. He was standing beside Captain the Hon, A. S. Chichester when he observed a Corporal fall wounded, and while endevouring to effect his rescue, met his own death. His step mother Mrs Darling, Chelsea Lodge, Duncannon, is prostrate with grief at his untimely fate, and following so soon after her husbands death, her grief is all the more poignant and has evoked the deepest sympathy.

From De Ruvigny's Roll of Honour:

eldest son of the late Rev, William Oliver Darling, Rector of Killesk, Duncannon, Co Waterford, by his wife, Edith, 2nd dau, of George Newman, Dunn, of Kinsale, Co Cork, M. D. ; and brother to Lieut Claude Henry Wish Darling (q.v.); b, Carham, Co

Northumberland, 11 Sept, 1892; educ, Braidlea, Stoke Bishop, Bristol; hailey-bury College, where he was a member of the O.T.C., and on the Medway, one of the Mercantile Marine Training vessels under Lord Brassey's scheme; entered the Mercantile Marine Service 1910; served under Messrs, Westcott and Laurence from Nov, 1913, but returned home on the outbreak of war to volunteer for Imperial Service; was gazetted 2nd Lieut, 14th batn, Royal Iriah Rifles 16th Sept, 1914; transferred to the 3rd battn, in April, 1915; went to France in Aug., attached to the 1st Battn, and was promoted Lieut, in the same month; he was killed in action whilst on patrol 16 Oct, following. Buried in Wye Farm Cemetery.

Grave or Memorial Reference: K. 30. Cemetery: Y Farm Military Cemetery, Bois-Grenier in France. He is also listed on the Haileybury Register.

DEEGAN, John Francis: Rank: Private. Regiment or Service: Royal Dublin Fusiliers. Unit: 1st Bn. Date of death: 29 March 1918. Service No: 20650. Formerly he was with the KSLI where his number was 32613. Born in Glenmore, Wexford. Enlisted in Wallasey while living in Poulton, Cheshire. Killed in action. Age at death: 20.

Supplementary information: Son of Joseph and Esther J. Deegan of 32 Balfour Road, Poulton, Wallasey, Cheshire. He has no known grave but is commemorated on Panel 79 and 80. Memorial: Pozieres Memorial in France.

DELANEY, James: Rank: Stoker. Regiment or Service: HMS *Indefatigable*.

Date of death: 31 May 1916. Service No: 5202S. During the Battle of Jutland the German Battlecruiser *Von Der Tann* fired 11-inch shells at the *Indefatigable*. The first two entered 'X' magazine area and blew out the bottom of the ship and she began sinking by the stern. More 11-inch shells from the Van Der Tann destroyed 'A' turret and also blew up the forward magazine and she then sank. There were only two survivors of her crew of 1017 men.

From an article in a Wexford newspaper, 'Stoker James Delaney, son of Mr Jas, Delaney, Cornmarket, Wexford, was killed in action on board HMS *Indefatigable* during the big encounter off Jutland, on 31 May. He volunteered for service just eighteen months ago, and much sympathy is felt for his family in the loss they have sustained.' Grave or Memorial Reference: 19. Memorial, Portsmouth Naval Memorial, UK.'

DELANEY, James: Rank: Corporal. Regiment or Service: Royal Irish Regiment. Unit: 1st Bn. Age at death: 35. Date of death: 23 March 1915. Service No: 8523. Born in Ballycanny, Co. Wexford. Enlisted in Enniscorthy. Died.

Supplementary information: Son of Patrick and Mary Delaney of Enniscorthy, Co. Wexford. Grave or Memorial Reference: I.E.12A. Cemetery: Wimereux Communal Cemetery in France.

DEMPSEY, Jack: Rank: Private. Regiment or Service: Canadian Infantry. Unit: 79th Bn. Age at death: 24. Date of death: 20 November 1916. Service No: 150880.

Supplementary information: Son of James and Johanna Dempsey of Glenview, Barntown, Co. Wexford. Information from

his enlistment documents: Eyes: grey. Hair: dark. Complexion: dark. Height: 5 Feet 5 inches. Date of birth: 1 January 1892. Age on enlistment: 23 years 8 Months. Place of birth: Wexford. Marital status: single. Name and address of next of kin, Mrs J. Dempsey, Wexford. Date of attestation: 10 September 1915. Location of attestation: Brandon, Manitoba. Occupation on enlistment: labourer. Cemetery: Blairmore (St Anne's) Roman Catholic Cemetery in Canada.

DEMPSEY James. Rank: Private. Regiment or Service: Royal Dublin Fusiliers. Unit: 9th Bn. Age at death: 38. Date of death: 31 March 1916. Service No: 13692. Born in Dublin. Enlisted in Dublin. Killed in action.

Supplementary information: Father of Mrs Margaret Furey of 2 Eugene Street, Dublin. From an article in a Wexford newspaper:

On Wednesday night Mr Patrick Dempsey, baker, John Street, Enniscorthy, received news of the death of his son, James Dempsey, who was serving with the Royal Irish at the front.

The deceased, at the outbreak of the war was working at his trade as a baker in Wicklow Town, where his wife and children reside. He joined the Royal Irish and has been in France for some months. No details have been furnished as to how he met his death. The deceased was a brother of Mr Aiden Dempsey, baker at Messrs James Donohoe and Co., Enniscorthy, while he has three other brothers – Ben, Paddy and Jack – also serving in the army. Much sympathy is felt with Mr Patrick Dempsey in the loss of his son.

Grave or Memorial Reference: C. 12. Cemetery: Bois-Carre Military Cemetery, Haisnes in France.

DEMPSEY, James: Rank: Private. Regiment or Service: Royal Irish Regiment. Unit: 2nd Bn. Age at death: 27. Date of death: 19 October 1914. Service No: 4347. Born in Ballinamore, Co. Wexford. Enlisted in Wexford while living in Ballybroker, Co. Wexford. Killed in action.

Supplementary information: Son of James and Margaret Dempsey of Ballybokes, Ballycogley, Wexford. From an article in the *Enniscorthy Guardian*:

> Tomhaggard Soldier Missing. Private James Dempsey, 2nd Battalion Royal Irish Regiment (4347) is the son of Mrs Dempsey, Ballyboker, Tomhaggard. When the first British Expeditionary Force landed in Flanders, amongst the gallant fellows was Private Dempsey.
>
> He took part in the heavy fighting during the opening stages of the war. In all these engagements in which the Royal Irish covered themselves with glory, Private Dempsey participated, but at the tragic retreat from Mons, after which so many of the Royal Irish failed to answer the roll call, it was learned that amongst the missing was Private Dempsey. Some time before last Christmas his parents were informed by the war office that their son had been missing since October 19th, and though anxious enquiries concerning him have been made repeatedly, we regret to say they have all been without avail.

Grave or Memorial Reference: Panel 11 and 12. Memorial: Le Touret Memorial in France.

DEMPSEY, James: Rank: Private. Regiment or Service: Royal Irish Regiment. Unit: 2nd Bn. Date of death: 10 May 1916. Service No: 11347. Born in Kilmore, Co. Wexford. Enlisted in Wexford while living in Bridgetown Co. Wexford. Killed in action. Grave or Memorial Reference: XV.M.6. Cemetery: Delville Wood Cemetery, Longueval in France.

DEMPSEY, Michael: Rank: Private. Regiment or Service: Royal Irish Regiment. Unit: 6th Bn. Date of death: 5 August 1917. Service No: 5753. Born in Bride Street, Wexford. Enlisted in Wexford. Killed in action. Grave or Memorial Reference: Has no known grave but is commemorated on Panel 33. Memorial; Ypres (Menin Gate) Memorial in Belgium.

DEMPSEY, Simon: Rank: Lance Corporal. Regiment or Service: Irish Guards. Unit: 1st Bn. Date of death: 9 June 1915. Killed in action. Service No: 6282. Born in Wexford, Co. Wexford. Enlisted in Dublin.

Supplementary information: Brother of Thomas Dempsey, of 'Mountain View' Castle Street Bray, Co. Wicklow. From an article in the *Enniscorthy Guardian*:

> There has been regret felt in Wexford this week when news was received that Mr Simon Dempsey, a well known native of Wexford, had been killed at the front. For a number of years My Simon Dempsey worked as a coach painter, and enjoyed an immense share of popularity. He joined the R.I.C. seven years ago.
>
> He was stationed for a number of

years at Kinvara, Co Galway and about two years ago he was transferred to Kildare, where he was stationed at the time, the authorities made the first call for volunteers for active service from members of the R.I.C. He immediately offered his services and entered the Irish Guards about 3rd January last. So eager was he to go to the front that during the period of training at Warley in Essex, that he applied specially to be allowed to go to France with one of the early drafts of his Regiment, as shown by the following extract from his letter to his brother, Mr T Dempsey of Bray dated 21st May 1915, from Warley Barracks; "There is a draft of 200 going on tomorrow morning (Saturday), and when I heard of it I volunteered, and was accepted. So o'er you receive this note I will be on my way to France. I have put your name down as next of kin, but please God, I will come back safe."

The sad tidings of Mr Simon Dempsey's death were conveyed in a

Simon Dempsey.

letter from Private Doyle of the same Battalion, a former employee of Bray County Council Electricity Works. The letter which is to his Father and Mother, Mr and Mrs Patrick Doyle Bray states "I am quite well. We have just come out of the trenches this morning, and as there was pretty hot work on I am not up to writing a long letter. I want my Father to tell Mr Tommy Dempsey (Dennehys Coach factory) that his brother, Simon was killed last night. I hate to be writing bad news as I was close by and know how it happened. I thought I would let his people know. He was a Corporal and he and two men went out in the sap, trench and as he was settling the sandbags, he got shot through the heart.

It may be some comfort for his people to know that he is buried in a proper graveyard. He and I were at Communion the morning before we went to the trenches and he died without any pain. I cannot let him out of my head, as I was very fond of him. However he is all right. They may not hear the official news for some time. In any case they would scarcely know the facts, so I think I am doing right to let them know. You may show Mr Dempsey this letter." In his last letter to his brother, Corporal Simon Dempsey, who was then attached to No 4 Company, 2nd Battalion, Irish Guards in France wrote "1st June 1915 Just a few lines to let you know that I am in the land of the living and in the best of form. We did not leave England as soon as I expected but left on Whit Monday and arrived in France the following morning.

We are now very close to the trenches but haven't seen any

Germans yet, though some of their shells dropped rather convenient to us. We may be ordered to the trenches at any moment as the Battalion has been resting for the past fortnight, so you may be sure I will do my best to dispose of a few Germans if I am not bowled over too soon."

Grave or Memorial Reference: D.44. Cemetery: Cambrin Churchyard Extension in France.

DEMPSEY, William: Rank: Private. Regiment or Service: Royal Dublin Fusiliers.

Unit: 2nd Bn. Date of death: 24 December 1917. Service No: 25282. Born in Monageer, Wexford. Enlisted in Enniscorthy. Died of wounds. Age at death: 21. Grave or Memorial Reference: III.G.31. Cemetery: Tincourt New British Cemetery in France.

DEMPSEY, William: Rank: Seaman. Regiment or Service: Royal Naval Reserve. Unit: HMS *Goliath*. Age at death: 18. Date of death: 13 May 1915. Service No: 5752A.

Supplementary information: Son of John and Mary Dempsey of Bride St (listed in the *Echo* and the *People* as Bride Place), Wexford. HMS *Goliath* was torpedoed in the Dardanelles. HMS *Goliath* was sunk by three torpedoes from German destroyer *Muvanet-I-Milet*, she blew up and capsized immediately taking 570 of her 750 crew including the Captain to a watery grave. Grave or Memorial Reference: 8. Memorial: Plymouth Naval Memorial UK.

William Dempsey.

DERRY, George Francis: Rank: Private. Regiment or Service: East Surrey Regiment. Unit: 8th Bn. Formerly he was with the Royal Engineers where his number was 125910. Age at death: 32. Date of death: 22 March 1918. Service No: 35563. Born in Wexford. Enlisted in Sandwich, Kent while living in Liverpool. Killed in action.

Supplementary information: Son of Mr and Mrs John Derry of Corn Market, Wexford. Grave or Memorial Reference: 3.B.15. Cemetery: Chauny Communal Cemetery British Extension in France.

DEVEREUX, James: Rank: Lance Corporal. Regiment or Service: Yorkshire Regiment. Unit: 13th Bn. Formerly he was with the Notts and Derby Regiment where his number was 32015. Date of death: 25 August

1916. Service No: 29783. Born in Enniscorthy. Enlisted in Enniscorthy. Killed in action. From an article in the *Enniscorthy Guardian*, December 1915:

Lance Corporal James Devereux, Duffery Hill, Enniscorthy, who was attached to the Yorkshire Regiment has been killed in action. The deceased was one of the many Enniscorthy men who follower the example of Capt. Thomas Ryan and other officers of the National Volunteers in joining the colours. He was interred by his Ennisorthy comrades. R.I.P.

From another article in the *Enniscorthy Guardian*:

His many friends will regret to learn of the death at the front of Lance Corporal James Devereux, Yorks Regiment, a native of Duffry Gate, Enniscorthy, who joined the colours about 12 months ago, following Captain Ryan, Lieutenant M Kelly, and other members of the National Volunteers, who joined about that time.

The Lance Corporal was a good all-round sportsman, a smart footballer, a clever boxer, and a good gymnast. He was buried by his Enniscorthy comrades, who shed many a tear at the loss of a sterling friend. May the soil of France rest lightly o'er him, and may his soul rest in peace.

Grave or Memorial Reference: I.J.37. Cemetery: Maroc British Cemetery, Grenay in France.

DEVEREUX, Patrick John: Rank: Lance Corporal. Regiment or Service:

Auckland Regiment. N.Z.E.F. Age at death: 20. Date of death: 10 August 1915. Service No: 12/2272.

Supplementary information: Son of James T and Jane Devereaux. Of Glenbrook, Waiuku, Aukland. Native of Ireland. From an article in the *Enniscorthy Guardian*:

The late Lance Corporal Devereux, who was killed in action on the 10th August inst, was the son of Mr and Mrs James Devereux, Patumahoe.

He was born on the 14th of November 1894 at Mount George, Ferns, Co. Wexford, and went to New Zealand with his parents in November 1910. Since his arrival he had been employed at Yates seed farm, Buckland, and on Mr Ivan Motion's and the late Captain Wilkerson's farm at Pukekohe Hill. Just previous to his departure for Trentham he was engaged in assisting his father in dairying on Mr J Henry's, Glenbrook Farm, Patumahoe, on account of his having previously been in the Territorial Forces, Lance Corporal Devereux was appointed to his position on his arrival at Trentham. He left New Zealand in June last with the 5th Reinforcements. The deceased was esteemed by all who knew him, his unassuming, yet, manly bearing and inherent courtesy being particularly noticeable in his new land where our rising manhood is careless of such outward manifestations of the inward man.

To anyone who had seen him in uniform he looked every inch a soldier and gave promise of rising to distinction in the service had not his career been brought to an untimely end. He had no misconception of the risks he was taking in volunteering to serve his country on the battle front in the

Patrick John Devereux.

Dardanelles. When he was reminded of his risk by his chums, he invariably replied that a man had to die but once, and someone had to take the risk. If the same spirit animated all the war eligibles of the empire the German menace would soon be a thing of the past. It's a pity that our voluntary system in this war is robbing us of this class of young men while the less desirable ones are left behind.

The heartfelt sympathy of the community is extended to Mr and Mrs Devereux in their loss of such an estimable son, and to the members of the Devereux family. A movement is on foot by the deceased's chums to erect a tablet to his memory in St Michael's Catholic Church, Patumahoe, where he was an attendant. Mr and Mrs Devereux and family resided in Borris where they held a shop for four years before they emigrated to New

Zealand. Lance Corporal Devereux was grandson to Mr John Buttle, Templeshannon, Enniscorthy, Grand Nephew to Mr Samuel Buttle, Royal Irish Rifles. Much sympathy is felt in Enniscorthy with the Buttle family in their bereavement. Prayers for the late Mr Devereux were offered up in Borris Church on Sunday last.

From an article in a Wexford newspaper:

On Friday 12th inst, Mr John Buttle, of Messrs, Buttle Bros, Enniscorthy, received news of the death of his eldest grandson, Lance Corporal Patrick John Devereux, who belonged to the New Zealand forces, and who was killed at Gallipoli on August 10th last.

The deceased young soldier had only reached his 20th year. Physically he was one of the finest men in the Colonial forces. Standing well over 6 feet in height, and built in proportion, he was a splendid type of Irish manhood, and not only his superb physique but his fine manly qualities attracted and held the admiration and affection of the many who had the pleasure of his acquaintance. The deceased, though living in New Zealand for some years, with his parents, was a Wexford man. He was born at Mount George, near Ferns, his Mother before her marriage to Mr James Devereux, being Miss Jennie Buttle, daughter of Mr John Buttle, one of Enniscorthy's most enterprising and successful merchants. The very deepest sympathy is felt with the parents of the deceased in their distant home in New Zealand, and with his Grandfather and other relatives in Enniscorthy.

Grave or Memorial Reference: 9. Chunuk Bair (New Zealand) Memorial in Turkey.

DEVEREUX, William: Rank: Corporal. Regiment or Service: Royal Irish Regiment. Unit: 2nd Bn. Age at death: 24. Date of death: 20 July 1918. Service No: 5520. Born in Rowe Street, Co. Wexford. Enlisted in Wexford. Killed in action.

Supplementary information: Son of James and Ellen Devereux of Gibson Street, Wexford. Grave or Memorial Reference: Panel 30 and 31. Memorial: Pozieres Memorial in France.

DEVINE, Joseph: Rank: Private. Regiment or Service: Royal Dublin Fusiliers. Unit: 'C' Coy. 9th Bn. Age at death: 21. Date of death: 7 February 1917. Service No: 22427. Born in Gorey, Co. Wexford. Enlisted in Gorey. Killed in action.

Supplementary information: Son of James and Annie Devine of Gorey. Husband of Mary Hayden (formerly Devine) of 1 Willam Street, Gorey. From an article in the *Enniscorthy Guardian*, June 1915:

> Joe Devine, William Street, Gorey, of the 2nd Battalion, Royal Irish Regiment, who was home in the early spring suffering from frostbitten fingers, has again returned home on sick leave. This time he has two fingers on the left hand blown off, and which he sustained at Hill 60, where the fighting was terrific. Although quite a young man, he has seen considerable service since the outbreak of the war.

Grave or Memorial Reference: N. 46. Cemetery: Kemmel Chateau Military Cemetery in Belgium.

DILLON, James Thomas: Rank: Corporal. Regiment or Service: Royal Irish Regiment. Unit: 2nd Bn. Age at death: 27. Date of death: 24 May 1915. Service No: 7248. Born in Meerut, Bengal in India. Enlisted in Spring Gardens, S.W. Middlesex. Killed in action. He was formerly with the Royal Marines for a few months when he joined up underage at thirteen years old.

Supplementary information: Son of the late Serjt. Maj. J.A. and Ellen Dillon of Wexford. Born in the 1st Bn. Royal Irish Regt. in India. Grave or Memorial Reference: Panel 33. Memorial: Ypres (Menin Gate) Memorial in Belgium.

DIXON, Alexander: Rank: Private. Regiment or Service: Australian Infantry, A.I.F. Unit: 15th Bn also listed as the 16th Bn. Age at death: 19. Date of death: 29 April 1915. Service No: 252.

Supplementary information: Son of William and Grace A. Dixon of Lake Brown, Nungarin, Western Australia. Native of Inch, Co. Wexford. Born in Inch, Gorey, Co. Wexford, 6 September 1895. Occupation on enlistment: lumper. Next of kin listed as Father, William Dixon, Coombe Street, Bayswater, WA. Enlisted: Blackboy Hill Camp, Western Australia on 20 October 1914. Weight: 130 lbs. Height: 5 feet 7¾ inches. Complexion: ruddy. Hair: dark brown. Eyes: blue. Monies due to his estate were collected by his mother, Grace Anne Dixon on the 6 December 1915, 68 Clarence Street, Highgate Hill, Perth, Western Australia. Previous address was 68 Alexander Street, Mt Lawley. Her application for a pension from the Military was 'Rejected not a dependant'. It was later changed and she received a pension of 40 shillings every fortnight from the 31 August 1915. Killed in action in Gallipoli. Grave or Memorial Reference: 52. Memorial: Lone Pine Memorial in Turkey.

DOBBS, James: Rank: Private. Regiment or Service: Royal Irish Regiment. Unit: 2nd Bn. Age at death: 34. Date of death: 8 May 1915. Service No: 7024. Born in St Mary's, Enniscorthy, Co. Wexford. Enlisted in Enniscorthy. Killed in action.

Supplementary information: Son of John Dobbs of Duffry Gate, Enniscorthy. Husband of Elizabeth Goff (formerly Dobbs, *née* Doolan) of Francis Row, Enniscorthy. Grave or Memorial Reference: Panel 33. Memorial: Ypres (Menin Gate) Memorial in Belgium.

DONELLY/DONNELLY, Patrick: Rank: Private. Regiment or Service: Royal Munster Fusiliers. Unit: 1st Bn. Formerly he was with the Royal Irish Regiment where his number was 2046. Date of death: 22 March 1918. Service No: 18085. Born in St Mark's, Newtownbarry, Co. Wexford. Enlisted in Newtownbarry while living in Enniscorthy. Killed in action. He has no known grave but is listed on Panel 78 and 79 on the Pozieres Memorial in France.

DONOHOE, Patrick: Rank: Sergeant. Regiment or Service: Irish Guards. Unit: 1st Bn. He won the Military Medal and is listed in the *London Gazette*. Date of death: 30 March 1918. Service No: 3056. Born in Monageer, Co. Wexford. Enlisted in Enniscorthy while living in Hammersmith in Middlesex. Killed in action. Age at death: 28.

Supplementary information: Son of the late John and Julie Donohoe. Husband of Agnes Juliana Donohoe of Hammersmith, London. Mobilized August 1914. He has no known grave but is listed in Bay 1 on the Arras Memorial in France.

DONOHUE, Patrick: Rank: Sergeant. Regiment or Service: Connaught Rangers. Unit: 1st Bn. Date of death: 10 October 1918. Service No: 7023. Born in Carlow. Enlisted in Naas while living in Gorey. Died in Egypt. Age at death: 38.

Supplementary information: Son of Patrick and Sarah Donohue. Husband of Sarah Williams (formerly Donohue) of 7 Newtown, Cwmbran, Mon. Served in the South African War. Born at Carlow. Grave or Memorial Reference: A. 87. Cemetery: Haifa War Cemetery in Israel.

DONOVAN, Michael: Rank: Lance Corporal. Regiment or Service: Irish Guards. Unit: 2nd Bn. Date of death: 13 September 1916. Service No: 2646. Born in New Ross, Co. Wexford. Enlisted in Waterford. Killed in action. Grave or Memorial Reference: VI.F.4. Cemetery: Guards Cemetery, Windy Corner, Cuinchy in France.

DOOLAN, Michael: Rank: Private. Regiment or Service: Royal Irish Regiment. Unit: 2nd Bn. Age at death: 26. Date of death: 26 April 1917. Service No: 4522. Born in New Ross, Co. Wexford. Enlisted in Waterford while living in New Ross. Died. He won the Military Medal and is listed in the *London Gazette*.

Supplementary information: Son of Edward and Kate Doolan of Barrack

Street, New Ross. Grave or Memorial Reference: IV.B.60. Cemetery: Longuenesse (St Omer) Souvenir Cemetery in France.

DOOLEY, James: Rank: Private. Regiment or Service: Royal Welsh Fusiliers. Unit: 13th Bn. Date of death: 31 July 1917. Service No: 66298. Born in Taghmon, Co. Wexford. Enlisted in Carmarthen. Killed in action.

Supplementary information: Father of Peter Dooley of Cottage Row, Taghmon, Co. Wexford. Grave or Memorial Reference: Panel 22. Memorial: Ypres (Menin Gate) Memorial in Belgium.

DORAN, Daniel: Rank: Private. Regiment or Service: Cheshire Regiment. Unit: 13th Bn. Date of death: 24 August 1916. Service No: 18234. Born in Wexford. Enlisted in Birkinhead. Killed in action. Grave or Memorial Reference: VII.B.6. Cemetery: Lonsdale Cemetery Authuile in France.

DORAN, Michael Daniel: Rank: Able Seaman and Quartermaster. Regiment or Service: Mercantile Marine. Unit: SS *Mercian* (Liverpool). Age at death: 39. Date of death: 3 December 1915. German Submarine U-38 fired at SS *Mercian*. It failed to sink her but killed twenty-three of her crew.

Supplementary information: Son of James and Catherine Doran of 71 Eldon Place, Liverpool. Born at Wexford. Memorial: Tower Hill Memorial UK.

DORAN, Myles: Rank: Private. Regiment or Service: Royal Irish Regiment. Unit: 1st Bn. Date of death: 9 April 915. Service No: 3723. Born in St Mary's, New Ross, Co. Wexford. Enlisted in Wexford while living in Campile, Co. Wexford. Killed in action. Age at death: 33. From an article in the *Enniscorthy Guardian*:

ANOTHER NEW ROSS MAN HAS SACRIFICED HIS LIFE FOR HIS COUNTRY.

This is Myles Doran of Mary Street, whose wife has received melancholy tidings of his death from the War Office. Myles, who was a Private of the 18th Royal Irish Regiment, was well known and much esteemed in his native town, and his death has caused widespread regret. He lost his life in the great battle of Neuve Chapelle. He leaves a widow and seven children.

Grave or Memorial Reference: Has no known grave but is commemorated on Panel 33 on the Ypres (Menin Gate) Memorial in Belgium.

DOWD, Jeremiah: Rank: Corporal. Regiment or Service: Royal Irish Regiment. Unit: 'B' Coy. 2nd Bn. Age at death: 26. Date of death: 19 October 1914. Service No: 9301. Born in Tralee. Enlisted in Wexford while living in Boherbee, Co Kerry. Killed in action.

Supplementary information: Husband of B.V. Dowd of Lower John Street, Wexford. Grave or Memorial Reference: Panel 11 and 12. Memorial: Le Touret Memorial in France.

DOWLING, Edward: Rank: Private. Regiment or Service: Irish Guards. Unit: 1st Bn. Date of death: 6 November 1914. Service No: 2648. Born in Goresbridge, Co. Wexford. Enlisted in Dublin. Age at death: 31.

Supplementary information: Son of the late James and Bridget Dowling. He has no known grave but is commemorated on Panel 11. Memorial; Ypres (Menin Gate) Memorial in Belgium.

DOWNEY, James: Rank: Private. Regiment or Service: The King's (Liverpool Regiment). Unit: 1st/6th Bn. Formerly he was with the Royal Army Service Corps where his number was T/293610. Age at death: 22. Date of death: 8 September 1918. Service No: 50323. Born in Clonroche, Co. Wexford. Enlisted in Wexford while living in Davidstown, Co. Wexford. Died of wounds.

Supplementary information: Son of Aidan and Margret Downey of Boolabawn, Davidstown, Enniscorthy, Co. Wexford. Grave or Memorial Reference: VI.B.8. Cemetery: Pernes British Cemetery in France.

DOWSE, Richard Henry: Rank: Chief Engineer. Regiment or Service: Mercantile Marine. Unit: SS *Towneley* (Newcastle). Date of death: 2 February 1918. Age at death: 48.

Supplementary information: Richard Henry Dowse was born on 12 October 1868 at Camolin RD, Wexford. He was the son of Richard Henry Dowse and Mary Halahan. Richard Henry Dowse and Mary Halahan appeared on the 1911 census at Scholarstown, Rathfarnham. Mary Dowse, head, 70, Richard Henry Dowse, 42, Richard Henry Dowse 23,

Anne Fleming 38, Samuel H.G. Fleming, 50, John R.W. Fleming. Son of Richard Henry Mary Dowse (*née* Halahan), of St John's Vicarage, York Road, Kingstown, Dublin. Born at Carnew, Co. Wicklow. He has no known grave but is listed on the Tower Hill Memorial, UK and St John's Mounttown Memorial in Monkstown Parish church, Dublin.

DOWSE, William Arthur Clarence: Rank: Lieutenant. Regiment or Service: Cheshire Regiment. Unit: 11th Bn. Age at death: 21. Date of death: 3 July 1916.

Supplementary information: Son of Dr Thomas J. Dowse and K. E. Dowse of 14 Lower George Street, Wexford. From an article in the *Enniscorthy Guardian*, 1915:

> Lance Corporal Edward Lacey, of the Royal Irish Regiment, son of Mr Edward Lacey, Selskar Street, Wexford, has written to Dr Thomas Dowse, George Street, Wexford, thanking him

William Arthur Clarence Dowse.

for papers, tobacco, and other articles sent to him from the Doctors family. He also acknowledges the receipt of a watch sent him by his mother.

Corporal Lacey adds; "I have been awarded the distinguished conduct medal for bravery in the field; I got my card from the General on the 12th April. I went very near winning the V. C., which you told me to win. I did my best when you told me to try and win it. Master Willie (Dr Dowse's son who has joined the service), I hope, will be out soon to make his name in the field. I am about the first Wexfordman to win the medal for bravery, and my father, I am sure, will be delighted to hear it. He always said to me that I was afraid of another fellow when I am at home, but I am not afraid of the Germans here.

Grave or Memorial Reference: Pier and Face 3C and 4A. Memorial: Thiepval Memorial in France.

DOYE/DOYLE, Edward: see DOYLE

DOYLE, Charles: Rank: Cook. Regiment or Service: Mercantile Marine. Unit: SV *Brandon* (Barrow-in-Furness). Age at death: 17. Date of death: 24 March 1917.

Supplementary information: Son of Thomas and Jane Doyle (*née* Hogan) of 6 Ashwood Walk, Wexford Road, Arklow, Co. Wicklow. Memorial: Tower Hill Memorial UK.

DOYLE, Christopher: Rank: Private. Regiment or Service: Royal

Army Medical Corps. Date of death: 8 December 1917. Service No: 7696. Born in Gorey, Co. Wexford. Enlisted in Dublin. Died at home. Grave or Memorial Reference: Screen Wall, Panel 2. Soldiers Circle 120912. Cemetery: West Ham Cemetery, UK.

DOYLE, Revd Denis: Rank: Chaplain, 4th Class. Regiment or Service: Army Chaplains Department, attached to the 2nd Battalion, Leinster Regiment. Date of death: 17 August 1916. From an article in the *Enniscorthy Guardian*:

Third Jesuit Chaplain Killed; Native of Co. Wexford. Father Denis Doyle, S.J. whose death has been announced, is the third member of the order to give his life in the service of Catholic soldiers at the front. He was born in 1878, entered the English Province of the Society of Jesus in 1896, and became Prefect of the Philosophers at Stoneyhurst College.

At the outbreak of war he was acting as minister at the Novitiate, Manrea House, Rochampton. While there he found time to devote himself to the spiritual needs of the Catholic soldier at Richmond Park, close by, and was so popular that the Provincial was requested to allow him to take up the regular work as Chaplain to the forces. He was one of the 60 Priests of the Irish and English Province sent out in response to the Cardinals appeal for Chaplains. Private W. J. Duffy, of the Leinster Regiment, who was well known in Wicklow and Wexford GAA circles, writing in reference to Father Doyle's death, says; Father Doyle belonged to Wexford, and was dearly loved by the Leinsters, to whom he was devotedly attached. Father Doyle told us one evening in the course of a short lecture that he had an Uncle shot in '48 because of his opposition to the then prevailing laws. He pointed out this fact as an example of the revolution of feeling which had taken place in Ireland.

Poor Father Doyle was most insistent in accompanying the Battalion for the purpose of attending the wounded and dying. Shells were falling with hellish fury at the time, whilst our lads continued to advance with unflinching courage. Some fragments caught him on the legs and body, lacerating his limbs badly. Although medical relief was instantly at hand and promptly administered, poor Father Doyle did not rally, but passed peacefully away the following day, a priest from another Division being with him when he died. He was a beloved soggart, saintly of soul and angelic of heart.

Grave or Memorial Reference: I.C.6. Cemetery: Dive Copse British Cemetery, Sailly-Le-Sec in France.

DOYLE/DOYE, Edward: Rank: Private. Regiment or Service: Royal Irish Regiment. Unit: 1st Bn. Age at death: 24. Date of death: 15 March 1915. Service No: 10346. Born in St Mary's, Co. Wexford. Enlisted in Wexford. Killed in action.

Supplementary information: Son of James and Anne Doyle of South Main Street, Wexford. From an article in the *People* newspaper:

Mr J. Doyle, saddler, South Main Street, Wexford, received an official account this week of the death of his son, Edward, at the battle of St Eloi.

Private Doyle belonged to the Royal Irish Regiment and was stationed in India up to the outbreak of the war when the Battalion was drafted to England. At that time he visited his home in Wexford where he spent a few days prior to his departure for the front. He was missing for some time and grave fears were entertained for his safety. Private Doyle was an extremely popular young man, and the sad news of his death, has caused a painful shock to his friends, but more particularly to his parents and relatives for whom the deepest sympathy is felt.

Grave or Memorial Reference: Panel 33. Memorial: Ypres (Menin Gate) Memorial in Belgium.

DOYLE, J.: Rank: Lance Corporal. Regiment or Service: Royal Munster Fusiliers. Unit: 3rd Bn. Date of death: 15 November 1918. Service No: 1385. Age at death: 35. Grave or Memorial Reference: I. 217. Cemetery, Wexford (St Ibar's) Cemetery, Wexford.

DOYLE, James: Rank: Private. Regiment or Service: Royal Irish Regiment. Unit: 2nd Bn. Date of death: 21 March 1918. Service No: 15020. Formerly he was with the Royal Dublin Fusiliers where his number was 25964. Born in Killamote, Co. Wicklow. Enlisted in Naas, Co Kildare while living in Duncormick, Co. Wexford. Killed in action. He has no known grave but is listed on Panel 31 and 31 on the Pozieres Memorial in France.

1385   PRIVATE
J. DOYLE
ROYAL MUNSTER FUSILIERS
15TH NOVEMBER 1918 AGE 35

J. Doyle.

DOYLE, James: Rank: Gunner. Regiment or Service: Royal Garrison Artillery. Unit: 80th Coy. Age at death: 39. Date of death: 8 May 1915. Service No: 29628. Born in Wexford. Enlisted in Wexford. Died in Singapore.

Supplementary information: Son of James and Jane Doyle of John Street, Wexford. Grave or Memorial Reference: 37.F.7. Cemetery: Kranji War Cemetery in Singapore.

DOYLE, James. Rank: Private. Regiment or Service: Irish Guards. Unit: 1st Bn. Age at death: 31. Date of death: 9 October 1917. Service No: 9918. Born in Kilanerin, Co. Wexford. Enlisted in Wicklow, Co. Wicklow. Killed in action.

Supplementary information: Son of James and Mary Doyle of Kilanerin, Gorey, Co. Wexford. From an article in the *Enniscorthy Guardian*:

Private James Doyle, aged 31 years, son of James and Mary Doyle, Kilanerin, who joined the Irish Guards on the 10th October, 1915, and went through a number of important engagements, was killed in action on the 9th October, 1917.

It was only three months ago that he had been awarded the Military Cross for bravery in the field. Before joining the colours he was a member of the Kilanerin Fife and Drum Band and Football Club, and they have sympathised with his relatives in their great loss.

Grave or Memorial Reference: Panel 10 to 11. Memorial: Tyne Cot Memorial in Belgium.

DOYLE, Jeremiah: Rank: Lance Corporal. Regiment or Service: Royal Dublin Fusiliers. Unit: 8th Bn. Date of death: 29 April 1916. Service No: 19972. Born in Wexford. Enlisted in Dublin while living in Wexford. Died of wounds.

Supplementary information: Son of John and Maria Doyle. From an article in the *Enniscorthy Guardian*:

On Monday, Mrs P Byrne, Market Square, Enniscorthy, received the sad intelligence of the death at the front of her nephew, the late Mr Jeremiah Doyle, Lance Corporal in the 18th Batt, Royal Dublin Fusiliers.

The deceased soldier was son of the late Mr Peter Doyle, Main Street, Enniscorthy. He was educated at the local Chirstian Brothers Schools, and closing a mercantile career was sent as apprentice to the drapery establishment of Mr John Bolger, George Street. Having completed his apprenticeship he filled some splendid appointments eventually securing the post of traveller to some of the largest Manchester and Leeds firms. He was travelling for a large wholesale Leeds house when he joined the army during the summer of of 1915. He was attached to the 8th Battalion, Royal Dublin Fusiliers, and went out with the 16th Irish Division last winter. He succumbed to the effects of an attack of gas poisoning at the front.

The late Lance Corporal was nephew to Mr P.J. Shaw town clerk, Enniscorthy, to Mrs P Byrne, Market Square, to Mrs Kehoe, Newtownbarry, and brother to Mrs Jordan, Newtownbarry. He was an accomplished singer, a leading member of the Cathedral choir, and always played a prominent part in the social and mercantile life of the town. No concert was complete if 'Jer' Doyles name did not

John Doyle.

stationed at Beggar's Bush military barracks as drill instructor. In March last he went to the front, and took part in the famous battle for hill 60, where he had some miraculous escapes from death from bullets andf shells. Although his Regiment suffered, they swept the positions with the utmost bravery. He took part in other stirring engagements and managed to write home regularly to hi people. He went with his Regiment to the Dardanelles, where whilst taking part in a vigorous fight he received a wound, and was taken to hospital where he died five days later.

appear on the programme. For some years past he resided in Dublin, where he married and settled down. He leaves a wife and three children to mourn the loss of a kind husband and fond father who fell nobly doing his duty at the early age of 36 years. RIP

DOYLE, John: Rank: Corporal. Regiment or Service: Royal Irish Regiment. Unit: 2nd Bn. Age at death: 34. Date of death: 19 May 1915. Service No: 9297. Born in Cloughbawn, Co. Wexford. Enlisted in New Ross, Co. Wexford while living in Clonroche, Co. Wexford. Died of wounds.

Supplementary information: Son of William and Mary Doyle (*née* Boland) of Clonroche. From and article in the *People* and the Enniscorthy *Echo*:

Amongst those who recently lost their lives at the Dardanelles is Corporal John Doyle of Clonroche, of the 18th Royal Irish Regiment. He joined in 1906 and served about 6 years in India, and after coming home was

Grave or Memorial Reference: VIII.D.27. Cemetery: Boulogne Eastern Cemetery in France.

DOYLE, John: Rank: Fireman. Regiment or Service: Mercantile Marine. Unit: SS *Lusitania* (Liverpool). The *Lusitania* was sunk by German Submarine U-20. Age at death: 35. Date of death: 7 May 1915.

Supplementary information: Son of Ann and Lawrence Doyle of 368 Vauxhall Road, Liverpool. Born at Glynn, Co. Wexford. Memorial: Tower Hill Memorial UK.

DOYLE, John: Rank: Seaman. Regiment or Service: Royal Naval Reserve. Unit: HMS *Laurentic*. Date of death: 25 January 1917. Age at death, 36. Service No: 5367B.

Supplementary information: Son of Annie Doyle, of Ballyhealy, Kilmore, Co. Wexford. Native of Rathaspick, Co. Wexford. From an article in the *People*, 1917:

News has been received from the Admiralty by Mrs Annie Doyle, Moorfield that her son, John Doyle, R. N. R., has been lost on the 'Laurentic', which was sunk by a mine. He was about 33 years of age and had been in the navy for 10 years previous to the outbreak of the war.

When the war broke out he was called up. He was on the Majestic when she was sunk in the Dardanelles and had a lucky escape at that time. He was then sent to the Canary, bringing troops from Canada and several other places. He was then sent to barracks to undergo some gunnery training and was then sent on the ill-fated Laurentic. The vessel sank in 1917 with the loss of 354 of its crew when it hit a mine at Fanad Head en route to Halifax, Nova Scotia. Some 121 crew members survived. The Laurentic was carrying the 1917 equivalent of £5 million in gold and a reported £3 million in silver coins to pay for arms for the British war effort.

John Doyle.

Also see **DOYLE, Patrick:** Rank: Sergeant. Grave or Memorial Reference: 23. Memorial, Portsmouth Naval Memorial, UK.

DOYLE, John: Rank: Sergeant. Regiment or Service: Royal Dublin Fusiliers. Unit: 9th Bn. Age at death: 31. Date of death: 16 April 1916. Service No: 14033. Born in Dublin. Enlisted in Dublin. Killed in action. From an article in the *Enniscorthy Guardian*:

> News has just been received of the death of Sergeant John Doyle, Twelveacre, Tagoat, who was killed in action at Verdun on Sunday 16th April.
>
> The sad news reached his Aunt, Miss Sarah Furlong, through Sergeant Kelly, a comrade, of the deceased, who stated that the poor fellow died quite happy, having previously made due preparation. Young Doyle, joined the 9th Battalion, Royal Dublin Fusiliers in September 1914, whilst working in Wales, where he had been residing for some months previously.

Grave or Memorial Reference: F. 19. Cemetery; Bois-Carre Military Cemetery, Haisnes in France.

DOYLE, John: Rank: Private. Regiment or Service: Royal Irish Regiment. Unit: 1st Bn. Date of death: 11 November 1915. Service No: 4373. Born in Gorey, Co. Wexford. Enlisted in Gorey. Killed in action. From an article in a Wexford newspaper:

> The death has been announced of Private John Doyle, of the Royal Irish Regiment, who was killed in action

in Flanders. He was a resident of William Street, Gorey, and had been home on a short furlough with his friends a few months ago. He had been in the principal engagements of the war and hitherto escaped without a scratch.

Grave or Memorial Reference: III. A.4. Cemetery: Houplines Communal Cemetery Extension, France.

DOYLE, Martin: Rank: Private. Regiment or Service: Irish Guards. Unit: 2nd Bn. Age at death: 22. Date of death: 28 September 1915. Service No: 6547. Born in New Ross, Co. Wexford. Enlisted in Enniscorthy, Co. Wexford. Killed in action.

Supplementary information: Son of Patrick and Margaret Doyle of Nunnery Lane, New Ross, Co. Wexford. From a Wicklow newspaper article:

Private Martin Doyle, Nunnery Lane, New Ross, son of Patrick Doyle, barber in the New Ross Workhouse was killed at the fighting in France on the 28th September.

He was 22 years of age and Volunteered in January last. He was a member of the 2nd Battalion of the Irish Guards and was in the same battle with young Daniel Hogan, who received seven of eight wounds. He fell during a stirring fight on the part of his Regiment, whilst driving the enemy from their entrenchments.

Grave or Memorial Reference: Panel 9 and 10. Memorial: Loos Memorial in France.

Michael Doyle.

DOYLE, Martin: Rank: Private. Regiment or Service: Royal Dublin Fusiliers. Unit: 1st Bn. Age at death: 19. Date of death: 5 October 1917. Service No: 40123. Born in Thornville, Co. Wexford. Enlisted in Maesteg. Killed in action. Formerly he was with the Royal Munster Fusiliers where his number was 7073.

Supplementary information: Son of Patrick and Mary Doyle of Yule Town, Ballycogley, Co. Wexford. Grave or Memorial Reference: Panel 144 to 145. Memorial: Tyne Cot Memorial in Belgium.

DOYLE, Michael: Rank: Private. Regiment or Service: Royal Irish Regiment. Unit: 7th Bn. Date of death: 21 March 1918. Service No: 4435. Born in Tomacork, Co. Wexford. Enlisted in Gorey, Co. Wexford while living in Carnew, Co. Wexford. Killed in action. Age at death: 30.

Supplementary information: Son of James Doyle of Collatton Row, Carnew, Co. Wicklow. From an article in the *Enniscorthy Guardian*:

> Private Michael Doyle, who was recalled to his regiment when hostilities were declared.
>
> He participated in the memorable retreat from Mons, in which the Royal Irish won undying fame. During the terrific struggle, when a mere handful kept the Hunnish hordes at bay, Mike was wounded, but recovered, and is again in the trenches since March last. Like his brother Jack, he is a well known exponent of the fistic art.

He has no known grave but is commemorated on Panel 30 and 31. Memorial: Pozieres Memorial in France.

DOYLE, Michael: Rank: Private. Regiment or Service: Leinster Regiment. Date of death: 18 January 1917. Service No: 4381. Born in Ballycarnew, Co. Wexford. Enlisted in Bray, Co. Wicklow. Killed in action. Grave or Memorial Reference: I.M.10. Cemetery: Maroc British Cemetery, Grenay in France.

DOYLE, N.: Rank: Private. Regiment or Service: Royal Irish Regiment. Unit: 3rd Bn. Date of death: 3 April 1919. Service No: 32018.
Supplementary information: Alternative Commemoration: buried in Skreen Catholic Churchyard, Co. Wexford. Grave or Memorial Reference: Addenda Panel (Screen Wall). Memorial: Grangegorman Memorial in Dublin.

DOYLE, Patrick: Rank: Private. Regiment or Service: Royal Irish Regiment. Unit: 2nd Bn. Age at death: 56. Date of death: 3 October 1917. Service No: 9100. Born in Enniscorthy. Enlisted in Enniscorthy. Killed in action.
Supplementary information: Son of Patrick and Mary Doyle of Kiltealy, Enniscorthy, Co. Wexford. Husband of Margaret Murphy (formerly Doyle, *née* Breen) of Clonroche, Co. Wexford. Grave or Memorial Reference: I.F.20. Cemetery: Croisilles British Cemetery in France.

DOYLE, Patrick: Rank: Sergeant. Regiment or Service: Royal Irish Regiment. Unit: 1st Bn. Date of death: 21 September 1918. Service No: 9102. Born in Kilmore, Co. Wexford. Enlisted in Wexford while living in Rosslare, Co. Wexford. Died of wounds in Palestine. From an article in the *Free Press*:

> Mrs Anne Doyle Moorfield, Rathaspeck, received news that her son, Sgt P. Doyle, Royal Irish Regiment, died in hospital from wounds received in action. He had been 3 times previously wounded. Native of Ballyhealy, Kilmore. Connected with the army for 12 years, 8 of them in India. Came home December, 1914. Spent 9 months in hospital in Salonika. Stationed in France for 1 year 9 months and was wounded in Palestine in the right arm and shoulder by a shell. Leaves a mother and sister.

Also see **DOYLE, John:** Rank: Seaman. He has no known grave but is listed on Panel 18 on the Jerusalem Memorial in Israel.

DOYLE, Patrick: Rank: Able Seaman. Regiment or Service: Mercantile Marine. Unit: SS *Formby* (Glasgow). The ship was lost with all hands and never located during a fierce storm. Supposed to have been torpedoed by German Submarine U-62. Very little wreckage ever from the Formby but the body of a Stewardess (Annie O'Callaghan) was washed up on the Welsh shore. Age at death: 55. Date of death: 16 December 1917.

Supplementary information: Son of James and Mary Doyle. Husband of Catherine Doyle (*née* Whitby) of 37 Doyce Street, Waterford City, Waterford. Born at Kilmore, Co. Wexford. Memorial: Tower Hill Memorial UK.

DOYLE, Patrick: Rank: Pantryman. Regiment or Service: Mercantile Marine. Unit: SS *Umgeni* (London). The ship was lost to German Submarine U-22 during very bad weather in Robin Hood Bay, Yorkshire. It was also supposed to have been lost at sea during bad weather while part of a convoy. Age at death: 39. Date of death: 9 December 1917.

Supplementary information: Son of Michael and Bridget Doyle. Husband of Kate Doyle (*née* MacDonald) of Great Island, Campile, Co. Wexford. Born at Tramore, Co. Waterford. Memorial: Tower Hill Memorial UK.

DOYLE, Patrick: Rank: Guardsman. Regiment or Service: Grenadier Guards. Unit: 4th Bn. Date of death: 7 August 1917. Service No: 26567. Born in Wexford. Enlisted in Bury. Died of wounds. He has no known grave but is listed on Panel 9 and 11 on the Ypres (Menin Gate) Memorial in Belgium.

DOYLE, Patrick: Rank: Private. Regiment or Service: Royal Irish Regiment. Unit: 2nd Bn. Age at death: 23. Date of death: 19 October 1914. Service No: 3965. Born in Ferns, Co. Wexford. Enlisted in Enniscorthy while living in Ferns, Co. Wexford. Killed in action.

Supplementary information: Son of Martin and Eliza Doyle of Tomsallagh, Ferns, Co. Wexford. From an article in the *Enniscorthy Guardian*, 1915:

> On Sunday last prayers were offered up in Monageer Church for the repose of the soul of Private Patrick Doyle, R.I.R., Tomsollagh, whose family were officially informed of the soldiers death by a rifle bullet in France lately. Much sympathy is felt with the Doyle family in their bereavment.

Grave or Memorial Reference: Panel 11 and 12. Memorial: Le Touret Memorial in France.

DOYLE, Peter: Rank: Leading Fireman. Regiment or Service: Mercantile Marine. Unit: SS *Lusitania* (Liverpool). The *Lusitania* was sunk by German Submarine U-20. Age at death: 32. Date of death: 7 May 1915.

Supplementary information: Son of Laurance and the late Annie Doyle. Husband of Bridget Doyle (*née* Kelly) of 70 Dryden Street, Liverpool. Born at Wexford. Memorial: Tower Hill Memorial UK.

DOYLE, Peter: Rank: Private. Regiment or Service: Royal Irish Regiment. Unit: 6th Bn. Date of death: 13 July 1916. Service No: 1458. Born in New Ross, Co. Wexford. Enlisted in Enniscorthy, Co. Wexford while living in New Ross. Killed in action. From an article in the *Enniscorthy Guardian*, 'New Ross Man Killed; Private Peter Doyle, The Bullawn, New Ross, is reported to have been recently killed at the front. It is reported that his brother Thomas was also wounded.' Grave or Memorial Reference: I.H.1. Cemetery: Dud Corner Cemetery, Loos in France.

DOYLE, Thomas: Rank: Private. Regiment or Service: Royal Irish Regiment. Unit: 1st Bn. Date of death: 28 August 1916. Service No: 8074. Born in Knockanare, Co. Wexford. Enlisted in Gorey while living in Courtown, Co. Wexford. Died in Salonika.

Supplementary information: Brother of Miss M. Doyle of 45 Upper Main Street, Gorey, Co. Wexford. Grave or Memorial Reference: 337. Cemetery: Salonika (Lembet Road) Military Cemetery in Greece.

DOYLE, Thomas: Rank: Sergeant. Regiment or Service: Argyll and Sutherland Highlanders. Unit: 10th Bn. Age at death: 44. Date of death: 3 April 1917. Service No: 7922 and S/7922. Born in Glasgow, Lanarks. Enlisted in Aldershot, Hants while living in, Glasgow, Lanarkshire. Killed in action.

Supplementary information: Son of Martin and Margaret Doyle of 26 South Shamrock Street, Glasgow. Born at Templetown, Co. Wexford. Grave or Memorial Reference: III. M.29. Cemetery: Faubourg D'Amiens Cemetery, Arras in France.

DOYLE, T.: Rank: Private. Regiment or Service: Royal Irish Fusiliers. Date of death: 23 March 1918. Service No: 16018 (16518 on his headstone).

Supplementary information: Husband of Mrs Murphy (formerly Doyle) of Wexford Street New Ross. Grave or Memorial Reference: South of main path. Cemetery: New Ross (St Stephen) Catholic Churchyard.

DOYLE, William: Rank: Private. Regiment or Service: South Lancashire Regiment. Reserve. Unit: 2nd Bn. Age at death: 23. Date of death: 25 January 1919. Service No: 12975.

Supplementary information: Son of Mrs Frances Doyle, of Grogan's Road., Wexford. From an article in the *Enniscorthy Guardian*, June 1916:

Mr and Mrs James Doyle, Grogan's Road, Wexford, have been informed that their son, James, belonging to the Royal Naval Brigade, has been wounded and is at present in hospital in Gosport, Hants. This young naval man, who belonged to the Naval Reserve, was called up at the outbreak of war.

He was in action with the division sent to Antwerp early in the struggle and for the past year he has taken part in many engagements in Gallipoli, where on two occasions he was wounded, but after treatment in hospital at Alexandria he took his place again in the fighting line. It is hoped that his injuries at present are not of a serious nature. He is one of four brothers serving with the colours. Michael, who belongs to the Royal Irish Regiment, was wounded at the battle of Mons, and is now at

T. Doyle.

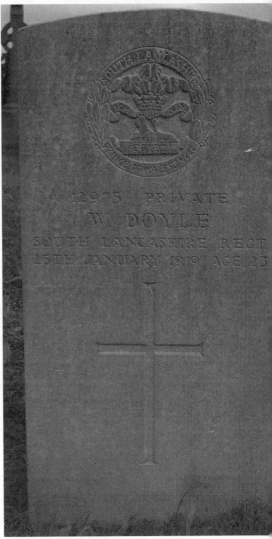

William Doyle.

Salonika; Jack is one of the crew of HMS *Umtali*; and William who volunteered shortly after the outbreak of hostilities is "somewhere in France". The latter has been on active service since July last and was once wounded. Two young brothers at home, Thomas aged nine and Joseph, aged eight, who sent contributions in aid of the Soldiers and Sailors Comforts Club, have been presented by the authorities with "Empire Day" certificates.

Grave or Memorial Reference: Cemetery, Wexford (St Ibars) Cemetery, Wexford.

DOYLE, William: Rank: Able Seaman. Regiment or Service: Royal Naval Volunteer Reserve. Unit: Nelson Bn. R. N. Div. Age at death: 20. Date of death: 20 January 1918. Service No: R/3979.

Supplementary information: (Served as **HIGGINS**), Son of Edward Doyle and Mary Barrington Doyle (*née* Higgins) of Kilanerin, Corey, Co. Wexford. Grave or Memorial Reference: Pier and Face 1 A. Memorial: Thiepval Memorial in France.

DOYLE, William: Rank: Private. Regiment or Service: Machine Gun Corps (Infantry). Unit: 8th Bn. Age at death: 24. Date of death: 11 December 1920. Service No: 48548.

Supplementary information: Son of Michael and Katherine Doyle of Creacon, New Ross, Co. Wexford. Grave or Memorial Reference: IV.Q.11. Cemetery: Basra War Cemetery in Iraq.

DOYLE, William: Rank: Lance Corporal. Regiment or Service: Machine Gun Corps (Infantry). Unit: 67th Bn. Formerly he was with the Royal Fusiliers where his number was 4715. Date of death: 20 September 1917. Service No: 20497 and 26497. Born in Arthurstown, Co. Wexford. Enlisted in Cardiff. Killed in action. From an article in a Wexford newspaper:

A Shelburne Soldier Killed; On Sunday last prayers were offered up for the repose of the soul of Lance Corporal Wm J Doyle, a native of Ballyhack, in St James Church in Ramsgrange, who has been reported killed in action.

He was a grandson of James Doyle, and about fifteen months ago joined a Sortsman's Battalion in Cardiff, where he had been a clerk in the Post Office. He was subsequently transferred to a Machine Gun Corps. Only 26 years of age, he was a good type of Irishman, and was popular in Waterford, when he served on the staff on the Post Office staff there previous to going to England. The news of his death was conveyed by letter from his Commanding Officer, who wrote; "He was a splendid young man, and my section seems incomplete without him. He was always brave, and I feel I shall never be able to replace him."

He was buried in front of 'Observatory Ridge', and a cross is being put on his grave. His comrades send their deepest sympathy, and I and the other Officers join with them.

Grave or Memorial Reference: VII.K.15. Hooge Crater Cemetery Zillebeke, Belgium.

DRAPER, John Robert: Rank: Rifleman. Regiment or Service: Royal Irish Rifles. Unit: 1st Bn. Age at death: 18. Date of death: 9 May 1915. Service No: 1314. Born in Kinsale, Co. Cork. Enlisted in Clonmel, Co. Tipperary. Killed in action.

Supplementary information: Son of John T. Draper of Ballina Park, Newtownbarry, Co. Wexford. Grave or Memorial Reference: Panel 9. Memorial: Ploegsteert Memorial in Belgium.

DRINKWATER, James: Rank: Private. Regiment or Service: East Surrey Regiment. Date of death: 7 June 1917. Service No: 9962. Born in Ballymoney, Co. Wexford. Enlisted in Kingston-on-Thames in Surrey while living in Hampton Wick in Middlesex. Killed in action. Age at death: 19.

Supplementary information: Son of George and Mary Drinkwater of 71 Wick Road, Teddington, Middlesex. He has no known grave but is commemorated on Panel 34. Memorial: Ypres (Menin Gate) Memorial in Belgium.

DRURY, George: Rank: Private. Regiment or Service: Royal Irish Fusiliers. Unit: 9th Bn. Date of death: 1 July 1916 (first day of the battle of the Somme). Service No: 20240. Born in Killegany, Co. Wexford. Enlisted in Newtownards, Co. Down while living in Cootehill, Co. Cavan. Killed in action. Age at death: 24.

Supplementary information: Son of Walter and Fanny Drury of 15 Citizen Road, Holloway, London. He has no known grave but is listed on Pier and Face 2 C on the Thiepval Memorial in France.

DUFFY, John: Rank: Gunner. Regiment or Service: Royal Field Artillery. Unit: 'C' Bty. 122nd Bde. Age at death: 29. Date of death: 31 July 1917. Service No: 1222. Born in Liverpool in Lancs. Enlisted in Bridgend, Glam. Killed in action.

Supplementary information: Nephew of Mathew Madden of Crossabeg, Co. Wexford. Grave or Memorial Reference: Panel 5 and 9. Memorial: Ypres (Menin Gate) Memorial in Belgium.

DUGGAN, George Robert: Rank: Drummer. Regiment or Service: Royal Irish Regiment. Unit: 2nd Bn. Date of death: 23 August 1914. Service No: 9981. Born in Wexford. Enlisted in Ashton-under-Lyne, Lancs while living in Manchester. Killed in action. Age at death: 19.

Supplementary information: Son of James and Marcella Duggan of 80 Beresford Street, Moss Side, Manchester. Grave or Memorial Reference: III.A.21. Cemetery: St Symphorien Military Cemetery in Belgium.

DUNBAR, Patrick Joseph: Rank: Private. Regiment or Service: Kings Liverpool Regiment. Unit: 19th Bn. Date of death: 9 April 1917. Service No: 48288. Born in Wexford. Enlisted in Liverpool while living in Liverpool. Killed in action. From an article in a Wexford newspaper:

FERNS GAEL KILLED IN ACTION
On Wednesday the relatives of Private Pat Dunbar, son of the late Mr and Mrs Martin Dunbar, merchants, Ferns, were officially informed that he had been killed in action on Easter Monday. Before leaving for England some years

ago, where he received a good commercial position, the late Pat Dunbar was a popular figure in hurling and football circles in his native county.

During the years he was engaged at business in Wexford and Enniscorthy he was a prominent member of the Young Ireland and Slaney Harriers Football Clubs and was Captain of the team which first brought county championship football honours to the Cathedral town. In a letter to his sister, Mrs S O'Connor, the Quay, Enniscorthy, written on Good Friday-three days before he was killed – he stated that he had just returned with the other members of his Regiment from Church, where all of them had received Holy Communionand assisted at the devotion of the Stations of the Cross.

The deceased had been in the army only about six months. His death, coming so soon after that of his father and mother, which occurred last year, is deeply regretted, and the greatest sympathy is felt for his brothers and sisters and other relatives in their bereavement. R.I.P.

Grave or Memorial Reference: I.A.9. Cemetery: St Martin Calvaire British, St Martin-Sur-Cojeul in France.

DUNLOP, Alexander: Rank: Sapper. Regiment or Service: Corps of Royal Engineers. Unit: 66th Div, Signal Company, R.E. Service No: 127903. Born in Johnstown, Co. Wexford. Enlisted in Dundalk, Co Louth. Died of wounds. Grave or Memorial Reference: IV.C.13. Cemetery; Perth Cemetery (China Wall) in Belgium.

DUNNE, James: Rank: Company Sergeant Major. Regiment or Service: London Regiment. Unit: 8th Bn (Post Office Rifles). Date of death: 1 March 1918. Service No: 371340. Enlisted in Wexford while living in Wexford. Died at home. From his headstone 'Sergt Major James Dunne, Parnell Street, 8th City of London Battn, Post Office Rifles. Died on the 1st of March 1918 at Cambridge Hospital, Aldershot. Aged: 42 Years'. Grave or Memorial Reference: P.66. Cemetery: Wexford (St Ibar's) Cemetery.

DUNNE, John Henry: Rank: Private. Regiment or Service: Royal Marine Light Infantry. Date of death: 17 March 1919. Service No: PLY/15707.

Supplementary information: Plymouth Div. Son of Mrs Bridget Dunne of Killencooby, Kilmuckridge, Co. Wexford. Grave or Memorial Reference: Screen Wall 1914/18 (RD. 273). Cemetery: Liverpool (Ford) Roman Catholic Cemetery UK.

DUNNE, Thomas: Rank: Private. Regiment or Service: Irish Guards. Unit: 2nd Bn. Age at death: 25. Date of death: 31 July 1917. Service No: 9506. Born in Enniscorthy, Co. Wexford. Enlisted in Enniscorthy. Killed in action.

Supplementary information: Son of Thomas and Winnie Dunne of John Street, Enniscorthy. Grave or Memorial Reference: Panel 11. Memorial: Ypres (Menin Gate) Memorial in Belgium.

DWYER, Albert: Rank Stoker 1st Class. Regiment or Service: Royal Navy. Unit: HMS *Natal*. Date of death:

ERECTED
IN LOVING MEMORY
OF
SERGT MAJOR JAMES DUNNE, *PARNELL ST*
8TH CITY OF LONDON BATTS POST OFFICE RIFLES
DIED ON THE 1ST MARCH 1918,
AT CAMBRIDGE HOSPITAL ALDERSHOT.
AGED 42 YEARS.
ALSO HIS WIFE KATHERINE.
DIED JUNE 5TH 1944,
AGED 62 YEARS.
ALSO THEIR BELOVED ELDEST DAUGHTER
MARGARET
DIED 15TH NOV. 1986.

MY JESUS MERCY

R.   I.   P.

James Dunne.

30 December 1915. Age at death: 25. Service No: K/18912.

Supplementary information: Husband of Margaret M. Dwyer. From a Wicklow Newspaper article:

Amongst the list of those who lost their lives by the explosion and sinking of HMS Natal in the name of Boatman Albert Dwyer of Gorey. He had been in the Navy for the past nine years and had made good headway in the service. He was a native of William Street Gorey and was well known in the town. He always proved himself a credit to his calling, and many are the expressions of regret at his untimely end. He was 24 years of age and had been attached to the NATAL for the past two years. A pathetic feature of the occurance is the fact that Mr Dwyer was married only 5 weeks ago in London to an Irish girl, who is now made a young widow.

Grave or Memorial Reference: 6 on the Plymouth Memorial. UK.

DWYER, Denis: Rank: Private. Regiment or Service: Royal Irish Regiment. Unit: 2nd Bn. Date of death: 20 October 1914. Service No: 10864. Born in Enniscorthy. Enlisted in Enniscorthy. Killed in action. He has no known grave but is listed on Panels 11 and 12 on the Le Touret Memorial in France.

DWYER, J.: Rank: Trimmer. Regiment or Service: Mercantile Marine. Unit: SS *Lusitania* (Liverpool). The *Lusitania* was sunk by German Submarine U-20. Age at death: 20. Date of death: 7 May 1915. Born in Wexford. Memorial: Tower Hill Memorial UK.

DWYER, James: Rank: Leading Seaman. Regiment or Service: Royal Navy. Unit: HMS *Shark*. Age at death: 30. Date of death: 31 May 1916. Service No: 228912.

Supplementary information: Son of John and Mary Dwyer of 8 Ross Road, Enniscorthy, Co. Wexford. HMS *Shark* was sunk during the Battle of Jutland while on service with the 4th Destroyer Flotilla. Around 6pm The HMS *Shark* destroyer led an unsuccessful torpedo attack on the German 2nd Scouting Group but was crippled by gunfire. The forecastle gun and its crew were blown away. The 4-inch gun was later destroyed with the bridge. Around 7pm the surviving crew were ordered to abandon ship and although about thirty got to the boats only five survived. Just as they left the ship she was sunk by a torpedo from German Submarine S54. She was commanded by Commander Loftus Jones who posthumously won the Victoria Cross in March 1917 Commander Jones had died in the boats as HMS *Shark* sank beneath the waves. Grave or Memorial Reference: 12. Memorial: Portsmouth Naval Memorial UK.

DWYER, Owen: Rank: Colour Sergeant. Regiment or Service: Royal Lancaster Regiment. Unit: 1st Bn. Attached to the Nigeria Regiment, W.A.F.F. Date of death: 18 May 1918. Service No: 6701. Born in Wexford. Enlisted in Manchester. Died at Sea. Age at death: 35.

Supplementary information: Son of Owen and Mary Dwyer. He has no known grave but is listed on the Memorial: Hollybrook Memorial, in Southampton, UK.

E

EARLE, Denis: Rank: Private. Regiment or Service: Royal Irish Regiment. Unit: 2nd Bn. Date of death: 9 May 1915. Service No: 6366. Born in Wexford. Enlisted in Waterford. Died of wounds. Grave or Memorial Reference: I.B.16. Cemetery: Bailleul Communal Cemetery Extension, (Nord). France.

EDWARDS, James: Rank: Private. Regiment or Service: Royal Irish Regiment. Unit: 7th Bn. Formerly he was with the Royal Munster Fusiliers where his number was G/1228. Date of death: 31 March 1918. Service No: 5207. Born in Ballycogley, Co. Wexford. Enlisted in Wexford while living in Ballycogley. Died of wounds. Grave or Memorial Reference: I.A.13. Cemetery: Le Cateau Military Cemetery in France.

EDWARDS, James: Rank: Private. Regiment or Service: Royal Irish Regiment. Unit: 2nd Bn. Date of death: 8 March 1917. Service No: 6856 and 3/6856. He was employed by Mr Doran, Johnstown. From an article in the *People*, 1917:

> rejoined the army in October, 1914; went to France in January, 1915; returned in June, 1915; went again to France, August, 1915, and returned in April, 1916, suffering from neuritis, from which he died 6th March, 1917. Private Edward [*sic*] was a native of Moorfield, Wexford.

Grave or Memorial Reference: Between the entrance and the ruin. Cemetery: Bannow Cemetery, 7 miles South West of Taghmon, Wexford.

EDWARDS, John: Rank: Private. Regiment or Service: Northumberland Fusiliers. Unit: 1/5th Bn (Territorial). Formerly he was with the Royal Dublin Fusiliers where his number was 17936. Date of death: 10 April 1918. Service No: 42892. Born in Wexford. Enlisted in Dublin. Died. He has no known grave but is listed on Panel 2 on the Ploegsteert Memorial in Belgium.

ELLIS, Alfred: Rank: Private. Regiment or Service: Army Service Corps. Unit: R.S.P. Depot. Formerly he was with the Cheshire Regiment where his number was 14984. Age at death: 25. Date of death: 2 April 1918. Service No: T/383773. Born in Runcorn, Cheshire. Enlisted in Runcorn while living in Runcorn. Died at home.

Supplementary information: Son of William and Elizabeth Ellis of Runcorn. Husband of M.E. Ellis of Haughton Place, New Ross, Co. Wexford. Grave or Memorial Reference: 12.939. Cemetery: Runcorn Cemetery UK.

ELLISON, Frederick John Gwynn: Rank: 2Lt. Regiment or Service: Royal Irish Rifles. Unit: 1st Bn attached to the 13th Bn. Date of death: 16 August 1917. Age at death, 20. Killed in action.

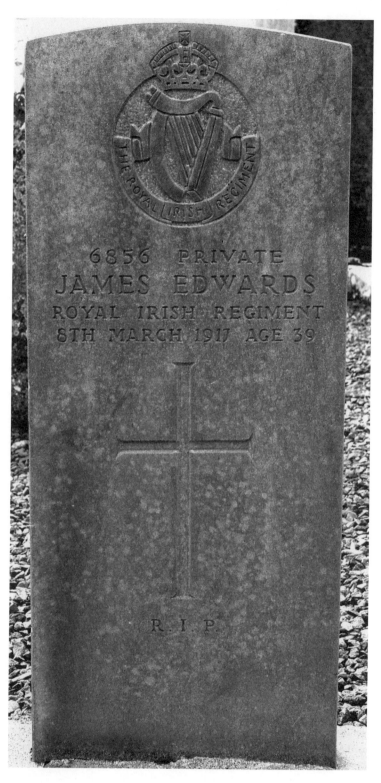

James
Edwards.

Supplementary information: Son of the Revd W.F.A. and Mrs Ellison, of 'The Observatory', Armagh. From an article in the *Enniscorthy Guardian* in 1917:

Second Lieutenant F.J.G. Ellison Killed in action on the 16th inst, was the eldest son of the Rev W. F. A. Ellison, Rector of Fethard, Co. Wexford.

He was educated at Mountjoy School, Dublin, where he won the senior grade intermediate medal as first in all Ireland in mechanics. He obtained a commission in the Royal Irish Regiment in February, 1915, and has been in the front line since that year. He has been through the battle of Messines-Wytschaete ridge, and was afterwards home on leave. He was transferred to the Royal Irish Rifles early in 1917.

From an article in a Wexford newspaper:

Lieut Ellison Killed; Lieut F.J. G. Ellison, killed in action while leading his men in an attack on the German positions behind Ypres, was eldest son of Rev Wm F.A. Ellison, Rector, Fethard, Co. Wexford.

The deceased had a distinguished career at the Mountjoy School, Dublin, and was granted a commission in the Royal Irish Regiment, but later was transferred to the Royal Irish Rifles. The Rev. Mr Ellison is a very popular gentleman, and needless to say every class and creed sympathises with him in his great bereavement.

Grave or Memorial Reference: Panel 138 to 140 and 162 to 162A and 163A. Memorial: Tyne Cot Memorial in Belgium.

ELMES, King: Rank: Captain. Regiment or Service: Royal Army Medical Corps. Secondary Regiment: London Regiment (Queen's Westminster Rifles). Secondary. Unit: attd. 2nd/16th Bn. Age at death: 25. Date of death: 28 September 1918. Killed in action.

Supplementary information: Son of Mr T. and Mrs M.R. Elmes of Robinstown House, Palace East, New Ross, Co. Wexford. Grave or Memorial Reference: I.D.3. Cemetery: Kandahar Farm Cemetery in Belgium.

ENNIS, James: Rank: Private. Regiment or Service: Irish Guards. Unit: 2nd Bn. Age at death: 29. Date of death: 19 October 1915. Service No: 7470. Born in Wexford. Enlisted in Wexford. Killed in action.

Supplementary information: Son of

James Ennis.

Peter and the late Margaret Ennis of 6 Upper King Street, Wexford. From an article in the *Enniscorthy Guardian*:

> Painfully sad is the news of the death of yet another young Wexfordman – Private James Ennis of the Irish Guards. This young soldier who enlisted about six months ago, was only a couple of weeks in action on the 19th of October – the date on which me met his untimely end by the bullet of a German sniper.
>
> Private Ennis, who was the third son of Mr Peter Ennis, King Street, was about 23 years of age.
>
> In his native town he was well known to a large number of comrades, amongst whom the announcement of his death has caused much regret. To deceased's father, his brother, Mr Patrick Ennis, "The People", and the other members of the family the genuine sympathy of their many friends are extended in their sad affliction.

Another article went:

> During the week Mr Ennis, of King Street, Wexford, was notified that his son James was killed in action while serving with the Irish Guards. Private Ennis volunteered for active service some time ago, and on being sent to Flanders participated in several engagements with the Irish Guards.
>
> For some years Private Ennis had been employed at the "Free Press" office. Much sympathy is felt with his respected family in the loss they have sustained. At the general meeting of the A. O. H. Insurance Section on Monday last, a resolution of sympathy with the Secretery, Mr Patrick Ennis,

John Henry Grattan Esmonde.

in his bereavement, occasioned by the death of his brother, Jas, was passed.

Grave or Memorial Referenc: I.K.9. Cemetery: Vermelles British Cemetery in France.

ESMONDE, John Henry Grattan: Rank: Midshipman. Regiment or Service: Royal Navy. Unit: HMS *Invincible*. Age at death: 17. Date of death: 31 May 1916. HMS *Invincible* was sunk during the battle of Jutland.

Supplementary information: Son of Sir Thomas Henry Grattan Esmonde, Bart. M. P. and Alice Barbara Donovan of Ballynastragh, Gorey, Co. Wexford. From an article in the *Enniscorthy Guardian*:

> A boy's brilliant writing. One of the personal losses on Wednesday's action that called for more than ordinary

sorrow in that it involves the sudden ending of a life of much more than ordinary promise is that of midship man, John H.G. Esmonde of the "Invincible".

The dead midship man was the son of Sir Thomas Esmonde M. P. and his brilliant account of the battle of the Falkland Islands can be forgotten by no-one who read it in the Daily News of the Manchester Guardian, the two papers to whom Sir Thomas Esmonde courteously supplied copies of his son's letter. The description of the battle – in particular the duel between the "Invincible" and "Scharnhorst"– as seen from the top of a turret, was characterised by many competent judges as the most effective narrative of a naval engagement that the war had, up to then, produced. Put at the lowest, it was a remarkable piece of writing for a boy under 16, arguing powers of observation and presentation that the future must have brought to a noteable maturity. "I hope I shall never have to go through it again," young Esmonde wrote of the scenes he witnessed on the sinking Gneisenam.

The words come back with an even more tragic ring today. But we cannot doubt that if the story of the Invincible's end could be known, the boy who flinched honourably at the death of others would be found to have gone unflinchingly to meet his own.

From an article in the *Enniscorthy Guardian*, 1916:

Much sympathy will be felt with Sir Thomas and Lady Esmonde on the death of their son in the Invincible.

He took part in the battle of the Falkland Island on the same ship. In Midshipman Esmonde the British Navy has lost an officer of rare promise, and Ireland a son who was worthy of his country. He was, it is true, only a boy – he had completed his seventeenth year on May 8th of the present year. But in his brief career he had shared in all the brilliant naval engagements of the war.

After the usual course at Osborne and Dartmouth, and a short period of training on board the Jupiter he was offered his choice of service in the Erin or the Invincible; he chose the latter vessel. He had barely joined the ship when she sailed to take part in the action at Helogoland. There he made his first acquaintance with the realities of war. After the battle the *Invincible* returned to port, and taking on Admiral Sturdee on board sailed for the Southern Atlantic in quest of the German squadron which had defeated Craddock at Coronel. With her sister ships she met the enemy at the Falkland Islands. In the fight that followed the Invincible was pitted against Von Spee's flagship, the Scharnhorst, which she sent to the bottom. From the turret to which he was assigned Midshipman Esmonde took minute notes of the incidents of the conflict, and these he set forth in a graphic letter to his father, which was widely published in the press.

The literary merits of this account of the destruction of the German squadron would do credit to a writer more experienced than a boy of 15. Returning to England the Invincible joined the cruiser fleet in the keeping of the North Sea, and the Midshipman shared to the full in the hardships that duty entails. On March of the present year he was again in action in the Schloswig-Holstein raid. On May 31st the Invincible sailed on her last voyage. We have not, as yet, the full account of her share in the Titanic battle which will make the name of Horn Reef famous in history. But we may take it she bore herself bravely. And we may also be assured that when her work was done she carried to the depths no stouter heart than that of John Henry Grattan Esmonde.

Grave or Memorial Reference: 11. Memorial: Portsmouth Naval Memorial UK.

EVANS, Richard: Rank: Private. Regiment or Service: The King's (Liverpool Regiment). Unit: 1st/5th Bn. Formerly he was with the North Lancashire Regiment where his number was 32827. Age at death: 37. Date of death: 26 September 1918. Service No: 90685. Born in Liverpool. Enlisted in Liverpool. Killed in action.

Supplementary information: Son-in-law of James Roche of Saltmills, Co. Wexford. Native of Liverpool. Grave or Memorial Reference: IV.G.15. Cemetery: Fouquieres Churchyard Extension in France.

EVOY, Michael: Rank: Private. Regiment or Service: Royal Dublin Fusiliers. Unit: 1st Bn. Date of death: 12 July 1915. Service No: 5632. Born in Wexford. Enlisted in Dublin while living in Wexford. Killed in action in Gallipoli. He has no known grave but is listed on Panel 190 to 196 on the Helles Memorial in Turkey.

F

FANNING, James: Rank: Private. Regiment or Service: Leinster Regiment. Unit: 3rd Bn. Formerly he was with the South Irish Horse where his number was 2996. Age at death: 33. Date of death: 30 December 1917. Service No: 6029. Born in Wexford. Enlisted in Ardeer, Co Louth. Died at Sea.

Supplementary information: Son-in-law of Mrs A. Cassidy of Adamstown, Co. Wexford. Native of Wexford. Grave or Memorial Reference: C.45. Cemetery: Alexandria (Hadra) War Memorial Cemetery in Egypt.

FANNING, John: Rank: Private. Regiment or Service: Royal Irish Regiment. Unit: 2nd Bn. Date of death: 5 July 1916. Service No: 6508. Born in St Mary's, Wexford. Enlisted in Enniscorthy. Killed in action. He has no known grave but is listed on Pier and Face 3A on the Thiepval Memorial in France.

FANNING, William: Rank: Private. Regiment or Service: Irish Guards. Unit: 2nd Bn. Date of death: 31 July 1917. Service No: 10868. Born in Ballymoney, Co. Wexford. Enlisted in Pembrey, Carmarthen while living in Ballymoney, Co. Wexford. Killed in action. He has no known grave but is listed on Panel 11 on the Ypres (Menin Gate) Memorial in Belgium.

FARMER, Franics Harry: Rank: Private. Regiment or Service: Devonshire Regiment. Unit: 9th (Service) Bn. Date of death: 1 November 1917. Service No: 31367. Born in Cahore Point. Enlisted in Devizes while living in Swindon. Died of wounds. Age at death: 19.

Supplementary information: Son of Joseph Richard and Sarah Jane Farmer, of 18 Regent Place, Swindon, Wilts. Grave or Memorial Reference: VI.F.15. Cemetery: Wimereux Communal Cemetery in France.

FARRELL, Francis: Rank: Warrant Officer, Class II (Company Sergeant Major) Regiment or Service: Royal Irish Regiment. Unit: 7th Bn. Formerly he was with the South Irish Horse where his number was 1074. Date of death: 21 March 1918. Service No: 25262. Born in Slane, Co Meath. Enlisted in Dublin while living in New Ross, Co. Wexford. Killed in action. Age at death: 23.

Supplementary information: Son of James and Christina Farrell of Lyons, Hazlehatch, Co. Kildare. He has no known grave but is listed on Panel 30 and 31 on the Pozieres Memorial in France.

FARRELL, Michael: Rank: Private. Regiment or Service: Royal Irish Regiment. Unit: 2nd Bn. Date of death: 24 May 1915. Service No: 4602. Born in St Mary's, Wexford. Enlisted in Wexford. Killed in action. From an article in a Wexford newspaper, 'Bandsman Michael Farrell, Royal Irish Regiment. He had over eight years service with the colours, and had been with the Royal

Irish in South Africa and India. Previous to his joining the colours he acted as an instructor to the Wexford Foresters Band, and his musical ability subsequently resulted in his being attached to the band of the regiment.' He has no known grave but is commemorated on Panel 33. Memorial; Ypres (Menin Gate) Memorial in Belgium.

FARRELL, Patrick: Rank: Private. Regiment or Service: Royal Dublin Fusiliers. Unit: 2nd Bn. Age at death: 22. Date of death: 24 May 1915. Service No: 11666. Born in Kilrush, Co. Wexford. Enlisted in Enniscorthy, Co. Wexford while living in Wexford. Killed in action.

Supplementary information: Son of Peter and Mary Farrell of Clohamon, Ferns, Co. Wexford (see below **FARRELL, Peter:** No; 3851) From an article in the *People*, 1915:

> Bunclody soldiers killed. Bunclody people generally regret to hear of the death of Private Peter O'Farrell of the Army Service Corps, who subsequently transferred into the R.I.R. some time ago and was killed in France. About the same time came the news of the death of his son, Private Patrick O'Farrell, R.I.R. who was killed in the trenches in France.

Grave or Memorial Reference: Panel 44 and 46. Memorial: Ypres (Menin Gate) Memorial in Belgium.

FARRELL, Peter: Rank: Private. Regiment or Service: Royal Irish Regiment. Unit: 2nd Bn. Age at death: 23. Date of death: 25 May 1915. Service No:

3851. Born in St Mary's, Co. Wexford. Enlisted in Wexford. Died of wounds. Son of Michael and Mary Farrell of King Street, Wexford. From an article in a Wexford newspaper:

DIED FROM GAS POISONING

> Since the Germans have adopted their cowardly tactics of sending noxious fumes to sweep away the brave soldiers who are undaunted by shot, shell or steel, several gallant young Wexfordmen have fallen victims to the savagery of the Huns. Each succeeding week brings sorrow to many homes, and the hearths of Wexford are not immune from grief for some dear ones who have gone to their last home. The latest victim of the foul fumes is Private Peter Farrell of the 4th Battalion of the Royal Irish Regiment. On Thursday morning, his father – Mr Michael Farrell, who resides at Stonebridge, Wexford, was officially notified that his son died from gas poisoning on the 25th May. With the letter conveying the sad news was a message of sympathy from the King and Queen and Lord Kitchener.
>
> Another brother of the deceased's, Private Michael Farrell, is serving in the same Regiment, and is fondly hoped that he will be spared to comfort his bereaved parents.

Grave or Memorial Reference: I. F.73. Cemetery: Bailleul Communal Cemetery Extension (Nord) in France.

FARRELL, Peter: Rank: Private. Regiment or Service: Royal Irish Regiment. Unit: 2nd Bn. Age at death: 46. Date of death: 19 October 1914. Service

No: 6712. Born in Kilrush, Ferns, Co. Wexford. Enlisted in Enniscorthy, Co. Wexford while living in Ferns. Killed in action.

Supplementary information: Husband of Mary Farrell of Clohamon, Ferns, Co. Wexford. Grave or Memorial Reference: Panel 11 and 12. Memorial: Le Touret Memorial in France.

FARRELL, Robert: Rank: Private. Regiment or Service: Royal Irish Regiment. Unit: 1st Bn. Date of death: 24 April 1915. Service No: 3739. Born in St Mary's, Wexford. Enlisted in Wexford. Killed in action. From an article in the *Enniscorthy Guardian*, 'Private Robert Farrell, Duke Street, Wexford, Royal Irish Regiment was killed in action on the 24 April in an engagement near Ypres. He leaves a wife and three children.' He has no known grave but is commemorated on Panel 33. Memorial; Ypres (Menin Gate) Memorial in Belgium.

Robert Farrell.

FENLON, Hugh: Rank: Private. Regiment or Service: Labour Corps. Formerly he was with the Royal Dublin Fusiliers where his number was 30284. Date of death: 28 October 1918. Service No: 620505. Born in Athy, Co Carlow. Enlisted in Dublin while living in Kellistown, Co Carlow. Died. Grave or Memorial Reference: C. 624. Cemetery: Enniscorthy New Catholic Cemetery, Wexford.

FENLON, Martin: Rank: Private. Regiment or Service: Royal Irish Fusiliers. Unit: 1st Garrison Bn. Formerly he was with the Royal Dublin Fusiliers where his number was 18471. Date of death: 5 October 1916. Service No: G/196. Born in Wexford. Enlisted in Wexford. Died in India. Age at death: 62.

Supplementary information: Son of Mr and Mrs Michael Fenlon. Husband of Margaret Fenlon. From an article in a Wexford newspaper:

> The death occurred in India on Oct 4th of Private Martin Fenlon of Distillery Road, Wexford. Though he was over fifty years of age, he volunteered for active service, joining the Royal Irish with which he had formerly served. The deceased who was one of the sixty-six children of the late Michael Fenlon, ex-schoolmaster, was a member of the Wexford Board of Guardians for some years.

He has no known grave but is listed on Face E of the Kirkee 1914-18 Memorial in India.

FERRIS, Charles: Rank: Lance Corporal. Regiment or Service: Irish

Hugh
Fenlon.

Guards. Unit: 1st Bn. Date of death: 25 October 1914. Service No: 2416. Born in Wexford, Co. Wexford. Enlisted in Dublin. Killed in action. He has no known grave but is listed on Panel 11 on the Ypres (Menin Gate) Memorial in Belgium.

FINN, Michael: Rank: Sergeant. Regiment or Service: Royal Garrison Artillery. Unit: 83rd Siege Bty. Age at death: 27. Date of death: 19 February 1918. Service No: 40718. Born in Rathgormack in Wexford and enlisted in Merthyr Tydfil in Wales while living in Waterford.
Supplementary information: Son of Thomas and Mary Finn, of Ballynock, Carrick-on-Suir, Co. Tipperary. Grave or Memorial Reference: XIII.E.20. Cemetery: Poelcapelle British Cemetery in Belgium.

FINN, William: Rank: Private. Regiment or Service: Royal Army Ordnance Corps. Unit: Depot. Age at death: 32. Date of death: 26 February 1916. Service No: 4666. Born in Fethard, Co. Wexford. Enlisted in Llanelly, Carm. Died at home.
Supplementary information: Son of Matthew and Henrietta Finn of Fethard, County Wexford. Served in Egypt. Grave or Memorial Reference: Screen Wall. G.B.18.135. Cemetery: Wandsworth (Earlsfield) Cemetery UK.

FITZGERALD, Gerald Hugh: Rank: Captain. Regiment or Service: 4th Dragoon Guards (Royal Irish). Age at death: 28. Date of death: 13 September 1914. Killed in action.

Supplementary information: Son of Lord and Lady Maurice Fitzgerald and of Johnstown Castle, Wexford. Husband of Dorothy Fitzgerald. From an article in the *Enniscorthy Guardian*:

Popular Wexford Officer Killed in action. The genuine sympathy of the people of the county of Wexford goes out to Lady Maurice Fitzgerald, Johnstown Castle, Wexford, on the death of her only son, Captain Gerald H. Fitzgerald, who was killed in the battle on the Aisne. The deceased officer, who was only 28 years old belonged to the 4th Royal Irish Dragoon Guards, with which he has been connected over six years. A splendid type of manhood possessing all the admirable qualities which have ever characterised the Johnstown family, he was held in the highest esteem by all who knew him and even those who had not the pleasure of his personal acquaintance cannot but realise the void which his death has created in the life of his ancestral home, and the intense pain and anguish caused to his sorrowing mother and young bride.

A decidedly pathetic feature of Captain Fitzgerald's death is the fact that he was only six weeks married to Miss Dorothy Charrington, daughter of Mr Spencer Charrington, Winchfield, Hants, the marriage ceremony having taken place quietly at Fedworth on the date of his departure with his Regiment for the front. His afflicted widow, who is at present staying at Johnstown, as well as the members of the family, was profoundly shocked on receiving the sad tidings in a wire from the War Office to the Castle on Friday evening. The news, on being circulated in Wexford town and throughout the

Gerald Hugh Fitzgerald.

county occasioned general expressions of regret. Amongst the populace of South Wexford Captain Fitzgerald was, perhaps, better known than in other districts, as he had made himself a favourite with everyone with whom he was associated.

On his periodical visits home he was identified with many forms of sport, and was particularly popular on the hunting field with the clubs of the Killinick Harriers and the Wexford Hounds. In the Military service he had distinguished himself as a soldier, and since the outbreak of hostilities, his regiment was engaged in many trying encounters with the enemy. Only about a fortnight previous to the news of his death the family were informed of his being slightly wounded while in action somewhere in the vicinity of Mons. His injury on this occasion, which was, fortunately slight, did not incapacitate him from action. Deceased was a first cousin of the Duke of Leinster.

Description of the sad affair;

Particulars of the fatal blow are contained in a letter received this week by Lady Maurice Fitzgerald from Captain H.S. Sewell, 4th Royal Irish Dragoon Guards. The following is a copy of the letter; American Ambulance, Lysee Paskur, Neiully, Paris, September 15th, 1914 – My Dear Lady Maurice, This is my most unhappy duty to write and tell you the terrible news of Gerald's death. He was shot through the head and died, I believe, almost at once.

We were in action fighting the German rearguard at Bourg, on the Aisne, on Sunday morning last. I was slightly wounded myself in the same action, and I could not see him. They buried him in the village cemetery. His personal property was collected and given to me, and I am sending it all to Mrs Fitzgerald, with the exception of his revolver and knife, which I shall also send on later, if possible by some wounded officer who is going home. To me personally and to every officer in the regiment Gerald's death was an awful loss. We have all been through dangers and some hardships, and Gerald was always the most cheery and happy companion. Once before he was very nearly hit while fighting his guns at Brulin, on August 22nd. Then the bullet hit the ground just in front of him and his face was cut by flying stones. At Bourg he was in action with his guns and was standing up to observe his fire when he received his fatal wound.

I know you will bear this bravely, and we all mourn with you the loss of so noble and gallant a comrade. Yours sincerely, H.S. Sewell.' During the week her Ladyship and Mrs Fitzgerald were the recipients of numerous messages of condolence in their bereavement, not only from friends in the county Wexford but throughout the country, and an instance of the widespread sympathy felt with Lady Maurice Fitzgerald is exemplified in the many sympathetic expressions from people with whom she is not personally acquainted. Their Majesties, the King and Queen, through their private secretary, wired as follows; 'Lady Fitzgerald, Johnstown, Wexford – The King and Queen deeply regret the loss you and the army have sustained by the death of your son in the service of his country. Their Majesties truly sympathise with you in your sorrow'.

Her Ladyship telegraphed in reply– "Please convey my most grateful thanks to their Majesties, the King and Queen, for their message of sympathy in the loss of my only son. I am proud to think that he died in the service of his King and country." A Memorial service will be held in Rathaspeck Church at 11.30am on Sunday.

From an article in the *Enniscorthy Guardian*, 1914:

CAPTAIN FORBES WOUNDED.
According to the casualty list dated on Wednesday night, Captain the Hon, F, Forbes, of the Royal Irish regiment, who some weeks ago was reported as missing, is now said to be wounded and a prisoner in charge of the Germans(sic). Captain Forbes is a half-brother of Lady Maurice Fitzgerald, Johnstown Castle, Wexford.

From an article in the *Enniscorthy Guardian*, 1915:

Corporal Gerald O'Doherty, R.I.R.

writing from the firing line some-where in France to the representitive of the "Enniscorthy Guardian" takes the opportunity of publicly thank-ing the good priests and nuns of Enniscorthy for their kindness to him whilst on leave last January, and in this, he says, he might also include the whole population of Enniscorthy. Corporal O'Doherty is the sol-dier who was by the side of the late Captain Fitzgerald, Johnstown Castle, and in whose arms the ill-fated young officer, expired when he received the fatal shot from a German rifle.

The Corporal seems in the best spirits, judging from the tone of his letter. He says all the boys from Town in his locality, and his whole battalion are all in the best of form. "They are confident" he says. "That in the coming fine weather, the Huns will have to go, and once we have them going," says the Corporal, "Will keep them on the move till we reach Berlin." He speaks highly of the British Commisariat – plenty of food, tobacco, clothing, and, in fact, the sol-diers could not be better looked after.

From De Ruvigny's Roll of Honour:

son of the late Lord Maurice Fitzgerald of Johnstown Castle, Co. Wexford, by his wife, Lady Adelaide, dau, of George Arthur Hastings Forbes, 7th Earl of Granard, K. P., and grandson of Charles William, 4th Duke of Leinster, P. C. ; b, Johnstowne Castle, 11 April, 1886, educ; Eton; joined the North Devon Hussars (Yeomanry) in November 1904; gazet-ted from them to the 4th Dragoon Guards, 11 Dec, 1907; promoted Lieut, 17 Nov, 1908 and Capt, 25 Nov, 1913; accompanied the Expeditionary

Force to France; was slightly wounded during the first week in Sept, and fell shot through the head in the Battle of the Aisne when in charge of a machine gun section of his battn, 13 Sept, 1914; buried in the cemetery ar Bourg, Col R. L. Mullins, his commanding officer wrote; "It happened early in the morning of the 13th.

We were fighting in the village of Bourg-et-Comin, about 17 miles east of Soissons, which is about 63 miles north-east of Paris. Herald was as always, hard working and doing good work with his maxims. Some Germans were on the canal bank about 500 yards away, and I had warned him and his men to keep their heads down. Some little time after I had to leave him to attend to other matters he was hit. Major Bridges was close to him at the time, but there was nothing to be done – the end was instantaneous ... His loss to the regt, is immense. He was universally popular and loved by his brother officers and men." Capt, Fitzgerald, was a keen sportsman, a fine rider, and took great interest in polo. He married at South Tidworth, 5th August, 1914, Dorothy Violet, yst, dau, Spencer Charrington, of Winchfield Lodge, Winchfield, Hants.

Grave or Memorial Reference: 8. Cemetery: Bourg-Et-Comin Communal Cemetery in France.

FITZGERALD, Michael: Rank: Private. Regiment or Service: Welsh Regiment. Unit: 2nd Bn. Age at death: 26. Date of death: 16 October 1914. Service No: 939. Born in Ballycanew,

Co. Wexford. Enlisted in Cardiff while living in Ballycanew. Died of wounds.

Supplementary information: Son of Michael and Margaret Fitzgerald. Grave or Memorial Reference: I. A. 11A. Cemetery: Bois Guillaume Communal Cemetery in France

FITZGIBBON, Michael Joseph: Rank: Lieutenant. Regiment or Service: Royal Dublin Fusiliers. Unit: 7th Bn. Date of death: 15 August 1915. Killed in action. From an article in the *People*:

Mr John Fitzgibbon, M.P., has been informed that his son, Captain Michael J Fitzgibbon, 7th Dublin Fusiliers, has been killed in action in the Dardanelles. Captain Fitzgibbon was 29 years of age on the day that he was killed. Prior to receiving his commission in the Dublin Fusiliers he was a law student.

He was Gazetted Captain on 6th March 1915 (his records in the CWGC and SDGW give his rank as Lieutenant). Deep regret is felt in Castlerea for the gallant young officer, who was greatly admired for his many sterling qualities.

He has no known grave but is listed on Panel 190 to 196 on the Helles memorial in Turkey.

FITZHENRY, James: Rank: Gunner. Regiment or Service: Royal Field Artillery. Unit: 'C' Bty. 62nd Bde. Age at death: 30. Date of death: 5 April 1917. Service No: 13140. Born in New Ross, Co. Wexford. Enlisted Newport, Monmouthshire. Killed in action.

Supplementary information: Son of Thomas and Mary Fitzhenry of Fair

Gate, New Ross, Co. Wexford. Grave or Memorial Reference: III.O.7. Cemetery: Faubourg D'Amiens Cemetery, Arras in France.

FITZHENRY, Michael: Rank: Private. Regiment or Service: Royal Irish Regiment. Unit: 1st Bn. Age at death: 21. Date of death: 8 May 1915. Service No: 4423. Born in Mulrankin, Co. Wexford. Enlisted in Wexford while living in Mulrankin, Co. Wexford Killed in action.

Supplementary information: Son of Edward and Margaret Fitzhenry of Kilmannon, Cleariestown, Co. Wexford. From an article in the *People*:

> Private Michael Fitzhenry of the 4th Battalion Royal Irish Regiment was killed near Ypres on the 8th of May last.
>
> His father Mr Edward Fitzhenry, carpenter, Kilmannon, and his mother were notified by the War Office about three weeks afterwards. Deceased, who was about 21 years of age, was a reservist; he worked as a black-smith prior to the war with Mr John White, Ballycapogue. He was a general favourite amongst all in the district and the nes of his death has caused wide-spread regret On the outbreak of hos-tilities he was called to the colours and was sent to the front in February last. He had only served about a fortnight in the trenches, when he was badly frost bitten and was invalided home.
>
> On his recovery towards the end of March he rejoined his Battalion and was again sent to Flanders about the 1st of May only to meet his death a week later. Much sympathy is felt for his parents and relatives.

Grave or Memorial Reference: Panel 33. Memorial: Ypres (Menin Gate) Memorial in Belgium.

FITZHENRY, Patrick: Rank: Rifleman. Regiment or Service: Royal Irish Rifles. Unit: 6th Bn. Formerly he was with the Royal Irish Regiment where his number was 1710. Date of death: 6 August 1915. Service No: 7305 and 7395. Born in New Ross, Co. Wexford. Enlisted in St Helen's, Lancs. Killed in action in Gallipoli. Age at death: 44.

Supplementary information: Husband of Catherine Fitzhenry of 11 Banner Street, St Helen's, Lancs. He has no known grave but is listed on Panel 177 and 178 on the Helles Memorial in Turkey.

FITZHENRY, Thomas: Rank: Private. Regiment or Service: Irish Guards. Unit: 2nd Bn. Age at death: 22. Date of death: 18 August 1918. Service No: 7110. Born in Wexford. Enlisted in Wexford. Died.

Michael Fitzhenry.

Thomas Fitzhenry.

Supplementary information: Son of Robert Fitzhenry and Annie Carty (formerly Fitzhenry) of 3 John's Gate Street, Wexford. From an article in the *People*, 1916:

Missing Wexford soldier now a prisoner of war. Private Thomas Fitzhenry, of the Irish Guards, who had been missing has now been heard of. His mother Mrs Fitzhenry, John's Gate Street, Wexford has received a letter from him dated July 5th, stating that he was a prisoner of war in Germany. All previous efforts to trace him failed, as the following letters to his mother from the British Red Cross show;

20th Sept, 1916. Dear Madam – In answer to your query we regret to tell you that we hear from Corporal N Greeling, 7971, 2nd Irish Guards, lately in a hospital in France, that he saw Fitzhenry lying, as he believes dead on the ground in No Man's Land when they were coming back from the raid under Lt Pym on the 2nd July, 1916. Greeling states that he knew Fitzhenry well, and describes him as being 5ft 8", fair, clean shaven, well built. We are continuing our inquiries on your behalf, and are also watching the Prisoner's Lists from Germany in case by any possible chance we may be obtain information for you from that source. Assuring you of our sincere sympathy in your great anxiety. – Yours Faithfully, Rosalind Lyell, for the Earl of Lucan.

22nd Sept, 1916. Dear Madam, Since writing to you yesterday, we are told by Private W. C. Egan, 7462, 2nd Irish Guards, now in hospital in France, that he was told by H. Beck, that he had seen your son wounded, and added that he was placed by two of our men on the German parapet. He mentions that he believes that Sergeant Anstey of No 3 Company (who is still alive) was in command of the party. We are trying to obtain some more information for you, and hope you will accept our most sincere with you in your great anxiety. – Yours Faithfully, Rosalind Lyell for the Earl of Lucan.

From another article in a Wexford newspaper:

Drowned in Switzerland. Wexford Soldiers Fate. In a recent issue we chronicled the death at Interlaken, Switzerland, of Private Thomas Fitzhenry, Irish Guards whose photograph is reproduced herewith. During the week his Mother Mrs Carty [*sic*] John's Gate Street, was notified by the officer in charge of the soldiers interned in Switzerland that her son accidentally drowned while bathing at Interlakin on Sunday, August 18th.

The young soldier ventured out of the shallow water and sank, and though his body was quickly recovered, efforts at resuscitation proved futile. Sympathy was also tendered by the officer on behalf of himself and the interned men, with whom the deceased was very popular. The deceased, who was only in his nineteenth year, had been a member of the Wexford Corps of the National Volunteers prior to enlisting in the Irish Guards. When on active service in France about a year he was badly wounded in the head, arms and legs during a raid on the enemy trenches.

Private Fitzhenry, while in this condition, was captured by the Germans, and on recovery was interned as a prisoner of war. He was one of a batch of prisoners recently sent to Switzerland, and while awaiting exchange lost his life as stated. A pathetic feature of the tragedy is that Private Fitzhenry, who had not been on leave since he volunteered, had written a few days before his death to his mother stating that he expected to reach home early in September. His untimely end is deeply regretted in his native town, and much sympathy with his relatives in their loss.

Grave or Memorial Reference: 32. Cemetery: Vevey (ST. Martin's) Cemetery in Switzerland.

FITZPATRICK, James Michael: Rank: Gunner/Driver. Regiment or Service: Australian Field Artillery. Unit: 1st Brigade. Date of death: 19 August 1917. Age ar Death, 35. Service No: 5816. Enlisted on 13 October 1915 in Sydney. Occupation on enlistment: bricklayer. Had previous service with the British Navy. Age on enlistment: 32 years 8 months. Height: 12 stone. Eyes: grey. Hair: fair. Complexion: florid. His next of kin details changed when his Mother died and he listed his new next of kin (19 July 1917) as his cousin Miss M. Porterfield/Paterfield, 4 Vine Street, Darlington, Sydney. His effects were to be given to Miss Dora Leary/O'Leary of Dining Rooms, Cornmarket, Wexford. Brother: John Fitzpatrick lived at Ballyslaney, Oylgate, Co. Wexford. In the 30th Divisional Artillery Routine Orders he was awarded the Military Medal (two weeks before he died) and is listed (List 231) in the Australian Gazette. Fifth Supplement, No 30287, 14 September 1917. Died of wounds (gunshot wound to the abdomen) at Casualty Clearing Station No 32. Killed in action in Ypres.

Supplementary information: Born Redmond's Town, Enniscorthy, (also listed as being born in Oylgate) Co. Wexford. Son of Thomas and Margaret Fitzpatrick. From an article in the *Enniscorthy Guardian*, 1917:

Intelligence has been received of the death in action of Private J. M.

James Michael Fitzpatrick.

Fitzpatrick of the Australian Force. Only a short time ago Private Fitzpatrick, who belongs to Oylegate, received the Military Medal for conspicuous gallantry on the field.

His death is deeply mourned by his comrades. He was a general favourite in his Regiment, as letters of sympathy from his brother soldiers go to show, and they all deeply deplore his death. The Chaplain of his Regiment, Rev J. J. Fitzpatrick, has written to his relatives stating that after getting his fatal wound Private Fitzpatrick lived long enough to receive the Last Sacraments and ensure his eternal salvation. He is buried in the military cemetery, where a nice wooden cross marks his grave. Father Fitzpatrick offers his sincere sympathy to his relatives in their great affliction. R.I.P.

Grave or Memorial Reference: II.E.4. Cemetery: Brandhoek New Military Cemetery in Belgium.

FITZPATRICK, Patrick: Rank: Driver. Regiment or Service: Royal Horse Artillery and Royal Field Artillery. Unit: A Battery, 62nd Brigade. Service No: 77557. Born in Askamore, Wexford. Enlisted in Bray, Wexford. Killed in action. Age at death: 19.

Supplementary information: Son of Jeremiah and Kate Fitzpatrick of Ballinaclea, Co. Wicklow. Grave or Memorial Reference: I.J.3. Cemetery: Tilloy British Cemetery, Tilloy-Les-Mofflaines in France.

FITZPATRICK, Patrick: Rank: Private. Regiment or Service: Canadian Infantry (Quebec Regiment) and Royal Field Artillery. Unit: 14th Battalion.

Service No: 448091. Born in Wexford on 23 November 1880. Occupation on enlistment, steel worker. Militia experience, served with the 3rd Field Battery for one year. Next of kin listed as his father, Peter Fitzpatrick. Enlisted in Montreal on the 12 June 1915. From an article in the *Enniscorthy Guardian*:

Patrick Fitzpatrick, son of Mr Peter Fitzpatrick, Ballinastraw, Bunclody, was killed in action with the Canadians some time ago.

He held a commission in that force, which he joined shortly after the outbreak of the war. He lies today in a soldier's grave in the north of France. Great sympathy is felt with his grief stricken parent and brothers and sisters, in their sad bereavement.

Grave or Memorial Reference: Panel 24-26-28-30. Memorial: Ypres (Menin Gate) Memorial in Belgium.

FITZPATRICK, Thomas: Rank: Private. Regiment or Service: Northumberland Fusiliers. Unit: 1/6th Bn (Territorial). Formerly he was with the Royal Inniskilling Fusiliers where his number was 29846. Date of death: 21 September 1918. Service No: 75746. Born in Wexford. Enlisted in Glasgow. Died of wounds. Grave or Memorial Reference: II.D17. Cemetery: Niederzwehren Cemetery in Germany.

FITZSIMONS/FITSIMONS, Frank: Rank: Private. Regiment or Service: Royal Irish Rifles. Unit: 1st Garrison Bn. Formerly he was with the Royal Dublin Fusiliers where his number was 18810. Date of death: 13

May 1916. Service No: 1058 and G/1058. Born in Navan, Co Meath. Enlisted in Naas, Co Kildare while living in Gorey, Co. Wexford. Died in India.

Supplementary information: Buried in Cawnpore Cantonment New Cemetery. Grave or Memorial Reference: Face 23. Memorial: Madras 1914-1918 War Memorial, Chennai, India.

FLANAGAN, Thomas: Rank: Private. Regiment or Service: Royal Dublin Fusiliers. Unit: 1st Bn. Age at death: 25. Date of death: 24 April 1917. Service No: 21651. Born in Wexford. Enlisted in New Ross. Killed in action.

Supplementary information: Son of John and Mary Flanagan of 13 Bullawn, New Ross, Co. Wexford. Grave or Memorial Reference: I.D.17. Cemetery: Monchy British Cemetery, Monchy-Le-Preux in France.

FLYNN, Thomas: Rank: Private. Regiment or Service: Irish Guards. Unit: 2nd Bn. Age at death: 22. Date of death: 13 August 1917. Service No: 10278. Born in New Ross, Co. Wexford. Enlisted in New Ross. Died of wounds.

Supplementary information: Son of Edward and Eliza Flynn of Mount Garret, New Ross, Co. Wexford. Grave or Memorial Reference: III. B.27. Cemetery: Abbeville Communal Cemetery Extension in France.

FOGARTY, James: Rank: Private. Regiment or Service: Machine Gun Corps. Unit: 55th Bn. Formerly he was with the Shropshire Light Infantry where his number was 204151. Age at death: 25. Date of death: 1 April 1918.

Service No: 122123. Born in Liverpool. Enlisted in Liverpool. Died of wounds.

Supplementary information: Son of Andrew and Mary Fogarty of Castlebridge, Wexford and Liverpool. Grave or Memorial Reference: VIII. I.178. Cemetery: Boulogne Eastern Cemetery in France.

FOGG, Frank: Rank: Private. Regiment or Service: Royal Munster Fusiliers. Unit: 'B' Coy. 1st Bn. Formerly he was with the Lancers of the Line where his number was 4227. Age at death: 22. Date of death: 17 August 1917. Service No: 5656. Born in Dovercourt, Essex. Enlisted in Colchester while living in North Fanbridge in Essex. Killed in action.

Supplementary information: Husband of Kathleen Fogg of Abbey Street, Wexford. From an article in a Wexford newspaper:

During the week Mrs Fogg, of Abbey Street, Wexford, was notified by the War Office that her husband, Frank had been killed in action in France on August 17th, while serving with the Munster Fusiliers.

The deceased, who was a native of Chigwell, Essex, volunteered shortly after the outbreak of war, joining the Munster Fusiliers, with which unit he was on active service until he was wounded. When convalescent he was sent to the detachment at Wexford, and while stationed in the town, he proved to be an extremely popular young soldier. Four months ago, at his request, he was sent to the front, and during the terrible engagement in which the Irish Regiments proved unlucky he made the supreme sacrifice. The news of his death was learned with much regret in Wexford, and much sympathy is felt with his young widow. By his superiors and comrades the gallant young soldier was held in high esteem, as is borne testimony to in a letter which his widow has received from his Company officer, Lieutenant, J.J. O'Shea, expressing the sympathy of both officers and men, and stating "Your husband was a splendid soldier and was loved by all his comrades and is sadly missed. He was a gallant, brave boy.

And his conduct was always exemplary. I knew him very well and had a great regard for him, just as all the men had, and I am sure it will be a comfort to you in your sorrow to know that everyone thought so highly of him.'

Grave or Memorial Reference: Panel 143 to 144. Memorial: Tyne Cot Memorial in Belgium.

FOLEY, Patrick: Rank: Private. Regiment or Service: Australian Infantry. Unit: 6th Bn. Date of death: 25 April 1915. Service No: 502. Born in Wexford. Age on enlistment: 34. Occupation on enlistment: seaman. Enlisted 24 August 1914 in Melbourne, Victoria. Next of kin: wife, Elizabeth Foley (*née* Graydon), Remarried now Mrs E. Harvey, 19 Grace Street, Yarraville, changed to 75 Simpson Street, Yarraville, changed to 162 Athol Street, Ascot Vale. Age on enlistment: 34 years 1 month. Height: 5 feet 6½ inches. Hair: brown. Eyes: grey. Complexion: dark. Weight: 11 stone. Reported missing, 24 April 1916. His wife was awarded a pension of £1 per week from 19 March 1916. He has no known grave but is listed on the Lone Pine Memorial in Turkey.

FORDE, Frank: Rank: Private. Regiment or Service: Royal Dublin Fusiliers. Unit: 'D' Coy. 10th Bn. Age at death: 16. Date of death: 10 September 1916. Service No: 26437. Born in Dungarvan, Co Waterford. Enlisted in Waterford while living in Wexford. Killed in action.

Supplementary information: Son of John and Margaret Forde of Patrick Square, Wexford. From an article in the *Enniscorthy Guardian*:

WEXFORD SOLDIER KILLED

The sad news of the death of Private Francis Forde, eldest son of Mr John Forde, St Patrick's Square, has been officially received by his parents on Sunday morning. Private Forde, who was barely 17 years old, joined the Pals battalion of

Frank Forde. Photograph courtesy of Mrs Margaret Walsh Themistocleous, Middlesex. (Frank Forde's niece).

the Royal Dublin Fusiliers in the end of March last, and he was only about a month on active service. Prior to his joining the army he was one of the clerical staff in the office of the Millroad Ironworks, and he was a great favourite with all his companions.

The deepest sympathy is felt for his sorrowing parents. Second Lieut, A.W. Henchy, in conveying the sad news to Private Fordes mother says; " I regret to have to inform you of the death of your son, Private Francis Forde, while in the execution of his duty on the morning of the 10th inst. He died on his way to the dressing station shortly after being wounded. I may mention that in the early morning of the day he entered the trenches he attended his religious duties and received Holy Communion. I attended the funeral service at which was present a number of his friends. He was buried in the cemetery behind the firing line and a wooden cross neatly inscribed marks his grave. You will be informed of his burial ground at some later time. As his platoon Commander, I assure you that I am indeed very sorry to lose such a fine courageous fellow and a gallant soldier of whom his family shoud be proud.

Grave or Memorial Reference: J. 9. Cemetery: Tranchee De Mecknes Cemetery, Aix-Noulette in France.

FORRESTAL, David: Rank: Private. Regiment or Service: Irish Guards. Unit: No. 2 Coy. 1st Bn. Age at death: 22. Date of death: 1 December 1914. Service No: 3517. Born in Enniscorthy, Co. Wexford. Enlisted in Enniscorthy. Killed in action.
Supplementary information: Son of John

and Bridget Forrestal of The Shannon, Enniscorthy, Co. Wexford. From an article in the *Echo*:

News has reached his parents, though not from official quarters, of the death at the front of David Forrestal, a private in the Irish Guards, son of Mr and Mrs J. Forrestal, Shannon, Enniscorthy.

Private Forrestal had been on the reserve and prior to his being called up at the outbreak of war had secured a post-office appointment in London. FORRESTAL – Killed in action on November 1st, David, son of Mr and Mrs John Forrestal, Shannon, Enniscorthy, and grandson of Mrs B Murphy, 15 Temple-shannon, aged 23 years – R.I.P.

From another article in a Wexford newspaper:

David Forestal, a nephew of Miss Murphy, the Shannon, was killed in a recent engagement at the front. He was a popular young man in town and much sympathy is felt for his relatives in their bereavment. Prior to his leaving for the front he had been attached to the London Post Office.

Grave or Memorial Reference: Panel 11. Memorial: Ypres (Menin Gate) Memorial in Belgium.

FORTUNE, James: Rank: Second Mate. Regiment or Service: Mercantile Marine. Unit: SS *Adela* (Dublin). Age at death: 55. Date of death: 27 December 1917. Torpedoed by German Submarine U-100 on her way from Dublin to Liverpool. Twenty-four crew lost.
Supplementary information: Son

of Christopher and Mary Fortune. Husband of Mary Anne Fortune (*née* Kane) of 8 Hasting Street, Ringsend, Dublin. Born at Courtown, Co. Wexford. Memorial: Tower Hill Memorial UK.

FORTUNE, Michael: Rank: Private. Regiment or Service: Royal Irish Regiment. Unit: 2nd Bn. Age at death: 21. Date of death: 9 May 1915. Service No: 10695. Born in Ferns, Co. Wexford. Enlisted in Enniscorthy while living in Ferns. Killed in action.

Supplementary information: Son of Thomas and Marcella Fortune of Clologue, Co. Wexford. Grave or Memorial Reference: Panel 33. Memorial: Ypres (Menin Gate) Memorial in Belgium.

FORTUNE, Thomas: Rank: Lance Corporal. Regiment or Service: Royal Irish Regiment. Unit: 6th Bn. Age at death: 26. Date of death: 3 September 1916. Service No: 2020. Born in Moonager, Co. Wexford. Enlisted in Gorey while living in Wexford. Killed in action.

Supplementary information: Son of Thomas and Ann Fortune of Gorey Hill, Gorey, Co. Wexford. From an article in a Wexford newspaper:

ENNISCORTHY SOLDIER DIES
The death is announced of Corporal Thomas Fortune, Dublin Fusiliers, second eldest son of Mr Wm Fortune, building contractor, Enniscorthy.

The sad event occurred in a military hospital in France, and much sympathy is felt with Mr W Fortune in his bereavment.

From an article in the *Enniscorthy Guardian* in 1916:

Lance Corporal Thomas Fortune, Gorey, was killed in action on 3rd September last. He joined in November, 1914, the 6th Battalion, Royal Irish Regiment and having undergone a course of training at Fermoy he and his company were sent straight to France, where he went through several important engagements, and in the Battle of Guillemont he met his death by a shell from a trench mortar. The deceased was an expert bomb-thrower and on more than one occasion came under the notice of the authorities, and it is stated that if he had survived he would have been recommended for distinction.

Grave or Memorial Reference: Pier and Face 3 A. Memorial: Thiepval Memorial in France.

FRENCH, Robert James: Rank: Petty Officer, 1st Class. Regiment or Service: Royal Navy. HMS *Snaefell*. Age at death: 48. Date of death: 2 November 1918. Service No: 125480.

Supplementary information: Husband of Catherine French. From an article in the *Enniscorthy Guardian*:

TAGOAT NAVAL MAN'S DEATH.
Mr Robert French, R. N. recently died in a London hospital, as a result of an operation. He was in the Navy, and at one time acted as gunner instructor at Rosslare Battery. Shortly after the outbreak of the war he was called upon to serve on board one of his Majesty's cruisers and the scene of his operations

was generally round the west coast of Scotland. He contracted a cold which necessitated an operation in the throat and he died on the 2nd November.

He was interred with full naval honours in St Patrick's Catholic Cemetery, Leyton. He was son-in-law of Mr Stephen Kinsella, Ballyell, Tagoat, and leaves a wife and two children to mourn his loss. Mr French during the time of his residence at Rosslare was extremely popular with all classes of the community, but especially amongst the large number of Navy Reserve men who came there from various parts of Ireland to do their months drill. R.I.P.

Grave or Memorial Reference: XI.A.5.37. Leytonstone (St Patrick's) Roman Catholic Cemetery. UK.

FULL, Arthur: Rank: Private. Regiment or Service: Middlesex Regiment. Unit: 1st Bn. Date of death: 18 July 1916. Service No: G/9708. Born in Duncannon, Co. Wexford. Enlisted in Cork while living in Cork. Killed in action. Grave or Memorial Reference: I.B.15. Cemetery: Flatiron Cemetery: Flatiron Copse Cemetery. Mametz in France.

FURLONG, Edward: Rank: Corporal. Regiment or Service: Royal Horse Artillery and Royal Field Artillery. Unit: 38th Bde. Ammunition Column. Age at death: 41. Date of death: 30 July 1915. Service No: 15932. Born in Taghmon, Co. Wexford. Enlisted in Wexford.

Supplementary information: Son of John and Annastatia Furlong of Foghmon, Co. Wexford. Husband of Elizabeth Furlong of 48 Slievekeale, Waterford.

Served in China (1900) and in the South African Campaign. Grave or Memorial Reference: I.G.3. Cemetery: Poperinghe New Military Cemetery in Belgium.

FURLONG, James: Rank: Private. Regiment or Service: Royal Dublin Fusiliers. Unit: 2nd Bn. Date of death: 30 March 1918. Service No: 18527. Born in Piercestown, Co. Wexford. Enlisted in Wexford while living in Redmondstown, Co. Wexford. Killed in action. From an article in the *Free Press*, 1916:

Private James Furlong, son of Mr James Furlong, Redmondstown, Johnstown, is serving with the Royal Dublin Fusiliers. He had been employed in Johnstown Castle, and after the outbreak of war he joined the colours. He has been in the trenches for over a year, and on his return to his native district a couple of weeks ago, when he was on a brief furlough, he was congratulated by his many friends on his survival of the

James Furlong.

many big encounters in which his regiment figured.

Grave or Memorial Reference: VIII. G.2. Cemetery: Heath Cemetery, Harbonnieres in France.

FURLONG, James. Rank: Stoker. Regiment or Service: Royal Naval Reserve. Unit: HMS *Indefatigable*. Age at death: 21. Date of death: 31 May 1916. Service No: 5241S.

Supplementary information: Son of Gregory and Margaret Furlong of Yoletown, Ballycullane, Co. Wexford. The Van Der Tann was scuttled in Scapa flow in June 1919. From an article in the *Enniscorthy Guardian*:

> Sergeant Thomas Furlong. Sergeant Thomas Furlong. Royal Welsh Fusiliers, was in Cardiff when the war broke out, and volunteered at once. He rose rapidly to the rank of Sergeant, and is at present engaged in one of the English Camps training the new recruits. He is a son of Mr Laurence Furlong, Yoletown, Ballycullane.

Grave or Memorial Reference: 19. Memorial: Plymouth Naval Memorial UK.

FURLONG, John: Rank: Gunner. Regiment or Service: Royal Garrison Artillery. Unit: 320th Siege Bty. Age at death: 32. Date of death: 15 December 1918. Service No: 31273.

Supplementary information: Son of Francis and Mary Furlong of Wexford. Husband of Elizabeth Jane Furlong of Rose Villa, Alfred Parade, St James, Bristol. Grave or Memorial Reference:

819. Cemetery: Mikra British Cemetery, Kalamaria in Greece.

FURLONG, Joseph, A.: Rank: Lieutenant. Regiment or Service: U.S. Medical Reserve attached to the British Forces. From an article in the *People*, 1918:

> Lieut, Joseph A. Furlong of the U.S.A. Medical Reserve, attached to the British Forces, nephew of Mr Clement Furlong and Miss Agnes Furlong, Lough, Duncormack, who was also lost in the disaster. Lieut, Furlong, was eldest son of Mr Michael Furlong, formerly of Lough, now at St Louis, Missouri, U.S.A. He joined the Medical Reserve Corps of the U.S.A. Forces and was returning to take up his duties with his regiment after spending a short time in his fathers native district which he visited for the first time. The remains were removed from the 5th hospital, Arbour Hill, Dublin, and were conveyed to Wexford on Monday night by the seven train, the American flag enshrouding the coffin, and were received by a guard of honour of armed American sailors, his Worship, the Mayor (Ald, W. H. McGuire, J. P.) wearing his chain of office, and eighteen members of the corporation, a large selection of the general public, and some members of the police force.
>
> They were borne from the mortuary van by members of the Major Redmond Memorial Committee. The funeral proceeded to the Church of the Immaculate Conception was a particularly sad spectacle. On reaching the Church the remains were received by Rev, Thos, Hore, Adm, and at the close of the ceremonies Mr Frank Breen, R.I.A.M. played the 'Dead March

in Saul'. On Tuesday after 10 o'clock Mass was offered up for the repose of his soul, the internment took place at Carrig-on-Bannow when there was a very large attendance of sorrowing friends and the general public. Rev, Thos, Hore. Adm, recited the prayers appropriate for the occasion before the remains were taken from the Church, and Rev M. O'Sullivan, P. P. received them at the cemetery.

The flag at Bannow Coastguard Station was at half mast. At the cemetery the U.S.A. detachment fired three volleys, and the Last Post was sounded. The chief mourners were – Messrs Clement Furlong, Lough, Duncormack (uncle), R. Murphy, Airhill; D. Scallan; Stephen Corish, Ballingly; Raymond Corish, Taghmon; P. and T. Furlong, Lacken; Philip Keating, M.C.C.; Mrs Corish, Lough; and Mrs Scallan, Lough (cousins).

Lieutenant Furlong's remains were identified by his uncle, Mr Clement Furlong, and his cousin, Mr R.P. Corish, amongst 149 victims of the disaster.

FURLONG, L.: Rank: Staff Sergeant. Regiment or Service: Royal Army Ordnance Corps. Unit: Ordnance Advanced Depot. Age at death: 28. Date of death: 4 August 1920. Service No: S/6942.

Supplementary information: Son of William and Mary Furlong of Clongeen, Foulksmills, Wexford. Grave or Memorial Reference: VIII.F.9. Cemetery: Baghdad (North Gate) War Cemetery in Iraq.

FURLONG, Michael: Rank: Private. Regiment or Service: Royal Irish

Regiment. Unit: 2nd Bn. Date of death: 15 October 1917. Service No: 4468. Born in St Mary's, New Ross, Co. Wexford. Enlisted in New Ross. Died. Grave or Memorial Reference: V.J.13. Cemetery: Niederzwehren Cemetery in Germany.

FURLONG, William: Rank: Gunner. Regiment or Service: Royal Marine Artillery. Unit: HMS *Defence*. Age at death: 24. Date of death: 31 May 1916. Service No: RMA/12643.

Supplementary information: Son of John and Anastasia Furlong of Crandaniel, Barntown, Wexford. HMS *Defence* was an armoured cruiser and was sent to the bottom by the Naval guns of a German battlehip during the battle of Jutland. There were no survivors. Grave or Memorial Reference: 21. Memorial: Portsmouth Naval Memorial UK.

FURNISS, James: Rank: Private. Regiment or Service: Royal Irish Regiment. Unit: 1st Bn. Age at death: 26. Date of death: 10 March 1918. Service No: 10063. Born in New Ross, Co. Wexford. Enlisted in Waterford while living in New Ross, Co. Wexford. Killed in action in Palestine. From an article in the *People*, 1915:

On Monday last Private James Furniss, of Neville Street, New Ross, who was a postman up to the time of volunteering, and who was recently invalided suffering from a dose of gas which he received in the trenches, left Ross for the front.

On the same day Private Peter Stafford, of Rosbercon, who was gassed in the trenches, came home recently, also returned to the front. Private

William Cass, who got a slight dose of gas and was wounded also, left Ross at the end of last week. He had been home for about a month.

From an article in the *Enniscorthy Guardian*, 1915:

On Friday of last week, James Furness, Neville Street, New Ross, who had been a postmaster previous to going to the front returned to Ross from an English hospital where he had been treated for some weeks for the effects of gas poison sustained in the trenches. He got a severe dose of the stuff and it was rumoured a few weeks ago that he was dead. He looks well and expects to be going back to the fighting line by the end of the week. He gives an interesting account of the manner in which the gas operates.

Sometimes one could see a number of Germans at a distance dressed in an attire resembling a divers suit, head and body completely covered, with an apparatus strapped to their backs like a man spraying a potato garden in July, walk hither and tither in the trenches and let off the gas in volumes. It floats along in the wind like a thick vapour and once it gets into a persons lungs it has a suffocating and painful effect. He says there are instances of German gunners being chained to the big guns to prevent them deserting their posts.

Supplementary information: Son of Mrs Margaret Hennessy of Church Lane, New Ross, Co. Wexford. Grave or Memorial Reference: J. 68. Cemetery: Jerusalem War Cemetery, Israel.

FURNISS, Martin: Rank: Gunner. Regiment or Service: Royal Field Artillery. Unit: Reserve Bde. Age at death: 23. Date of death: 21 March 1917. Service No: 69338. Born in New Ross, Co. Wexford. Enlisted in Waterford. Died of wounds at home.

Supplementary information: Son of James and Mary Furniss of Church Lane, New Ross, Co. Wexford. Grave or Memorial Reference: D. 127. Cemetery: Lincoln (Newport) Cemetery UK.

FURNISS/FURNESS, Patrick: Rank: Private. Regiment or Service: 4th (Queen's Own) Hussars. Date of death: 7 February 1916. Service No: 10985. Born in New Ross, Co. Wexford. Enlisted in Southampton while living in New Ross. Killed in action.

Supplementary information: Son of Mrs Furniss of Church Lane, New Ross, Co. Wexford. From an article in a Wexford newspaper, 'New Ross Soldier Killed; Private Patrick Furniss, New Ross, has been killed in the war. Patrick Furniss was in the Royal Artillery and joined the army prior to the outbreak of the war.' Grave or Memorial Reference: II.B.4. Cemetery: Vermelles British Cemetery in France.

FYFE, Thomas M.: Rank: Deck Hand. Regiment or Service: Royal Naval Reserve. Unit: HM Trawler *George Milburn*. Age at death: 27. Date of death: 12 July 1917. Service No: 11706/DA. Grave or Memorial Reference: Between the Church and the North Boundary. Cemetery, Templetown Graveyard, Wexford.

Thomas J. Fyfe.

G

GANNON, James. Rank: Boatswain (Bosun). Regiment or Service: Mercantile Marine. Unit: SS *Beacon Light* (Liverpool). Age at death: 44. Date of death: 19 February 1918. SS *Beacon Light* was attacked by a German Submarine on 19 February 1918.

Supplementary information: Son of the late Thomas and Martha Gannon. Husband of Margaret Gannon (*née* Downey) of 47 South Chester Street, Liverpool. Born in Co. Wexford. Memorial: Tower Hill Memorial UK.

GAUL, James: Rank: Leading Seaman. Regiment or Service: Royal Naval Reserve. Unit: SS *Emlyndene*. Age at death: 32. Date of death: 11 December 1917. Service No: 2424B.

Supplementary information: Son of Anne and James Gaul of Faythe, Wexford. Husband of Margaret Gaul of 20 Carrigeen Street, Wexford. *Emlyndene* O. N. 119961, 495 tons coaster, 171ft x 23. 6ft. Built 1904 by Murdoch & Murray, Port Glasgow as the *Llandaff* for Michael Murphy, Cardiff. 1913 sold to Wilson & Reid, Belfast renamed *Kilroot*. 1913 sold to Emlyn Line Ltd, Cardiff renamed *Emlyndene*. 11 December 1917 sailed from Cardiff for Granville with a cargo of coal and went missing. Grave or Memorial Reference: 23. Memorial: Plymouth Naval Memorial UK.

GAYNOR, Michael: Rank: Private. Regiment or Service: South Lancashire Regiment. Unit: 2nd Bn. Date of death: 3 September 1916. Service No: 3062. Born in Taymon, Co. Wexford. Enlisted in Penre, Glam while living in Clerastown, Co. Wexford. Killed in action.

Supplementary information: Brother of Mrs Kehoe of Shilmalier Common, Cleristown, Co. Wexford. From an article in the *Enniscorthy Guardian*, 1915:

Private Michael Gaynor, Son of Mrs Gaynor, Skeeter Park, Cleristown, has just been home on a brief furlough. He is attached to the 2nd South Lancashire Regiment, having volunteered his services shortly after the out break of the war.

He arrived in Wexford on Wednesday of last week having come direct from the trenches, the soil of Belgium and France still adhering to his boots and clothes. Private Gaynor looked fit and well considering his trying experience of the past twelve months. He has had some providential escapes and the only injury received by him is a slight wound in the knee caused by the explosion of an aerial torpedo. In the course of a conversation with a friend he related some of his adventures in the firing line. He had been in most of the big engagements, Kimmel, St Eloi, Ypres, Nerve Chapelle, Hill 60 etc. He related several instances of German savagery and barbarity, and of their treatment of the women of Ypres and other places. The Germans are a cowardly lot, he says, when it comes to a bayonet charge. The sight of the cold steel is enough for them.

He tells of one bayonet charge in which the Irish Rifles and his Regiment took part, and in which the Germans cried out "You English, Mercy", but the Irish Rifles greeted their appeals with cries of "Remember the Lusitania" when charging them. Private Gaynor served through the Boer war with distinction and in the present war has been recommended on three different occasions for his gallantry and effective work.

Grave or Memorial Reference: Special Memorial 16. Cemetery: Blighty Valley Cemetery, Authuile Wood in France.

GEDDES, George: Rank: Skipper. Regiment or Service: Royal Naval Reserve. Unit: HMS *Speedwell V*. Date of death: 28 October 1916. Age at death, 45.

Supplementary information: Husband of Margaret Jane Geddes, of 'Tarwathie' South Pringle Street, Buckie, Banffshire. Grave or Memorial Reference: South East of the Church. Cemetery: Kilscoran Church of Ireland Cemetery in Tagoat.

GEDDES, George: Rank: Trimmer. Regiment or Service: Royal Naval Reserve. Unit: HMS *Speedwell V*. Date of death: 28 October 1916. Age at death, 18. Service No: 2065TS.

Supplementary information: Son of Margaret Jane Geddes, of 'Tarwathie' South Pringle Street, Buckie, Banffshire, George Geddes (see above). From an article in the *People*, 1916:

Two bodies washed ashore. At Rosslare. Inquest and Verdict. In the early hours of Saturday morning the body apparently of a naval man was washed ashore near Rosslare Fort, the body being first observed by Walter Cousins, who was on watch at the time.

Later on in the day a second body was picked up almost opposite the White House by Joseph Duggan, Rosslare. Sergeant Gallagher, on being acquainted of the facts of the finding of the first body, at once proceeded to the Fort, and arranged for the conveyance of the body to Rosslare, and later on the second body on coming ashore was taken in charge by Sergeant Gallagher, and both conveyed to Kelly's Hotel, where an inquest was held on the same day by Mr Peter Ffrench, M.P. coroner for South Wexford. Both bodies were much decomposed, but identification was easy in the first case from the slip of paper found in one of the vest pockets of the deceased. The remains were subsequently identified as those of George Geddes, who was the skipper of the ill-fated 'Speedwell IV'. Identification was exceedingly difficult in the second instance, but from the description given to the constabulary of the lost crew, there seemed to be no room for doubt that the remains answered to the description of the son of the skipper, who was about 19 years of age.

It will be remembered that on October 27th the Speedwell IV, was lost with all hands about Greenore, and from the evidence given below it would appear that the second body found was that of the skipper's son, who was also named George Geddes. It was with much difficulty that the body of the skipper was removed to Rosslare, as owing to the high seas the approaches to the Fort were almost impassable. Sergeant Gallagher procured a horse and car to recover the body, and after a great struggle through the high seas, succeeded regaining the shore. Much assistance

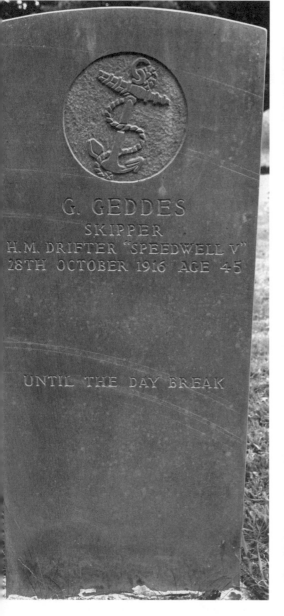

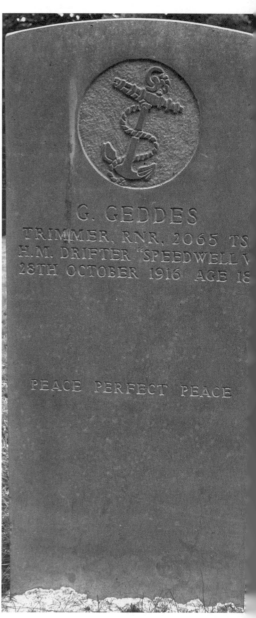

G. GEDDES
SKIPPER
H.M. DRIFTER "SPEEDWELL V"
28TH OCTOBER 1916 AGE 45

UNTIL THE DAY BREAK

G. GEDDES
TRIMMER, RNR, 2065 TS
H.M. DRIFTER "SPEEDWELL V
28TH OCTOBER 1916 AGE 18

PEACE PERFECT PEACE

George Geddes (Skipper).   George Geddes (Trimmer).

was rendered to the Police by several members of the lifeboat crew at the Fort, who it may be mentioned, were in extreme peril themselves at that particular time owing the heavy seas which swept over the embankment.

Dr J.H. Anglin, who had charge of the funeral arrangements, had both bodies interred in Kilscoran Cemetery on Sunday, both of the deceased being accorded a naval funeral. A large number of the members of the crews of the drifters at present lying at Rosslare Pier followed the remains to the last resting place. The prayers at the graveside were recited by the Rev T.E.G. Condell, Rector. The following are the details related at the inquest; Inquest at Kelly's Hotel on Saturday at 1.30pm by Mr P. Ffrench, J. P. coroner, on the bodies of George Geddes and an unknown man, apparently about 19 years of age. The following are sworn; Messrs J. Kelly, Hotel (foreman), John Cloke, W. Williams, Theobald Barlow, Nicholas Barry, Joseph Murphy, John Murphy, John Barrett, M. O'Brien, W. Shiel, Thomas Leary and J. Moran. Sergeant Gallagher was present on behalf of the police, and Mr E.T.M. Sandwith, J.P., the local representative of the National Lifeboat Institution and hon, sec of Ballygeary branch was also present.

The first witness sworn was Walter Cousins, who is a member of the lifeboat crew at Rosslare Fort. He deposed he was on watch at about 3 a.m. on Saturday morning. He found a dead body on the strand at the Fort. He told Mr E Wickham, the coxswain of the lifeboat, who assisted him in removing the body and he also reported the matter by telephone to the constabulary at Rosslare Strand. He then made

the body secure on the burrow. Asked by the coroner if the body was recognisable, he said it was not.

Joseph Cowey depose he was skipper of the drifter Buoywind, and that he know one body to be that of George Geddes but could not swear to the other, only that he was a member of the crew of the HMS *Speedwell IV,* which was lost at Greenore Point on the 27th October last. In reply to the coroner, he said he was personally acquainted with George Geddes but only knew the other by the uniform he wore. This concluded his evidence. Alexander Farquher [*sic*], mate of the H. M. Drifter Irene, was sword and examined. He deposed he knew George Geddes, but could not name the other man, who was greatly decomposed, but he identified the clothes he wore to be one of the crew of the *Speedwell IV.* He corroborated the statement of the last witness.

Joseph Duggan, Rosslare, deposed that he found the body of the unknown man about twelve noon on the strand on Warren Lower, and notified the coastguard at Rosslare. Sergeant Gallagher deposed that he was notified of the finding of a body at 6a.m. on Saturday morning by the local coastguards. He immediately proceeded to the Fort, where the dead body was tied on the burrow to a telegraph pole. He searched the body of the deceased, George Geddes, and found in a leather purse two Treasury notes, silver, and copper to the amount of 5s 11d and a slip of paper (produced), on which was written what was presumed to be the ages of his children. He also found a tobacco pouch (produced).

Dr J.H. Anglim, Ballyregan, deposed that he made a superficial examination of the two bodies, one of which was unrecognisable, the other largely decomposed, and from the evidence heard, he believed that death was due to drowning.

Grave or Memorial Reference: South East of the Church. Cemetery: Kilscoran Church of Ireland Cemetery in Tagoat.

GILL, John Joseph: Rank: Private. Regiment or Service: Royal Inniskilling Fusiliers. Unit: 7th Bn. Formerly he was with the Royal Dublin Fusiliers where his number was 13131. Age at death: 22. Date of death: 21 October 1916. Service No: 8/25750 and 25750. Born in Newbawn, Co. Wexford. Enlisted in St Helen's while living in Wexford. Died of wounds.

Supplementary information: Son of John Gill of Ballyclemock, Newbawn, Wexford. From an article in the *Enniscorthy Guardian*, 'Private Gill, Ballyclemock, Newbawn is home from the front where he took part in several engagements. He received a number of wounds, and has been compelled to wear glasses on account of injuries received to his eye.' Items from an article in a Wexford newspaper:

During the present week, Mr Gill, of Ballyclomack, Foulks Mills, received notification from the war office of the death in action of Lance Corporal John J. Gill, Inniskilling Fusiliers. Lance Corporal Gill, who comes from a family which has given several members to the army, was 22 years of age. Private William Gill, Irish Guards, 23 years of age, has been in all the recent severe fighting on the Somme

front, but so far escaped unscathed. He joined the army prior to the beginning of the war. Private Martin Gill is at present in hospital in Liverpool recovering from the effects of a severe wound received in the big push.

Private Martin Gill, who is 19 years old, has already been severely wounded on three occasions. He has been through the whole campaign in France since the commencement of the war.

Grave or Memorial Reference: III.A.253. Cemetery: Bailleul Communal Cemetery Extension (Nord) in France.

GLANVILLE, James: Rank: Petty Officer 1st Class. Regiment or Service: Royal Navy. Unit: HMS *Bayano*. Date of death: 11 March 1915. Service No: 126966. Age at death: 45.

Supplementary information: Son of Michael and Margaret Glanville (*née* McCarthy), of Goleen. Husband of Mary E. Glanville (*née* Wool), of Goleen, Skibbereen, Co. Cork. From an article in the *Enniscorthy Guardian*, 1915:

Victim of the *Bayano*. My John Glanville, principle light-house keeper on the Tuskar Rock, has received information that his brother, James, a torpedo instructor on the auxiliary curiser, *Bayano*, which was sunk off the Scotch coast, is amongst those drowned. The deceased, Mr Glanville, is a brother-in-law of Mr Henry Higginbotham mate of the Blackwater lightship.

Grave or Memorial Reference: 7. Memorial, Portsmouth Naval memorial, UK.

W. S. GLOVER
CHIEF OFFICER
S.S. "MESABA"
1ST SEPTEMBER 1916 AGE 39

DEARLY LOVED
NEVER FORGOTTEN
HOME AT LAST
GOD KNOWS BEST

William Stanmore Glover.

GLOVER, William Stanmore:
Rank: Chief Officer. Regiment or Service: Mercantile Marine. Unit: SS *Mesaba*. Age at death: 39. Date of death: 1 September 1918.

Supplementary information: Son of William and Mary Ann Glover, of London. Husband of Esther Mary Louise Glover, of 21 St Paul's Avenue, Cricklewood, London. From an article in the *Enniscorthy Guardian*:

LOSS OF LIVES AT SEA

Inquest and verdict. An inquest was held on Tuesday morning last by Mr J. J. Roche, J. P., coroner for South Wexford, upon the bodies of three young men whose ship was torpedoed by an enemy submarine, The following respectable jury was sworn upon the case, Messrs William B. Moncas (foreman) Ernest Cavey, William Duggan, Patrick Hogan, Isaac Scanlan. Patrick Furlong, Michael Ferguson, W. Pierce, John Metcalf, Patk Hayden, Stephen Ferguson, Edmund Doyle, Stephen Murphy, Andrew Parle. Lieutenant Michael John O'Neill stated; I received a wireless message from one of his Majesty's war ships that they had out at sea three apparently drowned men, and required medical assistance immediately.

Dr Anglim was at once sent for and taken out to the man of war by a steam drifter. As soon as the doctor saw the bodies he pronounced them dead. They were then brought on shore. We identified William Stanmore Glover as chief officer of the ship sunk by papers found upon the body and Henry O'Neill was identified assistant steward by documents found on him. The third body remains unidentified as the body was in a nude state when picked up, and there was nothing to lead to iden-

tification. I believe this unidentified body was also a member of the crew of the same torpedoed steamship, as he had been picked up in the same vicinity as the two other bodies. Dr. Anglim stated when he examined the bodies. Life was extinct. We tried artificial respiration on board the war ship upon the three bodies but without success. The cause of death was shock, due to immersion in the water, said immersion, I believe was caused by the action of an enemy submarine through firing a torpedo at the ship of which the deceased formed part of the crew, as told to me by some officers on board the warship. Coroner-Gentlemen, Dr Anglim's evidence is the last testimony you are to hear as to how these unfortunate young men met their deaths.

We have no direct evidence by anyone who saw the torpedo fired, but the circumstantial testimony leaves scarcely a doubt that these men were 'done to death' by murderers from the brigand empire of Germany, a nation whose brutal conduct of the war during the last four years is a disgrace to humanity. The doctor tells us the cause of death was shock due to immersion in the water, said immersion being caused through the action of an enemy submarine by firing a torpedo at the steamship, of which the deceased, according to the evidence, formed part of the crew. If you base your verdict upon these details of the disaster, you will be finding in accordance with the evidence, and arriving at the only conclusion in sympathy with the facts. The jury unanimously agreed with the coroner's view of the case, and returned the following verdict 'We find the said William Stanmore Glover, Henry O'Neill, and one unidentified man died from shock caused by immersion in the water, due to the action of an enemy submarine through firing a torpedo at the steamship, the deceased, we believe, being members of the crew.'

The Coroner returned thanks to the jury for their punctual attendance and close attention they gave to the details of the inquest. Immediately after the inquest the remains of the three young men were carried off the pier and removed in three hearses for burial at Kilscoran burial ground. Several long wagonettes carried parties of soldiers and bluejackets in the funeral cortege. The Rev Mr Condel read the funeral service at the graveside. In three coffins the bodies were interred in one grave and a military sergeant upon a coronet sounded 'The Last Post', after which all departed. Though the deceased belonged to the mercantile marine, they were accorded a military or naval funeral, with full military honours.

Grave or Memorial Reference: South East of the church. Cemetery: Kilscoran Church of Ireland Churchyard, Tagoat, Wexford.

GODSELL, Edward: Rank: Private. Regiment or Service: Royal Irish Regiment. Unit: 2nd Bn. Formerly he was with the Royal Munster Fusiliers where his number was 4864. Date of death: 3 September 1916. Service No: 18022. Born in St Michael's, Limerick. Enlisted in Limerick while living in Wexford. Killed in action. Age at death: 19.

Supplementary information: Son of Mrs J. Bennett of 45 St James Street, Doncaster, Yorks. He has no known grave but is listed on Pier and Face 3.A. on the Thiepval Memorial in France.

GOGGIN/GOGGINS, Michael: Rank: Private. Regiment or Service: Royal Irish Regiment. Unit: 'C' Coy. 2nd Bn. Age at death: 42. Date of death: 24 May 1915. Service No: 4272. Born in Ballybricken, Co Waterford. Enlisted in Wexford. Killed in action.

Supplementary information: Son of Patrick Goggins of Mary's Lane, Wexford and the late Catherine Goggins. Husband of Elizabeth Goggins of Wetherheld's Court, Bride Street, Wexford. A snippet from the *People*, 'A Wexford soldier, Private M Goggin, Watery Lane, who served with the Royal Irish Regiment, is reported missing since 26th of May last.' Grave or Memorial Reference: Panel 33. Memorial: Ypres (Menin Gate) Memorial in Belgium.

GOLDEN, Michael: Rank: Leading Seaman. Regiment or Service: Royal Naval Reserve. Unit: HMS *Louvain*. Age at death: 39. Date of death: 20 January 1918. Service No: 3276B.

Supplementary information: Son of John and Mary Golden. Husband of Mary E. Golden of Wygram Place, Wexford. From an article in the *People*, 1918: 'News has been received in Wexford that Leading Seaman Michael Golden, John Street, Wexford, aged 37 years, has been lost at sea. He leaves a wife and four children to mourn his loss.' Grave or Memorial Reference: 29. Memorial: Plymouth Naval Memorial UK.

GOODE, Henry William: Rank: Gunner. Regiment or Service: Royal Garrison Artillery. Unit: 177th Siege Bty. Age at death: 29. Date of death: 20 May 1917. Service No: 114682. Born in

Enniscorthy, Co. Wexford. Enlisted in Liverpool while living in Wavertree in Liverpool. Killed in action.

Supplementary information: Son of James and Lizzie Goode of Enniscorthy, Co. Wexford. Husband of Sarah Goode of 13 Ashfield, Wavertree, Liverpool. From an article in a *Enniscorthy Guardian*, 1917 (note they give his name as Harry):

The news of the death in action of Gunner Harry Goode, which was received in Enniscorthy on Tuesday, evoked much sorrow. The deceased, who had only reached the age of 27 years, was in the Royal Garrison Artillery, and was son-in-law of Mrs Jones, Slaney Street, and nephew of the late Mr Wm White, estate clerk in the office of Mr P. J. O'Flaherty and Sons, solicitors. Though not a native of Enniscorthy, the late Mr Goode spent many years in it, having been in the employment of Messrs Buttle and Messrs Davis and Co, and some years ago left to take up the position of accountant in the Liverpool butter firm. He visited Enniscorthy every year for his holidays, and maintained the many friendships he had formed there in previous years. The deepest sympathy is felt with Mrs Goode and her child-and only boy – Mrs Jones and family and other relatives in their bereavement. Mrs Goode has received the following letter from the commanding officer of the battery in which her late husband served. "It is my sad duty to inform you that your husband was killed in action on Sunday last, 20ᵗʰ May.

His loss is keenly felt by all, especially by myself, as he had been with me practically the whole time he had been in France. He was one of the best men in the battery, always bright and cheerful. It may interest you to know that he was given a military funeral and now lies in a British cemetery close to where he fell. Kindly accept my sincere sympathy in your great loss.'

Grave or Memorial Reference: I.C.14. Cemetery: Henin Communal Cemetery Extension in France.

GOODWIN, James: Rank: Able Seaman. Regiment or Service: Royal Navy. Unit: HMS *Monmouth*. Age at death: 23. Date of death: 1 November 1914. Service No: J/2496. HMS *Monmouth*. Was lost with all hands at Coronel in the Pacific when they were ambushed by Von Spee's Squadron.

Supplementary information: Son of Michael and Mary Goodwin of Loughgunnen, Ballycogley, Co. Wexford. Grave or Memorial Reference: 1. Memorial: Plymouth Naval Memorial UK.

GOODWIN, Michael: Rank: Private. Regiment or Service: Royal Inniskilling Fusiliers. Unit:. 9ᵗʰ Bn. Date of death: 1 July 1916 (First day of the battle of the Somme). Service No: 13521. Born in Wexford. Enlisted in Dublin. Killed in action. Grave or Memorial Reference: XIII.D.9. Cemetery: Mill Road Cemetery in France.

GORMAN, John: Rank: Private. Regiment or Service: Royal Irish Regiment. Unit: 1ˢᵗ Bn. Age at death: 26. Date of death: 2 May 1915. Service No: 8889. Born in Enniscorthy, Co. Wexford. Enlisted in Enniscorthy. Killed in action.

Supplementary information: Son of

Mary Murphy (formerly Gorman) and John Murphy (step-father) of Clonmore, Glenbrien, Enniscorthy. Grave or Memorial Reference: Panel 33. Memorial: Ypres (Menin Gate) Memorial in Belgium.

GORMAN, Patrick Joseph Francis: Rank: Sergeant. Regiment or Service: Devonshire Regiment. Unit: 8th (Service) Bn. Date of death: 27 September 1915. Service No: 8904 and 8704. Born in Wexford. Enlisted in Devonport. Died of wounds. Age at death: 25.

Supplementary information: Son of James and Susan Gorman of 29 Market Street, Devonport. Grave or Memorial Reference: I.C.20. Cemetery: Noeux-Les-Mines Communal Cemetery in France.

GRANT, Joseph: Rank: Gunner. Regiment or Service: Royal Field Artillery and Royal Horse Artillery. Unit: 117th Battery, 26th Brigade. Date of death: 2 December 1917. Service No: 76521. Born in Wexford. Enlisted in Manchester. Killed in action. Grave or Memorial Reference: X.A.2. Cemetery: Vlamertinghe New Military Cemetery in Belgium.

GREGORY, William Joseph: Rank: Leading Seaman. Regiment or Service: Royal Naval Reserve. Unit: SS *Fern*. Date of death: 22 April 1918. Age at death: 26. Service No: 5718A.

Supplementary information: Son of Thomas and Ellen Gregory, of 6 Coolgreney Road, Arklow, Co. Wicklow. Husband of Margaret Gregory, of Moires Farm, Kulnuney Grieg, Co. Wexford. Steam Ship *Fern* was sunk by a torpedo from German Submarine 5 miles east by north of the Kish lighthouse, there were no survivors. Grave or Memorial Reference: 29 on the Plymouth Naval Memorial, UK.

GROVES, Charles Henry: Rank: Sergeant. Regiment or Service; Middlesex Regiment. Unit: 4th Bn. Date of death: 21 October 1914. Chipping Norton, Oxon. Enlisted in Enniscorthy while living in Wexford. Killed in action. Age at death: 36.

Supplementary information: Husband of Hannah Mary Groves of 'The Cottage', Upper Dargle Road, Bray, Co. Wicklow. He has no known grave but is listed on Panels 31 and 32 on the Le Touret Memorial in France.

H

HADDEN, H.A.: Rank. Captain. From an article in a Wexford newspaper:

The news of the death of Capt, H.A. Hadden, R.A.M.C, which took place at the County Infirmary, Wexford, on Thursday, will occasion deep sorrow amongst his many friends in town and country. A native of Wexford, he was a member of a family which has been long and prominently identified with public and professional life. He was the son of the late John Hadden Hadden [*sic*], who filled the mayoral chair of his native town with dignity and credit to the community.

In sporting and social circles there was no more popular figure than the late Doctor 'Jer', as he was more familiarly known, and his amiable disposition and genial manner won him friend wherever he went. In his earlier days Captain Hadden was a doctor in the Mercantile Marine, and for some years filled the position of Commodore Surgeon to the Allan Line. He was a popular official on various local boards, being compounder of medicines to the different dispensaries in Wexford town and anaesthetist to the County Infirmary for a long period. In December, 1915, he, in response to the appeal for doctors for service at the front, volunteered and was gazetted to the Royal Army Medical Corps. For some time he was medical officer to the military in Dublin, and subsequently went to France, being given the rank of Captain, and was attached to an Indian Cavalry Division.

The rigours of active service undermined his constitution, and in the fierce fighting at the Somme, when heavy demands were made on his services, he contracted pleurisy. After a brief leave, though still suffering from the effects of the malary [*sic*], he undertook medical duties at Salisbury Plain, and complications setting in soon after, he was obliged to retire from the service. The military authorities showed their appreciation of his sterling worth and devotion to duty by conferring on him the title of captain which he carried with him into civilian life. His retirement, however, came too late, for after a brief interval his health completely broke down and he succumbed at the County Infirmary as stated. By his death Wexford is all the poorer, for a genial and kindly gentleman has passed way.

H.A. Hadden.

His demise at the age of 49 is deeply regretted, and much sympathy is felt with his relatives. The funeral will take place on Saturday, when a Memorial Service will be held in the Methodist Church (Rowe Street) at 2.30pm, after which internment will take place in Crosstown Cemetery.

He is not listed in any of the war dead databases.

HALL, James Joseph: Rank: Corporal. Regiment or Service: Royal Irish Regiment. Unit: 2nd Bn. Age at death: 19. Date of death: 24 May 1915. Service No: 10735. Born in Rowe Street, Wexford, Co. Wexford. Enlisted in Kilkenny while living in Wexford. Killed in action.

Supplementary information: Son of Philip and Mary Ellen Hall of 4 Carrigan Street, Wexford. Grave or Memorial Reference: Panel 33. Memorial: Ypres (Menin Gate) Memorial in Belgium.

HALLORAN, Thomas: Rank: Private. Regiment or Service: Connaught Rangers. Unit: 6th Bn. Date of death: 13 August 1918. Service No: 10615. Born in New Ross, Co. Wexford. Enlisted in New Ross while living in New Ross. Died of wounds at home. Age at death: 22.

Supplementary information: Son of Mrs Luke Halloran of 1 Chapel Lane, New Ross. From an article in the *Enniscorthy Guardian*:

WOUNDED NEW ROSS SOLDIER.

Private Thomas Halloran of the Connaught Rangers, has come home on sick furlough to Rosbercon. He went through the battles of Mons and then the Aisne, and in the latter fight received a bullet wound in the chest. The bullet went right through his body, just grazing his lung.

He is now convalescent.

From an article in the *People*, 1915:

New Ross man not dead but wounded. It was reported last week that Private Thomas Halloran, Chapel Lane, New Ross, had died of wounds received at the front. His people received a letter from a soldier at the front who knew him to that effect, but since they have received official notice that he is not dead and is progressing satisfactorily in hospital in England. He received sever wounds in a recent battle. This is the second time he has been wounded since the commencement of the war.

From an article in the *Enniscorthy Guardian*, November, 1915:

FAMILY OF THREE SONS

From one home in New Ross there are three of its members in the fighting line. They are the brothers Jeremiah, Thomas and Patrick Halloran, who is a postman, volunteered at the outbreak of the war, and is attached to the Royal Artillery. In the desperate fighting in Flanders he got wounded, and came home on a visit, and soon after going back received two more wounds in the legs, and on his second visit to Ross brought home a piece of shrapnel which had been extracted from his leg. He is presently in the firing line. The other brother, Thomas, who had been in the army about 1½ years before the outbreak of the war, went through several battles for nine months when he got wounded twice. He was

10615 PRIVATE
T. HALLORAN
CONNAUGHT RANGERS
13TH AUGUST 1918 AGE 22

Thomas Halloran.

at home about five weeks ago, and is gone back to the front again. He is not fully 20 years of age, and is attached to the Connaught Rangers. The third brother, Patrick, volunteered six months ago and joined the Connaught Rangers. He is presently at Kinsale. In their letters home they express the confident hope that they will see Ross safe and sound when the war is over.

Grave or Memorial Reference: South East of the Church. Cemetery: New Ross (St Stephen) Catholic Churchyard, Wexford.

HANDRICK, James: Rank: Private. Regiment or Service: Cheshire Regiment. Unit: 11th Bn. Age at death: 32. Date of death: 3 July 1916. Service No: XI/16355 and 16355. Born in Wexford. Enlisted in Birkinhead. Killed in action.
Supplementary information: Son of John and Elizabeth Handrick of Maudlins, New Ross, Co. Wexford. Grave or Memorial Reference: VI.2.6. Cemetery: Lonsdale Cemetery, Authuile in France.

HANLON, Henry: Rank: Acting Company Sergeant Major. Regiment or Service: Royal Dublin Fusiliers. Unit: 5th Bn. Date of death: 28 January 1916. Service No: 13570. Born in Glynn, Co. Wexford. Enlisted in Wexford. Died at home. Age at death: 48. Grave or Memorial Reference: H. III. Cemetery: Wexford (St Ibars) Cemetery in Wexford.

HANTON, Patrick: Rank: Stoker. Regiment or Service: Royal Naval Reserve. Unit: Anson Bn. R.N.Div. Age at death: 23. Date of death: 2 January 1916. Service No: 2440/S.
Supplementary information: Son of Thomas and Elizabeth Hanton of 9 Emmet Place, Wexford. He had three other brothers in the services, Corporal Peter Hanton who was wounded early in the war but recovered, Seaman Robert Hanton, Seaman Robert Hanton who served aboard the HMS *Prince Edward* and Private Thomas Hanton. From an article in the *People*, 'Seaman Patrick Hanton, died at the Malta Hospital from a wound in the head caused by a compound fracture of the skull received at the Dardanelles. Pictures of his three brothers in the newspaper article are not included here.' Grave or Memorial Reference: R.C.111. Cemetery: Malta (Capuccini) Naval Cemetery Malta.

HARDING, Alfred: Rank: Private. Regiment or Service: Royal Dublin Fusiliers. Unit: 10th Bn. Age at death: 20. Date of death: 21 July 1917. Service No: 26184. Born in New Ross, Co. Wexford. Enlisted in Wexford while living in New Ross. Died.
Supplementary information: Son of Frederick W. and Elizabeth Harding of Neville Street, New Ross, Co. Wexford. Grave or Memorial Reference: Screen Wall. B10.6.474C. Cemetery: Birmingham (Lodge Hill) Cemetery UK.

HARPER/HARPUR, Nicholas: Rank: Private. Regiment or Service: Royal Dublin Fusiliers. Unit: 1st Bn. Age at death: 21. Date of death: 4 June 1915. Service No: 18181. Born in Wexford. Enlisted in Haverfordwest while living in Wexford. Killed in action in Gallipoli.
Supplementary information: Son of

Henry Hanlon.

Thomas Harpur of Corn Market, Wexford. From an article in the *People*, 1915:

Four months ago Mr Nicholas Harpur, Cornmarket, Wexford, enlisted in the Royal Dublin Fusiliers, and the first intimation received by his parents as to his whereabouts was that contained in a notice from the war office on Thursday morning announcing that he had been killed in action with the Mediterranean Expeditionary Force at the Dardanelles on June 4th.

This young Wexfordman, who is a son of Mr Thomas Harpur, was popular amongst his companions in the town, and the news of his death in such a short time after his enlistment has caused much regret. He was formerly an employee at the Mill Road Iron Works, and was about 21 years of age. The greatest sympathy is felt with his parents.

Nicholas Harper.

Grave or Memorial Reference: Panel 190 to 196. Memorial: Helles Memorial in Turkey.

HARRIS, John: Rank: Private. Regiment or Service: Royal Dublin Fusiliers. Unit: 1st Bn. Date of death: 1 July 1916 (first day of the battle of the Somme). Service No: 22211. Born in Enniscorthy, Co. Wexford. Enlisted in Limerick. Killed in action. Grave or Memorial Reference: II.B.2. Cemetery: Auchonvillers Military Cemetery in France.

HARTE, Martin: Rank: Private. Regiment or Service: Royal Irish Regiment. Unit: 2nd Bn. Date of death: 7 January 1915. Service No: 3994. Born in Bride Street, Wexford. Enlisted in Wexford while living in South Main Street, Wexford. Died of pneumonia while a prisoner of war. From an article in the *Enniscorthy Guardian*, 'News reached Wexford on Tuesday morning announcing the death of Private Martin Harte, South Main Street, son of the late Mr John Harte, H. M. Customs, Wexford.' Deceased, who belonged to the Royal Irish Regiment, was interned as a prisoner of war in Germany for some months past. His death is due to pneumonia.' The *Echo* adds that his Aunt is Nurse Murphy from South Main Street.

Supplementary information: Grave or Memorial Reference: III.J.5. Cemetery: Niederzwehren Cemetery in Germany.

HATCHELL, Nicholas: Rank: Private. Regiment or Service: Leinster Regiment. Unit: 2nd Bn. Formerly he was with the Royal Irish Regiment where his number was 5490. Date of death: 12 April 1917. Service No: 15022. Born in Wexford. Enlisted in Wexford. Killed in action. Age at death: 22.

Supplementary information: Son of Martin Hatchell and Kate Hatchell. Husband of Margaret Atkinson (formerly Hatchell) of 3 Fleming's Court, Castle Lane, Lurgan, Co. Armagh. From an article in the *People*, 1917:

> It is officially announced that Private Nicholas Hatchell, of the Leinster Regiment, has been killed in action. Private Hatchell, who belongs to Dodd's Lane, Wexford, where his widow resides, was on active service practically since the outbreak of the war. He took part in some of the recent big engagements, and received the fatal blow on 12th of April. The sympathy and regret of his friends are extended to his widow and family.

Grave or Memorial Reference: Bay 9. Memorial: Arras Memorial in France.

HAWKINS, George: Rank: Leading Signalman. Regiment or Service: Royal Canadian Navy. Unit: HMCS *Rainbow*. Age at death: 24. Date of death: 22 September 1914. Service No: O/118.

Supplementary information: Son of the late William and Francis Hawkins of Killegney, Clonroche, Enniscorthy, Co. Wexford. Grave or Memorial Reference: 136. Cemetery: Esquimalt (Veternas) Cemetery in Canada.

HAWNICK, Augustus: (Soldiers died in the Great War) **HORNICK, John Augustus** (Commonwealth War Graves Commission). Rank: Private.

Regiment or Service: Labour Corps. Date of death: 18 December 1917. Service No: 4299117. Born in Wexford. Enlisted in Glasgow. Died at home.

Supplementary information: Youngest son of William Thomas Hornick of Wexford. Grave or Memorial Reference: Screen Wall. BB. 4. 631E. Cemetery: Dundee (Balgay) Cemetery in UK.

HAYDEN, James: Rank: Private. Regiment or Service: Royal Irish Regiment. Unit: 2nd Bn. Date of death: 9 October 1914. Service No: 6637. Born in Camolin, Co. Wexford. Enlisted in Newtownbarry, Co. Wexford while living in Ferns, Co. Wexford. Killed in action. In a short item in the *Enniscorthy Guardian* his address is given as Clohamon. He has no known grave but is listed on Panels 11 and 12 on the Le Touret Memorial in France.

HAYDON, Patrick: Rank: Private. Regiment or Service: Royal Dublin Fusiliers. Unit: 2nd Bn. Date of death: 9 May 1915. Service No: 8501. Born in Carlow. Enlisted in Carlow while living in Gorey, Co. Wexford. Killed in action. Grave or Memorial Reference: III.H.24. Cemetery: Ypres Town Cemetery Extension in Belgium.

HAYES, Robert: Rank: Private. Regiment or Service: Grenadier Guards. Unit: 2nd Bn. Age at death: 26. Date of death: 15 December 1915. Service No: 19483. Born in Kilmannin, Co. Wexford. Enlisted in Malstig. Died.

Supplementary information: Grandson of Mrs Ann Hayes of Kilmannore, Cleariestown, Co. Wexford. Grave or

Memorial Reference: II.A.8. Cemetery: La Gorgue Communal Cemetery in France.

HEALEY, Maurice Kevin: Rank: Corporal. Regiment or Service: Machine Gun Corps (Infantry). Unit: 177th Coy. Formerly he was with the D.C.L.I. where his number was 18687. Age at death: 28. Date of death: 28 September 1917. Service No: 83381. Enlisted in Tipperary. Died of wounds.

Supplementary information: Son of Tom and Kathleen Healey of Wexford. Husband of Marjorie E. Healey of Peter Street, Nenagh, Co. Tipperary. From De Ruvigny's Roll of Honour:

HEALY, MAURICE KEVIN, Corpl., No. 83381, Machine Gun Corps, 3rd s. of Thomas Joseph Healy, Solicitor, of Callan, by his wife, Kathleen E., dau. Of Mathew Forrest Shine; b. Wexford, 7 March, 1889; educ. Wexford College, was a Bank Clerk; joined the Duke of Cornwall's Light Infantry in March, 1915; served with the Expeditionary Force in France and Flanders from Jan. 1916; was wounded at Delville Wood in July and taken prisoner, but managed to escape; transferred to the Machine Gun Corps about Sept. 1916, and died in the No. 12 Casualty Clearing Station 28 Sept. 1917. From wounds received in action on the 27th. Buried in the Military Cemetary at Mendinghem. He m. in Dublin, 26 Nov. 1914, Marjorie Elixabeth (Peter Street, Nenagh), dau. Of the late Charles Albert Sprent, and had a dau., Joan, b. 9 Sept 1915.

Grave or Memorial Reference: VI.F.18. Cemetery: Mendinghem Military Cemetery in Belgium.

HEALY/HEALEY, Joseph: Rank: Irish Guards. Unit: 2nd Bn. Date of death: 21 April 1916. Service No: 4742. Born in Wexford. Enlisted in Wexford. Died of wounds. From an article in the *Enniscorthy Guardian*, 'Private Joseph Healy, Bail Street, Wexford, Irish Guards, who was wounded in France, and subsequently died at Boulogne on April 21st 1916. He was the son of the late Mr Michel Healy. Before the Army Private Healy was engaged at Kelly's Hotel, Rosslare.' Grave or Memorial Reference: VIII.A.98. Cemetery: Boulogne Eastern Cemetery in France.

HEALY, Thomas: Rank: Private. Regiment or Service: Royal Irish Regiment. Unit: 2nd Bn. Age at death: 26. Date of death: 26 May 1915. Service No: 5674. Born in Gorey, Co. Wexford. Enlisted in Clonmel, Co Tipperary while living in Gorey, Co. Wexford. Killed in action of gas poisoning.

Supplementary information: Son of James and Mary Healy of Knockinagh, Gorey, Co. Wexford. Grave or Memorial Reference: I.C.25. Cemetery: Le Touquet-Paris Plage Communal Cemetery in France.

HEALY, Timothy: Rank: Private. Regiment or Service: Royal Irish Regiment. Unit: 2nd Bn. Date of death: 25 May 1915 Age at death: 26. Service No: 5674. Born in Gorey. Enlisted in Clonmel, Co. Tipperary. Killed in action.

Supplementary information: Son of James and Mary Healy of Knockinagh, Gorey, Co. Wexford. From an article in the *Echo*:

Official information reached Gorey during the week of the death of

Timothy Healy at the front from the effects German poisonous gasses.

Tim who had been employed by Mr P.J. Dolan for upwards of 14 years, was well known in Gorey, and was a popular favourite with all classes.

Grave or Memorial Reference: I.C.25. Cemetery: Le Touquet-Paris Plage Communal Cemetery in France.

HENDRICK, Peter: Rank: Private. Regiment or Service: Royal Irish Regiment. Unit: 1st Bn. Date of death: 6 May 1915. Service No: 9164. Born in Ferns, Co. Wexford. Enlisted in Gorey while living in Camolin, Co. Wexford. Killed in action. He has no known grave but is listed on Panel 44 on the Ypres (Menin Gate) Memorial in Belgium.

HENNEBERRY, James: Rank: Private. Regiment or Service: Royal Irish Regiment. Unit: 2nd Bn. Age at death: 47. Date of death: 22 March 1918. Service No: 6842. Born in St Mary's, New Ross, Co. Wexford. Enlisted in Enniscorthy, Co. Wexford while living in New Ross. Died of wounds.

Supplementary information: Son of James and Elizabeth Henneberry. Husband of Bridget Henneberry of Church Lane, New Ross. From an article in the *People*, 1915:

Private James Henneberry, Charlton Hill, New Ross, who is home on a short visit from the trenches last week, has had remarkable escapes.

He was on the reserve, and has been out in the fighting line since the beginning of the war practically, and

escaped all through with the exception of a slight wound from a piece of shell which necessitated his being away from the trenches but a few days.

Grave or Memorial Reference: Marchelepot Brit. Cem. Mem. 81. Cemetery: Roye New British Cemetery In France.

HENNESSY, Edward: Rank: Winchman. Regiment or Service: Mercantile Marine. Unit: SS *Formby* (Glasgow). The ship was lost with all hands and never located during a fierce storm. Supposed to have been torpedoed by German Submarine U-62. Very little wreckage ever from the Formby but the body of a Stewardess (Annie O'Callaghan) was washed up on the Welsh shore. Age at death: 32. Date of death: 16 December 1917.

Supplementary information: Son of the late James and Mary Hennessy. Husband of Mary Hennessy (*née* Culleton) of 3 Bank Lane, Waterford. Born at New Ross. Memorial: Tower Hill Memorial UK.

HICKEY, John: Rank: Gunner. Regiment or Service: Royal Field Artillery. Unit: 122nd Bty. Age at death: 19. Date of death: 26 August 1914. Service No: 72955. Born in New Ross, Co. Wexford. Enlisted in Waterford. Killed in action.

Supplementary information: Son of John and Anastasia Hickey of 1 Cross Lane, New Ross. From an article in the *Enniscorthy Guardian*, 1914:

The sad news reached Mrs Hickey, Cross-Lane, New Ross, on Tuesday morning that her only son, John aged

John Hickey.

122nd Battery of the RFA. He was at home on furlough about six months ago. The sympathy of all classes in the town goes to Mrs Hickey in her terrible affliction.

Memorial: La-Ferte-Sous-Jouarre Memorial in France.

HIGGINS, Michael: Rank: Private. Regiment or Service: Royal Dublin Fusiliers. Unit: 6th Bn. Age at death: 38. Date of death: 9 December 1915. Service No: 22239. Born in Wexford. Enlisted in New Ross. Killed in action in the Balkans.

Supplementary information: Husband of Bridget Higgins of Chapel Lane, New Ross, Co. Wexford. Memorial: Doiran Memorial in Greece.

nineteen and a Private in the Royal Field Artillery, was killed in action at Mons. The letter came direct from the War Office, and enclosed was a note from Lord Kitchener conveying the deepest sympathy of his Majesty to the bereaved Mother. Needless to say the news came as a terrible shock to Mrs Hickey, and indeed has caused a painful sensation throughout the town. The deceased boy was her only son, and a circumstance which adds to the painfulness of the tragedy is that her husband, who was also a soldier, and served in the Boer War, died only a short time ago. John Hickey, was a very popular young man, and his death in the flower of his youth, is deplored by numerous friends.

He was a fine handsome lad, of a genial disposition and high character. He enlisted in the Artillery about 18 months ago, and was attached to the

HOGAN, Patrick: Rank: Private. Regiment or Service: Irish Guards. Unit: 1st Bn. Age at death: 19. Date of death: 10 October 1917. Service No: 10589. Born in Taghmon, Co. Wexford. Enlisted in Wexford. Died of wounds.

Supplementary information: Son of Mr and Mrs Henry Hogan of Back Street, Taghmon, Co. Wexford. Grave or Memorial Reference: VII.C.40. Cemetery: Mendinghem Military Cemetery in Belgium.

HOLBROOK, Patrick: Rank: Private. Regiment or Service: Household Cavalry and Cavalry of the line including the Yeomanry and Imperial Camel Corps. Unit: 12th (Prince of Wales) Lancers. Date of death: 20 May 1917. Service No: 1042. Born in Wexford, Co. Wexford. Enlisted in Dublin while living in Wexford. Killed in action. From an article in a Wexford newspaper:

The news of the death of Private Patrick Holdbrook, youngest son of Mrs Holdbrook, South Main Street, Wexford, and brother of Very Rev Henry Holbrook, Chancellor of the Diocese of Aukland, New Zealand, will be learned with extreme regret by the many friends of his family in Wexford. Private Holdbrook, who was serving with the Lancers for the past ten years, had been on active service since the outbreak of war. Last October he was seriously wounded, and during his convalescence, returned to his native town. Shortly after he went back to the firing line, and during an engagement on May 30th, was killed.

Patrick Holbrook.

The first intimation of his death conveyed in a letter from his comrade Lance Corporal Phillips, of Bridgetown, and the sad news was later confirmed by the War Office. Much sympathy is felt with his relatives in their bereavement.

Grave or Memorial Reference: E.80. Cemetery: Villers-Faucon Communal Cemetery in France.

HOLDEN, J.: Rank: Private. Regiment or Service: Royal Irish Regiment. Unit: Depot. Age at death: 21. Date of death: 14 February 1915. Service No: 10003.
Supplementary information: Son of James Holden, of Barrack Street, New Ross. From another article in the *People*, 1915:

Private John Holden, New Ross, arrived home on Tuesday invalided, and in the charge of a soldier of the Red Cross. He was in the army reserve and went to the front with his regiment at the outbreak of the war. During the fierce fighting in Flanders he was taken prisoner and had been held in the German camp for nearly a year, when he was recently let home following an exchange of prisoners.

From another article in the *People*, January, 1915:

Private James Holden, School House Place, New Ross, was at home on a short visit from the front last week. He volunteered after the outbreak of the war and has been practically at the seat of war since and escaped unhurt through such engagement. He had

J. Holden.

been with the colours before and his time had expired before the outbreak of war when he volunteered.

He was a famous rugby player. This man is not in Soldiers died in the Great war nor is he listed in Ireland's Memorial records. [I was not sure if the man above is one and the same however I include the articles for your reference. – Author].

Grave or Memorial Reference: About centre of the west part. Cemetery, New Ross (St Stephen) Catholic Churchyard.

HOLDEN, Patrick: Rank: Private. Regiment or Service: Royal Irish Regiment. Unit: 7th (South Irish Horse) Bn. Age at death: 19. Date of death: 21 March 1918. Service No: 5314. Born in St Mary's, New Ross, Co. Wexford. Enlisted in Wexford. Killed in action.

Supplementary information: Son of Patrick and Bridget Holden of Military Barracks, Michael Street, New Ross. Grave or Memorial Reference: Panel 30 and 31. Memorial: Pozieres Memorial in France.

HOLLIGAN, John: Rank: Private. Regiment or Service: South Lancashire Regiment. Unit: 2nd Bn. Date of death: 13 March 1915. Service No: 10613. Born in Wexford, Co. Wexford. Enlisted in Warrington in Lancs while living in Widnes in Lancs. Died of wounds. Grave or Memorial Reference: H.55. Cemetery: Kemmel Chateau Military Cemetery in Belgium.

HOWIE, James: Rank: Private. Regiment or Service: Labour Corps.

Unit: Training Reserve, 77th Bn. Formerly he was with the Royal Scots Fusiliers where his number was 29423. Date of death: 16 September 1917. Service No: 123330 and TR/2/20792. Born in Monkland, Ayr. Enlisted in Glasgow while living in Dennistown, Co. Wexford. Died of wounds. Age at death: 41.

Supplementary information: Son of John and Mary Lambie Howie of Gaswork Row, Mauchline, Ayrshire. Grave or Memorial Reference: I.A.3. Cemetery: Nine Elms Military Cemetery, Thelus in France.

HOWLIN, James: Rank: Private. Regiment or Service: Royal Irish Regiment. Unit: 6th Bn. Age at death: 39. Date of death: 25 December 1915. Service No: 3/7509 and 7509. Born in St Mullin's, Co Carlow. Enlisted in Enniscorthy, Co. Wexford. Died at Sea.

Supplementary information: Son of Patrick and Stasia Howlin of Goolin, Co. Carlow. Husband of Bridget Howlin of Grange, Rathnure, Enniscorthy. Grave or Memorial Reference: C.106. Cemetery: Alexandria (Chatby) Military and War Memorial Cemetery in Egypt.

HUGHES, Peter: Rank: Private. Regiment or Service: Irish Guards. Unit: 1st Bn. Date of death: 8 May 1918. Service No: 11590. Born in Camolin, Co. Wexford. Enlisted in Dublin. Killed in action. Grave or Memorial Reference: B.10. Cemetery: Ayette British Cemetery in France.

HUMPHREYS, John Henry: Rank: Private. Regiment or Service: Royal Irish

John Henry Humphreys.

Regiment. Unit: 2ⁿᵈ Bn. Date of death: 19 October 1914. Service No: 10643. Born in Kilnamanagh, Co. Wexford. Enlisted in Enniscorthy while living in Gorey, Co. Wexford. Killed in action. He has no known grave but is commemorated on Panel 11 and 12. Memorial: Le Touret Memorial in France.

HUMPHREYS, Thomas Tector: Rank: Private. Regiment or Service: Irish Guards. Unit: 1ˢᵗ Bn. Age at death: 21. Date of death: 8 December 1914. Service No: 3311. Born in Kilnamanagh, Co. Wexford. Enlisted in Enniscorthy, Co. Wexford. Died of wounds in a French Hospital. Occupation on enlistment: farmer.

Supplementary information: Son of Richard and Amelia Humphreys of Ballinahoun Wells, Gorey, Co. Wexford. Grave or Memorial Reference: A.7. Cemetery: Halluin Communal Cemetery in France.

I

IEVERS(also listed as **JEVERS**), **Edwin:** Rank: Private. Regiment or Service: Northumberland Fusiliers. Unit: 1st/7th Bn. Age at death: 32. Date of death: 26 October 1917. Service No: 205130. Born in Carlow. Enlisted in Sunderland. Killed in action.

Supplementary information: Son of E. and A. Ievers of Ballyanne, New Ross, Co. Wexford. Husband of Gertrude Ievers of 58 Ridley Street, Southwick, Sunderland. Grave or Memorial Reference: Panel 19 to 23 and 162. Memorial: Tyne Cot Memorial in Belgium.

IEVERS, R W. (also listed as **IVERS, Walter Robert**): Rank: Private. Regiment or Service: Durham Light Infantry. Unit: 10th Bn. Age at death: 27. Date of death: 9 April 1917. Service No: 21481. Born in Duckets Grove, Co. Carlow. Enlisted in Newcastle while living in Wexford. Killed in action.

Supplementary information: Born in Co. Carlow. Son of Edwin and Annie Ievers of Ballyanne House, New Ross, Co. Wexford. Grave or Memorial Reference: B.24. Cemetery: Hibers Trench Cemetery, Wancourt in France.

J

JACKMAN, James: Rank: Rifleman. Regiment or Service: Rifle Brigade. Unit: 16th Bn. Date of death: 3 September 1916. Service No: S/14487. Born in Wexford, Co. Wexford. Enlisted in Bargoed, Glam while living in Clohamon, Co. Wexford. Killed in action. He has no known grave but is listed on Pier and Face 16B and 16C on the Thiepval Memorial in France.

JAMES, Edward: Rank: Quartermaster Sergeant /Instructor. Regiment or Service: Corps of Royal Engineers. Unit: No. 6 Depot Coy. R.E. Training Centre (Deganwy). Date of death: 3 December 1916. Service No: 52202. Born in Gorey, Co. Wexford. Enlisted in Chatham in Kent. Died at home.

Supplementary information: Grave or Memorial Reference: N. 74. Cemetery: Llandudno (Great Orme's Head) Cemetery, UK.

JAMES, John: Rank: Private. Regiment or Service: The King's (Liverpool Regiment). Unit: 4th Bn. Age at death: 36. Date of death: 27 March 1916. Service No: 31307. Born in Wexford, Co. Wexford. Enlisted in Liverpool while living in Wexford. Died of wounds.

Supplementary information: Son of John and Ellen James of Distillery Road, Wexford. Served twelve years in India with Royal Irish Regiment. From an article in a Wexford newspaper:

Intelligence reached Wexford during the week that Private John James, of Distillery Road, Wexford, had died of wounds on March 27th, received in action, while serving with the King's Liverpool Regiment. Private James volunteered for active service shortly after the outbreak of war. Much sympathy is felt with his parents who reside at Distillery Road, Wexford.

Grave or Memorial Reference: Plot 2. Row L. Grave 2B. Cemetery: Le Treport Military Cemetery in France.

JAMES, Thomas: Rank: Lance Corporal. Regiment or Service: Royal Dublin Fusiliers. Unit: 8th Bn. Date of death: 9 September 1916. Service No: 24535. Born in Enniscorthy, Co. Wexford. Enlisted in Dublin while living in Ballycumber, King's County. Killed in action. From an article in a Wexford newspaper, 'Killed in action; Much sympathy is felt with Mr and Mrs J. James, Ballinapierce, Enniscorthy, in the loss they have sustained by the death of their third eldest son, Lance Corporal Thomas James who was killed in action on the 9th September last.' He has no known grave but is listed on Pier and Face 16C on the Thiepval Memorial in France.

JEFFARES, Reginald Isaac: Rank: Private. Regiment or Service: Royal Dublin Fusiliers. Unit: 9th Bn. Date of death: 16 August 1917. Service No: 26218. Formerly he was with the Leinster Regiment where his number was 1976. Born in Rosbercon,

New Ross, Co. Wexford. Enlisted in Waterford while living in Dalkey, Co. Dublin. Killed in action.

Supplementary information: Son of the late Sheppard French Jeffares. Husband of Margaret S. Jeffares of 2 Mont Alto, Dalkey, Co. Dublin. From De Ruvigny's Roll of Honour:

JEFFARES, REGINALD ISAAC, Private, No. 26218, 9th (Service) Battn. The Royal Dublin Fusiliers, eldest s. of the late Sheppard French Jeffares, Gentleman Farmer and Landowner, by his wife, Kate Elizabeth (Tinneranny, New Ross, co. Wexford) dau. Of William Clapham: b. The Rower, co. Kilkenny, 8 May, 1893; educ. John Ivory School, New Ross; was a Farmer and Landowner; joined the Cadet Corps of the 7th Battn. The Leinster Regt. In Dec. 1914, but, owing to a series accident, was unable to go to the front with the 16 Division; transferred to the Dublin Fusiliers in Feb. 1916; took part in the Dublin Rebellion in April, served with the Expeditionary Force in France and Flanders from the following Aug.; came home in the spring of 1916, but returned to France early in June, and was killed in action at Ypres 16 Aug. following. One of his officers wrote: "He was popular with all ranks, and one on whom they could always rely on assistance, and it will be a long while before he is forgotten by the battalion." He m. at Monkstown, 9 May, 1916, Margaret Susan (2, Mont Alto, Dalkey, co. Dublin), dau. Of the late William Crawley, of Bloomfield Park, Lorrha, co. Tipperary.

Grave or Memorial Reference: VI.S.22. Cemetery; Railway Dugouts Burial Ground in Belgium.

JOLLY, Andrew Gordon: Rank: Lance Corporal. Regiment or Service: Royal Sussex Regiment. Unit: 4th Bn. Date of death: 29 July 1918. Service No: G/4702 and G/4782. Born in Duncannon Fort, Co. Wexford. Enlisted in London. Killed in action. Age at death: 30.

Supplementary information: Son of Julia Jolly of 'St Leonard's' 31 Beach Road, Southsea and the late Andrew Jolly. Grave or Memorial Reference: He has no known grave but is listed on the Soissons memorial in France.

JONES, Charles: Rank: Private. Regiment or Service: Royal Dublin Fusiliers. Unit: 1st Bn. Age at death: 32. Date of death: 7 June 1915. Service No: 7233. Born in Enniscorthy, Co. Wexford. Enlisted in Athlone while living in Enniscorthy. Died of wounds in Gallipoli. From an article in the *Enniscorthy Guardian*:

Mrs Jones, Slaney Street, Enniscorthy, received intelligence of the death of her son, Private Charles Jones of the Dublin Fusiliers. He was wounded at the Dardanelles about a month ago, and died in hospital on June 5th. Much sympathy is felt with Mrs Jones and the Misses Jones in their bereavement.

Supplementary information: Son of Mrs J. Jones of Slaney Street, Enniscorthy, Co. Wexford. Grave or Memorial Reference: Prot. 246. Cemetery: Malta (Capuccini) Naval Cemetery in Malta.

JORDAN, Patrick: Rank: Private. Regiment or Service: Royal Irish Regiment. Unit: 1st Bn. Age at death: 20. Date of death: 20 January 1915. Service

No: 10426. Born in Enniscorthy, Co. Wexford. Enlisted in Enniscorthy. In the *Enniscorthy Guardian* he is listed as **James JORDAN**.Killed in action. From an article in the *Echo* newpaper:

DIED IN HIS ARMS

Private Thomas Smith of Enniscorthy who is home suffering frostbite in the foot belongs to the R. I. Regiment. He was in some two of three engagements since going to the front. He was within 30 yards of Private P Jordan, of the same Regiment, another Enniscorthy man, when the latter was shot dead in the trenches a few weeks past.

Supplementary information: Son of James and Ellen Jordan of Ross Road, Enniscorthy, Co. Wexford. Grave or Memorial Reference: Panel 33. Memorial: Ypres (Menin Gate) Memorial in Belgium.

JOYCE, John Ulick: Rank: Corporal. Regiment or Service: Royal Marine Light Infantry. Unit: HMS *Bulwark*. Date of death: 26 December 1914. Service No: PO/13059.

Supplementary information: Son of John Evans Joyce and Margaret Aphra Joyce of of Tagmon. Husband of Josephine Joyce of Aughfal House, Tagmon, Co. Wexford. From an article in the *Enniscorthy Guardian*, November 1914:

British Battleship blown up. Terrible loss of life, London, Thursday.

It was announced in the House of Commons this afternoon that the battleship 'Bulwark' was blown up in Sheerness Harbour this morning. Only twelve lives were saved. The 'Bulwark' was a battleship of fifteen thousand tons. She was completed in 1902 and re-commissioned at Chatham in June, 1912. She had a compliment of seven hundred and fifty men, and carried four twelve inch guns. The 'Bulwark' cost £997,846. It is believed that the cause of the disaster was an internal magazine explosion, which rent the ship asunder. There was no upheaval of water, and when the smoke cleared, the ship had entirely disappeared. An inquiry into the affair will be held tomorrow.

Grave or Memorial Reference: 6. Memorial: Portsmouth Naval Memorial UK.

K

KANE, Denis Joseph: Rank: Private. Regiment or Service: Tank Corps. Unit: 11th Bn. Age at death: 31. Date of death: 2 September 1918. Service No: 302818 also down as 302813. Born in Fairview in Dublin. Enlisted in Dublin. Killed in action. Formerly he was with the King Edward's Horse where his number was 1457.

Supplementary information: Son of Timothy and Dora Kane of Gorey, Co. Wexford. Husband of Mary T. Kane of 6 Spring Garden Passage, Ballybough Road, Dublin. Grave or Memorial Reference: III.C.26. Cemetery: Dury Crucifix Cemetery in France.

KANE, John Francis Aloysius: Rank: Captain. Regiment or Service: Royal Flying Corps. Unit: Secondary Unit. Devonshire Regiment. Date of death: 22 March 1915. From an article in the *Echo*:

Capt. John Kane, of the Royal Flying Corps, was killed while flying at Brooklands, London, on Monday. He was the third son of the late Mr. John Kane, formerly of Saunderscourt, Wexford, and a nephew of the Rev Robert Kane, S J the famous preacher. In 1899 he joined the Devonshire Regiment, and was appointed captain in 1907.

In the South African War he was engaged in the defence of Ladysmith, and he was in action at Lombard's Kop, Belfast, and Lydenburg. He received both medals, with six clasps. During the present war he has been serving in the Flying Corps in France and Flanders, and was recently appointed to the command of a squadron of twelve machines.

Grave or Memorial Reference: 3. 2927. Cemetery: Kensal Green (St Mary's) Roman Catholic Cemetery, UK.

KANE, Patrick: Rank: Private. Regiment or Service: Royal Berkshire Regiment. Unit: 1st Bn. Formerly he was with the Northumberland Fusiliers where his number was 75716. Age at death: 24. Date of death: 8 October 1918. Service No: 50765. Enlisted in Clonmel, Co. Tipperary while living in Gorey, Co. Wexford. Killed in action. This man is also listed a **KEANE, Patrick.**

Supplementary information: Son of Patrick and Kattern Kane of Church Street, Gorey, Co. Wexford. Grave or Memorial Reference: I.E.4. Cemetery: Rumilly-En-Cambresis Communal Cemetery Extension in France.

KANE, Patrick: Rank: Private. Regiment or Service: Labour Corps. Unit: 746th Area Deployment Company. Date of death: 12 October 1918. Service No: 377340. Formerly he was with the Royal Irish Rifles where his number was 5942 and 3/5942. Born in Tagoat, Co. Wexford. Enlisted in Wexford. Died. Grave or Memorial Reference: V.E.31. Cemetery: Longuenesse (St Omer) Souvenir Cemetery in France.

KANE, Robert Henry: Rank: Sergeant. Regiment or Service: Royal

Fusiliers. Unit: 'D' Coy. 19th Bn. Age at death: 33. Date of death: 2 January 1916. Service No: PS/560. Born in Wexford, Co. Wexford. Enlisted in Westminister while living in London E.C. Killed in action.

Supplementary information: Son of John Francis Kane and Mary Kane of Wexford. From an article in the *Enniscorthy Guardian,* 'Sergeant R.H. Kane, 19th Battalion, Royal Fusiliers, youngest son of the late J.F. Kane, formerly of Saunderscourt, Wexford, was killed in action on 2nd January, according to information received by his relatives.' Grave or Memorial Reference: E. 27. Cemetery: Cambrin Military Cemetery in France.

Patrick Kavanagh.

KAVANAGH, Kevin: Rank: Private. Regiment or Service: Leinster Regiment. Unit: 1st Bn. Date of death: 30 December 1917. Service No: 2813. Born in Wexford, Co. Wexford. Enlisted in Newtownbarry. Died at Sea. He has no known grave but is listed on the Chatby Memorial in Egypt.

KAVANAGH, Martin: Rank: Private. Regiment or Service: Royal Inniskilling Fusiliers. Unit: 7th Bn. Age at death: 17. Date of death: 27 April 1916. Service No: 27704. Born in Glynn, Co. Wexford. Enlisted in Enniscorthy while living in Macmine. Died of wounds. Formerly he was with the Royal Irish Regiment where his number was 11272.

Supplementary information: Son of Martin and Johanna Kavanagh. Native of Co. Wexford. Grave or Memorial Reference: I.D.6. Cemetery: Philosophe British Cemetery, Mazingarbe in France.

KAVANAGH, Patrick: Rank: Private. Regiment or Service: Irish Guards. Unit: 1st Bn. Date of death: 6 November 1914 Age at death, 24. Service No: 3509. Born in Kilanerin, Co. Wexford. Enlisted in Dublin while living in Tomcoyle, Co. Wexford. Killed in action.

Supplementary information: Son of John and Briget Kavanagh of Tomcoyle, Kilanerin, Gorey, Co. Wexford. From an article in the *Enniscorthy Guardian* and the *People*:

Patrick Kavanagh, 2st Battalion, Irish Guards, killed in action at Ypres on 6th November 1914, was the fourth son of John and Brigid Kavanagh, Seaview, Tomcoyle, Kilanerin, and was aged 22 years. Some years ago he held an important position in Dublin, and subsequently joined the Irish Guards, in which he spent three years.

Returning to his native place, he took a very active part in the volunteer question, and he was instrumental in starting a branch of the movement in Kilanerin and Pallas, and he certainly, while he was in charge of them, brought them to a good state of efficiency. At the outbreak of the war, he being in the reserve, he was called to his old Regiment, and was sent straight to the front after a few months training. He had been through several engagements, and came clear of all, but came by his death from shell fire at the battle of Ypres on the above date.

His parents, who thought that he was either in hospital or a prisoner of war in Germany, not hearing from him, were much startled on getting the sad news on Saturday morning, the 10th inst, from the proper authorities, that he had been killed in action as far back as the 6th of November last.

He has no known grave but is listed on Panel 11 on the Ypres (Menin Gate) Memorial in Belgium.

KAVANAGH, Patrick: Rank: Seaman. Regiment or Service: Royal Naval Reserve. Unit: HMS *Goliath*. Age at death: 23. Date of death: 13 May 1915. Service No: 5729A.

Supplementary information: Son of Patrick and Mary Kavanagh of Kildermott, Ballymoney, Gorey, Co. Wexford. HMS *Goliath* was sunk by three torpedoes from German destroyer *Muvanet-I-Milet*, she blew up and capsized immediately taking 570 of her 750 crew including the Captain to a watery grave. Grave or Memorial Reference: 8. Memorial: Plymouth Naval Memorial UK.

KAVANAGH, William: Rank: Corporal. Regiment or Service: Royal

Irish Regiment. Unit: 2nd Bn. Age at death: 27. Date of death: 7 June 1917. Service No: 9494. Born in St Mary's, Enniscorthy, Co. Wexford. Enlisted in Enniscorthy. Killed in action.

Supplementary information: Son of Aiden and Sarah Kavanagh of Fairfield, Enniscorthy, Co. Wexford. From an article in a Wexford newspaper:

ENNISCORTHY SOLDIER KILLED
The relatives of Corpoal William Kavanagh, Royal Irish, who belonged to Fairfield, Enniscorthy, have been notified of his death which occurred on Thursday last in Belgium.

The deceased had been at the front since the outbreak of the war. He was gassed once, and wounded once. Much sympathy is felt for his relatives in their bereavement. R.I.P.

From another article:

Killed in action; In a letter to the mother of Corporal W Kavanagh, RIR., who belonged to Fairfield, Enniscorthy, the Lieutenant in charge of the platoon in which deceased served, states that Corporal Kavanagh, who was killed on 17th inst, died like a soldier and a man, gallantly leading his section and inspiring all around him by his coolness and devotion to duty. The men loved the deceased, which was saying a good deal for an N.C.O., and all ranks were his friends.

Grave or Memorial Reference: Panel 33. Memorial: Ypres (Menin Gate) Memorial in Belgium.

KAVANAGH, William: Rank: Private. Regiment or Service: Irish Guards. Unit:

1st Bn. Date of death: 1 November 1914. Service No: 1258. Born in Castletown, Co. Wexford. Enlisted in Liverpool, Lancs while living in Cloneraney, Co. Wicklow. Killed in action. He has no known grave but is listed on Panel 11 on the Ypres (Menin Gate) Memorial in Belgium.

KEANE, J.: Rank: Sapper. Regiment or Service: Royal Engineers. Age at death: 42. Date of death: 13 July 1920. Service No: 15021.

Supplementary information: Son of Mr J. Keane of 4 High Street, Wexford. Grave or Memorial Reference: G. 48. Cemetery: Wexford (St Ibar's) Cemetery.

John Keane.

J. Keane.

KEANE, John: Rank: Private. Regiment or Service: South Lancashire Regiment. Unit: 2nd Bn. Date of death: 22 March 1918. Service No: 40461. Born in Holdman Hill, Co. Wexford. Enlisted in Widnes in Lancashire while living in Holdman Hill. Killed in action. The following article is supplied by his grand-nephew Stephen Foley from Coolcotts, Wexford:

Jack Keane was born in 1897 in Holdmanhill, near Duncormick, to Michael Keane and Kate Quinn. His father was a stonemason. There were quite a large number of children in the family and in his late teens, he moved to Widnes in Lancashire, England.

The war was already in full course at this stage. It was in Widnes that Jack enlisted in the South Lancashire Regiment (Prince of Wales Volunteers), and was eventually posted to France to serve with the 2nd Battalion of that Regiment. I believe he joined with his unit in France in October 1917. In March 1918, the German Army launched its last great offensive of the war, which became known as the German Spring Offensive. At this time, Jack's unit was in the line near Lagnicourt, a town near Bapaume. The offensive was very unexpected by British units and much confusion reigned in the following days with units being flung into the line to try and repel the German assault.

It is believed that on the 22nd March 1918, at Bois de Vaux, Jack was killed in action. There is somewhat of a mystery surrounding the exact circumstances of his death, as there was with many soldiers whose remains were never recovered. Jack's sister Kate, whom he corresponded with a great deal while he was at the front was at this time working in London. Having not heard from him in some time, she sought information from the Red Cross as to his whereabouts. In August 1918, she received a letter from a Lance Corporal Lambe, who was in the same platoon as Jack. He was in hospital in Camberwell, and stated that he and Jack had bee captured together on 23rd March and that Jack was a prisoner of war in Germany. This was never officially confirmed by the army authorities.

He has no known grave but is commemorated on Panel 48 and 49. Memorial: Pozieres Memorial in France.

KEANE, Patrick: Rank: Private. Regiment or Service: Royal Berkshire Regiment. Unit: 1st Bn. Formerly he was with the Northumberland Fusiliers where his number was 75716. Age at death: 24. Date of death: 8 October 1918. Service No: 50765. Enlisted in Clonmel, Co Tipperary while living in Gorey, Co. Wexford. Killed in action. This man is also listed a **KANE, Patrick.**

Supplementary information: Son of Patrick and Kattern Kane of Church Street, Gorey. Grave or Memorial Reference: I.E.4. Cemetery: Rumilly-En-Cambresis Communal Cemetery Extension in France.

KEANE, Thomas: Rank: Lance Corporal. Regiment or Service: Machine Gun Guards. Unit: 4th Bn. Age at death: 30. Date of death: 30 March 1918. Service No: 1115. Formerly he was with the Irish Guards where his number was 9055. He won the Military Medal and is listed in the *London Gazette*. Born in Elphin, Co Roscommon. Enlisted in Clonmel, Co Tipperary. Killed in action.

Supplementary information: Son of Michael Keane of Scurbeg, Boyle, Co. Roscommon. Husband of May M. Keane of Thomas Street, Gorey, Co. Wexford. Served in the Royal Irish

Constabulary. From an article in a Wexford newspaper:

A GOREY HERO

During the week Mrs M Keane, Thomas Street, Gorey, widow of Lance Corporal Thomas Keane, Machine Gun Corps, received the Military Cross and ribbon which was awarded to her husband for conspicuous bravery. He was killed in action on April 1st, but had previously been awarded the medal for an act of great bravery during the Somme battles of last October. His Commanding Officer, writing to Mrs Keane, says; "I am very sorry to inform you that your husband was killed in action on the 1st April. He worked his gun till the whole of his team had become casualties, and behaved with the greatest gallantry. I have had the pleasure of knowing your husband for fifteen months and can assure you that there was no more popular man in the whole company.

He was a favourite with everyone and was always most cheerful under all circumstances and one of the best gunners we had. I always had the greatest confidence in him as a thoroughly reliable N.C.O. and I always knew that he would do his duty to the end. Will you please accept from all the officers and men in the whole company our most sincere sympathy in your great loss." Mrs Keane had the option of having this medal presented to her in Dublin or London, but she preferred no ceremony. It is the first medal of this kind which has actually been received in the town up to the present. Mrs Keane is the daughter of Mrs William Fitzpatrick, Thomas Street Gorey.

Grave or Memorial Reference: Special Memorial 3. Cemetery: Bucquoy Road Cemetery, Ficheux in France.

KEANE, William: Rank: Private. Regiment or Service: Royal Irish Regiment. Unit: 2nd Bn. Date of death: 17 May 1915. Service No: 6709. Born in Ladys Island, Wexford. Enlisted in Porth, Glam while living in Broadway, Co. Wexford. Died. From an article in the *Enniscorthy Guardian,* June 1915:

BROADWAY MAN DIES A PRISONER IN GERMANY.

The Very Rev, Canon Doyle, P. P. Tagoat, has handed the following letter to the relatives of Private Wm Keane, 18th Royal Irish Regiment, which he has recently received. It explains itself; "Kriegsenlangen, Limburg, Lahn, Germany, 18th May, 1915,

Dear Rev Father, Please inform relatives of the death of Private William Keane, of the 18th Royal Irish Regiment, which took place here on yesterday morning;- the 17th of May, after a brief illness. One of his companions gave me your address as I did not know the names of the deceased's relatives."

Grave or Memorial Reference: III.K.5. Cemetery: Niederzwehren Cemetery in Germany.

KEARNS, Thomas: Rank: Private/ Lance Corporal. Regiment or Service: Royal Irish Regiment. Unit: 5th Bn. Date of death: 7 July 1916. Service No: 5766. Born in Bride Street, Wexford. Enlisted in Wexford. Died in Salonika. Grave or Memorial Reference: 215.

Cemetery: Salonika (Lembet Road) Military Cemetery in Greece.

KEATING, David: Rank: Lt (TP). Regiment or Service: York and Lancaster Regiment. Unit: 14th Bn also listed as 1st/4th Bn. Date of death: 21 April 1918. Died of wounds. From an article in a Wexford newspaper:

POPULAR WEXFORD
OFFICER'S DEATH

Lieut. Tim Keating makes the supreme sacrifice. His many friends in Wexford will deeply regret to learn of the death of Lieut David Timothy Keating, of the York and Lancaster Regiment. The sad announcement of the demise of the popular young officer was conveyed in a letter from the War Office to his respected father, Mr D.R. Keating, T. C. Ardara, on Tuesday intimating that his son had died of wounds on the 21st inst. The news of his untimely end caused a painful impression in his native town, where "Tim" Keating, as he was more popularly known, was a favourite in social and sporting circles.

Though he had only reached his 22nd year he had a more stirring than that experienced by many of more mature years. He was educated at St Peter's College, Wexford, and Clongowes Wood College, and even in his boyhood he was an athlete of no mean prowess. He was an adept at most popular games, but it was in rowing circles that he earned an enviable fame. When in his seventeenth year he was stroke of the famous Wexford junior four which held an unbeaten record on Irish waters and defeated the crack Irish crews in the 1913 rowing season. He was a popular member of the Wexford Boro' Batt. Irish National Volunteers in 1914, and shortly after the outbreak of war volunteered for active service.

He applied for a commission in the Irish Brigade, but was gazetted to the York and Lancashire Regiment. Soon after he was drafted out in charge of a detachment of the Lincolns to Gallipoli, where his brother Lieut J. J. Keating, was already serving with the Pals Battalion of the Royal Dublin Fusiliers. During that ill-starred campaign the brothers Keating had many narrow escapes, and Lieut Tim, with his Colonel, were the two last to leave the peninsula. On the vacation of Gallipoli he was sent to the Suez Canal and was placed in charge of the water supply to the troops.

Having seen some service in Egypt with a Camel Corps, he was sent to France about a year and a half ago, and since then he had been in the thick of the fight, but escaped unscathed until the 21st, when he was mortally wounded. To his sorrowing parents and relatives, in their hour of affliction, the heartfelt sympathy of the citizens is spontaneously tendered, and to the chorus of regret at the gallant young officer's fate we desire to add our voice.

Grave or Memorial Reference: V.C. 33. Cemetery: Haringhe (Bandaghem) Military Cemetery in Belgium.

KEEGAN, George: Rank: Private. Regiment or Service: Royal Dublin Fusiliers. Unit: 8th Bn. Date of death: 10 February 1917. Service No: 23072. Born in Wexford. Enlisted in Aberdeen while living in Gorey, Co. Wexford. Killed in action. Grave or Memorial Reference: II.K.14. Cemetery: Queens Cemetery, Buoquoy in France.

KEENAN, Micheal: Rank: Private. Regiment or Service: Leinster Regiment. Unit: 2nd Bn. Date of Death: 4 September 1918. Service No: 3366. Born in Granford, Co Wexford. Enlisted in Dublin while living in Arklow, Co Wicklow. Killed in Action. From an article in the *Enniscorthy Guardian*, June 1916:

> Tis a far cry back to those dark days when the prowess of Irish soldiers on many a hard-fought field in Flanders turned the scale of victory and brought glory to French arms, wringing a curse from an English King on the laws that deprived him of such brave subjects, but time has not changed the Irish soldier, and though, thank God, the fell laws of the Penal Days have long been repealed, and happier, more tolerant times now find him fighting side by side with the impulsive, dashing way as the soldiers of the 'Wild Geese'. Nothing can daunt his cheeriness, nothing daunt his courage, nothing weaken his power of endurance, and surely nothing can shake his faith in God's providence. These were my reflections after reading a bundle of letters from Private Michael Keenan of the 7th Leinsters.
>
> They were all written to his old neighbour and friend, Mrs Andrew Leonard of Kilmichael, Castletown. I think I am fair in assuming that young Keenan is a fair type of the thousands of young Irishmen who voluntarily

joined the army since the war broke out. The names of many occur to me, all intelligent, active, well-placed young men who gave up good positions to take part in the great fight. I may just instance the registrar of the Co Infirmary, Mr Michael Kavanagh, who long ago joined, Messrs, Tommy Doyle, Michael Kavanagh and Arthur Smyth of Gorey; Pat Kavanagh of Tomcoyle (who fell bravely fighting); the Hall boys of Tomnahely (of whom there are four at the front), only to mention a few. Taking these as an average it is gratifying to believe that the Irish regiments in personnel can at least hold their own with the English and Scotch.

I am certain that after perusing the following excerpts from Mike Keenan's letters, which I have had the privilege of reading, through Mrs Leonard's kindness, and which I am kindly allowed to give to you for publication, your readers will agree with me that we may well be proud of our fellow countrymen at the front. I may just add that Private Keenan is the son of an evicted tenant – Mr. Keenan, formerly of Glandoran, Gorey, a man who was esteemed by all who knew him. He had the good fortune some short time before his death to be reinstated in the Kilmichael farm which Private Michael Keenan holds at present. I may also add that another brother of Michael's, Willie Keenan, is also at the front, and neither knew of the other's whereabouts till they met most dramatically on the battlefield. I delete dates and names of places, indeed as a matter of fact he gives no place names.

A Correspondant.

P. S. The revulsion of feeling amongst

Nationalists during the past few weeks was particularly exemplified by Mr Dillon, a man who, next to Mr John Redmond, has been, for many years the principal target of Sinn Fein attacks. The few hundred rash youths whose suicidal conduct incensed Irish Nationalists, incomparably more than Carsons bluster of a few years seemed to judge by the British papers as well as our own Tory sheets, a far greater object of hatred than the German enemy.

Well now Mrs Leonard I have had a trying experience since I wrote you last indeed. It was near finishing me, and I am sure if it were not for your prayers and the prayers of all my good friends I should not have been saved. I will try to tell you about it, but I have no words to describe what I felt through it all. There were about 20 of us laying a mine under the German trenches. Everything was fairly quiet, when all of a sudden the enemy exploded a mine of theirs just beside us. The shock caused ours to cave in and we were buried. We were about 500 yards from the mouth of our shaft and about 50 feet underground.

After a long time we got clear of the stuff on top of us, but our rifles and all our equipment were lost. We made our way up to the surface with difficulty, and the sight that then met our eyes was something beyond description. Shells were falling and exploding like continuous thunder, not to mention machine gun fire, bombs, etc, and, worst of all, they were using the accursed gas and liquid fire. Our trenches were all levelled, and the poor fellows who were holding them were all dead or wounded. We gave

up all hopes, as you could not imagine anyone could survive in the hell that was raging; but life is sweet, and we made a dash for it, and, my God, that race for life will live in my memory till I die.

Half dazed with the flashes and shock of shells, scorched and blinded, we ran on, sometimes falling perhaps five or six feet in a shell hole, out again, and after what seemed an age we reached a place where there was a little protection, but out of the 20 that started on that terrible race only four got safe, and, thank God, I was one. The remaining 16 were all killed. We are having terribly severe weather – snow and frost, and we are up to our waists in mud in the trenches. I often wonder how we stick it, but I suppose one can get accustomed to anything, but we will all be glad when this terrible war is over and we get home once more.

I know some will say that those who volunteered are not to be pitied, but if they were here to see how the German savages treated the country and heard the tales of how they used the poor women and children they would think better of those who came and stopped the Kaiser and his army from getting to Ireland, and I believe he would be there now were it not for those who volunteered. Give my best wishes to ——— and ———and all the neighbours. How is ———? Is he married yet? Tell him to volunteer and come over here and I will introduce him to a nice, dark, slender, good looking, gay French widow with a pub. There is nothing but widows here from 18 years to 80. I have a notion of settling down myself after the war, that is if the Kaiser don't settle me down in it first. I laughed when I read your letter that I was reported a prisoner of war. I think they don't bother much about taking you alive now, at least we didn't give them the chance that night. It was too risky. I must now close as my time is up, and I must have a bang or two at Fritz.

Here are further extracts from other letters of his:

As you remark, 'tis a queer world. Just imagine Willie [his brother] and me meeting on a battlefield of far-off Flanders. Well, such is life. I received "The Enniscorthy Guardian" and the "Wicklow People" which you sent me, and was glad to get them; also a lot of cigarettes from the AOH Castletown. It was indeed, very kind of them, also a cheering letter from Father O'Keefe. I can only say, God bless you all.

In another letter he says:

I wish we had the Kaiser and his crowd cleared off the earth till we'd get back to civilisation again. When I do go back there is one thing will not trouble me and that is paying rent for a house. I will dig a dug out in the 'Big-Bed' (one of his fields in Kilmichael). I wish I was there now, but still it is more exciting shooting Germans than rabbits.

Here is another one:

I was sorry to hear of poor ———'s death, but I was going down myself a few nights ago. We blew up a mine right under the German trenches (this is done by making a tunnel from our trenches underneath the Germans, where the explosives-five tons-are placed and exploded by means of an electric wire). The hole made, by, the explosion was as big as the 'Station Field' [another field in Kilmichael]. It is called a crater. Well, of course, a lot of Germans... you cannot realise the desolation that they have wrought. Whole cities, towns and villages without a house standing and poor little refugees like Charlie (Mrs Leonards eight year old son) their fathers and mothers all gone. It is something beyond expression.

Don't forget writing, you and Pat. I will write at every opportunity. When my letters cease you will know I am down and out, but, please God, they won't.

Another

France was a beautiful country before this terrible war, but now, alas, it is a land of desolation and sorrow. There is not a tree, even for hundreds of miles, but shows sign of the havoc wrought with shell-fire, and every few miles one see a graveyard with hundreds of little wooden crosses to mark the spot where the poor soldier sleeps his last sleep far away from home and friends. I have heard many say – and God knows I have felt the same myself – that they would be satisfied to die if they could live to see Ireland and to know that they would be buried there.

And again he writes:

You can have no idea of what those desolate fields of Flanders are like. The snow has hidden a lot of ghastly sights. There are hundreds of poor fellows lying within a few yards of our trenches un-buried. To try and bury them means death, as the Germans allow no respite.

At night time here all parties, friends and enemies send up rockets, searchlights, etc, and the battlefield is lit up as if the sun was shining. Then the roar and flash of shells bursting makes the scene so awful that words cannot explain it. But, thank God, we have one great consolation – we receive Absolution and Holy Communion frequently – so that if the worst happens we are prepared to go. The Priest told us yesterday that this is the third time that this privilege was granted (the dispensing with confession and fasting, I presume he means) so you see we have a great deal to be thankful for. There is one thing very remarkable here, and that is that the life size images of the Crucifixion which are to be met at every cross-roads, village and farmhouse, had an extraordinary immunity from injury where ruin spreads all around. The villages and houses are all in ruins, the ground torn up, but the Crucifix stands untouched by shot or shell. I have seen one in particular, and right around it was fought the greatest battle since the war started.

There were 20,000 casualties. It was in a cemetery and the dead were torn up with shells and heavy tombstones blown hundreds of yards away, but there is not a mark on this Crucifix!

Here is the first letter he wrote after going out to the front:

I have been in the trenches for some time past. I may tell you it is a lively place, but thank God I have been very lucky so far. I have not got a scratch, although many a poor fellow went down beside me. It is a matter of luck perhaps, my turn may come at any moment. The continual roar of the artillery, the whiz of shrapnel and rifle fire, is something awful. There are times when it lasts day and night without a moment's intermission, but the cold is the worst of all. I believe Jack Clancy of the rock, lost an eye a few weeks ago. He had bad luck, whilst on the march up to the trenches. We were halted in a town, six miles from the firing line just beside a chapel when a shell dropped in the middle of us.

There were ten of our lads badly wounded. They were all in my section, three of them in fact were standing beside me, so this, although it is only one on the many hair breadth escapes a fellow has, will show you how near death is to us all out here. But God is good and I will live to see you all again. It is strange how one gets accustomed to the shell-fire, etc. Just imagine going to cook your grub and sleep in the cellar of a house and the shells going fast and furious through the roof above you. Well this happens every night [unreadable] It is called a crater. Well of course, a lot of Germans were blown sky-high (they often blow us up too). But the main thing is to get possession of the crater, and it was in a charge for this that I got hit with a bit of shrapnel. It was only a slight wound, and, thank God, I am all right again.

They attacked us three times that night, but we beat them and held the crater. There was a terrible lot killed on both sides. The weather is very bad, snow and frost every day. We are up to our waists in the trenches, as you may guess we would be glad if it was all over. It is sickening to see all the poor fellows bodies lying unburied, food for the rats, which are here in millions. Death comes very suddenly here. A chum of mine named Nichols had just got a letter from home. He had started reading it when a shell burst and took his head clean off. He was only 18 years old. I had the unpleasant duty to write and let his mother know. Hundreds of similar cases happen daily. We have been resting here for 48 hours. In the morning our time is up and we go up to the trenches again. We are about six miles from the firing line, but even as I write this there are shells falling like hail from both guns and aeroplanes in the street below. I must conclude, as we are all going to confession and Holy Communion at five o'clock.

This is a strange life here compared to Kilmichael but I suppose one must go through whatever is allotted one, but please God, I will survive it and see you all again. I know you will do the praying and we will do the fighting.

From an article in the *Enniscorthy Guardian* in 1916:

PRIVATE MICHAEL KEENAN, CASTLETOWN, WOUNDED.

Your readers will perhaps remember some months ago extracts from Private Keenan's very interesting letters from France to his friend, Mrs Andrew Leonard, Kilmichael. He is now lying wounded, poor fellow, in the War Hospital, Whitechurch, Cardiff.

He received his wounds in an action near Loos in June last. He is making satisfactory progress towards recovery. Private Keenan is and adept with the brush and pencil and, as I think I told your readers before, there is many a souvenir of his art amongst his friends and neighbours around Castletown. The greater number of these are pencil and pen and ink sketches dashed off in a few minutes and are marvellous and lifelike likenesses of these friends. He painted a small seascape in water colours a few weeks ago in the hosipital. From a bundle of sketches of his which I had the privilege of seeing a few years ago I often thought it was a pity that he was not on some of our few(too few indeed) illustrated Irish Papers.

His work in my opinion, and my opinion is founded on 30 years observation of Irish art, for what passes as Irish art, as interpreted in our picture papers – is far above the average of our small number of black and white artists. The accompanying photo of Private Keenan in Whitechurch War Hospital. – A correspondant.

Grave or Memorial Reference: Bristol. Castle Cem Mem 2. Messines Ridge British Cemetery in Belgium.

KEHOE, Edward: Rank: Private. Regiment or Service: Royal Lancaster Regiment. Unit: 1/5th Bn. Date of death: 5 May 1915. Service No: 1576. Born in Wexford, Co. Wexford. Enlisted in Fleetwood. Killed in action. Age at death: 33.

Supplementary information: Husband of the late Margaret Kehoe. Native of New Ross. From an article in a Wexford newspaper, 'The news arrived on Wednesday evening that Private Edward Kehoe, a native of New Ross, was shot on Hill 60. The deceased was prayed for in the Augustinian Church on Thursday (Holy Ascension) morning.' Grave or Memorial Reference: VIII.E 4. Cemetery: Tyne Cot Cemetery in Belgium.

KEHOE, Francis: Rank: Seaman. Regiment or Service: Mercantile Marine. Unit: SS *Leinster* (Dublin). Motor Vessel *Leinster* was the biggest maritime disaster of the Irish Sea when she went to the bottom by German Submarine UB-123. She was on her way to Hollyhead with 770 passengers and crew. 501 of them died. Age at death: 25. Date of death: 10 October 1918.

Supplementary information: Son of Catherin Kehoe (*née* Murphy) of 2 Eden Terrace, Kingstown, Co. Dublin and the late John Kehoe Born at Wexford. From

Francis Kehoe.

an article in the *Enniscorthy Guardian*:

Seaman Frank Kehoe, Kingstown. Seaman Frank Kehoe, a member of the crew of the *Leinster* who went down with his ship, was son of Mr John Kehoe, Kingstown, and formerly of Bride Place, Wexford, and nephew of Mr Charles Kehoe, Bride Place. Like his fathers [*sic*] before him, the deceased answered the call of the sea and for some years had been sailing in the Dublin Steampacket Company's boats. In his native Wexford, where many of his relatives reside, the deceased was well known, particularly among the seafaring community, and his death on duty has evoked considerable sorrow.

A cousin of his, Seaman Lar Kehoe, who, sailing on another line of steamers, had procured a berth on the SS *Leinster*, and had not, fortunately for himself, taken up duty when the vessel set out on her last tragic trip. With his respected relatives much sympathy is felt.

Memorial: Tower Hill Memorial UK.

KEHOE, James: Rank: Leading Stoker. Regiment or Service: Royal Navy. Unit: HMS *Defence*. Age at death: 42. Date of death: 31 May 1916. Service No: 287130. HMS *Defence*'s magazine exploded when it was hit by a German shell during the Battle of Jutland. The magazine explosion triggered off other explosions which almost blew the ship apart and she went down with the entire crew of 903 men.

Supplementary information: Son of William and Catherine Kehoe of Oldhall, Bridgetown, Wexford. From an article in a Wexford newspaper, 'Leading Stoker

James Kehoe.

James Kehoe, of HMS *Defence*, whose parents Mr and Mrs Wm Kehoe, reside at Oldhall Cottage, Bridgetown. He had almost 21 years service with the Fleet, when he was killed in the big Naval Battle off the coast of Jutland.' Grave or Memorial Reference: 15. Memorial: Plymouth Naval Memorial UK.

KEHOE, James: Rank: Seaman. Regiment or Service: Royal Naval Reserve. Unit: HMS *Caesar* Age at death: 32. Date of death: 10 September 1918. Service No: 2942A.

Supplementary information: Son of Micheal Kehoe of Riverchappel, Courtown Harbour, Gorey, Wexford. Grave or Memorial Reference: General L.16.2. Cemetery: Ford Park Cemetery (formerly Plymouth Cemetery) (Pennycomequick) UK.

KEHOE, James: Rank: Private. Regiment or Service: Royal Irish Regiment. Unit: 2nd Bn. Age at death: 33. Date of death: 13 May 1915. Service No: 6969. Born in Kilmore, Co. Wexford. Enlisted in Goodwick in Pembrokeshire while living in Ballymitty, Co. Wexford. Died of wounds.

Supplementary information: Son of James and Bridget Kehoe. Husband of Mary Doran (formerly Kehoe) of Rochestown, Taghmon, Co. Wexford. Born at Kilmore Co. Wexford. Grave or Memorial Reference: I.C.4. Cemetery: Le Touquet-Paris Plage Communal Cemetery in France.

KEHOE, John: Rank: Private, Lance Corporal. Regiment or Service: Royal Irish Regiment. Unit: 2nd Bn. Date of death: 24 May 1915. Service No: 10137. Born in St Mary's, New Ross, Co. Wexford. Enlisted in New Ross. Killed in action. From an article in the *Enniscorthy Guardian*:

> Another New Ross man was killed in the trenches last week, Private Jack Kehoe, Bewley Street. He was on the regulars and was a cornet player in the New Ross, St Mary's Band some few years ago.
>
> One of his uncles Joseph Knight of the High Hill volunteered for the front last week and left a few days ago to join the Regiment he is to be attached to. Young Kehoe was only 20 years of age and his parents are dead.

Grave or Memorial Reference: Panel 33. Memorial: Ypres (Menin Gate) Memorial in Belgium.

KEHOE, Michael Joseph: Rank: Private. Regiment or Service: Army Pay Corps. Unit: Army Pay Office Nottingham. Age at death: 57. Date of death: 31 October 1918. Service No: 23359. Born in New Ross, Co. Wexford. Enlisted in Liverpool. Died at home.

Supplementary information: Son of Pierce and Anne Kehoe. Husband of Kathleen Kehoe of 49 Byerley Street, Seacombe, Wallasey, Cheshire. Born at New Ross, Co. Wexford. Grave or Memorial Reference: IVB. 51. Cemetery: Liverpool (Yew Tree) Roman Catholic Cemetery UK.

KEHOE, Nicholas: Rank: Private. Regiment or Service: Grenadier Guards. Unit: 4th Coy. 1st Bn. Age at death: 27. Date of death: 26 October 1914. Service No: 13331. Born in New Ross, Co. Wexford. Enlisted in Pontypridd. Killed in action.

Supplementary information: Son of Thomas and Margaret Kehoe. Husband of Margaret Kehoe of 18 Milford Street, Splotlands, Cardiff. From and article in the *Echo,* 'Official news reached Ross on Saturday that Private Nicholas Kehoe, of the Irishtown, was killed in Belgium. He was out scouting with a few others when they were surprised by Germans and shot. Private Thos Neill, Neville street, has arrived home. He was seriously wounded at the Yser. Grave or Memorial Reference: XVIII.D.14. Cemetery: Harlebeke New British Cemetery in Belgium.

KEILTHY, James: Rank: Private. Regiment or Service: Royal Irish Regiment. Unit: 6th Bn. Date of death: 2 June 1916. Service No: 8797. Born in Clonroche, Co. Wexford. Enlisted in New Ross, Co. Wexford. Killed in action. James is the father of Thomas Keilthy listed below and he was an employee of the Urban District Council before he enlisted. Grave or Memorial Reference: II.K.3. Cemetery: Dud Corner Cemetery, Loos in France.

KEILTHY/KIELTHY, Thomas: Rank: Private. Regiment or Service: Royal Dublin Fusiliers. Unit: 'C' Company, 10th Bn. Formerly he was with the Royal Irish Regiment where his number was 8089. Date of death: 28 April 1917. Service No: 40346. Born in Wexford, Co. Wexford. Enlisted in New Ross. Killed in action. Age at death: 23.

Supplementary information: Son of Mrs Ellen Kielthy of 5 Haughton Place, New Ross, Co. Wexford. Thomas is the son of James Keilthy above. Grave or Memorial Reference: Bay 9. Memorial: Arras Memorial in France.

KELLY, James: Rank: Private. Regiment or Service: Irish Guards. Unit: down as 1st bn and 2nd Bn. Age at death: 23. Date of death: 24 June 1916. Service No: 6255. Born in Wexford, Co. Wexford. Enlisted in Wexford. Died.

Supplementary information: Husband of Mary Kelly of Corn Market, Wexford. From an article in the *Enniscorthy Guardian,* 'The relatives of Private James Kelly, of Keyser's Lane, were officially notified during the week, that whilst serving with the Irish Guards, he had died from pneumonia.' Grave or Memorial Reference: VIII.B.14. Cemetery: Lijssenthoek Military Cemetery in Belgium.

KELLY, Mark: Rank: Private. Regiment or Service: Royal Irish Regiment. Unit: 2nd Bn. Date of death: 19 October 1914. Service No: 5870. Born in Tagoat, Co. Wexford. Enlisted in Wexford while living in Tagoat. Killed in action. From an article in the *Enniscorthy Guardian*:

During the past week news has been received at Tagoat of the death of Private Mark Kelly, R.I.R., Twelveacre. The news was not altogether unexpected, because no word of any kind had been received from him for over twelve months and the general belief was that he had been taken prisoner by the Germans.

The notification recently received from the headquarters of his Regiment stated that as no trace of him could be ascertained it was probable that he was killed in action on or about the 19th October, 1914. The late Private Kelly was a fine soldier, and himself and his brother Tim enlisted shortly after the war begun. His father, Edward Kelly, is also with the colours, stationed at Templemore, whilst a third brother, Jack is in the Navy. It is many months also since news of the whereabouts of Tim has been received by his mother, and it is feared that the worst has happened, though no official notification has been received. Both brothers were drafted out to France early in October, 1914 with an Irish Regiment, very few of whom returned. Much sympathy if felt for Mrs Kelly and family in their bereavement. Private Edward Kelly was recently home on furlough, having been out at the Dardanelles. He brought home with him many interesting reminiscences of a visit to a Turkish camp under the guise of a 'friend' and told many anecdotes of how he outwitted the enemy on several occasions.

Grave or Memorial Reference: Has no known grave but is commemorated on Panel 11 and 12. Memorial: Le Touret Memorial in France.

KELLY, Michael: Rank: Corporal. Regiment or Service: Royal Irish Regiment. Unit: 6th Bn. Date of death: 17 March 1918. Service No: 1958. *Supplementary information*: Husband of Bridget Kelly, of 12 Usher's Island, Dublin. Grave or Memorial Reference: M 108. Cemetery, Wexford (St Ibars) Cemetery, Wexford.

KELLY, Michael: Rank: Lance Corporal. Regiment or Service: Irish Guards. Unit: 1st Bn. Date of death: 6 November 1914. Service No: 1936. Born in Killane, Co. Wexford. Enlisted in Wexford while living in Tranmere, Cheshire. Killed in action. Grave or Memorial Reference: Has no known grave but is commemorated on Panel 11. Memorial; Ypres (Menin Gate) Memorial in Belgium.

KELLY, Michael: Rank: Private. Regiment or Service: Royal Irish Regiment. Unit: 6th Bn. Date of death: 16 August 1917. Age at death: 33. Service No: 1198. Born in St Mary's, Enniscorthy, Co. Wexford. Enlisted in Enniscorty while living in Bray, Co. Wicklow. Died of wounds. *Supplementary information*: Son of Steven and Margaret Kelly. Grave or Memorial Reference: II.B.14. Cemetery: Brandhoek New Military Cemetery in Belgium.

1958 CORPORAL
M. KELLY
ROYAL IRISH REGIMENT
17TH MARCH 1918 AGE 35

REST IN PEACE

Michael Kelly.

KELLY, Thomas: Rank: Private/Lance Corporal. Regiment or Service: Royal Irish Regiment. Unit: 2nd Bn. Date of death: 4 January 1915. Service No: 5904. Born in Gorey, Co. Wexford. Enlisted in Gorey while living in Dublin. Died. Grave or Memorial Reference: IV.B.13. Cemetery: Mons (Bergen) Communal Cemetery in Belgium.

KELLY, Thomas: Rank: Private. Regiment or Service: Royal Irish Regiment. Unit: 2nd Bn. Date of death: 24 May 1915. Service No: 5943. Born in Tagoat, Co. Wexford. Enlisted in Wexford while living in Tagoat. Killed in action. [See **KELLY, Mark** compare both entries and form your own conclusions.] He has no known grave but is listed on Panel 33 on the Ypres (Menin Gate) Memorial in Belgium.

KENEALY/KENEALLY, William Stephen: Rank; Lance Sergeant. Regiment or Service: Lancashire Fusiliers. Unit: 1st Bn. Date of death: 29 June 1915. Service No: 1809. Born in Wigan in Lancs. Enlisted in Bury in Lancs while living in Ashton-in-Makerfirld, Lancs. Died of wounds in Gallipoli. Age at death: 29.

Supplementary information: Son of John and Margaret Kenealy, of 361 Bolton Road, Stubshaw Cross, Ashton-in-Makerfield, Lancs. An extract from *The London Gazette* (No. 29273) dated 24 August 1915,

> On 25th April, 1915, three companies, and the Headquarters of the 1st Bn. Lancashire Fusiliers, in effecting a landing on the Gallipoli Peninsula to the West of Cape Helles, were met by a very deadly fire from hidden machine guns which caused a great number of casualties. The survivors, however, rushed up to and cut the wire entanglements, notwithstanding the terrific fire from the enemy, and after overcoming supreme difficulties, the cliffs were gained and the position maintained. Amongst the many very gallant officers and men engaged in this most hazardous undertaking, Capt. Willis, Serjt Richards, and Private Kenealy have been selected by their comrades as having performed the most signal acts of bravery and devotion to duty.

Grave or Memorial Reference: C.104. Cemetery: Lancashire Landing Cemetery in Turkey.

KENNEDY, Edward: Rank: Private. Regiment or Service: Royal Irish Regiment. Unit: 2nd Bn. Date of death: 19 October 1914. Service No: 3880. Born in St Michael's in Gorey, Co. Wexford. Enlisted in Marlfield, Co.– Tipperary while living in Gorey, Co. Wexford. Killed in action. Age at death: 20.

Supplementary information: Son of Owen and Sarah Kennedy of Centenary Place, Gorey, Co. Wexford. He has no known grave but is commemorated on Panel 11 and 12. Memorial: Le Touret Memorial in France.

KENNEDY, William: Rank: Private. Regiment or Service: Royal Irish Regiment. Unit: 1st Bn. Age at death: 27. Date of death: 10 March 1918. Service No: 10053. Born in Ramsgrange, Co. Wexford. Enlisted in Waterford while living in Ramsgrange. Killed in action in Palestine.

Supplementary information: Son of Patrick and Bridget Kennedy of Newtown, Ramsgrange, Co. Wexford. Grave or Memorial Reference: A. 44. Cemetery: Jerusalem War Cemetery, Israel.

KENNY, Edward: Rank: Seaman. Regiment or Service: Royal Naval Reserve. Unit: HMS *Canopus*. Age at death: 19. Date of death: 25 April 1915. Service No: 5733A.

Supplementary information: Son of Mary Anne Kenny of Ballinatray, Courtown Harbour, Co. Wexford. From an article in a Wexford newspaper:

> Killed in the Dardanelles; On Wednesday, the Admiralty notified Mr Patrick Kenny, Ballinatray, of the death of his son, Edward, who was killed on April 25th in the attack on the Dardanelles. He was serving on HMS *Canopus*.
>
> Though only a year in the service, young Kenny had participated in several fights having through the Pacific and Falkland Islands engagements.

Grave or Memorial Reference: Panel 7. Memorial: Helles Memorial in Turkey.

KENNY, John: Rank: Private. Regiment or Service: Irish Guards. Unit: 2nd Bn. Age at death: 31. Date of death: 12 September 1917. Service No: 4955. Born in Gorey, Co. Wexford. Enlisted in Dublin while living in Gorey. Killed in action.

Supplementary information: Son of Micheal and Mary Kenny of 9 William Street, Gorey. Irish Guards War diary extract courtesy of Brian Kenny:

At 2.15 pm 12 hostile aeroplanes flew quite low over the camp and dropped a large number of bombs. There were 20 casualties in the battalion. At 5, 30 pm the battaliom paraded to go up the line. Some of the Coldstream Guards got lost during the relief and it took longer than expected. It was reported complete with only 2 casualties at 11.40 pm."

John Kenny was one of these 22 casualties. His body was never recovbered. His family received three medals, the Victory Medal, the War Medal and the 1915 Star. According to his medal index card the 1915 star was returned. Grave or Memorial Reference: Panel 10 to 11. Memorial: Tyne Cot Memorial in Belgium.

KENT, Patrick Joseph: Rank: Private. Regiment or Service: Irish Guards. Unit: 1st Bn. Age at death: 33. Date of death: 24 September 1916. Service No: 9232. Born in New Ross, Co. Wexford. Enlisted in Tonypandy, Glam while living in New Ross. Died of wounds.

Supplementary information: Son of Patrick and Mary Kent of Mary Street, New Ross. Grave or Memorial Reference: II.C.55. Cemetery: Dartmoor Cemetery, Becordel-Becourt in France.

KEYES, Michael: Rank: Private. Regiment or Service: Leinster Regiment. Unit: 2nd Bn. Formerly he was with the Royal Field Artillery where his number was 100213. Age at death: 18. Date of death: 26 September 1915. Service No: 10407. Born in Ballinastraw,

Co. Wexford. Enlisted in Enniscorthy, Co. Wexford. Died.

Supplementary information: Son of John and Eliza Keyes of Bree, Co. Wexford. From and article in the *Enniscorthy Guardian*:

> Micheal Keyes, 2nd Leinster Regiment, a native of Bree, who prior to enlisting in May last had been employed at Major Beatty's of Borodale, Enniscorthy, died of wound received in France on the 19th of September last.
>
> He had been only 16 days at the front when he received his death wound. The sad event occurred at a hospital in France. The deceased had only reached the age of 19 years and his parents and relatives, for whom much sympathy is felt, were only aquainted with his death last Wednesday.

Grave or Memorial Reference: I.G.17. Cemetery: Poperinghe New Military Cemetery in Belgium.

KIELTHY/KEILTHY, Thomas: Rank: Private. Regiment or Service: Royal Dublin Fusiliers. Unit: 'C' Company, 10th Bn. Formerly he was with the Royal Irish Regiment where his number was 8089. Date of death: 28 April 1917. Service No: 40346. Born in Wexford, Co. Wexford. Enlisted in New Ross. Killed in action. Age at death: 23.

Supplementary information: Son of Mrs Ellen Kielthy of 5 Haughton Place, New Ross, Co. Wexford. Thomas is the son of James Keilthy KIA in 1916. Grave or Memorial Reference: Bay 9. Memorial: Arras Memorial in France.

KILBRIDE, Edward: Rank: Private. Regiment or Service: Irish Guards. Unit: 1st Bn. Date of death: 29 October 1914. Service No: 4520. Born in Tomacork, Co. Wicklow. Enlisted in Enniscorthy, Co. Wicklow. Killed in action. Age at death: 24.

Supplementary information: Son of Edward and Mary Kilbride, of Bullingate, Carnew, Co. Wicklow. From and article in the *Echo* and *Enniscorthy Guardian*:

> Edward Kilbride, Coolmeelagh, Bunclody, formerly in the employment of Mr R.W. Hall-Dare, J P, D L, was killed in action at the front. His father has been notified by the War Office.
>
> A number of other Bunclody men, at the front are missing. Martin Brien, Chapel lane, Bunclody, a private in the 18th R.I. Regiment, brother to Messrs James and Laurence Breen, well known in GAA circles was wounded at the battle of the Aisne and is at present in a hospital in Paris.

He has no known grave but is listed on Panel 11 on the Ypres (Menin Gate) Memorial in Belgium.

KINCH, Joseph: Rank: Sapper. Regiment or Service: Royal Engineers. Unit: 146th Army Troops Coy. Age at death: 59. Date of death: 11 June 1916. Service No: 94126. Born in Gorey, Co. Wexford. Enlisted in Gorey, Co. Wexford. Died.

Supplementary information: Son of Henry and Mary Kinch of Gorey. Husband of Elizabeth Kinch of 4 Centenary Place, Gorey, Co. Wexford. From an article in a Wexford newspaper:

The sad news reached his relatives in Gorey during the week of the death of Private Joseph Kinch, of the Royal Enginieers, which took place some days ago in a field hospital in Flanders.

He formerly belonged to Centenery Place, Gorey, and was for a number of years in the employment of Messrs Bates and Sons, coach builders. He went to France with his Regiment at the very outbreak of the war, and had been through the whole campaign. He was slightly wounded in an engagement near St Eloi, while cutting down wire. He was a quiet, industrious young man, and was very popular among his associates in Gorey, where the news of his death was heard with much sorrow. He leaves a widow and two children.

Grave or Memorial Reference: I.B.2. Cemetery: St. Hilaire Cemetery, Frevent in France.

KINGSBURY, Thomas: Rank: Able Seaman. Regiment or Service: Mercantile Marine. Unit: SS *Kalibia* (Glasgow). Torpedoed by a German Submarine and sunk 29 miles West of the Lizard. Age at death: 47. Date of death: 30 December 1917. Twenty-five of her crew died.

Supplementary information: Son of the late George and Elizabeth Kingsbury. From an article in the *People*, 1915, 'Mr Thomas Kingsberry, a sailor on HMS *Ranmazan* (Troopship) is under treatment in hospital in Malta for injuries recently received in the right arm, which, fortunately, are not serious. Mr Kingsberry, is a brother of Mr Joseph Kingsberry, Castlehill Street, Wexford.'

Born at Wexford. Memorial: Tower Hill Memorial UK.

KINSELLA, John: Rank: Private. Regiment or Service: Royal Irish Regiment. Unit: 2nd Bn. Age at death: 20. Date of death: 14 July 1916. Service No: 4866. Born in New Ross, Co. Wexford. Enlisted in Kilkenny while living in New Ross. Killed in action.

Supplementary information: Son of John and Ellen Kinsella of Fairgate, New Ross. Grave or Memorial Reference: Pier and Face 3.A. Memorial: Thiepval Memorial in France.

KINSELLA, Matthew: Rank: Sergeant. Regiment or Service: Connaught Rangers. Unit: 6th Bn. Age at death: 26. Date of death: 25 January 1917. Service No: 3965. Born in Adamstown, Co. Wexford. Enlisted in Galway while living in Glynn, Co. Wexford. Killed in action.

Supplementary information: Son of John and Margaret Molly Kinsella of Polehore, Glynn. Grave or Memorial Reference: I.15. Cemetery: Pond Farm Cemetery in Belgium.

KINSELLA, Michael: Rank: Private. Regiment or Service: Royal Irish Regiment. Unit: 2nd Bn. Age at death: 42. Date of death: 24 May 1915. Service No: 6812. Born in Suttons, Co. Wexford. Enlisted in Waterford while living in Suttons, Co. Wexford. Killed in action.

Supplementary information: Son of Thomas and Margaret Kinsella of Fisherstown, Campile. Husband of Catherine Kinsella (*née* Grace) of Kilmanock, Campile, Co. Wexford.

Michael Kinsella.

Grave or Memorial Reference: Panel 33. Memorial: Ypres (Menin Gate) Memorial in Belgium.

KINSELLA, Michael: Rank: Private. Regiment or Service: Australian Infantry, A.I.F. Unit: 25th Bn. Date of birth: 5 February 1884. Date of death: 27 June 1918. Service No: 6152. Born in Gorey, Co. Wexford. Next of kin listed as: mother, Mrs Bridget Kinsella, Bolacreen, Gorey. Enlisted in Enoggera and Kackay, Queensland on 6 October 1916. Age on enlistment: 26 years 6 months. Height: 5 feet 5 inches. Weight: 146 lbs. Hair: brown. Eyes: grey. Complexion: medium. Occupation on enlistment: labourer. Suffered with the mumps, retention of urine, chancroid, diphteria and trench fever during his service. Received a shotgun wound (22 September 1917) to the thigh and was transferred to Middlesex War Hospital in England. Treated and after a period of convalescence was returned to the battlefields on 9 January 1918. Admitted with a gunshot wound

(while in action) to the thigh (again)on 12 June 1918 and was initially treated at the 61 Casualty Clearing Station. Transferred to the 8th Stationary Hospital where he died of his wounds sixteen days later. His personal effects were sent to Dora Carthy, Ballyconlore, Gorey, Co. Wexford on 31 July 1918. From an article in the *Enniscorthy Guardian*, 1918:

Private Michael Kinsella, Australian Imperial Force, second eldest son of the late Denis Kinsella and Mrs Brigid Kinsella, Bolacreen, Gorey, aged 32 years, and who died on the 27th June, 1918, in a French Hospital from a gunshot wound received in action whilst serving with the British Expeditionary Force. The deceased was buried in a British Cemetery three miles north of Boulogne. Private Kinsella left this country for Australia about ten years ago, and about two years ago joined up at Sydney, where, after a short training, he was sent straight to France, where he went through several engagements, particularly in the early part of the present year, and came out unscathed each time till the early part of June last, when he was fatally wounded.

Before emigrating to Australia he went in for all kinds of sport in his native district, and was a first class gunman. He was a favourite with the boys around, and the deepest sympathy is extended to sorrowing relatives in their great loss. Office and high Mass for the repose of his soul were held in Craanford Parish Church on Thursday, 24th October. The celebrant of the Mass was the Rev Gregory Petitt, C.C. Monaseed, The very rev Canon Murphy. P.P. Craanford presided. There were eight other clergymen in attendance. A number of relatives and friends of the deceased were present at the solemn ceremonies.

Grave or Memorial Reference: I.B.42. Cemetery: Terlincthun British Cemetery, Wimille in France. He is also listed on the family headstone in Craanford Cemetery, Wexford.

KINSELLA, Patrick: Rank: Private. Regiment or Service: Royal Irish Fusiliers. Unit: 9th Bn. Formerly he was with the Royal Irish Rifles where his number was 22581. Date of death: 2 October 1918. Service No: 42506. Born in Ferns, Co. Wexford. Enlisted in Glasgow while living in Parkhead in Glasgow. Killed in action. Age at death: 30.

Supplementary information: Son of John and Mary Kinsella of Ballycooge, Woodenbridge, Co. Wicklow. Husband of Mary Kinsella of 129 Brook Arklow, Co. Wicklow. He has no known grave but is listed on Panel 140 to 141 on the Tyne Cot Memorial in Belgium.

KINSELLA, Patrick: Rank: Corporal. Regiment or Service: Royal Irish Regiment. Unit: 6th Bn. Age at death: 26. Date of death: 9 September 1916. Service No: 4035. Born in Gorey, Co. Wexford. Enlisted in Wexford while living in Gorey. Killed in action.

Supplementary information: Husband of Bridget Kinsella of Lower Wexford Street, Gorey. Grave or Memorial Reference: Pier and Face 3.A. Memorial: Thiepval Memorial in France.

KINSELLA, Patrick: Rank: Private.

Regiment or Service: Irish Guards. Unit: 1st Bn. Age at death: 29. Date of death: 30 September 1916. Service No: 8114. Born in Woodenbridge, Co. Wicklow. Enlisted in Dublin. Died of wounds.

Supplementary information: Son of Thomas Kinsella of Croghan, Ballyfadd Inch, Co. Wexford. Husband of Margaret Kinsella of 4 Affleck Street, Pentonville Road, London. Grave or Memorial Reference: I.K.22. Cemetery: Grove Town Cemetery, Meaulte in France.

KIRWAN, John T.: Rank: Private. Regiment or Service: Irish Guards. Unit: 2nd Bn. Age at death: 22. Date of death: 30 September 1915. Service No: 6954. Born in Wexford, Co. Wexford. Enlisted in Wexford. Killed in action.

Supplementary information: Son of John T. and Eliza T. Kirwan of John's Street, Wexford. From an article in the *Enniscorthy Guardian:*

During the week Mrs J. Tyghe-Kirwan, South Main Street Wexford, was notified by the War Office that her son, Mr James Kirwan, who volunteered for active service and joined the 2nd Batt of the Irish Guards, had been missing since September 30.

Mr Kirwan was a well know athlete, being a fine performer at the 100 and 120 yards sprint.

From an article in the *People*, 1915:

Wexfordmen in the big advance. Writing to Mr Simon Hore, South Main Street, Wexford, Private T Roche, (Mary Street, Wexford) of the Irish Guards states he had some dreadful experiences in action on the Western front recently, but so far he has escaped injury. Speaking of the big advance at Loos he says "When we advanced into the German trenches is was a sickening sight to see the bodies of Germans heaped up in hundreds and were mangled in every shape and form by our artillery fire. Their trenches were squashed into matchwood. Poor Ennis of King Street was killed the other night. He was knocked out instantly." T Foley, Mary Street was alongside him in the trench at the time.

He describes how in an attack with bombs they gained a good piece of ground. Jemmie Rossiter of Mary Street, was badly wounded. Private Rossiter, it may be mentioned, has since died. Private Kirwan, South Main Street, he states is missing.

Grave or Memorial Reference: Panel 9 and 10. Memorial: Loos Memorial in France.

KIRWAN, Patrick: Rank: Able Seaman. Regiment or Service: Royal Navy. Unit: HMS/M E14. Age at death: 23. Date of death: 28 January 1918. Service No: J/11213.

Supplementary information: Son of John and Annie Kirwan of Bolacrean, Gorey, Co. Wexford. Grave or Memorial Reference: 27. Memorial: Plymouth Naval Memorial UK.

KIRWIN/KIRWAN, Matthew: Rank: Private. Regiment or Service: Irish Guards. Unit: 2nd Bn. Date of death: 19 May 1916. Service No: 7230. Born in Enniscorthy, Co. Wexford. Enlisted in Dublin, while living in Arklow, Co.

Wicklow. Died of wounds. Age at death: 36.

Supplementary information: Husband of C. Kirwan of 22 Whitefriars Street, Dublin. Grave or Memorial Reference: II.C.20. Cemetery: Ration Farm (La Plus Douve) Annexe in Belgium.

KNOX, Francis Willaim White: Rank: Private. Regiment or Service: Royal Inniskilling Fusiliers. Unit: 12th Bn. Age at death: 37. Date of death: 27 April 1916. Service No: 27861. Born in Delgany, Co. Wicklow. Enlisted in Bray while living in Greystones. Died of wounds at home.

Supplementary information: Son of Francis W. White Knox and the late Mrs A.C. Knox. Born at Kilmannock, Co. Wexford. Grave or Memorial Reference: 5.172. Cemetery: Breandrum Cemetery Wexford.

KNOX, James: Rank: Private. Regiment or Service: Royal Dublin Fusiliers. Unit: 10th Bn. Date of death: 26 February 1917. Service No: 24713. Born in Ferns, Co. Wexford. Enlisted in Dublin. Killed in action. Age at death: 19.

Supplementary information: Son of George W. and Brigid Knox of Rosario, Ballyfermot, Chapelizod, Dublin. From De Ruvigny's Roll of Honour:

KNOX, James, Private, no. 24713, Lewis Machine Gun Section, 10th (Service) Battn. The Royal Dublin Fusiliers, 4th s. of George Wilson Knox, of Rosario, Ballyfermot, Motor Engineer, by his wife, Bridget, dau. Of the late John Doyle, of Ballyfad, Inch; b. Rathpierce, Ballyfad, Inch, Gorey, co. Wexford, 25 Feb. 1898; educ.

National School there, and Christian Brothers' School, Dublin; was a Clerk; enlisted in Nov. 1915; served with the Expeditionary Force in France and Flanders from Aug. 1916, and was killed in action near Miraumont 26 Feb. 1917. Buried there, Lieut. Higgins, M. C., wrote to Capt. Wilson; "His death was a grave loss to my party, and was much regretted by the officers and men of his company for, as you know, he was most popular with all who knew him. He was a plucky man, and I am unable to describe my appreciation of his gallant conduct and good work while under fire, save that he died the death of a gallant Irish soldier.

Grave or Memorial Reference: Has no known grave but is commemorated on Pier and Face 16 C. Memorial: Thiepval Memorial in France.

L

LACEY, John: Rank: Private. Regiment or Service: Royal Irish Regiment. Unit: 2nd Bn. Date of death: 19 October 1914. Age at death, 44. Service No: 6533. Born in Enniscorthy, Co. Wexford. Enlisted in Enniscorthy. Killed in action. Son of Patrick and Mary Lacey. Husband of the late Annie Lacey. Listed missing in the *Enniscorthy Guardian* on 20 March 1915 where his address was given as The Folly. Has no known grave but is commemorated on Panel 11 and 12. Memorial: Le Touret Memorial in France

LACEY, Nicholas: Rank: Private. Regiment or Service: Royal Dublin Fusiliers. Unit: 1st Bn. Date of death: 13 July 1915. Service No: 11251. Born in Kilrush, Co. Wexford. Enlisted in Carlow while living in Kilrush. Killed in action in Gallipoli. From an article in the *Enniscorthy Guardian*, 'Mr Brian Leacy, Chapel Lane, Bunclody received a communication from the War Office on Tuesday last that his brother Private Nicholas Leacy, 1st Royal Dublin Fusiliers was wounded on the 13th July last and is missing.'

From an article in the *Enniscorthy Guardian* 1917:

> Bunclody soldier Killed. Mr B Lacey, Chapel Lane, Bunclody received during the week information from the Infantry Record Office Dublin, of the death of his brother, Private N Lacey, Royal Dublin Fusiliers, who is missing since the landing at Gallipoli

on July 13th, 1915.

Private Lacey was prayed for at both Masses in Bunclody on Sunday. The news of his death caused widespread regret amongst his companions in Bunclody with whom he was very popular. Deep sympathy is felt for his mother, sisters and brothers in their bereavement.

He has no known grave but is listed on Panel 190 to 196 on the Helles Memorial in Turkey.

LACY/LEACY, Patrick: Rank: Lance Corporal. Regiment or Service: Royal Irish Regiment. Unit: 'B' Coy. 1st Bn. Age at death: 28. Date of death: 14 February 1915. Born in Enniscorthy, Co. Wexford. Enlisted in Wexford while living in Enniscorthy. Service No: 8845. Killed in action.

Supplementary information: Son of John and Johanna Lacy of 9 Duffry Street, Enniscorthy, Co. Wexford. From an article in the *Echo*:

ENNISCORTHY MAN KILLED AT THE FRONT.

The parents of Lance Corporal Patrick Lacey who resided at the Duffry gate, Enniscorthy, received intimation from the War Office on Tuesday morning that their son had been killed at the front. The deceased belonged to the Royal Irish Regiment. He was serving in India at the time of the outbreak of the war, and was amongst those sent with the Indian draft to the front. At all the masses in the Cathedral and Shannon Chapel on St Patrick's Day prayers were offered for the happy repose of his soul.

Grave or Memorial Reference: Panel 33. Memorial: Ypres (Menin Gate) Memorial in Belgium.

LACEY, William: Rank: Private. Regiment or Service: Irish Guards. Unit: 1st Bn. Age at death: 22. Date of death: 27 September 1918. Service No: 10770. Born in Wexford. Enlisted in Wexford. Killed in action.

Supplementary information: Son of Michael and Margaret Lacey (*née* Kehoe) of 12 Hill Street, Wexford. Grave or Memorial Reference: I.B.7. Cemetery: Sanders Keep Military Cemetery, Graincourt-Les-Havrincourt in France.

LAMBERT, John: Rank: Private. Regiment or Service: Royal Irish Fusiliers. Unit: 1st Bn. Formerly he was with the Royal Irish Regiment where his number was 1840. Age at death: 33. Date of death: 12 October 1916. Service No: 16498. Born in Wexford, Co. Wexford.

William Lacey before he joined the army. Courtesy of Margaret and John Tierney.

Enlisted in Wexford. Killed in action.

Supplementary information: Son of John and Maggie Lambert of Sell Row, Wexford. Husband of Margaret Lambert of 9 Bride Street, Wexford. Grave or Memorial Reference: Pier and Face 15 A. Memorial: Thiepval Memorial in France.

LAMBERT, Nicholas John: Rank: Private. Regiment or Service: Welsh Regiment. Unit: 8th Bn. Date of death: 4 July 1916. Service No: 43013. Born in Wexford, Co. Wexford. Enlisted in Fishguard while living in Tagoat, Co. Wexford. Died in Mesopotamia. He has no known grave but is listed on the Shaikh Saad Old Cemetery Memorial. Cemetery: Grave or Memorial Reference: XVI.C.13. Amara War Cemetery in Iraq.

LANE, Patrick John: Rank: Private. Regiment or Service: Royal West Surrey Regiment. Unit: 1st Bn. Formerly he was with the Royal Fusiliers where his number was 31391. Date of death: 14 April 1918. Service No: G/23699. Born in Wexford, Co. Wexford. Enlisted in Fulham while living in Fulham. Killed in action. He has no known grave but is commemorated on Panel 1 and 2. Memorial: Ploegsteert Memorial in Belgium.

LANGLANDS, Alan: Rank: Second Lieutenant. Regiment or Service: South Wales Borderers. Unit: 3rd Bn. attd. 1st Bn. Age at death: 19. Date of death: 9 May 1915. Killed in action

Supplementary information: Son of the late Major J. S. Langlands and of Mrs eatty of Borodale, Co. Wexford. From De Ruvigny's Roll of Honour:

son of the late Major John Shakespear Langlands, 43rd Oxfordshire L. I., sometime Adjutant, Montgomeryshire Militia, by his wife, Lucy Alice (now wife of Major Charles Harold Longfield Beatty, of Borodale, Co. Wexford, D. S. O.), dau, of the late Patrick Edward Peck; b, longwood, Rugby, 25 Sept, 1895; educ, Stubbington and Wellington College; gazetted 2nd Lieut, 3rd South Wales Borderers, 7 Oct, 1914; transferred to the 1st Battn., went to France in March, 1915, and was killed in action near Bethune, 9 May, 1915; unm. Buried at St.Vaast's Post.

Grave or Memorial Reference: II.B.2. Cemetery: St. Vaast Post Military Cemetery, Richebourg-L'Avoue in France.

LANNON, Martin: Rank: Rifleman. Regiment or Service: Royal Irish Rifles. Unit: 'A' Coy. 8th Bn. Age at death: 19. Date of death: 7 August 1917. Service No: 5538. This man is also listed as **LENNON, Martin:** Born in New Ross, Co. Wexford. Enlisted in New Ross. Killed in action.

Supplementary information: Son of John and Kate Lennon of Dunganstown, New Ross, Co. Wexford. Grave or Memorial Reference: Panel 40. Memorial: Ypres (Menin Gate) Memorial in Belgium.

LANNON, Thomas Francis: Rank: Lance Corporal. Regiment or Service: Royal Munster Fusiliers. Unit: 2nd Bn. Date of death: 4 October 1918. Service No: 4815. Born in Lacken, Co. Wexford. Enlisted in Swansea, Glam while living in Swansea. Killed in action.

Grave or Memorial Reference: I.H.21. Cemetery: Templeux-Le-Guerard British Cemetery in France.

LARKIN, James: Rank: Private. Regiment or Service: Royal Irish Regiment. Unit: 2nd Bn. Date of death: 24 May 1915. Service No: 8120. Born in Killaloe, Co Clare. Enlisted in Wexford while living in Sallystown, Co. Wexford. Died of wounds. From an article in the *Enniscorthy Guardian*:

> Private James Larkin, Som of Mr John Larkin, D.C., Sallystown, Murrintown, was the victim of gas poisoning in an engagement near Ypres on 24th of May. He died while being removed to the Base Hospital on the same day. Larkin joined the Royal Irish Regiment about 12 years ago and after service of about seven years, the greater part of which was spent in India, he retired and subsequently emigrated to Australia.
>
> Being still attached to the reserve he was called up at Brisbane on the outbreak of hostilities. He afterwards took part in the New Guinea Campaign and came to Clonmel in January whence he proceeded to the front. At the time he paid a brief visit to his parents at Murrintown. Private Larkin, who was scarcely 29 years old was of fine physical stature. The deepest sympathy is felt for his parents and relatives in their great loss.

Grave or Memorial Reference: III.B.6. Cemetery: Vlamertinghe New Military Cemetery in Belgium.

LAWLER, George: Rank: Private. Regiment or Service: Royal Irish

George Lawler.

Regiment. Unit: 2nd Bn. Age at death: 28. Date of death: 31 May 1915. Service No: 8636. Born in St Bridget's, Wexford. Enlisted in Camp Drinagh, Wexford while living in Wexford. Died of wounds.

Supplementary information: Son of Denis and Mary Lawler of Carrigeen Street, Wexford. From an article in The *Enniscorthy Guardian*:

In Wexford the greatest sympathy is felt for his parents and relatives. The sad announcement was conveyed to his parents by an officer of the 15th Hussars, who enclosed a letter found in his pocket after he had received the fatal blow. The letter was addressed to his sister and was written a short time previously, and in it he expressed surprise at some rumours that were circulated at home to the effect that he was killed or wounded. The following are some extracts from the letter —"My brave old regiment has been hard at it for a considerable time and indeed they have done splendidly.

They have shown the Germans that they can fight and fight well. We have been holding them back for the past nine days and repulsed every attack that they made to retake the ground we had won. We went for them at 4.15am on the 25th of May, and the fight lasted the whole day. We were subjected to the fiercest artillery fire my ears ever heard, but our brave lads held on until darkness brought relief. We then dug ourselves in position for the next day, when they attacked us again, and this time they used gas shells. Although our men were practically suffocating from the poisonous fumes the great spirit which the Irish race has inherited never for a moment left us.

We got them on the run, and you should see the way our brave lads shot them down as they retired leaving their dead strewn around in all directions. Farther he expresses thanks to God and His Blessed Mother for surviving some of the most fierce engagements, and in conclusion says; "If I get home, as I hope for with God's help, I will be able to tell you all the news" But an All-wise providence willed otherwise.

Grave or Memorial Reference: Div. 19.D.7. Cemetery: Ste. Marie Cemetery, Le Havre in France.

LAWLER, Guy Feinaigle: Rank: Lieutenant. Regiment or Service: 2nd Lancers (Gardner's Horse). Unit: 'C' Sqdn. Age at death: 22. Date of death: 22 April 1920.

Supplementary information: Son of Joseph Edward and Lucy Catherine Lawler. Educated at Elleray Park, Wallasey, Drogheda Grammar School and Newton College. Born at Kilcormack, Co. Wexford. Grave or Memorial Reference: B.9. Cemetery: Haifa War Cemetery in Israel.

LAWLOR, John: Rank: Private. Regiment or Service: Royal Irish Regiment. Unit: 2nd Bn. Age at death: 30. Date of death: 19 October 1914. Service No: 4551. Born in Piercestown, Co. Wexford. Enlisted in Wexford while living in Piercestown. Killed in action.

Supplementary information: Son of Thomas and Bridget Lawlor of Kilmacree, Killinick, Co. Wexford. Grave or Memorial Reference: Panel 11 and 12. Memorial: Le Touret Memorial in France.

LAWLER, Thomas: Rank: Private. Regiment or Service: Royal Irish Regiment. Unit: 1st Bn. Date of death: 22 February 1915. Service No: 10472. Born in Rowe Street, Wexford. Enlisted in Wexford. Died of wounds. Grave or Memorial Reference: III.C.67. Cemetery: Boulogne Eastern Cemetery in France.

LAWLER/LAWLOR, William: Rank: Lance Corporal. Regiment or Service: Royal Irish Regiment. Unit: 2nd Bn. Date of death: 14 July 1916. Service No: 10409. Born in Tacumshane, Co. Wexford. Enlisted in Wexford, Co. Wexford while living in Tacumshane. Killed in action. Age at death: 24. From an article in the *Enniscorthy Guardian*, 'William Lawler, a Private in the Royal Irish Regiment,

and son of Darby Lawlor, Ballyminane near Gorey, has been killed at the front. He had been with the colours since the outbreak of the war and went through several engagements.'

Supplementary information: Son of Mrs Bridgid Lawler. Grave or Memorial Reference: He has no known grave but is listed on Pier and Face 6C on the Thiepval Memorial in France.

LAWLOR, William: Rank: Private. Regiment or Service: Royal Dublin Fusiliers. Unit: 1st Bn. Date of death: 15 June 1915. Service No: 10230. Born in Gorey, Co. Wexford. Enlisted in Arklow while living in Gorey. Killed in action in Gallipoli. Grave or Memorial Reference: XI.E.15. Cemetery: Twelve Tree Copse Cemetery in Turkey.

LEACH, James. Rank: Petty Officer Stoker. Regiment or Service: Royal Navy. Unit: HMS *Rocket*. Date of death: 2 April 1921. Service No: K/11874.

Supplementary information: Husband of Mrs Henneberry (formerly Leach), of Kilmokea. Grave or Memorial Reference: About twenty-five yards southwest of the entrance. Cemetery, Kilmokea Cemetery, Campile.

LEACY, NICHOLAS. See **LACEY, NICHOLAS**.

LEACY/LACY, Patrick: Rank: Lance Corporal. Regiment or Service: Royal Irish Regiment. Unit: 'B' Coy. 1st Bn. Age at death: 28. Date of death: 14 February 1915. Born in Enniscorthy, Co. Wexford. Enlisted in Wexford while

J. LEACH
S.P.O. K/11874 R.N.
H.M.S. "ROCKET"
2ND APRIL 1921 AGE 31

James Leach.

living in Enniscorthy, Co. Wexford. Service No: 8845. Killed in action.

Supplementary information: Son of John and Johanna Lacy of 9 Duffry Street, Enniscorthy, Co. Wexford. From an article in the *Echo*:

> The parents of Lance Corporal Patrick Lacey, who resided at the Duffry Gate, Enniscorthy, received intimation from the War Office on Tuesday morning that their son had been killed at the front. The deceased belonged to the Royal Irish Regiment.
>
> He was serving in India at the time of the outbreak of the war, and was amongst those sent with the Indian draft to the front. At all the Masses in the Cathedral and Shannon Chapel on St Patrick's Day prayers were offered for the happy repose of his soul.

Grave or Memorial Reference: Panel 33. Memorial: Ypres (Menin Gate) Memorial in Belgium.

LEARED, Frank Harvey: Rank: Trooper. Regiment or Service: 1st King Edward's Horse. Age at death: 43. Date of death: 9 April 1918. Service No: 1443. Born 7 November 1877. Enlisted in London while living in Wexford. Died of wounds.

Supplementary information: Son of Mr R.H. Leared and Mrs S.M. Leared of Glenville, Wexford. Grave or Memorial Reference: B.5. Cemetery: Haverskerque British Cemetery in France.

LEARED, Paul Lupus: Rank: Major. Regiment or Service: 7th Gurkha Rifles. Age at death: 37. Date of death: 7 March

1918.

Supplementary information: Youngest son of R.E. Leared. Husband of J.K. Leared of 6 Gillsland Road, Edinburgh. Born at Wexford 22 July 1880. Mentioned in the London Gazette, May 3 1910. From an article in the *Enniscorthy Guardian*:

> The late Major Leared. Major Paul L Leared, Indian Infantry, who died in hospital at Baghdad on March 7th was the youngest son of the late R. H. Leared of Glenville, Wexford, and was born in 1880.
>
> He was educated at Harrow and Trinity College, Dublin, obtained a commission in the Rorset [*sic*] Regiment in 1900, and served in the South African War. In 1905 he exchanged into a battalion of the Gurkha Rifles, from which he gained one of the three nomination to the Staff College, Camberley, which were allotted annually to the Indian Army. When the present war broke out he was appointed G.S.O., third grade, to the 53rd Division, and went to Suvla Bay. For his services there he was mentioned in dispatches and was awarded the Cross de Guerre by the French Government.
>
> He died on active service in Mesopotamia as the result of amputation after gas-gangrene. He married Kathleen, second daughter of Mr and Mrs Bertram, of Glencairn Crescent, Edinburgh, and leaves a daughter.

Grave or Memorial Reference: X.F.4. Cemetery: Baghdad (North Gate) War Cemetery in Iraq.

LEARY, James. Rank: Stoker 1st Class. Regiment or Service: Royal Navy. Unit: HMS *Formidable*. Age at death: 28. Date of

James Leary,

death: 1 January 1915. Service No: 310039.

Supplementary information: Son of James and Elizabeth Leary of Wexford. From an article in the *Echo* entitled 'Lost with the 'Formidable'' 'On Wednesday morning Mr Jas Leary Faythe, received notification that his son, James, who was a stoker on HMS Formidable, blown up in the Channel, was amongst the members of the crew who were missing.' From an article in the *Enniscorthy Guardian*, 1915:

Mr James O'Leary, son of Mr Jas. O'Leary, of Castle Hill Street, Wexford who also went to his doom on the same occasion. Mr O'Leary was a splendid type of young fellow who had a very promising career before him. He was leading stoker on the ill fated ship, and was held in the highest regard by his superior officers. A few weeks prior to his death he had rendered great assistance in the work of rescuing he survivors of the 'Bulwark'

in Sheerness Harbour. In the town of Wexford the news of the sad death was learned with feelings of unfeigned regret, and much sympathy is felt for his family in their bereavement.

Grave or Memorial Reference: 11. Memorial: Chatham Naval Memorial UK.

LEARY, P.: (O'Leary on the headstone) Rank: Private. Regiment or Service: Leinster Regiment. Unit: 2nd Bn. Age at death: 32. Date of death: 10 January 1920. Service No: 7904.

Supplementary information: Son of John Leary, of Shannon Hill, Enniscorthy. He won the Military Medal and is listed in the *London Gazette*. Grave or Memorial Reference: D.25. Cemetery: Enniscorthy New Catholic Cemetery, Wexford.

LEARY/O'LEARY, Thomas: Rank: Stoker 1st Class. Regiment or Service: Royal Navy. Unit: (RFR/PO/B/3391). HMS *Good Hope*. Age at death: 31. Date of death: 1 December 1914. Service No: SS/101169.

Supplementary information: Son of John and Margaret Leary of Shannon, Enniscorthy. Husband of Bridget Leary of 15 Duffey Gate, Enniscorthy, Co. Wexford. From an article in the *Enniscorthy Guardian*:

He was for years a member of the Catholic Workingman's Club and of the brass band attached to that institution with which he played the first cornet. He was a member of AOH, Enniscorthy up to the time of his departure to join the Navy as a reserv-

7904 PRIVATE
P. O'LEARY MM.
LEINSTER REGIMENT
10TH JANUARY 1920 AGE 32

P. Leary.

ist at the outbreak of the war. When called on to join the Navy he was engaged as a porter in the Munster and Leinster Bank. Since the engagement in question with the German Squadron on the 1st of November hopes were entertained that he might have escaped but the official news received this week has dashed them to the ground.

Much sympathy is felt with the wife and family of the dead sailor who is son-in-law to Mr P Hendrick of the Town tenants Association. He leaves a wife and one child to mourn the loss of a kind father and good husband. It is hoped that the naval authorities will make ample provision for the widow and child. RIP.

Grave or Memorial Reference: 4. Memorial: Portsmouth Naval Memorial UK.

LEE, Thomas: See **LEIGH, Thomas**.

LEECH, James Alexander: Rank: Second Lieutenant. Regiment or Service: Royal Inniskilling Fusiliers. Unit: 12th Bn. Age at death: 23. Date of death: 10 October 1918. Killed in action.

Supplementary information: Son of George and Emily Leech of Tomfarney, Clonroche, Co. Wexford. From an article in a Wexford newspaper:

Lieut Leech Killed. His relatives have received intimation of the death in action on October 10th of Lieut Leech, of the Royal Inniskilling Fusiliers. Lieut Leech has been with his Majesty's forces for the past three years and his many friends will regret that when the war was so near won he was not spared to share in the triumph. There will be a Memorial Service for Lieut Leech at Killegney Church on Thursday, 5th December at 3pm.

Grave or Memorial Reference: 9. Cemetery: Reumont Churchyard in France.

LEIGH, Edward: Rank: Major. Regiment or Service: Hampshire Regiment. Unit: 2nd Bn. Age at death: 47. Date of death: 1 May 1915. Killed in action.

Supplementary information: Son of Mr and Mrs Francis Augustine Leigh of Rosegarland, Co. Wexford. Husband of Mary Meade Leigh of Clareinch, Claremont, Cape Peninsula, South Africa. 29 years of service in the 1st, 2nd

James Alexander Leach.

and 7th Bns. of the Hampshire Regt. Served in the South African Campaign and in India, Malta and the British West Indies. From De Ruvigny's Roll of Honour:

LEIGH, EDWARD, Major, 2nd Battn. Hampshire Regt., yr. s. of the late Francies Augustine Leigh, of Rosegarland, co. Wexford, Ireland, J.P., D.L., formerly Lieut., 10th Hussars, by his wife, Augustine, dau. Of Charles Perrier, of Metz, Lorraine; b. Rosegarland, 25 Aug. 1867; educ. St. Coluna's, co. Dublin; gazetted 2nd Lieut., from the Militia, to the Hampshire Regt., 9 May, 1888, but transferred in 1897 to the 1st Battn, then serving on the Indian Frontier at Mooltan, Lundi Kotal, Peshawar, etc. ; volunteered for active service in the South African War, in which he was employed with the Mounted Infantry, taking part in the operations in the Transvaal, 30 Nov. 1900 to Jan. 1902; in Orange River Colony, Dec. 1900 to Oct. 1901; in Cape Colony, Feb. to March, 1901; commanded the 7th (Hampshire) Mounted Infantry in the operations against De Wet, until he was severely wounded at Onverwacht, near Emelo, 4 Jan. 1902 (mentioned in Despatches (London Gazette, 25 April, 1902), Queen's medal with three clasps and King's medal with two clasps.); was Adjutant to 4th (Volunteer) Battn. Hampshire Regt., from 20 May, 1904, to 21 July, 1905, when, on promotion to the rank of Major, he rejoined 2nd Battn.

As second in command and served with it (temporarily commanding at various times during 1909, 1912, 1913, 1914 and at the time of his death) whilst in Bermuda, South Africa, Mauritius, India and Gallipoli; left for the Dardanelles, 19 March 1915; took part in the landing there on 25 April, and was killed in action during the Turkish attack on the Allied trenches S.W. of Krithia, Gallipoli, on the night of 1-2 May, 1915. Buried close to where he fell. Major Leigh m. at Christ Church, Lancaster Gate, London, 11 April, 1912, Mary Meade (Ladies' Empire Club, 69, Grosvenor Street, W.), only dau. Of the Hon. Sir John Buchanan, of Clareinch, Claremont, South Africa, LL. D., Knight of Grace of St. John of Jerusalem, and has a son, Edward Buchanan, b. at Vacoas, Mauritius, 19 June, 1913.

Grave or Memorial Reference: I.A.18. Cemetery: Redoubt Cemetery, Helles in Turkey.

LEIGH, Thomas: Rank: Private. Regiment or Service: Royal Irish Regiment. Unit: 1st Bn. Age at death: 28. Date of death: 10 March 1915. Service No: 6970. Born in Broadway, Co. Wexford. Enlisted in Swansea, Glamorgan while living in Taghmon. Died at home.

Supplementary information: Son of William Leigh of Taghmon, Co. Wexford. From and article in the *People* dated 27 March 1915:

THE LATE PRIVATE THOMAS LEE.

A Bristol newspaper of the last week contains the following: "Another brave soldier had been laid to rest at Arno's Vale cemetery-Private Thomas Lee of the 1st Royal Irish Regiment-who died at Bishop's Knoll Hospital Infirmary. The body was taken to the Pro-Cathedral on

Thursday evening, and Mass was celebrated on Friday morning. The funeral included a contingent of the Royal Scottish Fusiliers, the officers present being Lieutenants A. L. Ritchie, J.F. Campbell and J.P. Halcrow. Mr and Mrs R.E. Rush and the matron at Bishop's Knoll were also in attendance." Private Lee was a native of Taghmon, and the news of his death has come as a shock to his many friends and relatives. He was highly esteemed in his native district for his many sterling qualities.

On the outbreak of the war he volunteered for the 1st Royal Irish Regiment, and about Christmas was sent to the front. Not being at any time of a robust constitution, he did not long withstand the rigours of war, and after a short time was sent back to Bishop's Knoll Hospital, Bristol, where he breathed his last about ten days ago, notwithstanding the tender care of the skilled nurses of the institution. In his last moments he received all the consolations of the Holy Catholic Church. R.I.P.

Grave or Memorial Reference: Screen Wall. War Plot. C. Cemetery: Bristol (Arnos Vale) Roman Catholic Cemetery UK.

LENNAN, Dennis: Rank: Private. Regiment or Service: Royal Dublin Fusiliers. Unit: 8th Bn. Date of death: 9 April 1916. Service No: 16251. Born in New Ross, Co. Wexford. Enlisted in Swansea while living in Plasmart, Swansea. Died of wounds. Grave or Memorial Reference: III. G. 46. Cemetery: Bethune Town Cemetery in France.

LENNON, Martin: Rank: Rifleman. Regiment or Service: Royal Irish Rifles. Unit: 'A' Coy. 8th Bn. Age at death: 19. Date of death: 7 August 1917. Service No: 5538. This mas is also listed as **LANNON, Martin:** Born in New Ross, Co. Wexford. Enlisted in New Ross. Killed in action.

Supplementary information: Son of John and Kate Lennon of Dunganstown, New Ross. Grave or Memorial Reference: Panel 40. Memorial: Ypres (Menin Gate) Memorial in Belgium.

LEO, Francis: Rank: Corporal. Regiment or Service: Kings Liverpool Regiment. Unit: 2nd Bn. Date of death: 1 September 1915. Service No: 11095. Born in Wexford, Co. Wexford. Enlisted in Clonmel while living in Liverpool. Died in India. He has no known grave but is listed on Face 1 on the Delhi (India Gate) Memorial in India.

LEWIS, Thomas Norman: Rank: Corporal and Acting Corporal. Regiment or Service: Royal Garrison Artillery. Unit: 321st Siege Battery. Date of death: 8 August 1917. Service No: 56682. Born in Courtown Harbour. Enlisted in Shepherd's Bush in Middlesex while living in Dawlish, Devonshire. Killed in action.

Supplementary information: Son of Thomas Norman and Mary Lewis of 3 Iddesleigh Terrace, Dawlish, Devon. Grave or Memorial Reference: XIV.B.I. Cemetery: Voormezeele Enclosure No 3 in Belgium.

LIEBERMAN, Frederick Victor: Rank: Gunner. Regiment or Service:

Australian Field Artillery. Unit: 6th Bde. Date of death: 11 August 1918. Service No: 8197.

Supplementary information: Son of Adolf and A.E. Lieberman of 33 Russell Street, Camberwell, Melbourne. Native of Wexford. Went to St Paul's Cathedral Choir School. Emigrated from Wexford when he was two years old. Enlisted in Melbourne, Victoria on 19 June 1915. Height: 5 Feet 10 inches. Weight: 153lbs. Age on enlistment: 33 years and two months. Complexion: ruddy. Eyes: hazel. Hair: dark brown. It states in his records that he died of multiple shell wounds but also adds a note beside this saying 'gas'. Born in Wexford. Occupation on enlistment: Accountant and Commercial Traveller. On his death his effects were to be given to his sister, Gertrude Ellen Lieberman, of Broadway Camberwell. The witness to his will was A.E. Leibermann, 53 Broadway, Camberwell. Buried by Revd Lt Causton attached to the 20th Casualty Clearing Station. Next of kin, Mother, Mrs A.E. Lieberman, Broadway, Camberwell, Victoria. In a later letter (21 July 1919) to records her address was 33 Russell Street Camberwell. Father died November 1911. Grave or Memorial Reference: VI.A.9. Cemetery: Vignacourt British Cemetery in France.

LONG, Patrick: Rank: Private. Regiment or Service: Royal Dublin Fusiliers. Unit: 1st Bn. Age at death: 42. Date of death: 29 June 1915. Service No: 17722. Born in Piercestown, Co. Wexford. Enlisted in Piercestown. Killed in action in Gallipoli.

Supplementary information: Husband of May Long of Barntown, Co. Wexford.

Served nearly fifteen years with 1st Bn. Royal Irish Regt. Also served in the South African War. From an article in a Wexford newspaper:

Barntown Soldier Killed. Mrs Long of Barntown, was notified by the War Office last week that her husband, Patrick Long, who was a Lance Corporal in the Dublin Fusiliers had been killed in action whilst fighting with the Mediterranean Expeditionary Force on June 29th near the Dardanelles. Lance Corporal Long had been fourteen years with the colours altogether, and during his term of service had assisted in the quelling of a mutiny in India in 1896, and subsequently participated in the South African campaign. After the Boer War, his term of service having been completed, he returned to civil life, but in December last he volunteered for active service.

He rejoined his old Regiment, the Dublin Fusiliers on May 29th, was sent out some time after to the Dardanelles, where the Dublins lost heavily but earned a glorious fame. Amongst those who fell during a fierce engagement exactly a month later was lance Corporal Long. Much sympathy is felt with his widow in the loss she has sustained.

Grave or Memorial Reference: Panel 190 to 196. Memorial: Helles Memorial in Turkey.

LOUGHLIN, William: Rank: Private. Regiment or Service: Royal Irish Regiment. Unit: 2nd Bn. Age at death: 34. Date of death: 24 August 1914. Service No: 6583. Born in St Mary's, Enniscorthy, Co. Wexford. Enlisted in

Enniscorthy. Killed in action.

Supplementary information: Son of Patrick and Mary Anne Loughlin of Clonroche, Co. Wexford. Served in the South African War. I include the following article for your reference. I do not know if the writer is related to William Loughlin. From a *Free Press* article 1916:

KILANERIN SOLDIER
IN EAST AFRICA.

An interesting letter was recently received from East Africa, form Corporal Harry Loughlin, Maxin Gunner, 1st royal Dublin Fusiliers, who is attaché to the 29th Division Transport R. A. M. C. stationed in that region. He formerly belonged to Ballynestragh, Kilanerin, where his relatives reside. The letter, which was written to Mr Michael Byrne, of Inch, and old associate of his, runs as follows:

Dear Mick,

I hurry a few scribbled lines to let you know I am again near the operation quarter. I left Alexandria a few days ago, and now I am travelling in the land of lions and tigers. I was on Gallipoli Peninsula, and was in the trenches at the great battle of Chocolate Hill, on August 28, 1915.

I send you some lines of poetry I composed in the trenches the night before the battle. I hope you will like them. The country about here is very wild and barren. It is nearly as bad as Gallipoli Peninsula. The weather here is very hot now, but cold dews fall at night time. I travelled a few days ago by camel over the great Imolian lands. It is wonderful the country we get over and the natives here are nearly wild. With kind wishes from East Africa, and remind all the boys in Incha and Kilanerin of my good wishes. Yours sincerely, Harry Loughlin.

Lines on the battle of Chocolate Hill, Suvla Bay, 28 August 1915. Composed by Harry Loughlin, Maxim Gunner, 1st Royal Dublin Fusiliers.

There are fellows I'm now meeting
that I never met before,
But all are in good spirits as when
leaving Irelands shore,
Who knows tomorrows bringing,
who knows what deadly shell
May tear its way right through our
front line and send us all to h----

Lets think not of horrid gas shells that
stink our trenches here,
But think of the bliss of a sweethearts
kiss and a glass of good old beer,
I'll think not of the Huns and Turks as
into the trench I'll swing,
But I'll not think of the charms of my
Nora's arms as my maxim I'll make ring.

That's how my hearts now singing
and the action is drawing near,
How my Maxim gun will smash the
Hun, oh' I'll make it speak out clear,
We must hold the Turks and take the
hill, our Division give three cheers,
"Fix bayonets, boys, and charge them
down, We're the Dublin Fusiliers."

It was three o'clock in the morning,
the hill was hard to find,
And our engineers had worked for
hours to get it completely mined.
Just as a great explosion the mines
went up like a kite,
and we made our preparations for the
coming desperate fight.
The gallant lads with bayonets fixed
dashed straight into the fray,

The Hants, The Lancs, and the Munsters did splendid work that day,
The fighting was most terrific and we gave the Turks his due,
Thought the battled on like demons we killed more than a few.

Though we beat them back they swarmed on in overwhelming hoardes,
To gain the hill, cost what it may with bayonets guns and swords.
The shrapnel screamed above out heads and many bit the dust,
But no matter what the cost might be, we knew to win, we must.

Our numbers ever smaller grew, by hundreds we saw their loss.
Yes, every man that fought that day should get the Victoria Cross.
Our brave officer McDermott who was wounded very bad,
Was one of the best leaders the Dublins ever had.

Although severely stricken he would not leave the fight,
But bravely threw the hand grenades till he went deadly white,

At last a bullet caught him and robbed him of lifes breath,
He nobly did his duty and he died a glorious death.

It was a glorious victory, we think of it with pride,
and we'll cherish in our memory our brave comrades who died.

Grave or Memorial Reference: II.B.16. Cemetery: St Symphorien Military Cemetery in Belgium.

LYONS, John: Rank: Corporal. Regiment or Service: Royal Dublin Fusiliers. Unit: 2nd Bn. Date of death: 17 November 1915. Service No: 9030. Born in Wexford, Co. Wexford. Enlisted in Dublin. Died.

Supplementary information: Husband of M. Lyons of 9 William Place, Sheriff Street, Dublin. Grave or Memorial Reference: 582. Cemetery: Curragh Military Cemetery in Co Kildare.

M

MADDOCK, Matthew: Rank: Sailor. Regiment or Service: Mercantile Marine. Unit: SS *Welbeck Hall* (London). Age at death: 30. Date of death: 22 April 1918.

Supplementary information: Son of John and Elizabeth Maddock (*née* Kavanagh) of Duncormick, Co. Wexford. Born at Wexford. Memorial: Tower Hill Memorial UK.

MAGUIRE, Matthew Laurence: Rank: Lieutenant. Regiment or Service: Royal Flying Corps. Unit: 30 Sqdn. Secondary Regiment: Connaught Rangers. Secondary. Unit: and 1ˢᵗ Bn. He is also listed as being attached to the Royal Flying Corps. Age at death: 22. Date of death: 28 April 1917. Killed in action. He won the Military Cross and is listed in the *London Gazette*.

Supplementary information: Son of the late James Maguire, J.P. and of Dora Maguire of Tomgar, Ballycanew, Gorey, Co. Wexford. Ex-official of the Irish Civil Service. Entered Sandhurst August, 1915; gazetted to a permanent commission, December 1915. From an article in a Wexford newspaper before he died:

> It will be pleasing news to everyone in Gorey district to learn that Matthew L Maguire, has obtained a well-merited commission in the Army. He is the son of Mr James Maguire, J. P., Tomgar House, Ballycanew, and he pluckily threw up a very promising position under the Congested Districts Board, for which he had taken first place in all Ireland, in order to join the Army and to serve his country in her hour of danger. He joined as a Private, but his exceptional ability soon brought him very prominently under the notice of his superior officers, and he has now been permanently appointed as a Lieutenant in the Connaught Rangers and attached to the Royal Flying Corps. Mr Maguire received his training for this important position while in Camberley College, where he had undergone a course of military training.
>
> He is a young man of exceptional ability, and good accounts should be heard from him at the front in the near future.

Another article continues:

Matthew Laurence Maguire.

Mr Maguire whose age is only 20 years, obtained first place at the Congested Districts Board Examination held in October 1913 and secured 21st place in the United Kingdom at the Woolwich-Sandhurst Open Competitive Army Entrance Competition, held in June-July 1915, with a brilliant aggregate total marks to his credit. Prior to his recent appointmen this young gentleman concluded a further most successful course of advance studies in the Royal Military College, camberley, Surrey. He is a brother of Mr Wm J Maguire, Inland Revenue Officer, Custom House, Dublin, who is the well known Editor of the Civil Service Department in the Irish Christian Brothers highly popular and excellent monthly magazine""Our Boys".

Grave or Memorial Reference: Panel 6 and 61. Memorial: Basra Memorial in Iraq.

MAGUIRE, Patrick: Rank: Rifleman. Regiment or Service: Royal Irish Rifles. Unit: 2nd Bn. Age at death: 17. Date of death: 10 August 1917. Service No: 9697. Born in Clonroche, Co. Wexford. Enlisted in Wexford. Killed in action.

Supplementary information: Son of John and Rose Anne Maguire of Clonroche, Co. Wexford. Grave or Memorial Reference: Panel 40. Memorial: Ypres (Menin Gate) Memorial in Belgium.

MAGUIRE, Robert: Rank: Leading Seaman. Regiment or Service: Royal Naval Reserve. Unit: SS *Kalibia.* Age at death: 28. Date of death: 30 December 1917. Service No: 2306A.

Supplementary information: Son of

James Maguire of Seamount, Courtown Harbour, Co. Wexford. Grave or Memorial Reference: 23. Memorial: Plymouth Naval Memorial UK.

MAHER, Thomas: Rank: Private. Regiment or Service: Australian Infantry. A. I. F. Unit: 11th Bn. Date of death: 3 June 1918. Age at death: 32. Service No: 7192. Born in Enniscorthy, Wexford. Age on enlistment: 30 years 7 months. Occupation on enlistment: labourer. Enlisted in Rifle Range Camp, Brisbane on 5 July 1916. Weight: 175 lbs. Hair: dark brown. Eyes: blue. Complexion: dark. Next of kin: Mother, Annie Maher, 61 John Street Valley, Brisbane, Queensland. Parents were deceased and he had no brothers so his medals were sent to his sister Mrs Mary J. Flynn, 56 Kennigo Street Valley, Brisbane in 1921. His other sister (Margaret Bowles) wanted the medals but the Authorities decided they should go to Mrs M. J. Flynn, his other sister. Killed in action in Merris while bringing in a wounded comrade.

Supplementary information: Son of Phillip and Anne Maher. Born at Enniscorthy. He has no known grave but is listed on the Villiers-Bretonneux Memorial in France.

MAHER, William: Rank: Private. Regiment or Service: Royal Munster Fusiliers. Unit: 1st Bn. Age at death: 28. Date of death: 22 March 1918. Service No: 1041. Born in Kilmuckridge, Co. Wexford. Enlisted in Merthyr, Glamorgan. Killed in action.

Supplementary information: Son of Patrick and Elizabeth Maher of Tenacre, Kilrane, Co. Wexford. Husband of

Elizabeth Griffen (formerly Maher) of Monamolin, Co. Wexford. Grave or Memorial Reference: Panel 78 and 79. Memorial: Pozieres Memorial in France.

MAHON, Patrick: Rank: Sergeant. Regiment or Service: Kings Liverpool Regiment. Unit: 8th Bn. Date of death: 14 August 1918. Service No: 305169. Born in Enniscorthy, Co. Wexford. Enlisted in Liverpool while living in Liverpool. Died. Won the D. C. M. Age at death: 23.

Supplementary information: Husband of Mary Mahon of 65 Eldon Street, Liverpool. Grave or Memorial Reference: V.D.3. Cemetery: Hamburg Cemetery in Germany.

MALONE, Joseph: Rank: Corporal. Regiment or Service: Devonshire Regiment. Unit: 1st Bn. Formerly he was with the (Queen's Own) Hussars where his number was 10644. Age at death: 23. Date of death: 7 November 1918. Service No: 31192. Born in Gorey, Co. Wexford. Enlisted in Enniscorthy, Co. Wexford. Killed in action.

Supplementary information: Son of Patrick and Catherine Malone of Gorey, Co. Wexford. From an article in the *Enniscorthy Guardian,* 1918:

Corporal Joseph Malone, aged 23 years, who was killed in action at the front on the 7th Nov., was the third son of Patrick and Catherine Malone, formerly of Thomas Street, Gorey. The January previous to the outbreak of the hostilities he joined the 8th Hussars and went through several engagements, being wounded three times, once severely. He was home on furlough on the 28th October, and met his death

on the above date, which ws four days before the signing of the armistice. The Rev, F.E. Walker. Chaplain of the 1st Devon Regiment, B.E.F., to which the deceased was some time ago transferred, writing to his relatives in St Michael's Place, Gorey, stated that he was killed by shell fire, and his remains were interred in a military cemetery at Pantigney, a village east of the River Sombre.

He was, he stated, a brave and efficient soldier, trusted alike by officers and men who greatly regret the loss of such a brave comrade and leader, and they all sympathised with his relatives in their great sorrow. Lieut, Pook, writing to his relatives, also stated that deceased was in his platoon and he was killed in action on the 7th Nov., death being instantaneous. He was a great favourite amongst the boys, and he led his section forward with great courage, and was buried with military honours. The deceased, it may be mentioned, was a very steady young man, and was held in the highest respect by the people of his native town.

Grave or Memorial Reference: B.2. Cemetery: Pont-Sur-Sambre Communal Cemetery in France.

MALONE, Laurence: Rank: Private. Regiment or Service: Royal Dublin Fusiliers. Unit: 2nd Bn. Age at death: 24. Date of death: 23 October 1916. Service No: 25259. Born in New Ross, Co. Wexford. Enlisted in Waterford while living in New Ross. Killed in action.

Supplementary information: Son of Laurence and Mary Malone of Houghton Place, New Ross. Grave or Memorial Reference: Pier and Face 16 C. Memorial: Thiepval Memorial in France.

MANGAN/MUNGAN, Andrew:
Rank: Private. Regiment or Service:
Middlesex Regiment. Unit: 2nd Bn.
Date of death: 1 July 1916 (First day of
the battle of the Somme). Service No:
G/1102. Born in Wexford, Co. Wexford.
Enlisted in London. Killed in action.
Age at death: 21.

Supplementary information: Son of
William and Catherine Mangan of 3
Abbey Street, Wexford. From an article in the *People*, 1916, 'Wexford soldier
missing. Private Andrew Mangan of the
Middlesex Regiment, aged 20 years, a
son of Mr and Mrs Wm Mangan, Abbey
Street, Wexford, who had been on active
service in France for nearly a year. He
was in Paris when the war broke out.'
He has no known grave but is listed
on Pier and Face 12 D and 13 B on the
Thiepval Memorial in France.

MANN, Wilfred Oates: Rank: Private.
Regiment or Service: Kings Royal
Rifle Corps. Unit: 12th Bn. Formerly
he was with K.E.H. where his number
was 1543. Date of death: 2 April 1918.
Service No: R/34568. Born in Rosslare,
Ireland. Enlisted in London while living
in Orford, Suffolk. Killed in action. Age
at death: 29.

Supplementary information: Son of
Isaac John and Wilhelmina Mann of
Orford, Suffolk. He has no known grave
but is listed on Panel 61 and 64 on the
Pozieres Memorial in France.

MARSH, John Michael: Rank:
Private. Regiment or Service: King's
Own Scottish Borderers. Unit: 2nd Bn.
Date of death: 14 October 1914. Service
No: 7633. Age at death: 33. Born in
Darwen in Lancs. Enlisted in Retford,

John Michael Marsh.

Notts while living in Retford, Notts.
Killed in action.

Supplementary information: Son of
Edward and Anne Marsh of Black Pad,
Moorgate, Retford, Notts. From an arti-
cle in the *Enniscorthy Guardian*:

Much sympathy is felt with Mrs
Corrigan, Licenced Grocer,
Blackwater on the death of her
brother, Private J. M. Marsh of the K.
O. S. B., the sad event being recorded
in a recent casualty list.

He had served in India, Egypt, and
on home service and had been three
years on the reserve when the war
broke out and was one of the very
first draft of the Expeditionary Force
to go to France. He took part in the
famous retirement from Mons and
fought in several engagements until
meeting his death early last month.

He has no known grave but is commemorated on Panel 15. Memorial: Le Touret Memorial in France.

MARTIN, Richard: Rank: Surgeon Lieutenant. Regiment or Service: Royal Navy. Unit: HMS *Grenville*. Age at death: 35. Date of death: 25 December 1919.

Supplementary information: Son of Harvey Martin of Wexford. Grave or Memorial Reference: 31. Memorial: Plymouth Naval Memorial UK.

MATES, Patrick: Rank: Private. Regiment or Service: Royal Inniskilling Fusiliers. Unit: 8th Bn. He was previously with the Royal Dublin Fusiliers where his number was 19264. Date of death: 15 July 1916. Age at death: 26. Service No: 25218. Born in Barndarrig, Co. Wicklow. Enlisted in Dublin while living in Wexford. Killed in action.

Supplementary information: Son of John and Annie Mates of Barndarrig, Wicklow. Grave or Memorial Reference: VII.H.2. Cemetery: Cabaret Rouge British Cemetery, Souchez in France.

McCARTHY, Bartholomew: Rank: Fireman. Regiment or Service: Mercantile Marine. Unit: SS *Lusitania* (Liverpool). The *Lusitania* was sunk by German Submarine U-20. Date of death: 7 May 1915.

Supplementary information: Son of the late Bartholomew and Margaret McCarthy. Born at Wexford. Memorial: Tower Hill Memorial UK.

McCLEAN, William: Rank: Private. Regiment or Service: Machine Gun Corps. Unit: Infantry, 72nd Coy. Formerly he was with the Manchester Regiment where his number was 16147. Date of death: 1 September 1916. Service No: 8815. Born in Enniscorthy and enlisted in Enniscorthy, Co. Wexford. Killed in action. Age at death: 20.

Supplementary information: Son of Mrs Alice McClean of 437 West Derby Road, Liverpool. Grave or Memorial Reference: Pier and Face 15A and 15B. Memorial: Thiepval Memorial in France.

McCORMICK, J.: Rank: Guardsman. Regiment or Service: Irish Guards. Age at death: 46. Date of death: 22 February 1919. Service No: 6871.

Supplementary information: Husband of Mary McCormick of Duke Street, Wexford. Grave or Memorial Reference: C.160. Cemetery: Wexford (St Ibar's) Cemetery.

McDONALD, Edward: Rank: Private. Regiment or Service: Royal Irish Regiment. Unit: 1st Bn. Date of death: 15 May 1917. Service No: 8788. Born in Enniscorthy and enlisted in Enniscorthy, Co. Wexford. Died of wounds in Salonika.

Supplementary information: Husband of Katie McDonald of Shannon Hill, Enniscorthy. From an article in a Wexford newspaper:

The relatives of Edward McDonald, aged 28, a native of Shannon, Enniscorthy, who was serving with the 1st Royal Irish Regiment at Salonika, have been notified of his death from wounds. The deceased had spent six months with his Regiment in France before leaving for Salonika two years ago.

His father, James McDonald, is serving with the Royal Engineers in France at the present time, while his uncle, Christopher Toole, who also belonged to the Royal Irish Regiment, has been a prisoner in Germany for the past two years. For the widow and child of the deceased, his parents and sisters much sympathy is felt in their bereavement.

From an article in the *People*, 1915:

Private L McDonald, Shannon Hill, Enniscorthy is home for a brief furlough. He has been out in France almost since the war started. He lost one finger by a German bullet last Autumn, but he again returned to the fighting line, where he has been for many months. He has to go back to the front in a few days.

Grave or Memorial Reference: VI.B.11. Cemetery: Struma Military Cemetery in Greece.

McDONALD, James. Rank: Private. Regiment or Service: Royal Irish Regiment. Unit: 2nd Bn. Date of death: 25 May 1915. Service No: 8189. Born in Kilrush, Co. Wexford. Enlisted in Wexford while living in Ferrybank, Co Kilkenny. Died of wounds. Age at death: 35.
Supplementary information: Husband of Mary Anne McDonald of Glasshouse, Ferrybank, Waterford. Grave or Memorial Reference: I.F.75. Cemetery: Bailleul Communal Cemetery Extension (Nord) in France.

McDONALD, Peter: Rank: Private. Regiment or Service: Irish Guards. Unit: 'A' Coy. 2nd Bn. Age at death: 23. Date of death: 9 October 1917. Service No: 6493. Born in Wexford, Co. Wexford. Enlisted in Wexford. Killed in action.
Supplementary information: Son of Murray and Dora McDonald of Upper John Street, Wexford. Grave or Memorial Reference: VIII.F.16. Cemetery: Artillery Wood Cemetery in Belgium.

McDONALD, William: Rank: Driver. Regiment or Service: Royal Horse Artillery and Royal Field Artillery. Unit: D Battery, 32nd Brigade. Date of death: 14 November 1916. Service No: 76647. Born in River Chapel, Wexford. Enlisted in Dublin. Killed in action. From a snippet in a Wexford newspaper:

The photograph produced here is that of Private Wm, McDonald, of Ballinagran, Courtown Harbour, Gorey, who was killed in action on November 14th.

Deceased, who was only in his 24th year, volunteered for active service shortly after the outbreak of war, and had been in the fighting line for a long while. During an engagement on the date above McDonald was killed by shell fire. His death is regretted by his many friends in Gorey district, and much sympathy is felt with his relatives.

He has no known grave but is commemorated on Pier and Face ! A and 8 A on the Thiepval Memorial in France.

McEVOY, James: Rank: Private. Regiment or Service: Royal Dublin

Fusiliers. Unit: 10th Bn. Age at death: 35. Date of death: 20 December 1917. Service No: 22384. Born in Dublin. Enlisted in Dublin. Killed in action.

Supplementary information: Son of Mary Underwood (formerly McEvoy) of The Faythe, Wexford and the late Thomas McEvoy. Grave or Memorial Reference: Bay 9. Memorial: Arras Memorial in France.

McEVOY, John: Rank: Private. Regiment or Service: Royal Dublin Fusiliers. Unit: 9th Bn. Date of death: 7 September 1916. Service No: 15741. Born in Wexford, Co. Wexford. Enlisted in Gorey while living in Wexford. Killed in action. He has no known grave but is listed on Pier and Face 16.C. on the Thiepval Memorial in France.

McFADYEN, George: Rank: Private. Regiment or Service: Gordon Highlanders. Unit: 'C' Company, 1st Bn. Date of death: 14 June 1917. Service No: S/2528. Born in Cohane, Co. Wexford. Enlisted in Glasgow. Killed in action. Age at death: 29.

Supplementary information: Son of George and Rebecca McFadyen of 22 Portugal Street, South Side, Glasgow. Grave or Memorial Reference: Bay 8 and 9. Memorial: Arras Memorial in France.

McGEE, Thomas: Rank: Private. Regiment or Service: Royal Dublin Fusiliers. Date of death: 16 August 1915. Service No: 16375. Born in Ballintubber, Co. Wexford. Enlisted in Wexford. Died of wounds in Gallipoli. Grave or Memorial Reference: II.G.13. Cemetery: Hill 10 Cemetery in Turkey.

McGRATH, James: Rank: Private. Regiment or Service: Cheshire Regiment. Unit: 1st Bn. Date of death: 20 March 1915. Service No: 12212. Born in Gorey, Co. Wexford. Enlisted in Liverpool. Killed in action. He has no known grave but is listed on Special Memorial 8. Cemetery: Kemmel Churchyard in Belgium.

McGRATH, John: Rank: Private. Regiment or Service: Irish Guards. Unit: 1st Bn. Date of death: 17 September 1916. Service No: 8688. Born in Tacumshane, Co. Wexford. Enlisted in Wexford. Killed in action. Grave or Memorial Reference: Pier and Face 7.D. Memorial: Thiepval Memorial in France.

McGRATH, Martin: Rank: Private. Regiment or Service: Cameronians (Scottish Rifles). Unit: 1st/7th Bn. Age at death: 21. Date of death: 2 December 1917. Service No: 265797. Born in Tenton, Co. Wexford. Enlisted in Glasgow. Killed in action in Egypt.

Supplementary information: Son of James and Julia McGrath of 8 Bishop Street, Anderston, Glasgow. Born in Co. Wexford. Grave or Memorial Reference: XVI.A.15. Cemetery: Gaza War Cemetery in Israel.

McGRATH, Michal/ Michael: Rank: Private. Regiment or Service: Royal Inniskilling Fusiliers. Unit: 8th Bn. Age at death: 28. Date of death: 26 April 1916. Service No: 26158. Born in Clongeen, Co. Wexford. Enlisted in Wexford. Died of wounds. Formerly he was with the Royal Irish Regiment where his number was 1874.

Supplementary information: Son of William and Bridget McGrath of Redmoore Cottage, Duncormick, Co. Wexford. Grave or Memorial Reference: III.H.31. Cemetery: Bethune Town Cemetery in France.

McGRATH, Thomas: Rank: Corporal. Regiment or Service: Royal Dublin Fusiliers. Unit: 1ˢᵗ Bn. Age at death: 19. Date of death: 21 April 1917. Service No: 17877. Born in Wexford, Co. Wexford. Enlisted in Wexford. Killed in action.

Supplementary information: Son of John and Elizabeth McGrath (née Leary) of 31, Monument Place, Wexford. From an article in the *People*, 1917:

> It is announced, though not officially that Corporal Thomas McGrath, of the Royal Irish Fusiliers has been killed in action. He was a son of Mr John McGrath, Monument Place. He enlisted about two years ago and for the past year he took part in some of the severest fighting. Corporal McGrath was about twenty years of age. The deepest sympathy is felt for his father and relatives. The news of his death will be learned with regret by his many friends in Wexford.

Grave or Memorial Reference: Bay 9. Memorial: Arras Memorial in France.

McIVER, John: Rank: Lance Corporal. Regiment or Service: Royal Inniskilling Fusiliers. Unit: 13ᵗʰ Bn. Date of death: 27 August 1918. Service No: 47681. Formerly he was with the Seaforth Highlanders where his number was 7364. Born in New Ross. Enlisted in Storoway. Killed in action.

Grave or Memorial Reference: II.H.54. Cemetery: Outtersteene Communal Cemetery Extension, Bailleul in France.

McLENNON/McLENNAN, Farquhar John: Rank: Lt and 2ⁿᵈ Lt (TP). Regiment or Service: Gordon Highlanders. Unit: 1ˢᵗ Bn. Date of death: 18 August 1916. Age at death, 24. Born in Wexford. Killed in action at Gillemont. Son of John McLennan of Killough House, Bray, Co. Wicklow. He has no known grave but is listed on Pier and Face 15 B and 15 C of the Thiepval memorial in France.

McLOUGHLIN, James: Rank: Private. Regiment or Service: South Lancashire Regiment. Unit: 'D' Coy. 11ᵗʰ Bn. Age at death: 19. Date of death: 29 June 1917. Service No: 20883. Born in St Helens in Lancs. Enlisted in St Helen's. Died of wounds.

Supplementary information: Son of John and Mary McLoughlin of Co. Wexford. Grave or Memorial Reference: XIV. C.12A. Cemetery: Lijssenthoek Military Cemetery In Belgium.

McNAMARA, Michael: Rank: Trimmer. Regiment or Service: Mercantile Marine. Unit: SS *Ausonia* (Liverpool). Torpedoed and sunk by shellfire. 44 lives lost. Age at death: 39. Date of death: 30 May 1918.

Supplementary information: Son of Mary and John McNamara. Husband of Mary Anne McNamara (*née* Hogan) of Irishtown, New Ross, Co. Wexford. Born in Dublin. Memorial: Tower Hill Memorial UK.

McSORLEY, Andrew: Rank: Private. Regiment or Service: Royal Inniskilling Fusiliers. Unit: 1st Bn. Date of death: 30 July 1915. Service No: 9630. Born in Wexford, Co. Wexford. Enlisted in Castlederg. Killed in action in Gallipoli. Age at death: 25.

Supplementary information: Son of Robert and Sarah McSorley of 6 McAlpine Street, Glasgow. He has no known grave but is listed on Panel 97 to 101 on the Helles Memorial in Turkey.

MELIA, James: Rank: Private. Regiment or Service: Durham Light Infantry. Unit: 2nd Bn. Formerly he was with the Lancashire Fusiliers where his number was 5681. Date of death: 2 April 1918. Service No: 58360. Born in New Ross, Co. Wexford. Enlisted in St Helen's. Died of wounds. Age at death: 30.

Supplementary information: Son of Charles and Catherine Melia of 66 Phythian Street St Helen's, Lancs. Grave or Memorial Reference: B.20. Cemetery: Gent City Cemetery in Belgium.

MENELAWS, Willliam Ferguson: Rank: Sergeant. Regiment or Service: Royal Irish Regiment. Unit: 2nd Bn. Age at death: 20. Date of death: 27 May 1915. Service No: 10615. Born in Fort George, Invernesshire. Enlisted in Wexford while living in Enniscorthy, Co. Wexford. Died of wounds.

Supplementary information: Son of Serjt. William Ferguson Menelaws (2nd Bn. Seaforth Highlanders) and Mary Menelaws of 7 Redmond Street, Enniscorthy, Co. Wexford. Previously wounded at Ypres, October 1914. From an article in the *Enniscorthy Guardian*:

The friends of Sergt Menelans [*sic*], R.I.R., a native of Ross Road, Enniscorthy have received the sad tidings of the young soldier's death which took place last week.

He was one of a force that were attacked by the German poisonous gas, which has wrought such havoc amongst the British and French troops. He succumbed to its effects after about two days illness. Sergt Menelans, who was only 20 years of age, had just received his promotion, and was a most promising and dashing soldier. He was stepson to Mr James Doherty, Ross Road, one of the staff of the D. and S. E. Railway, Enniscorthy. Much sympathy is felt with Mrs Doherty and family on the death of her son in such cruel circumstances.

From a later article in the *Enniscorthy Guardian*, 'With reference to the death of Sergeant Menelaus [*sic*], who was reported to have died from gas poisoning, it is now officially announced that the immediate cause of death was wounds in the head from a bursting shell.' Grave or Memorial Reference: VIII.D.49. Cemetery: Boulogne Eastern Cemetery in France.

MERCER, Samual Alexander: Rank: Corporal and Acting Corporal. Regiment or Service: Royal Engineers. Unit: Inland Water Transport. Age at death: 29. Date of death: 22 May 1918. Service No: WR/552234 and also down as 168453. Born in Gorey, Co. Wexford. Enlisted in Gorey. Died in Mesopotamia.

Supplementary information: Son of George and Anna Mercer. of Gorey. Grave or Memorial Reference: I.T.21. Cemetery: Basra War Cemetery in Iraq.

J. Mernagh.

MERNAGH, J.: Rank: Gunner. Regiment or Service: Royal Garrison Artillery. Unit: 10th Siege Bty. Date of death: 1 December 1917. Service No: 21202.

Supplementary information: Son of Margaret Mernagh of Upper Mary Street, New Ross, Co. Wexford. Grave or Memorial Reference: XXI.C.C.12. Cemetery: Lijssenthoek Military Cemetery in Belgium.

MERNAGH, James. Rank: Stoker 2nd Class. Regiment or Service: Royal Navy. Unit: HMS *Invincible*. HMS *Invincible* was sunk during the battle of Jutland. Age at death: 27. Date of death: 31 May 1916. Service No: K/30267.

Supplementary information: Son of James and Eliza Mernagh of Clonroche, Co. Wexford. From the *Free Press*, 1915:

A fond father send us the following letter received from a son in the Navy; " You want to know how we get paid. Well, here is how it is done. Every month, punctually, at half past

twelve, on the first – except when the first happens to fall on Sunday – the men gather on the upper deck for their dinner smoke, and to wait for their call to the pay table. There are, as a rule, nearly a thousand men to be paid in any single modern battleship, and in order that they shall be robbed of as little of their spare time as possible, they are split up into what is known as 'hundreds,' and in these 'hundreds' they muster, as they are required. All the morning men have been making preparations for this half hour. Down in the ships office the paymaster and assistants have been counting out the cash required to pay all hands, and placing the amount due to each man in an envelope and in a tray.

The tray is split up into a number of little compartments, each bearing a certain number – a number which corresponds to the ship's books number of the man himself. This numbering is very necessary, for there might be seven Smiths in one ship, and if they had no numbers, Ordinary Seaman Smith, whose monthly pay runs to about thirty two shillings, might get the envelope which is really meant for Chief Stoker Smith, and which contains about four pounds. The writers and the remainder of the ship's clerical staff have been checking the figures in the great ledgers, and reckoning up the totals to be extracted from the ships safe to pay the month's wages with. So much for the clerical side. There is a certain traditional routine connected with the payment of the sailor, which is the same in every battleship, and the like of which is absolutely unknown in the distribution of wages in any firm ashore.

Just forward of the quarter deck a table is rigged, and behind it the paymaster and his writer ensconce them-selves, the Commander of the ship being at the side to superintend the payment of the cash. The men to be paid are drawn up in four lines, and facing aft, and when all is ready the paymaster opens the ball. 'John Jones' he calls. John Jones – an elderly chief gun-ners mate – steps forward smartly, and removes his cap. 'No. six, sir,' he says. 'Five pound thirteen.' Says the writer of the ledger, and the paymaster digs into the little hole in the pay tray, which is number six. He places the cash he finds therein on the table. John Jones sweeps it on the upturned crown of his cap, turns right, and walks quietly away, and so it goes on every man removing his cap as his name is called, and calling out his number as a check on his identity. Sometimes, especially in the case of a lesser rating – a bitter disappointment awaits as he steps up to the table.

For some reason or other he is not entitled to any pay that day, and the gloomy aspect of his countenance as he moves away tells his comrades that a 'stiff-nor'-easter' was blowing for him at the table that day. The term, like all sailors nicknames, is exceed-ingly appropriate for the initials N. E., stand for not entitled, and also for Nor' Easter, see? As each man steps up to the table from the front section of fours, the man behind him takes a pace forward and fills the gap in the rank vacated by him, so that the front section is always complete, and so that each man is always the same distance from the table as his pred-ecessor. Counting the cash served out to him, the newly paid man walks across the upper deck to the other battery where the stewards are wait-ing with the soap and tobacco. Here

again he has top take his turn, these commodities being issued to every man in strict rotation, and according to his number. At last our man's turn comes. 'Number six, John Jones,' he says, 'Two of brown and six of white.'

A steward hands him up two pounds of leaf tobacco, while his colleague issues half a dozen bars of soap, a third steward entering the quantities in a book kept for that very purpose. With his month's pay in his pocket, two pounds of baccy in one hand and six of soap in the other, our sailor makes his way forward, meet-ing with many adventures on his way. The first persons that waylay him are the 'baccy firm'. These men, generally a couple of pals, are willing to relieve him of the job of making that leaf tobacco into a plug for the small sum of three-pence, and as they take his name they place the weed in a huge sack they have obtained from the canteen. A little fur-ther forward, note-book in hand, stand the man who has done all our sailors washing during the last month, and to this 'Dobeying firm' John Jones wends his way. 'Three and three pence', says the firm in answer to his query. 'How much?' and with a willing heart he pays over the amount demanded. You see washing clothes is tedious work at the best of times, and apt to become a nuisance in a battleship, so the major-ity of the men are perfectly willing to pay others – usually married men with families – to keep their wardrobe clean. He has not finished paying out, though yet, for still further forward his tailor or 'sewing firm' (all combination of work-ers are called firms by the sailors), awaits with his little bill. Perhaps he has made our sailor a new serge suit during the month, and he is to receive payment for it on this universal naval settling day, 'the glorious first of the moon'.

Cash again changes hands and his little claims settled the sailor makes his way to his bag, where, in a little linen sack specially made for soap, he stows away his 'six of white'. The next place he visits is the mess, and here again he dips his hand into his pocket. The first thing he is called upon to pay is his private canteen bill. This bill consists of the small luxuries he has had for breakfast and tea during the month, and for which the mess has allowed him credit. It may run to any amount between two shillings and a pound, but beyond this latter limit men seldom, if ever, go. Then he has to pay his mess bill. The latter is the amount which the mess has spent at the canteen over the allowance it has from the paymaster and the men in the mess subscribe to it in equal shares. This paid his liabilities are all settled, and often then the sailor discovers that fully half of his pay has been disbursed to pay his just debts. Still he does not grudge the cash, for he has either food or clothes, or service for it, and, as he says, 'It's worth it all'.

Grave or Memorial Reference: 16. Memorial: Plymouth Naval Memorial UK.

MERNAGH, Patrick: Rank: Private. Regiment or Service: Royal Irish Regiment. Unit: 6th Bn. Age at death: 32. Date of death: 3 September 1916. Service No: 3834. Born in St Mary's, New Ross, Co. Wexford. Enlisted in New Ross. Died of wounds.

Supplementary information: Son of James Memagh of Enniscorthy. Husband of Mary James (formerly Mernagh) of 11 Patrick Street, Enniscorthy, Co. Wexford. Grave or Memorial Reference: Pier and Face 3A. Memorial: Thiepval Memorial in France.

MERNAGH, William: Rank: Private. Regiment or Service: Royal Irish Regiment. Unit: 2nd Bn. Date of death: 19 October 1914. Service No: 4381. Born in New Ross, Co. Wexford. Enlisted in New Ross. Killed in action. From an article in the *People*, 1916:

Another New Ross family has contributed three sons to the fighting forces in the war as also a son in law. They are the three sons of Mrs Margaret Mernagh, Mary Street. Gunner James Mernagh, of the Royal Garrison Artillery, has been at the front almost since the beginning of the war and has gone through many hard fought battles and escaped without serious injuries of any kind. Before the outbreak of the war he was a maltser in the firm of Messrs P. J. Roche and Son, New Ross. His brother, John Mernagh, who is in the Army Service Corps, volunteered about nine or ten months ago and is at present at the front. A third son, William Mernagh, of the 2nd Royal Irish, was killed in action in one of the engagements after the outbreak of the war.

Previous to joining the army this young man was engaged by Messrs Cherry Bros, Creywell Brewery, New Ross. Lance Corporal Power of the 3rd Royal Irish, who is a brother in law of the Mernaghs, has been in France for over twelve months, but returned to England last week and is at present lying ill in a private hospital in

Southampton. He has been through some of the biggest engagements and luckily escaped without a scratch, his present illness due to frostbite. He was also an employee of Messrs Cherry Bros, Creywell Brewery.

He has no known grave but is commemorated on Panel 11 and 12. Memorial: Le Touret Memorial in France.

MERNER, Patrick: Rank: Private. Regiment or Service: Royal Field Artillery and Royal Horse Artillery. Unit: 30 Div, H.Q. Date of death: 4 July 1916. Service No: 5233. Born in Bridgetown, Wexford. Enlisted in Neath, Glam. Died. Grave or Memorial Reference: II.A.26. Cemetery: Dive Copse, British Cemetery, Sailly-Le-Sec in France.

MERRIGAN, Patrick: Rank: Able Seaman. Regiment or Service: Mercantile Marine. Unit: SS *Lapwing* (Arbroath). Age at death: 23. Date of death: 10 December 1917. While on a voyage from Rotterdam to London she hit a mine laid by German Submarine UC-4.

Supplementary information: Son of Patrick and Mary Merrigan (*née* Maddick) of 5 Old Post Office Lane, New Ross, Co. Wexford. Memorial: Tower Hill Memorial UK.

MERRIMAN/MERRYMAN, Edward: Rank: Private. Regiment or Service: Royal Munster Fusiliers. Unit: 6th Bn. Age at death: 24. Date of death: 17 August 1915. Service No: 3183. Enlisted in the Curragh camp, Co Kildare while living in Wexford. Died of wounds in Gallipoli.

Edward Merryman.

Supplementary information: Son of Edward and Mary Merriman of 52 Faythe Street, Wexford. From an article in the *Enniscorthy Guardian*:

Corporal [*sic*] Edward Merryman of the Munster Fusiliers, son of Mr Edward Merryman, the Faythe, Wexford, has been killed in action at the Dardanelles on August 17th.

The sad announcement was received by his parents on Friday last. Corporal Merryman was 24 years old, was connected with the telegraph department of the Wexford Post Office for nearly 8 years. Subsequently he went to Wales, where shortly after the outbreak of hostilities he joined the colours. He had been scarcely a month in action when he was fatally wounded. Much sympathy is felt parents, family and relatives. At the monthly meeting of Wexford Corporation on Monday, the Mayor (Presiding), Alderman Corish said he would like to draw the attention of the Corporation to the fact that one of their employees, Mr Edward Merryman, had lost his eldest and best son in action at the Dardanelles.

He proposed that the sympathy of the Corporation be conveyed to Mr Merryman and family in their affliction. Mr O'Brien seconded. Mayor – Every member of the Corporation sympathises with Mr Merryman in the loss of his noble boy. He has done a noble part, the highest it is possible for any man to do, in laying down his life in defence of his country. The resolution was passed in silence.

Grave or Memorial Reference: Panel 185 to 190. Memorial: Helles Memorial in Turkey.

MERRIMAN, Thomas: Rank: Lance Corporal. Regiment or Service: Leinster Regiment. Unit: 2nd Bn. Date of death: 12 April 1917. Service No: 7974. Born in Enniscorthy and enlisted in Enniscorthy, Co. Wexford. Killed in action. From an article in the *Enniscorthy Guardian* in 1917:

Lance Corporal T Merriman, Kilcannon, Enniscorthy, is one of those gallant "boys of Wexford" of whom, it may truly be said, has sustained the reputation of the Model County for bravery during the vigorous prosecution of the world's great war on the sanguinary fields of France.

Lance Corporal Merriman is of the 2nd Leinster Regiment and was decorated with the military medal for exceptional courage and strenuous devotion to duty in the battles of the Somme and elsewhere in the capacity of stretcher bearer. He was openly

exposed to dangers and assault unprecedented for their savagery, but he went through his perilous plight unflinchingly in the face of such soul-torturing experiences, removing some hundreds of wounded to dressing stations.

He has no known grave but is listed in Bay 9 on the Arras Memorial in France.

MEYLER, Michael: Rank: Armourer (Pensioner). Regiment or Service: Royal Navy. Unit: HMS *Goliath*. Age at death: 55. Date of death: 13 May 1915. Service No: 110470. On the 13 May 1915 sunk by three torpedoes fired from the Turkish torpedo boat Muavenet which was manned by a German crew at the time. 570 of her complement were lost. From an article in the *Enniscorthy Guardian*, June 1915:

WEXFORDMAN RECOMMENDED FOR D.C.M.
Driver Laurence Meyler, Royal Field Artillery, son of Mr Laurence Meyler, Trimmers Lane, Wexford, in a letter which was received by his parents on Saturday last, states he has been recommended for the Distinguished Service Medal for bravery in action. Two days ago his parents were notified that he had been wounded, but as far as can be ascertained his injuries are slight. Mr Meyler has two other sons in the Naval Service.

Grave or Memorial Reference: 7. Memorial: Plymouth Naval Memorial UK.

MIDDLETON, Patrick: Rank: Private. Regiment or Service: Royal Irish Regiment. Unit: 2nd Bn. Date of death: 29 October 1914. Service No: 5866. Born in Kilmuckridge, Co. Wexford. Enlisted in Wexford while living in Liverpool. Died of wounds. Grave or Memorial Reference: A.9. Cemetery: Sainghin-En-Weppes Communal Cemetery in France.

MILLAR, James Joseph Francis: Rank: Second Lieutenant. Regiment or Service: Royal Irish Rifles. Unit: 5th Bn. Age at death: 25. Date of death: 12 June 1919.

Supplementary information: Son of Samuel and Julia Millar of Wexford. Husband of Mary Josephine Millar of 'Rockfield' Spawell Road, Wexford. Grave or Memorial Reference: IX.F.16. Cemetery: Cologne Southern Cemetery in Germany.

MILLER, James Charles: Rank: Corporal. Regiment or Service: Royal Engineers. Unit: Motor Cyclist Section and 'L' Company, Royal Engineers. Age at death: 23. Date of death: 7 January 1915. Service No: 30247.

Supplementary information: Son of Robert and Catherine Miller of 96 North Main Street. Native of Kilkenny. Grave or Memorial Reference: Div.14. J.I. Cemetery: Ste. Marie Cemetery, Le Havre in France.

MILLER, Joseph: Rank: Private. Regiment or Service: Australian Infantry, A.I.F. Unit: 16th Bn. Date of death: 7 July 1917. Service No: 6297. Born in Armagh, 17 February 1884 also listed a being born in Killinahue, Gorey, Wexford. Enlisted in Black Boy Hill on St Patrick's Day 1916 while living in

Joseph Miller. Courtesy of Richard Miller.

Beverley, West Australia. Next of Kin: wife, Lurline Meroula Miller, 3 Brown Street, Subiaco, West Australia. Age on enlistment: 29 years 1 month. Height: 5 feet 8 inches. Complexion: fresh. Eyes: blue. Hair: brown. Occupation on enlistment: dairy worker and farm hand. Reported missing on 11 April 1917 and later reported as wounded and a prisoner of war. The following is an extract from a statement made by the above named repatriated prisoner (Private Tomley, E.W. 2370, 16th Bn, A.I.F.):

While at St Saulve Private Miller of the 16th Bn was shot by the Germans; he was in a starved condition and broke out of camp to get potatoes from a neighbouring garden. It was on his return to camp that he was shot through the head by a sentry from a distace of a few yards at 11pm.

Another report states:

The English prisoners Battalion, Denain. Prisoner of War, Joseph Miller, 6297, escaped in the night of 6

July 1917 from St Saulve Prison camp and was shot in flight by the sentry because he did not obey the order to halt.

Death occurred consequent on the shot-wound between 12.15 and 12.30am on 7 July 1917. That death occurred consequent on the wound is established by the Judicial inquest. Miller is buried in the local soldiers cemetery". From Private Jury, 2937 "At St Saulve Private Mullins was shot dead by a German sentry. He was climbing a wall after being out of the compound to get food from the French." From Private, Private Kyle, H. B. 2012, 16th Bn 'At Valenciennes, Private Miller, 16th Bn who was in a starving condition attempted to take some potatoes from a field close by and was shot dead by one of the sentries'. From Corporal Rilat. L 1231, 15th Bn, ' On the Lager at this place (St Saulve) 6297 Private Miller, J 16th Bn jumped over a low wall to collect some potatoes (nearly).

He was starving. On entering the lager again he was shot by a sentry. I saw his dead body being removed the next morning by the French'. From Private Giese, 3786. While working behind enemy lines in France I saw Private Miller shot dead by a German sentry while trying to get food'.

The Prisoners of War Directorate certifies the cause of death as 'Shot while attempting to escape'. Grave or Memorial Reference: IV.D.26. Cemetery: Valenciennes (St Roch) Communal Cemetery, Nord in France.

MITTEN, Thomas: Rank: Pte. Regiment or Service: South Lancashire Regiment. Unit:2nd Battalion. Date of death: 2 August 1917. Service No:18027. Enlisted in Maesteg while living in Coolballow, Wexford. Formerly he was with the Manchester Rgiment where his number was 16009. Killed in action. Grave or Memorial Reference: LX.D.15. Cemetery. Poelcapelle British Cemetery in Belgium.

MOLLOY, Patrick Joseph: Rank: Sergeant. Regiment or Service: Australian Infantry, A.I.F. Unit: 24th Bn. Age at death: 23. Date of death: 8 June 1918 also listed as 9 June 1918. Service No: 1550. Awards: Military Medal (A.I.F. routine orders No 16 dated 9 April 1918) and is listed in the Commonwealth Gazette No 175 (173?) dated 7 November 1918:

For conspicuous gallantry and keen initiative near WARNETON on the 13th March, 1918. This N.C.O. was of great assistance to his Officer in accounting for 3 of the enemy who had previously been observed in No Man's Land. He crawled out in company with Lieutenant GRAHAM to secure identifications and discover what had happened to the enemy party. Seeing movement in a shell hole Corporal MOLLOY rushed the place, wrestled with the enemy who was armed with 2 rifles, S. A. A. and bombs and succeeded in capturing him. This cool act of courage in broad daylight, when identifications were urgently required was of great value and set a fine example to his comrades. Corporal MOLLOY as Scout N.C.O. has on many occasions rendered most valuable service to his Battalion.

Notice of Military Medal sent to his

Father Mr John Molloy (Farmer), Askinch, Coolgreaney, Co. Wexford. Occupation on enlistment: labourer. Age on enlistment: 20. Place and date of enlistment: Pyramid Hill, Victoria 3 April 1915. Height: 5 feet, 6½ inches. Weight: 9st 7. Complexion: dark. Hair: black. Eyes: blue. Wounded in the field on 5 May 1917 (gunshot wound to his back) and 21 September 1917 (shell wound to the head) 23 February 1918. Illnesses while in service: dysentry, mumps, orchitis, nephritis and rheumatism. When asked to make a will he declined and signed papers to this effect.

Supplementary information: Born in Garristown, Co. Dublin. Schooled in Swords, Co. Dublin. Son of John and Rachel Molloy of Askinch, Coolgreany, Wexford. Buried by Revd T.A. Campbell attached to the 24th Battalion. A.I.F. Grave or Memorial Reference: VI. G.4. Cemetery: Warloy-Baillon Communal Cemetery Extension in France.

MOLLOY, Valentine: Rank: Petty Officer Stoker. Regiment or Service: Royal Navy. Unit: HMS *Europa I.* Age at death: 35. Date of death: 7 August 1915. Service No: 287306. From a Wexford newspaper article, 'Mrs Valentine Molloy, Saltmills, received information from the Admiralty on Tuesday evening that her husband had been killed in action at the Dardanelles. He was a seaman on board the Battleship Queen Elizabeth.'

Supplementary information: Son of Valentine and Kate Molloy of Grange, Fethard, Co. Wexford. Husband of Annie Molloy of Tintern Saltmills, Co. Wexford. Grave or Memorial Reference: 6. Memorial: Plymouth Naval Memorial UK.

MONAGHAN, Bernard: Rank: Private (Acting Corporal). Regiment or Service: Royal Irish Regiment. Unit: 2nd Bn. Date of death: 24 May 1915. Service No: 4087. Born in St Mary's, Enniscorthy, Co. Wexford. Enlisted in Enniscorthy. Killed in action. From an article in a Wexford newspaper:

Berney Monaghan, a native of Shannon, Enniscorthy, has died as the result of gas poisoning at the front. His parents and relatives were informed of the sad event on Thursday morning. The deceased, who was only a little over 20 years of age, enlisted in the Royal Irish Regiment after the outbreak of the war, and prior to that he had been employed at Mr George Lett's, the Brewery.

Grave or Memorial Reference: III.C.2. Cemetery: Roeselare Communal Cemetery in Belgium.

Thomas Monaghan.

MONAGHAN, Thomas: Rank: Lance Corporal. Regiment or Service: Royal Munster Fusiliers. Unit: 'D' Coy. 6th Bn. Age at death: 28. Date of death: 9 August 1915. Service No: 3186. Born in Taghmon, Co. Wexford. Enlisted in Maesteg, Glamorgan. Killed in action in Gallipoli.

Supplementary information: Son of John and Elizabeth Monaghan of Taghmon, Co. Wexford. From an article in a Wexford Newspaper:

> Four sons with the colours. Taghmon's contribution to the fighting forces is fairly large, and amongst the brave boys at the front are the four sons of Mr and Mrs John Monaghan, of Taghmon … Adam Monaghan who was working in Wales at the outbreak of war, joined the Wiltshire Regiment and is at present on active service.
>
> He was a talented young man and composed poems of happenings in his native district. Since he went to the firing line he wrote an excellent poem entitles "Tommy in the Trenches" which we published in our issue of April 24th. Tommy Monaghan is at present with the Munster Fusiliers at the operation on Gallipoli Peninsula. Though he participated in the landing where the Munsters performed great deeds, and the subsequent engagements, has escaped unscathed. The many friends of the gallant lads will join with us in wishing them a safe return from the war. James Monaghan was engaged at his trade in Manchester when war was declared. He rejoined his regiment, with which he had some years previously served in India. He has been in the thick of the fray since the outbreak of hostilities, but has escaped with a whole skin.
>
> He served his apprenticeship to the tailoring business with Mr L. O'Grady, of High Street, Wexford, and here, as with his comrades in the army, he was exceedingly popular. Henry Monaghan is at present engaged with the very important unit, the Army Service Corps. Prior to joining the colours he was employed by Mr O'Ryan, Tomcoole, and, like his brothers, he was a great favourite.

Grave or Memorial Reference: Panel 185 to 190. Memorial: Helles Memorial in Turkey.

MOORE, James: Rank: Private/ Lance Corporal. Regiment or Service: Royal Irish Regiment. Unit: 5th Bn. Date of death: 17 October 1918. Service No: 10952. Formerly he was with the Royal Irish Rifles where his number was 10370. Born in Bride Street, Wexford. Enlisted in Wexford. Died of wounds. From an article in a Wexford newspaper:

> Brave brothers at the front. The two brave sons of Mrs Moore, Well Lane (Selskar), Wexford, have undergone thrilling experiences in Flanders. They are both serving in the Royal Irish and have participated in many engagements in which the regiment figured conspicuously since the outbreak of the war… Private William Moore Royal Irish Regiment was sent out with the first British Expeditionary Force when war was declared.
>
> His regiment was hurried to the support of the brave Belgians and participated in the memorable struggle at Mons. During the famous strategic retreat many of the gal-

James Moore.

furlough he returned to Flanders and is again in the thick of the fray. Private James Moore, Royal Irish Regiment went on active service at the outbreak of war and, like his brother, took part in the many engagements in the Autumn and Winter seasons in which the Royal Irish won a glorious fame. At the battle of Ypres he was wounded in the right leg, and is at present home in Wexford on furlough recuperating.

From an article in the *People*, 1915:

> Private James Moore, Selskar Street, Wexford, 2nd Battalion, Royal Irish Regiment, is in hospital suffering from a bullet wound in the right leg. Private Moore has been on active service in France since the outbreak of the war.
>
> He has another brother, William, also in the firing line.

See William Moore below. Grave or Memorial Reference: I.B.6. Cemetery: Roisel Communal Cemetery Extension in France.

lant Royal Irish fell, but from the memory of the deeds performed by them on that occasion will not speedily be forgotten. Private William Moore was one of a party in charge of a Lieutenant which held the Germans at bay. Though opposed by overwhelming numbers, they stuck to their post till their task was received. Through force of numbers, they were cut off from the main body and only six men and the Lieutenant remained. They refused to give in, however, and fought till their ammunition agve out, when after a desperate struggle they were captured. They were hurried to a house several miles behind the German lines, but the little band succeeded in overpowering their captors and made good their escape. After enduring many privations the party regained the British lines.

He fought with the remnants of the regiment up to May last, when he was sent home on sick leave. After a brief

MOORE, Matthew: Rank: Private. Regiment or Service: Royal Irish Regiment. Unit: 2nd Bn. Age at death: 32. Date of death: 19 October 1914. Service No: 7555. Born in Bree, Co. Wexford. Enlisted in Wexford while living in Bree. Killed in action.

Supplementary information: Son of Laurence and Annie Moore (*née* Cullen) of Bree, Enniscorthy, Co. Wexford. Husband of Mary Cogley (formerly Moore) of 4 'C' Block, The Barracks, Newbridge, Co. Kildare. Grave or Memorial Reference: Panel 11 and 12. Memorial: Le Touret Memorial in France.

William Moore.

MORGAN, Charles: Rank: Private. Regiment or Service: Household Cavalry and Cavalry of the line including the Yeomanry and Imperial Camel Corps. Unit: 5th Dragoon Guards (Princess Charlotte's Own). Date of death: 24 August 1914. Service No: 6842. Born in York, Birmingham. Enlisted in Middlesborough. Age at death: 20. From an article in the *People*, 1915:

MORAN, John: Rank: Private. Regiment or Service: Royal Irish Fusiliers. Unit: 7th/8th Bn. Formerly he was with the Royal Irish Regiment where his number was 464. Age at death: 43. Date of death: 3 January 1917. Service No: 13718. Born in New Ross, Co. Wexford. Enlisted in Cardiff while living in New Ross. Killed in action.

Supplementary information: Husband of Mary Anne Moran of 7 Windmill Lane, New Ross, Co. Wexford. Grave or Memorial Reference: X.5. Cemetery: Kemmel Chateau Military Cemetery in Belgium.

MOORE, William: Rank: Private. Regiment or Service: Royal Irish Regiment. Unit: 1st Bn. Date of death: 21 November 1916. Service No: 10534. Born in Bride Street, Wexford, Co. Wexford. Enlisted in Wexford while living in Bagenalstown, Co Carlow. Killed in action in Salonika. Age at death: 23.

Supplementary information: Son of Laurence and Anastatia Moore. From an article in the *People*, 1915:

> Private James Moore, Selskar Street, Wexford, 2nd Battalion, Royal Irish Regiment, is in hospital suffering from a bullet wound in the right leg. Private Moore has been on active service in France since the outbreak of the war. He has another brother, William, also in the firing line.

He has no known grave but is listed on the Doiran Memorial in Greece.

> Mrs Morgan, Trinity Place, Wexford, has been notified by the war office that her husband, Private Charles Morgan, Dragoon Guards, was killed in action about the 24th of August, 1914. At that time a report from the Cavalry Office, Canterbury, stated he was missing, but all efforts to trace him in the meantime have been unsuccessful. Private Morgan was a native of Middlesborough, and his widow is a Wexford woman, a daughter of Private John Mernagh, Connaught Rangers now stationed at Kinsala [*sic*]. One of her brothers, Private Joseph Mernagh, belong to the Australian Light horse and is stationed at Liverpool Camp Sydney.

Grave or Memorial Reference: Memorial: La-Ferte-Sous-Jouarre Memorial in France.

MORRIS, Arthur Russell: Rank; Private. Regiment or Service: Princess Patricias Canadian Light Infantry (Eastern Ontario Regiment). Age at death: 22. Date of death: 8 May 1915. Service No: 51344.

Supplementary information: Son of J. R. Russel and Annie F. Morris. Killed in action. From an article in the *Enniscorthy Guardian*:

> He was son of Mr Joseph R Morris, Somerville, Wexford and was only 21 years of age. Having spent 2½ years in Canada, at the outbreak of the war he resigned a good position in the bank there and joined the colours. On the completion of his training in England he left Southampton for France on the 29th of April, and was killed on the 8th of May.

Grave or Memorial Reference: Panel 10. Memorial: Ypres (Menin Gate) Memorial in Belgium.

MORRIS, James: Rank: Private. Regiment or Service: Black Watch (Royal Highlanders). Unit: 1st Bn. Date of death: 25 September 1915. Service No: S/7549. Born in Bartluckin, Co. Wexford. Enlisted in Cowdenbeath, Fifeshire. Killed in action. Grave or Memorial Reference: III.D.17. Cemetery: Dud Corner Cemetery, Loos in France.

MORRIS, Patrick: Rank: Private. Regiment or Service: Royal Dublin Fusiliers. Unit: 1st Bn. Age at death: 21. Date of death: 4 June 1915. Service No: 18057. Born in Wexford, Co. Wexford. Enlisted in Wexford. Killed in action in Gallipoli.

Supplementary information: Son of Patrick and Mary Morris of Alma Park, Wexford. From an article in the *People*:

> Mrs Morris, Hospital Road, Wexford, received a letter on the 10th of July from the Infantry Office, Dublin saying that her husband, Patrick Morris, has been missing since an engagement on the 4th of June with the Mediterranean Expeditionary Force at the Dardanelles. Private Morris volunteered last January and was attached to the 1st Batt, Royal Dublin Fusiliers.

Grave or Memorial Reference: Panel 190 to 196. Memorial: Helles Memorial in Turkey.

MORRISSEY, Thomas: Rank: Saddler. Regiment or Service: Army Service Corps. Unit: Remount Depot. Age at death: 43. Date of death: 12 August 1918. Service No:TS/6823. Born in New Ross, Co. Wexford. Enlisted in New Ross. Died in the Balkans.

Supplementary information: Husband of Mrs M. Morrissey of New Ross, Co. Wexford. Grave or Memorial Reference: 1481. Cemetery: Salonika (Lembet Road) Military Cemetery in Greece.

MUNGAN/MANGAN, Andrew: Rank: Private. Regiment or Service: Middlesex Regiment. Unit: 2nd Bn. Date of death: 1 July 1916 (First day of the battle of the Somme). Service No:

Albert Murphy.

G/1102. Born in Wexford, Co. Wexford. Enlisted in London. Killed in action. Age at death: 21.

Supplementary information: Son of William and Catherine Mangan of 3 Abbey Street, Wexford. He has no known grave but is listed on Pier and Face 12D and 13B on the Thiepval Memorial in France.

MURPHY, Albert: Rank: Private. Regiment or Service: Royal Inniskilling Fusiliers. Unit: 7th Bn. Date of death: 27 April 1916. Service No: 27700. Formerly he was with the Royal Irish Regiment where his number was 9451. Born in Newbridge, Co Kildare. Enlisted in Wexford. Killed in action by gas. Grave or Memorial Reference: I.C.29. Cemetery: Philosophe British Cemetery, Mazingarbe in France.

MURPHY, Alexander: Rank: Private. Regiment or Service: Royal Scots Fusiliers. Unit: 6th/7th Bn. Date of death: 5 April 1917. Service No: 19211. Born Bellettsbridge, Kilkenny. Enlisted in Ardrossan, Ayrshire. Killed in action.

Supplementary information: Son of John and Ellen Murphy of Broadway, Co. Wexford. Grave or Memorial Reference: Bay 5. Memorial: Arras Memorial in France.

MURPHY, Daniel: Rank: Private. Regiment or Service: Middlesex Regiment. Unit: 16th Bn. Age at death: 18. Date of death: 1 July 1916 (First day of the battle of the Somme). Service No: 2911 and P. S. 2911. Born in Wexford, Co. Wexford. Enlisted in London while living in Strand, Middlesex. Killed in action.

Supplementary information: Son of John and Catherine Murphy of Kellystown, Adamstown, Co. Wexford. Grave or Memorial Reference: A.34. Cemetery: Hawthorn Ridge Cemetery No. 1, Auchonvillers in France.

MURPHY, Edward: Rank: Fireman. Regiment or Service: Mercantile Marine. Unit: SS *Laconia* (Liverpool). Torpedoed and sunk by a German Submarine. Age at death: 56. Date of death: 25 February 1917.

Supplementary information: Husband of Catherine Murphy. Born in Wexford. Memorial: Tower Hill Memorial UK.

MURPHY, Edward: Rank: Private. Regiment or Service: Grenadier Guards. Unit: 1st Bn. Age at death: 21. Date of death: 14 March 1915. Service No: 17235. Born in Barnmoney, Co. Wexford.

Enlisted in Cardiff. Killed in action.

Supplementary information: Son of Patrick and Catherine Murphy of Barmoney, Bree, Co. Wexford. Grave or Memorial Reference: Panel 2. Memorial: Le Touret Memorial in France.

MURPHY, Edward: Rank: Private. Regiment or Service: Royal Irish Regiment. Unit: 1st Bn. Age at death: 39. Date of death: 16 March 1915. Service No: 4319. Born in Wexford, Co. Wexford. Enlisted in Wexford. Killed in action.

Supplementary information: Son of Nicholas and Jane Murphy. Husband of Mary Ann Murphy of 3 Well Lane, Wexford. From an article in a Wexford newspaper:

In this column we publish a photograph of Private Edward Murphy, who was killed at St Eloi, while serv-

Edward Murphy.

ing with the Royal Irish Regiment. He had been in the army for a number of years, and had been on active service in India and South Africa. He was a native of Well Lane, Wexford, where his wife and two children at present reside.

Grave or Memorial Reference: Panel 33. Memorial: Ypres (Menin Gate) Memorial in Belgium.

MURPHY, George: Rank: Private. Regiment or Service: Kings Liverpool Regiment. Unit: 11th Bn. Date of death: 20 July 1915. Service No: 12384. Born in Ross, Co. Wexford. Enlisted in Seaforth in Lancashire while living in Waterford. Died of wounds. From an article in the *Echo* 1915, 'New Ross still continues to contribute to the roll of victims claimed in the last year, the latest casualties announced being Private George Murphy, a native of Bewley Street, who had been previously in the army and had been working in Wales before hostilities commenced.' Grave or Memorial Reference: III.B.8A. Cemetery: Lijssenthoek Military Cemetery in Belgium.

MURPHY, Henry Arthur: Rank: Sergeant. Regiment or Service: Royal Irish Regiment. Unit: 5th Bn. Age at death: 35. Date of death: 5 December 1915. Service No: 5266. Born in Halifax in Yorkshire. Enlisted in Wexford. Died in Egypt.

Supplementary information: Son of Bandsmaster Murphy. Husband of Elizabeth Murphy of Bridge Row, Gorey, Co. Wexford. Article from a Wexford newspaper in 1915:

Henry Arthur Murphy.

During the week, Mrs Murphy, of the Park, Wexford, was notified that her husband, who was a Colour Sergeant in the Royal Irish Regiment, had died at a hospital in Alexandria, Egypt. He had been on active service in Gallipoli, but as he was found to be suffering from a heart disease he was removed to Alexandria for treatment.

Colour Sergeant Murphy was son of the late Colour Sergeant James Murphy, who was on the staff of the Wexford Militia for many years. The deceased had 21 years service. Much sympathy is felt for his widow in the loss she has sustained ... Colour Sergeant Harry [*sic*] Murphy of the Royal Irish Regiment, who recently died at a hospital in Alexandria. He had been on active service in Gallipoli, but as he was found to be suffering from a heart disease he was removed for treatment to Alexandria where he succumbed.

The deceased who had 21 years service with the colours, was son of the late Patrick Murphy of Barrack Street, a former bandmaster of the 3rd Batt, Royal Irish Regiment. Much sympathy is felt with his widow who resides at Park, in her sad bereavement.

Grave or Memorial Reference: C.35. Cemetery: Alexandria (Chatby) Military and War Memorial Cemetery in Egypt.

MURPHY, Hugh Patrick: Rank: Fifth Engineer Officer. Regiment or Service: Mercantile Marine. Unit: SS *San Urbano* (London). Age at death: 22. Date of death: 1 May 1917.

Supplementary information: Son of Hugh and Elizabeth Francis Murphy of Beaufield, Enniscorthy, Wexford. Born at Kilcullen. From an article in a Wexford newspaper:

Widespread sympathy is felt with Mr and Mrs Hugh Murphy, Beaufield, Enniscorthy, in the loss they have sustained by the death of their second eldest son Hugo. On Wednesday they were officially informed the vessel on which deceased served as a marine engineer had been torpedoed, and that he, with some others had been lost. The deceased, who was only 22 years of age, served the first years of his engineering apprenticeship at the Star Works, Wexford. He then secured a position with Messrs, Harland and Wolfe, and was employed at their works on the Clyde until October of last year, when he secured a good an appointment as a marine engineer.

A young fellow of frank and engaging manners, the deceased made many friends everywhere he went, and his death under such tragically sad circumstances is sincerely regretted. The greatest sympathy is felt for his bereaved parents, brothers, sisters and other relations. R.I.P.

He has no known grave but is commemorated on the Tower Hill Memorial, UK.

MURPHY, James: Rank: Corporal. Regiment or Service: Royal Engineers. Unit: 2nd Field Coy. Age at death: 35. Date of death: 12 October 1918. Service No: 13988. Born Kiltealy, Co. Wexford. Enlisted in Lixnaw, Co Kerry. Killed in action.

Supplementary information: Son of James and Annie Murphy of New Ross, Co. Wexford. Husband of Ellie Murphy of Kilflynn, Co. Kerry. From an article in the *Enniscorthy Guardian*, June 1915:

Interesting Letter from the Front. Writing home to his parents at New Ross last week from the front, James Murphy of the Royal Engineers, and son of Mr James Murphy, Neville Street, New Ross, gives very interesting details. He has been at the front since the war commenced and has gone through several battles, having miraculous escapes on several occasions. Previous to joining the Royal Engineers he was a prison warder and his great mechanical knowledge quickly attracted the attention of the authorities of his Regiment and he was offered promotion in a comparatively short time. The following is part of his letter -"Dear Parents, Even though many miles from you and on the battlefield, I don't forget you and never will. Distance or circumstance will never make me forget the affection I owe my parents, whose prayers are being offered each day for my welfare along with the prayers of my dear and beloved wife. I write to my dear wife every day to keep her in good spirits, and with a devoted love to her as my wife, and with God's help when the war is over we will all meet again, and I have made up my mind to spend my holidays with ye all, particularly as those holidays shall be the most enjoyable ones of my life, and away from the continuous roaring of weapons and spattering of shells, all of which I may say is second nature to me now. But give me peace, that beautiful peace that should always reign and which would be a blessing-one of the greatest blessings that ever came during our time from Almighty God. I attend Benediction every night since I have been out here, and go to Holy Communion every Sunday.

Conscription is not far off in my opinion, and it is time to pull a lot of the slackers out of their feather beds. I am sure the poor class have well contributed their position, and, dear parents, you can say that you have contributed one son who is in the thick of the fight. Germany will be beaten if it was to take us years to do it, and there shall be no surrender to the Kaiser and his outlaws. I can tell you straight he will get something this month that he has not got since the beginning of the war, and he will get something twice as hot in July and treble as hot in October, or maybe sooner, and before the New Year I am sure peace will shine o'er the earth again, and in my opinion the Kaiser will then be fast on his way back to where he came from. May God send peace soon and dispose of the Kaiser as He wishes. We are not the Kaiser's judge, and it is a good job he is not ours either. As the French man says, he is no bonn (no good)." The writer gives me further interesting passages, and winds up by saying that he is in the best of health, and hopes to meet his parents, wife and child and his brothers and sisters when the war is over.

Grave or Memorial Reference: II.A2. Cemetery: Level Crossing Cemetery, Fampoux in France.

MURPHY, James: Rank: Private. Regiment or Service: Royal Irish Regiment. Unit: 2nd Bn. Date of death: 24 May 1915. Service No: 5491. Born in Enniscorthy and enlisted in Wexford while living in Ballaghkeen, Co. Wexford. Killed in action. He has no known grave but is listed on Panel 33 on the Ypres (Menin Gate) Memorial in Belgium.

MURPHY, James: Rank: Private. Regiment or Service: Irish Guards. Unit: 1st Bn. Age at death: 36. Date of death: 18 May 1915. Service No: 5666. Born Castlebridge, Co. Wexford. Enlisted in Wexford. Killed in action.

Supplementary information: Son of Thomas and Catherine Murphy of Ardcavan, Castlebridge, Wexford. From and article in the *Enniscorthy Guardian*:

An Ardcavan soldier killed. Private S Fitzpatrick, 7th Battalion, 3rd Company, King's Own Highland Light Infantry who is with the British Expeditionary Force, wrote on October 11th as follows to Mrs Murphy, Ardcavan, Wexford, in reference to the death of her son James – "I am sorry to inform you about your son whom I found behind our lines today.

I picked up his pay book, and saw the address of his next of kin in it, so I thought it my duty to let you know about him, if you have not heard before, as I thought you would think he was a prisoner. I will bury him in a quiet spot nearby to-morrow. Accept my sympathy. The late Private Murphy was very popular with his friends and comrades. He took great interest in Gaelic games, particularly hurling. He was an only son and his poor widowed Mother and sisters will feel their loss keenly. That the sod of that quiet spot"– that sod reddened with his own and his comrades blood-may rest lightly o'er his manly bosom, and that his soul may rest in peace, is the wish of his numerous friends who will really miss him.

Grave or Memorial Reference: Panel 4. Memorial: Le Touret Memorial in France.

MURPHY, James Charles: Rank: Private. Regiment or Service: Royal Irish Regiment. Unit: 2nd Bn. Date of death: 4 July 1916. Service No: 10907. Born in Bride Street, Wexford. Enlisted in Wexford while living in Doonooney, Co. Wexford. Killed in action. Grave or Memorial Reference: Pier and Face 3.A. Memorial: Thiepval Memorial in France.

MURPHY, James Edward: Rank: Boy, 1st Class. Regiment or Service: Royal Navy. Unit: HMS *Albion*. Date of death: 25 April 1915. Service No: J/27313. Died of wounds. Age at death, 17.

Supplementary information: Born in Williamstown, Co, Dublin. Son of Patrick and Margaret Murphy, of 28 St Ives Grove, Stanley, Old Swan, Liverpool. From the *People*:

YOUNG LIVERPOOL SAILOR

News has been received by his parents who reside at 28 St Ives Grove, Stanley, Liverpool, of the death of James E. Murphy, only child of Patrick Murphy, Common Quay Street, Wexford, from wounds received in action in the Dardanelles.

He was serving on HMS *Albion*, and was wounded on April 24th dying in Malta Hospital. He was only 17 years of age, and entered the Navy in his 16th year, and is deeply regretted by his family. HMS *Albion* was supporting the allied troops landing at the tip of the peninsula at the Dardanelles at the time James was fatally wounded.

Grave or Memorial Reference: 10. Chatham Memorial. UK.

MURPHY, James Patrick: Rank: Private. Regiment or Service: Royal Irish Regiment. Unit: 2nd Bn. Age at death: 24. Date of death: 7 June 1917. Service No: 11538. Born in Bannow, Co. Wexford. Enlisted in Wexford while living in Bannow. Killed in action.

Supplementary information: Son of James and Annie Murphy of Balloughton, Bannow, Co. Wexford. Grave or Memorial Reference: Panel 33. Memorial: Ypres (Menin Gate) Memorial in Belgium.

MURPHY, John: Rank: Rifleman. Regiment or Service: Royal Dublin

John Murphy.

Fusiliers. Unit: 6th Bn. Date of death: 16 August 1915. Service No: 18445. Born in Rosbercon, Co Kilkenny and enlisted in Seaforth while living in Bootle. Killed in action in Gallipoli. From an article in the *Enniscorthy Guardian*:

Private John Murphy, of Resbercon, New Ross, was killed at the Dardanelles on 16th of August last. He was 31 years of age, and volunteered at Brikinhead where he had a good position with a ship building firm. Sixteen others of the same firm volunteered along with him. He joined the Dublin Fusiliers in February last. He served his time with his uncle Mr Shanahan, ship builder, Rosbercon, before going to England where he married a Wexford lady about four years ago.

He was very popular and held in high esteem by the owners of the firm in which he worked. He wrote several letters to his wife and his parents and sisters, and in the last ones he wrote before going into action he related how he prepared by going to confession and holy Communion, and was not afraid to die. He was a brother in Hants, London, a member of the Army Service Corps.

He has no known grave but is listed on Panel 190 to 196 on the Helles Memorial in Turkey.

MURPHY, John: Rank: Rifleman. Regiment or Service: Royal Irish Rifles. Unit: 2nd Bn. Date of death: 27 October 1914. Service No: 7073. Born in Enniscorthy and enlisted in Gorey, Co. Wexford. Killed in action. Age at death: 36.

Supplementary information: Son of James and Mary Murphy (*née* Buttle). Extract from the war diary:

24 October1914. Neuve Chapelle: The enemy's fire became ... with increasing casualties. The recoil's firing of the field gun in the centre of the front line of trenches broke and went out of action. The field gun in the trenches on the left remained in action.

The enemy commenced a severe bombardment of Neuve Chapelle from the heavy guns at La Basse and from a heavy gun to our left front. The shells from La Basse arriving in series of fours. A ... of ... was fired but chiefly high explosive. Soon after dark a determined attack was made by the enemy in considerable strength but was repulsed with heavy casualties judging by the noise made by German wounded lying in front of the trenches. Some prisoners wounded and unwounded were taken. Our casualties were not heavy.

He has no known grave but is listed on Panels 42 and 43 on the Le Touret Memorial in France.

MURPHY, John: Rank: Lance Corporal. Regiment or Service: Royal Irish Regiment. Unit: 2nd Bn. Age at death: 21. Date of death: 7 August 1917. Service No: 4708. Born in Wexford, Co. Wexford. Enlisted in Wexford. Died of wounds.

Supplementary information: Son of Patrick and Mary Murphy of Wexford. Grave or Memorial Reference: IV.F.5. Cemetery: Brandhoek New Military Cemetery in Belgium.

MURPHY, J.J.: Rank: Air Mechanic 3rd Class. Regiment or Service: Royal Air Force. Unit: Training Depot Station. Age at death: 26. Date of death: 6 February 1919. Service No: 287199.

Supplementary information: Son of John Murphy, of 65 Faythe, Wexford. Grave or Memorial Reference: H.153. Cemetery: Wexford (St Ibars) Cemetery, Wexford.

MURPHY, John J.: Rank: Private. Regiment or Service: The King's (Liverpool Regiment). Age at death: 22. Date of death: 24 June 1921. Service No: 102041.

Supplementary information: Son of John and Julia Murphy of Ballingarry, Gorey, Co. Wexford. Grave or Memorial Reference: 34. RC. 888. Cemetery: St Helen's Cemetery, UK.

MURPHY, John Kilrosh: Rank: Private. Regiment or Service: Leinster Regiment. Unit: 1st Bn. Date of death: 13 March 1915. Service No: 3683. Born in Co. Wexford. Enlisted in Maryborough, Queen's County. Killed in action. Age at death: 20.

Supplementary information: Son of

J.J. Murphy.

Aidan and Mary Murphy. He has no known grave but is listed on Panel 44 on the Ypres (Menin Gate) Memorial in Belgium.

MURPHY, Laurence: Rank: Private. Regiment or Service: Royal Scots Fusiliers. Unit: 2nd Bn. Age at death: 22. Date of death: 4 December 1914. Service No: 9774. Born in Irvine, Ayrshire. Enlisted in Saltcoats, Ayrshire. Died of wounds.

Supplementary information: Son of John and Ellen Murphy of Broadway, Co. Wexford. Native of Ayrshire. Grave or Memorial Reference: IV.C.4. Cemetery: Larch Wood (Railway Cutting) Cemetery in Belgium.

MURPHY, Martin: Rank: Signalman. Regiment or Service: Royal Naval Volunteer Reserve. Unit: HMS *Paxton*. Age at death: 18. Date of death: 20 May 1917. Service No: Bristol Z/1731.

Supplementary information: Son of William and Mary Ellen Murphy of 27 Oldfield Road, Cumberland Basin, Bristol. Native of Wexford. From an article in a Wexford newspaper:

At the Pro-Cathedral Bristol, a special requiem Mass was celebrated by Canon Lee, in the presence of a large congregation for Martin Murphy, a signaller in the Navy who lost his life when his vessel was torpedoed last month. Murphy, who was only 19 years of age, was the only son of Mr and Mrs William Murphy, of 27 Oldfield Road, Hotwells (Late of Wexford), and grandson of Mrs Murphy, 96 Faythe, Wexford. Before joining he served as an alter boy at the Pro-Cathedral and

was a mitre bearer to the Bishop when he Pontificated at the Cathedral.

It was on Whit-Sunday morning that the first news of the youth's death was received, and at the evening service the Bishop of Clifton, after administering the Sacrament of Confirmation, referred to Murphy's death and asked all to remember him in their prayers. Dr Burton also added that he remembered him as a boy who always waited on him and "always turned up smiling".

Grave or Memorial Reference: 25. Memorial: Plymouth Naval Memorial UK.

MURPHY, Matthew: Rank: Fireman. Regiment or Service: Mercantile Marine. Unit: SS *Lusitania* (Liverpool). The *Lusitania* was sunk by German Submarine U-20. Age at death: 58. Date of death: 7 May 1915.

Supplementary information: Son of James and Ellen Murphy. Husband of Margaret Murphy (*née* Donelly) of 19 Southey Street, Marsh Lane, Bootle, Lancs. Born at Wexford. Memorial: Tower Hill Memorial UK.

MURPHY, Matthew: Rank: Private. Regiment or Service: Royal Irish Regiment. Unit: 2nd Bn. Age at death: 20. Date of death: 19 October 1914. Service No: 4068. Born in Rowe Street, Wexford. Enlisted in Wexford. Killed in action.

Supplementary information: Brother of John Murphy of Duke Street, Wexford. From an article in a Wexford newspaper, 'Reported Killed; Matthew Murphy, of Duke Street, Wexford, a Private in the 2nd Battalion, Royal Irish

Regiment, who is missing since the battle of Mons, has been given up as killed, and his sister who resides at High Street, Wexford, has been notified to this effect.' Grave or Memorial Reference: Panel 11 and 12. Memorial: Le Touret Memorial in France.

MURPHY, Michael: Rank: Private. Regiment or Service: Royal Dublin Fusiliers. Unit: 2nd Bn. Age at death: 30. Date of death: 30 December 1914. Service No: 9542. Born in Kilrush, Co. Wexford. Enlisted in Carlow while living in Ryland Road, Bunclody. Killed in action.

Supplementary information: Son of Michael and Bridget Murphy of 2 Ryland Road, Newtownbarry, Co. Wexford. Grave or Memorial Reference: I.C.2. Cemetery: Prowse Point Military Cemetery in Belgium.

MURPHY, Michael: Rank: Private. Regiment or Service: Royal Irish Regiment. Unit: 7th Bn. Date of death: 15 July 1918. Service No: 8751. Born in Ballymurrin, Wexford. Enlisted in Enniscorthy. Died. Grave or Memorial Reference:VII.C.20. Cemetery:Tincourt New British Cemetery in France.

MURPHY, Moses: Rank: Rifleman. Regiment or Service: Royal Irish Rifles. Unit: 2nd Bn. Date of death: 27 January 1916. Service No: 2290. Born in Blackford, Co. Wexford. Enlisted in Wexford. Killed in action.

Supplementary information: Husband of Catherine Murphy of Duke Street, Wexford. Grave or Memorial Reference: I.A.20. Cemetery: Tancrez Farm Cemetery in Belgium.

MURPHY, Myles Joseph: Rank: Private. Regiment or Service: Irish Guards. Unit: 1st Bn. Age at death: 28. Date of death: 23 October 1915. Service No: 5402. Born in Clonegal, Co. Wexford. Enlisted in Dublin, while living in Johnstown, Co. Wexford. Killed in action.

Supplementary information: Son of James and Bridget Murphy of Johnstown. Clonegal, Co. Wexford. From and article in the *Enniscorthy Guardian*:

It was with sad regret the news was heard in Clonegal of the death of Private Myles Murphy, Irish Guards, who was killed in action by a shell on October 23. The gallant young Guardsman had been through several engagements with his company, 1st Irish Guards; of which Lieutenant M. O'Leary, V. C., was Sergeant, and the late Father Gwynne was chaplain. His mother Mrs James Murphy has received many expressions of sympathy in her severe loss, chief amongst them being the deep sympathy of the King and Queen and Lord Kitchener, The Army Service Council, and also Father Knapp, who fortified him with the last rites of the Roman Catholic Church.

Not only was he a member of the National Volunteers, Clonegal, and the local Gaelic Football Club, but also a member of the St Brigid's Fife and Drum Band, Clonegal. He was through the battle of Festubert, Bethune, Givenchy and the bloody battle of Ritcheburg. The gallant young Guardsman sleeps to-day the sleep of the brave in a French Military Cemetery, and may he rest in peace.

Grave or Memorial Reference: I.H.1. Cemetery:Vermelles British Cemetery in France.

Owen Francis Murphy.

MURPHY, O.F.: Rank: Second Engineer. Regiment or Service: Mercantile Marine. Unit: SS *W. M. Barkley* (Belfast). Age at death: 28. Date of death: 12 October 1917. SS *W. M. Barkley* was a Guinness boat and was sunk at 7p.m. by a German Submarine. Five of the crew lost their lives. From a snippet in a Wexford newspaper, 'The late Mr Owen Francis Murphy, Stonebridge Wexford, who lost his life when his ship was torpedoed. The late Mr Murphy was a maritime Engineer, and secured his Chief's ticket a couple of years ago. Much sympathy is felt with his family in Wexford, where he was very popular.'

Supplementary information: Son of Mr Murphy of 105 South Main Street, Wexford. Born at Wexford. Memorial: Tower Hill Memorial UK.

MURPHY, Patrick: Rank: Seaman. Regiment or Service: Royal Naval Reserve. Unit: HMS *Orbita*. Age at death: 25. Date of death: 31 August 1915.

Service No: 4317A.

Supplementary information: Son of James and Kate Murphy of Wexford. Husband of Mary Kate Murphy of Abbey Street, Wexford. Drowned on the East coast of Africa. He had two brothers who also served, see **MURPHY, Thomas.** Serial Number; 9929. Royal Irish Regiment. From an article in the *People*, 1915:

Mrs Murphy, Abbey Street, Wexford, has been notified, that her husband, Patrick Murphy, a seaman on board HMS *Orbita* was drowned on the 31st of August.

No particulars are to hand as to where, or under what circumstances he met his death. Mr Murphy who was a naval reservist, was called up at the beginning of the war. About two months ago he was home on leave, and only a few days prior to the sad announcement, his wife received a letter from him in which he stated he

Patrick Murphy.

was quite well and in a rather hot climate. He was only 21 years of age. The deepest sympathy is felt for his widow and two young children. His brother, Private Murphy (Barrack Street, Wexford) Royal Irish Regiment, was killed in action a short time ago, and another, Private James Murphy is at present serving with the Irish Guards at the front.

Grave or Memorial Reference: 8. Memorial: Plymouth Naval Memorial UK.

MURPHY, Patrick: Rank: Private. Regiment or Service: Royal Irish Regiment. Unit: 2nd Bn. Date of death: 19 October 1914. Service No: 4316. Born in New Ross, Co. Wexford. Enlisted in New Ross while living in Durrow, Queen's County. Killed in action. He has no known grave but is commemorated on Panel 11 and 12. Memorial: Le Touret Memorial in France.

MURPHY, P J.: Rank: Sailor. Regiment or Service: Mercantile Marine. Unit: SS *Hesperian* (Glasgow). Age at death: 30. Date of death: 4 September 1915.

Supplementary information: Born in Wexford. Torpedoed by German Submarine U-20 85 miles south west of Fastnet. Memorial: Tower Hill Memorial UK.

MURPHY, Patrick Joseph: Rank: Private. Regiment or Service: North Staffordshire Regiment. Unit: 7th Bn. Date of death: 20 September 1917. Service No: 47126. Formerly he was

with the Royal Army Service Corps where his number was T4/214989. Born in Castlebridge, Co. Wexford. Enlisted in Woolwich in Kent while living in Bootle in Lancs. Died in Mesopotamia. Grave or Memorial Reference: III.B.5. Cemetery: Basra War Cemetery in Iraq.

MURPHY, Richard: Rank: Private. Regiment or Service: Leinster Regiment. Unit: 2nd Bn. Date of death: 1 September 1916. Service No: 10016. Born in Wexford, Co. Wexford. Enlisted in Wexford. Killed in action. He has no known grave but is commemorated on Pier and Face 16C. Memorial: Thiepval Memorial in France.

MURPHY, Richard: Rank: Private. Regiment or Service: Irish Guards. Unit: 1st Bn. Date of death: 27 September 1918. Service No: 11334. Born in Screen, Co. Wexford. Enlisted in Wexford. Died of wounds. Grave or Memorial Reference: II.B.9. Cemetery: Sanders Keep Military Cemetery, Graincourt-Les-Havrincourt in France.

MURPHY, Stephen: Rank: Bombardier. Regiment or Service: Royal Field Artillery. Unit: 37th Trench Mortar Bty. Date of death: 17 March 1918. Service No: 78142. Born in Liverpool. Enlisted in Liverpool. Died of wounds.

Supplementary information: Husband of Mary Ann Murphy of 3 Abbey Street, Wexford. Grave or Memorial Reference: XXVII.E.E.21. Cemetery: Lijssenthoek Military Cemetery in Belgium.

MURPHY, Thomas: Rank: Private. Regiment or Service: New Zealand

Expeditonary Force. Unit: Auckland Regiment, 1st Battalion. Date of death: between 26/27 March 1918. No: 34403. From an article in the *People* 1918:

RAMSGRANGE MAN KILLED

Thomas Murphy, a native of Ramsgrange, had been killed in action. He joined in New Zealand.

He was most popular in that country where he had a lucrative position, and was made the recipient of a valuable presentation by a number of his friends prior to his departure for Europe. Office and High Mass were held for the repose of his soul at Ramsgrange parish church on Friday, at which there was a good number of priests and a large number of his relatives and friends of the deceased.

Grave or Memorial Reference: He had no known grave but is listed on the Grevillers (New Zealand) Memorial in France.

MURPHY, Thomas: Rank: Private. Regiment or Service: Duke of Wellington's (West Riding Regiment). Unit: 2nd/5th Bn. Age at death: 41. Date of death: 25 August 1918. Service No: 34457. Enlisted in Enniscorthy. Killed in action.

Supplementary information: Son of Martin and Johanna Murphy of Enniscorthy, Co. Wexford. Husband of Margaret Murphy of 5 Cathedral Street, Enniscorthy. From an article in a Wexford newspaper:

ENNISCORTHY SOLDIER KILLED

Deep regret was felt in Enniscorthy when the intimation was received during the week that Thomas Murphy, Cathedral Street, who joined

the Sherwood Foresters in 1916, had been killed in France in the month of August.

The deceased, prior to joining the army, had been sacristan in Cathedral, a position which brought him into intimate relation with the townspeople with all of whom he was deservedly popular. He had also acted for a time as Secretary of the local branch of the A.O.H. His death is deeply regretted, and much sympathy is felt for his wife and six young children. His eldest little boy who is only eleven years is a clever Irish speaker, and spent two weeks in the Ring Irish College this year. R.I.P.

Grave or Memorial Reference: IV.A.7. Cemetery: Douchy-Les-Ayette British Cemetery in France.

MURPHY, Thomas: Rank: Private. Regiment or Service: Royal Dublin Fusiliers. Unit: 2nd Bn. Age at death: 28. Date of death: 1 July 1916. Service No: 19545. Born in Ballidaggan, Co. Wexford. Enlisted in Wexford while living in Kitealy, Co. Wexford.

Supplementary information: Brother of James Murphy of Cloroguemore, Kiltealy, Enniscorthy, Co. Wexford. Grave or Memorial Reference: Plot 1. Row G. Grave 18. Cemetery: Bertrancourt Military Cemetery in France.

MURPHY (Alias)**, Thomas:** (Correct name is **CULLEN, Thomas**): Rank: Private. Regiment or Service: Royal Irish Regiment. Unit: 6th Bn. Age at death: 25. Date of death: 6 June 1916. Service No: 8926. Born in Enniscorthy and enlisted in London while living in Enniscorthy.

Supplementary information: Killed in

action. Son of Robert and Mary Cullen of 20 Irish Street, Enniscorthy, Co. Wexford. Grave or Memorial Reference: I.J.20. Cemetery: Dud Corner Cemetery, Loos in France.

MURPHY, Thomas: Rank: Private. Regiment or Service: Royal Dublin Fusiliers. Unit: 1st Bn. Date of death: 7 August 1915. Service No: 19233. Born in Wexford, Co. Wexford. Enlisted in Maryhill while living in Wexford. Killed in action in Gallipoli. Grave or Memorial Reference: VII.F.10. Cemetery: Twelve Tree Copse Cemetery in Turkey.

MURPHY, Thomas: Rank: Private. Regiment or Service: Royal Irish Regiment. Unit: 1st Bn. Date of death; 3 May 1915. Serial Number; 9929. Born in Bridge Street, Wexford. Enlisted in Wexford. Killed in action in the batlle of St Julien. He was aged twenty-three years and was known as one of the best boxers in the army. A chum who was close to him when he was knocked over writing to a friend in Wexford said, 'He died as he lived, game to the last.' Son of James Murphy, Barrack Street, Wexford. From an article in the *Enniscorthy Guardian*:

WEXFORD SOLDIER KILLED.
Private Thomas Murphy, Barrack Street, Wexford, 1st Battalion, Royal Irish Regiment, was killed at St Julien on May 3rd. Lord Kitchener wrote to his parents conveying the sympathy of the King and Queen on the death of Private Murphy, who has a brother in the army and another in the navy. His brother Patrick Murphy drowned off the East coast of Africa with the

Thomas Murphy.

British Navy serving on boards the 'Orbita'.

From an article in the *People*, 1915:

Mrs Murphy, Abbey Street, Wexford, has been notified, that her husband, Patrick Murphy, a seaman on board HMS 'Orbita' was drowned on the 31st of August. No particulars are to hand as to where, or under what circumstances he met his death. Mr Murphy who was a naval reservist, was called up at the beginning of the war. About two months ago he was home on leave, and only a few days prior to the sad announcement, his wife received a letter from him in which he stated he was quite well and in a rather hot climate.

He was only 21 years of age. The deepest sympathy is felt for his widow and two young children. His brother,

Private Murphy (Barrack Street, Wexford) Royal Irish Regiment, was killed in action a short time ago, and another, Private James Murphy is at present serving with the Irish Guards at the front.

He has no known grave but is commemorated on Panel 33. Memorial: Ypres (Menin Gate) Memorial in Belgium.

MURPHY, Thomas: Rank: Private. Regiment or Service: Welsh Regiment. Unit: 1/6th Bn. Date of death: 1 May 1915. Service No: 1800. Born in Bannow, Co. Wexford. Enlisted in Clydach, Glam. Killed in action. From an article in the *Echo*, 1915:

> During the week a labourer named Michael Murphy, residing in a labourers cottage at Danescastle, Carrig-on-Bannow received intelligence from the War Office that his son Thomas Murphy had been killed 'somewhere in France'. Young Murphy who was a fine type of manhood, joined the army in Wales where he had been working previous to the outbreak of the war.

He has no known grave but is listed on Panel 77 and 78 on the Loos Memorial in France.

MURPHY, W.: Rank: Sapper. Regiment or Service: Royal Engineers. Date of death: 25 March 1920. Service No: 94684. Age at death: 26. Grave or Memorial Reference: C. 217. Cemetery, Enniscorthy New Catholic Cemetery, Wexford.

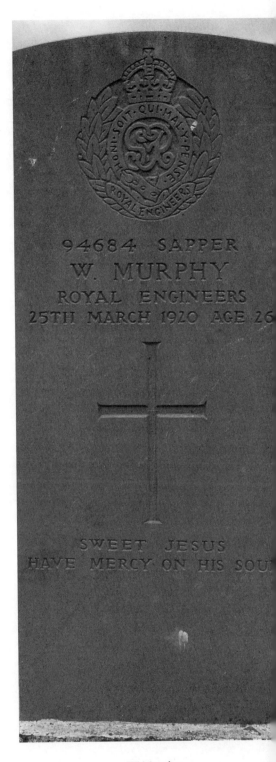

W. Murphy.

Cecil William Murray.

MURRAY, Cecil William: Rank: Private. Regiment or Service: Royal Dublin Fusiliers. Unit: 7th Bn. Date of death: 16 August 1915. Service No: 14125. Born in Bannow (also listed as Bannon), Co. Wexford. Killed in action in Gallipoli. Privately educated at Rosse College, Dublin. Occupation on enlistment; Clerk, Bank of Ireland, Dublin. Son of Revd W.D. Murray. He has no known grave but is listed on Panel 190 to 196 on the Helles Memorial in Turkey.

MURPHY, William John: Rank: Guardsman. Regiment or Service: Scots Guards. Date of death: 26 October 1914. Service No: 9213. Born in Ballyought, Wexford. Enlisted in Maryburgh, Aberdeen while living in Mount Wilson, Edenderry. Killed in action. Brother of Mrs Mary Walsh of Mount Wilson, Edenderry, King's Co. Age at death: 38. Grave or Memorial Reference: Has no known grave but is commemorated on Panel 11. Memorial: Ypres (Menin Gate) Memorial in Belgium.

MYLES, Peter: Rank: Stoker 1st Class. Regiment or Service: Royal Navy. Unit: HMS *Genista*. Age at death: 31. Date of death: 23 October 1916. Service No: K/27782. Flower Class Sloop was torpedoed in the North Sea by German Submarine U-57.

Supplementary information: Son of Peter and Margaret Myles of Mary Street, New Ross, Co. Wexford. Grave or Memorial Reference: 19. Memorial: Portsmouth Naval Memorial UK.

N

NEILL, Henry: Rank: Sergeant. Regiment or Service: Royal Irish Regiment. Unit: 2nd Bn. Date of death: 29 October 1914. Service No: 6369. Born in Enniscorthy and enlisted in Waterford while living in Enniscorthy, Co. Wexford. Died. From an article in the *Enniscorthy Guardian*, 1915:

> On Monday Mrs Neill, Island Road, Enniscorthy, received official information of the death of her son, Henry Neill, a corporal in the Royal Irish Regiment who was killed in action last November. Mrs Neill had five sons serving in the army and navy, three in the army and two in the navy. One of the navy men was accidentally drowned whilst going aboard his ship last autumn, and the other, William Neill, gunner on 'The Lion' was home a few weeks ago. Her two remaining sons in the army are still well and hearty.

Grave or Memorial Reference: A.7. Cemetery: Sainghin-En-Weppes Communal Cemetery in France.

NEILL, James: Rank: Private. Regiment or Service: Royal Dublin Fusiliers. Unit: 2nd Bn. Formerly he was with the Royal Irish Regiment where his number was 5307. Date of death: 16 August 1917. Service No: 43039. Born in Enniscorthy and enlisted in Gorey while living in Carrickduff, Co. Wexford. Killed in action. He has no known grave but is commemorated on Panel 154 to 144 and 145. Memorial: Tyne Cot Memorial in Belgium.

NEILL, John Henry: Rank: Able Seaman. Regiment or Service: Royal Navy. Unit: (RFR/DEV/B/5497), HMS *Severn*. Age at death: 35. Date of death: 6 December 1914. Service No: 210584.

Supplementary information: Son of John Henry and Mary Grace Neill of Abbeyleix, Queen's Co. Native of Enniscorthy, Co. Wexford. Grave or Memorial Reference: 2. Memorial: Plymouth Naval Memorial UK.

NEILL, Michael: Rank: Private. Regiment or Service: Irish Guards. Unit: 1st Bn. Age at death: 19. Date of death: 1 February 1915. Service No: 4802. Born in Wexford, Co. Wexford. Enlisted in Wexford in June 1914. Killed in action. From an article in the *Enniscorthy Guardian*:

> Private Michael Neill, of the Irish Guards, was killed in action on the 6th Inst. He was a son of Mr Michael Neill, Hill Street, Wexford, and had only enlisted in June last.
>
> Prior to his joining the army he was for some years connected with

Micheal Neill.

the printing business in Wexford. He was only 19 years of age. The sad news reached his parents early this week in a letter from his Uncle, Private Joseph Healy, of the Irish Guards, who stated that a detachment of the Regiment was after retaking trenches, and when proceeding further across a field the enemy opened fire with fatal results to young Neill. Much sympathy is felt for his parents and family.

Supplementary information: Son of Michael and Hannah Neill of 30 Hill Street, Wexford. Grave or Memorial Reference: Panel 4. Memorial: Le Touret Memorial in France.

NEILL, Patrick: Rank: Private, Lance Corporal. Regiment or Service: Royal Irish Regiment. Unit: 2nd Bn. Date of death: 16 March 1915. Service No: 8691. Born in St Mary's, New Ross, Co. Wexford. Enlisted in Clonmel, Co Tipperary. Killed in action. From an article in the *Enniscorthy Guardian*:

Patrick O'Neill, a native of New Ross, was killed at the front recently.

He had been brought up in the workhouse and some years ago he was assistant baker there and joined the army. Having served some years in India he returned to Liverpool where he had been until the outbreak of the war. He went through the battle of Mons and in a subsequent engagement got wounded. Shortly after leaving ... went to the firing line again and was killed.

Grave or Memorial Reference: Panel 33. Memorial: Ypres (Menin Gate) Memorial in Belgium.

NEVILLE, Martin: Rank: Private (Lance Corporal). Regiment or Service: Royal Irish Regiment. Unit: 7th Bn (South Irish Horse). Date of death: 21 March 1918. Service No: 11537. Born in Bannow, Co. Wexford. Enlisted in Wexford while living in Bannow. Died. Grave or Memorial Reference: Has no known grave but is commemorated on Panel 30 and 31. Memorial: Pozieres Memorial in France.

NEWSOM, W.: Rank: Lance Corporal. Regiment or Service: 13th Hussars. Age at death: 22. Date of death: 24 January 1920. Service No: 80213.

Supplementary information: Son of James and Bridget Newsom of 7 John Street, Enniscorthy, Co. Wexford. Grave or Memorial Reference: R. 362. Cemetery: Aldershot Military Cemetery UK.

NOCTOR, James: Rank: Private. Regiment or Service: Royal Dublin Fusiliers. Unit: 6th Bn. Date of death: 8 October 1918. Service No: 25284. Born in Monamolin, Co. Wexford. Enlisted in Enniscorthy, Co. Wexford while living in Ferns, Co. Wexford. Killed in action. Grave or Memorial Reference: III.C.17. Cemetery: Prospect Hill Cemetery, Gouy in France.

NOLAN, Aiden: Rank: Private. Regiment or Service: Connaught Rangers. Unit: 2nd Bn. Date of death: 13 January 1919. Service No: 9454. Born in Enniscorthy and enlisted in Enniscorthy while living in Enniscorthy, Co. Wexford. Died at home. Age at death: 30. Grave or Memorial Reference: C240. Cemetery: Enniscorthy New Catholic Cemetery.

NOLAN, James: Rank: Corporal. Regiment or Service: Royal Munster Fusiliers. Unit: 1st Bn. Formerly he was with the Royal Dublin Fusiliers where his number was 21659. Date of death: 28 September 1918. Service No: 1026 and G/1026. Born in St Mary's, Wexford. Enlisted in New Ross, Co. Wexford while living in New Ross. Killed in action.

Supplementary information: Son of William Nolan of Irish Town, New Ross, Co. Wexford. Grave or Memorial Reference: D.2. Cemetery: Cantaing British Cemetery in France.

NOLAN, James: Rank: Corporal. Regiment or Service: Machine Gun Corps (Infantry). Unit: 21st Coy. Age at death: 23. Date of death: 24 March 1918. Service No: 8225. Formerly he was with the Royal Irish Regiment where his number was 5161. He won the Military Medal and is listed in the *London Gazette*. Enlisted in Gorey while living in Ballycanew. Killed in action.

Supplementary information: Son of James and Margaret Nolan of Ballinamona, Ballycanew, Co. Wexford. Grave or Memorial Reference: Panel 90 to 93. Memorial: Pozieres Memorial in France.

NOLAN, John: Rank: Private. Regiment or Service: Leinster Regiment. Unit: 7th Bn. Date of death: 18 April 1916. Service No: 3552 Born in Enniscorthy and enlisted in Ballinasloe while living in Enniscorthy, Co. Wexford. Died of wounds. Grave or Memorial Reference: III.H.6. Cemetery: Bethune Town Cemetery in France.

NOLAN, Joseph Patrick: Rank: Private. Regiment or Service: New Zealand Expeditionary Force, Canterbury Regiment. Date of death: 7 June 1915. Service No: 6/1670. From an article in a Wexford newspaper:

WEXFORD SOLDIER KILLED.

News has been received of the death of Private Patrick Nolan, only son of the late Patrick Nolan and Mrs Nolan, 3 Clifford Street, Wexford. Many years ago Private Nolan adopted the career of a sailor, but finally settled in New Zealand. He married there, his wife being a native of Scotland.

At the outbreak of the war he volunteered and was sent to the Dardanelles with the New Zealand Forces. He was brought down by a sniper on the 22nd [*sic*] June last. The Deceased, who was 35 years of age, leaves his wife and daughter to mourn his loss. He was brother of Mrs Patrick Sinnott, Bellefield, Enniscorthy, and of Mrs Dora Breen, 3 Clifford Street, Wexford.

Grave or Memorial Reference: III.A.1. Cemetery: Shrapnel Valley Cemetery in Turkey.

NOLAN, Michael: Rank: Private. Regiment or Service: Royal Fusiliers. Unit: 3rd Bn. Date of death: 17 July 1917. Service No: 16565. This man does not appear in 'Ireland's Memorial Records' or in 'Soldiers died in the Great War'. Grave or Memorial Reference: D.18. Cemetery: Wexford (St Ibars) Cemetery, thirteen miles from Wexford Town, close to the north bank of the Slaney river.

Aiden Nolan.

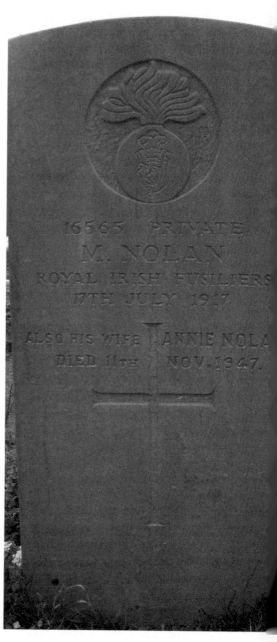

Michael Nolan.

NOLAN, Michael: Rank: Private. Regiment or Service: Connaught Rangers. Unit: 5th Bn. Date of death: 8 October 1918. Service No: 15218. Formerly he was with the Leinster Regiment where his number was 684. Born in Newtownbarry, Co. Wexford. Enlisted in Tullamore, King's County while living in Enniscorthy. Killed in action. From an article in a Wexford newspaper:

> The death, which occurred on active service, of Private Michael Nolan, aged 38 years, late of the Ross road, Enniscorthy, and son of the late Matthew and Bridget Nolan, formerly of Island road, has been announced. The deceased had a distinguished military record. He joined the army in the first year of the war, was at the landing at the Dardanelles, and fought in Serbia in 1915, as well as in Salonika, Palestine and Jerusalem. He then obtained a short leave, and, returning to France, took part in the last big advance in the Autumn, when he met his death.
>
> His brother, Private John Nolan, was also killed in France; his brother Aiden was taken a prisoner of war, and his brother Patrick won the military medal for bravery in the field, this distinction being conferred on him last January in Wexford. The greatest sympathy is felt for the deceased's sorrowing wife and three children, three sisters and other relatives.

Grave or Memorial Reference: A.20. Cemetery: Serain Communal Cemetery Extension in France.

NOLAN, Patrick: Rank: Private. Regiment or Service: Royal Irish Regiment. Unit: 2nd Bn. Age at death: 24. Date of death: 21 August 1918. Service No: 4806. Born in Enniscorthy and enlisted in Clonmel, Co. Tipperary while living in Enniscorthy, Co. Wexford. Killed in action.

Supplementary information: Son of Patrick and Bridget Nolan of 5 Mernagh Street, Enniscorthy, Co. Wexford. Grave or Memorial Reference: Panel 5. Memorial: Vis-En-Artois Memorial in France.

NOLAN, Patrick: Rank: Sergeant. Regiment or Service: Royal Irish Regiment. Unit: 2nd Bn. Age at death: 34. Date of death: 28 October 1917. Service No: 182. Born in New Ross in Wexford and enlisted in Leith while living in Carrick-on-Suir. Died.

Supplementary information: Brother of Margaret Hanlon of Upper Bally Richard Road, Carrick-on-Suir, Co. Tipperary. Grave or Memorial Reference: VIII.I.86. Cemetery: Boulogne Eastern Cemetery in France.

NOLAN, Patrick: Rank: Private. Regiment or Service: Royal Irish Fusiliers. Unit: 5th Bn. Formerly he was with the Royal Irish Regiment where his number was 1846. Date of death: 8 December 1915. Service No: 16489. Born in Wexford, Co. Wexford. Enlisted in Wexford. Died of wounds in Salonika. From an article in the *Enniscorthy Guardian* and the *People*, 1915:

> Another young Wexfordman, Private Patrick Nolan, Back Street, belonging to the Royal Dublin Fusiliers, was fatally wounded in action and died on the field in the Balkan Peninsula. He

volunteered for service about fourteen months ago and was in action for some months past. He leaves a widow to mourn his loss.

Another article went:

Last week Mrs Nolan, of Back Street, was notified by the War Office that her husband Patrick, who was a private in the Royal Dublin Fusiliers, had died from wounds received in action whilst serving in the Balkans. He volunteered for service about fourteen months ago. Much sympathy is felt for his widow in the loss she has incurred.

He has no known grave but is listed on the Doiran Memorial in Greece.

NOLAN, Richard: Rank: Private. Regiment or Service: Royal Irish Regiment. Unit: 2nd Bn. Date of death: 19 October 1914. Service No: 5406. Born in Gorey, Co. Wexford. Enlisted in Wexford while living in Gorey. Killed in action. He has no known grave but is listed on Panels 23 and 24 on the Le Touret Memorial in France.

NORRIS, Stanley Jephta: Rank: Lance Corporal. Regiment or Service: Duke of Cornwalls Light Infantry. Unit: 1st Bn. Date of death: 23 July 1916. Service No: 8606. Born in Wexford, Co. Wexford. Enlisted in Callington in Cornwall. Killed in action. He has no known grave but is listed on Pier and Face 6B on the Thiepval Memorial in France.

NORRIS, Thomas: Rank: Private. Regiment or Service: Irish Guards. Unit: 1st Bn. Age at death: 23. Date of death: 6 December 1914. Service No: 3647. Born in Newtownbarry, Co Kilkenny. Enlisted in Dublin. Killed in action.

Supplementary information: Son of William and Anne Norris of Kilbranish, Newtownbarry, Co. Wexford. Grave or Memorial Reference: Panel 11. Memorial: Ypres (Menin Gate) Memorial in Belgium.

NUNN, John Henry: Rank: Major. Regiment or Service: Royal Field Artillery. Unit: 'A' Bty. 149th Bde. Age at death: 32. Date of death: 1 April 1917. Died of wounds.

Supplementary information: Son of J.L. Nunn of Alma, Wexford. Husband of Doris Nunn (*née* Gregory) of 3 Ravensbourne Gardens, Ealing, London. From an article in the *Enniscorthy Guardian*:

Distinguished Wexford Officer Killed at the front; Much regret was expressed in Wexford town and county when the sad news was wired on Tuesday that Major J.H. Nunn, late of the Royal Field Artillery, was killed in action. Major Nunn was a sodier by profession, like many of his relatives.

Ten years ago he joined the Royal Field Artillery. His service was of a most distinguished character at home and on the field, as a result of which his promotion was rapid, and last year he was promoted Major at the early age of 30 years. It is very rarely that an officer reaches his majority at such an early age, and his promotion to that high rank when he was so young is the best testimony of his work as a gallant soldier. The last time he was home he never looked better, nor never felt in better spirits, and spoke cheerily of the ultimate and immediate success of the Allied flags. He was a great sportsman, a good shot, and rode well to hounds. His death is all the more sad since only two years ago he married Miss Gregory, whom he met in India, whilst he was serving with the colours there. Hi father, Mr. J. L. Nunn, belongs to one of the oldest families in the county, and is himself one of the most respected men in the county.

Items from an article in a Wexford newspaper:

Captain John Nunn is another son of Mr Joshua L. Nunn, serving with the colours.

At an early age Capt, Nunn entered the army and adopted for his profession the noble one of arms. By his ability he earned rapid promotion in that difficult branch of the Service the Royal Horse Artillery, with which he has been on active service since shortly after the outbreak of war.

Another article:

Our readers will be glad to know that Capt, John Nunn, son of Mr and Mrs J.L. Nunn, of Alma, Wexford, who has been at the front since the war started, has greatly distinguished himself. He was one of the first regiments drafted to the fighting line. He has been promoted and put in charge of a battery, and has been ordered back to England to train specially a battery there. He has been in the very midst of the fighting, he never sustained a scar. His brother, Lieutenant Dick Nunn, of the King's Own Royal Lancashire Regiment, has also done right well although he is only 19 years of age.

Like his elder brother he has been in the thick of the fight from the start. He has not escaped as well as Capt, John, for he was gassed in the last big engagement, but he was not one of the worst; on the contrary, we are glad to know he escaped pretty well and is on the high road to recovery. The Nunn's belong to one of the oldest and most distinguished families in County Wexford. They have always had a representative with the fighting forces for many centuries. We congratulate the two distinguished soldiers for their gallantry and success.

Grave or Memorial Reference: V.G.4. Cemetery: Warlincourt Halte British Cemetery, Saulty in France.

O

OAKES, William: Rank: Private. Regiment or Service: Manchester Regiment. Unit: 11th Bn. Date of death: 8 November 1915. Service No: 24083. Born in Wexford, Co. Wexford. Enlisted in Manchester. Died in Malta. Grave or Memorial Reference: E. EA. A. 669. Cemetery: Addolorata Cemetery in Malta.

O'BRIEN, Arthur: Rank: Sergeant and Acting Sergeant. Regiment or Service: Royal Munster Fusiliers. Unit: 'C' Coy. 8th Bn. Formerly he was with the Royal Irish Regiment where his number was 1820. Age at death: 29. Date of death: 4 September 1916. Service No: 4172. Born in Wexford, Co. Wexford. Enlisted in Wexford. Died of wounds.

Supplementary information: Husband of Mrs A. O'Brien of 8 Upper Bride Street, Wexford. From an article in a Wexford newspaper:

> The news of the death of Sgt Arthur O'Brien, son of Mr Patrick O'Brien of John Street, Wexford, was received in town on Tuesday last and gave rise to feelings of deep regret. The popular young soldier volunteered for active service shortly after the outbreak of war, and, joining the Royal Munster Fusiliers, was speedily promoted to the rank of Sergeant. For a lengthy period he was in the firing line and took part in many big engagements. During the recent big offensive in France, Sergeant O'Brien was mortally wounded and succumbed shortly afterwards.
>
> The deceased, who is a son-in-law

of Mr Thos O'Brien, T.C., P.L.G., Wexford, leaves a widow and three young children to mourn his loss, and with them and the other members of his family much sympathy is felt.

From an article in the *People*, 1916:

> Official information has been received on Tuesday morning of he death of Sergeant Arthur O'Brien, son of Mr Patrick O'Brien, John Street. He belonged to the Royal Munster Fusiliers, which regiment he joined shortly after the outbreak of the war and his death is due to serious wounds received in a recent engagement in France.
>
> Sergt O'Brien was well and popularly known amongst a large circle of friends in Wexford, and his death is deeply regretted. He leaves a widow and three young children to mourn their loss. He was a son in law of Mr Thomas O'Brien, T. C.

Grave or Memorial Reference: Plot 2. Row B. Grave 6. Cemetery: Corbie Communal Cemetery Extension in France.

O'BRIEN, John: Rank: Sergeant. Regiment or Service: Royal Irish Regiment. Unit: 3rd Bn. Date of death: 25 March 1915. Service No: 5739. Born in Wexford, Co. Wexford. Enlisted in Clonmel. Died at home. Age at death: 42.

Supplementary information: Husband of M. O'Brien of 5 Davis Road, Clonmel.

From an article in a Wexford newspaper:

> During the week the wife of John Brien [sic], Drumgoold, Enniscorthy, received word from the War Office Authorities in France that her husband had died in an hospital there as the result of wounds received some weeks ago. The deceased belonged to the Royal Irish and was called up at the outbreak of the war. He was sent to France in October, where he was wounded and invalided home, but as soon as he had recovered he was again sent to the firing line.

Grave or Memorial Reference: 4.D.128. Cemetery: Cemetery, Clonmel, St Patricks Cemetery, Co Tipperary.

O'BRIEN, Patrick: Rank: Private. Regiment or Service: Royal Irish Regiment. Unit: Depot. Age at death: 32. Date of death: 8 August 1916. Service No: 8093. From an article in a Wexford newspaper:

> ENNISCORTHY SOLDIERS DEATH
> Private P. O'Brien, who died at home, Patrick Street, Enniscorthy, was accorded the honours of a military funeral, a party of the Connaught Rangers stationed in town walking behind the remains with arms reversed, under the command of Lieut. Knox.
> The deceased who belonged to the Royal Irish Regiment, was present at the battle of Mons. He was taken prisoner and spent almost twenty months in the German camps. There his health became delicate, and about six weeks ago he arrived home with a batch of exchanged prisoners. He was present on the occasion when the Late Roger Casement visited the Irish prisoners

> in Germany abd addressed them on the desirability of forming themselves into an Irish Brigade for the purpose of fighting England.

Grave or Memorial Reference: C. 561. Cemetery, Enniscorthy New Catholic Cemetery, Co. Wexford.

O'BRIEN, Peter: Rank: Greaser. Regiment or Service: Mercantile Marine. Unit: SS *Arabic* (Liverpool). Age at death: 61. Date of death: 19 August 1915

Supplementary information: Son of the late John and Mary O'Brien. Husband of Johanna O'Brien (*née* Sheehan) of 5 Athol Terrace, Athol Street, Liverpool. Born in Co. Wexford. Torpedoed and sunk by German Submarine U-24 just of the Old Head of Kinsale. From an article in the *People* newspaper:

> Wexfordman saves child's life. Cargo Boat sunk, Wexfordman Killed. Mr Michael Murphy, Francis Street, Wexford, who was a Steward on the ill-fated Liner was fortunately saved. Early on Friday morning his sister received a wire from Queenstown stating that her brother was saved, but no communication was received from himself until Saturday evening when he wired from Liverpool stating that he had been saved after a terrible struggle. It seems that Mr Murphy, who is very popular in his native town, is suffering from chill and shock as a result of his terrible experience. His children who are still mourning for their mother who died but a few months ago were staying in Wexford last week and they set out for Liverpool on Saturday Morning where they arrived quite safely. One of them writing to their Aunt, Miss Murphy, on

8093 PRIVATE
P. O BRIEN
ROYAL IRISH REGIMENT
8TH AUGUST 1916 AGE 32

Patrick
O'Brien.

Monday, stated that her father was quite prostrated and was suffering from chill and shock. He was in the water for two hours and managed to save the life of a little child.

He will never forget the frightful experience he had as long as he lives. Mr Patrick McCormick, R. N. R., who is serving at Queenstown on HMS Colleen writing to his mother, Mrs Annie McCormick on Friday last said "We had a terrible night all last Thursday night carrying the wounded and survivors of the SS *Arabic* to hospital. Mr Mike Murphy, who was formerly at Godkins was one of those saved."

Memorial: Tower Hill Memorial UK.

O'BRIEN, Thomas: Rank: Private. Regiment or Service: Royal Welsh Fusiliers. Unit: 9th Bn. Date of death: 8 November 1915. Service No: 13264. Born in Kilmurrybricam, Co Clare. Enlisted in Tonypandy while living in

Thomas O'Brien.

Shandrum. Killed in action. From an article in a Wexford newspaper:

Wexford Soldier Killed; It has been officially announced that Private Thomas O'Brien, of the Welsh Fusiliers, a brother of Mr James O'Brien, merchant, South Main Street, Wexford, has been killed in action in France. He resided in Wales for some years and joined the colours after the outbreak of war. Much sympathy is felt with his relatives.

Grave or Memorial Reference: Panel 50 to 52. Memorial: Loos Memorial in France.

O'CALLAGHAN, James: Rank: Second Lieutenant. Regiment or Service: Cheshire Regiment. Unit: 13th Bn. Age at death: 25. Date of death: 21 October 1916. Killed in action.

Supplementary information: Son of Mrs. O'Callaghan (*née* O'Connor) of 'Rochford', Edermine, Enniscorthy, Co. Wexford. From an article in a Wexford newspaper:

As we go to press we learn with regret of the death of Lieut, James O'Callaghan, of the 13th Cheshire Regiment. The painful news of the death of this popular young officer was received on Thursday night by his uncle, Mr M.J. O'Connor, Solicitor, Wexford, in the form of a wire from the Secretery of War, as follows: "Deeply regret to inform you that Lieut James O'Callaghan, of the 13th Cheshire Regiment was killed in action on October 21st. The Army Council express their deep sympathy." The circumstance under which Lieut,

James O'Callaghan.

O'Callaghan met his untimely end have not yet reached us, but all who had the pleasure of his aquaintance are very sure that the gallant young officer met his death with that same bravery and fearlessness that character-ised his whole life. For though Lieut, O'Callaghan was but 26 years of age, he had crowded into his brief career more stirring exploits and exciting experiences than usually fall to the lot of those of far more mature years.

His love of the strenuous life is not to be wondered at, seeing that he came from a fighting race, one of his ances-tors being second in command during the rebellion of famed '98. In 1906, when the Zulu race rebelled, though he was only a lad of sixteen years of age, Mr O'Callaghan volunteered for active service, and took part in that great campaign. When the revolt was subdued he returned to his home in Johannesburg, but soon after joined the British Navy from pure love of adventure, and whilst serving on board HMS *Arrogance* was congratulated by Prince Louis of Battenberg on being the only man in the Navy wearing the Zulu rebellion medal. Having served his term, Mr O'Callaghan again

returned to Johannesberg and took up a lucrative position in the Municipal Council Offices in that city. When war was declared in August, 1914, and the appeal for men resounded through the Empire, amongst the sons of South Africa who quickly answered the call to arms was Lieut, O'Callaghan.

Having volunteered for active serv-ice it was only natural that he should elect to serve in a Regiment in the raising of which a fellow country-man played a conspicuous part -The South African Irish Horse. When that Regiment was attached to the infantry, Mr O'Callaghan, who pre-ferred the cavalry, was transferred at his own request to the 1st Imperial Light Horse. He joined the Regiment at Johannesberg, and from Prisca to Groofontein, a distance of 2,000 miles, was in the thick of the fray. When the campaign was ended and the forces demobilised, Mr O'Callaghan decided to do his share in driving the Germans back across the Rhine, and came to this country and volunteered for service in France. His services were accepted by the War Office, and he was immediately granted a commis-sion and Gazetted to the Cheshires. He was soon in France where he was allotted the perilous task of officer in charge of a bombing squadron, which was popularly known in the Army as the 'Suicide Club', and as such became conspicuous on many occasions.

As he had had ample opportu-nity during the sixteen years he spent with the different fighting forces of the Empire of studying the art of war both in theory and practice, he realised the dangers that beset the path of the bomb thrower. As those engaged in that arduous work have to approach within very close range of the enemy trenches, when after an assault at night they were exposed to the fire of the enemy, he endeavoured to lessen the dangers with which his men were surrounded, and in this he was successful. With remarkable ingenuity he hit on the plan of having the faces of his men blackened preparatory to an attack, and, the bombing raid accomplished, he instructed them to lie flat amongst the dead, and in this manner they escaped the terrific fusillade to which they would have otherwise have been exposed.

His example was quickly followed, and the practice, we understand, is now very prevalent amongst bombing squadrons. In these attacks Lieut, O'Callaghan displayed great daring, and only a couple of weeks before he received his death blow had been personally commended for his bravery and resource by his Commanding Officer. Despite the arduous life in the trenches, he regularly wrote cheery letters to his uncle, and a few days before he fell he wrote as follows "We are having a rough time but have the Boche well in hand. I hope the weather keeps favourable, as we will then be able to do some good work." The late Lieut, O'Callaghan was gifted with many excellent qualities which won him the affections of all with whom he was acquainted.

Amongst his brother officers and his men he was deservedly a favourite, and we are sure they deeply deplore his loss. In South Africa, too, where he spent his boyhood, he will be genuinely regretted, and in Wexford, where during his all too brief sojourn he made many friends, deep sorrow will be occasioned by his loss. He was the son of the late Mrs Maggie O'Callaghan, formerly of Rochfort, Enniscorthy, and nephew of Rev, Thos O'Connor, S. SS. R., who is at present serving as Chaplain in France; of Mr James O'Connor, Solicitor General for Ireland and of Mr M. J. O'Connor, solicitor, Wexford, with whom deep sympathy is felt.

From De Ruvigny's Roll of Honour:

O'CALLAGHAN, James, Lieut., 13 (Service) Battn. The Cheshire Regt., s. of the late Richard O'Callaghan, of co. Wexford, and Johannesburg, South Africa, by his wife, Margaret, dau. Of Michael Joseph O'Connor, of Wexford; and nephew of the Right Hon. James O'Connor K. C., Attorney-General for Ireland, also of the Rev. Thomas O'Connor, C. Ss. R., Army Chaplain; b. Rochford, Enniscorthy, 2 March, 1890; educ. At Durban, South Africa. On the outbreak of the Zulu Rebellion in 1906, he volunteered for active service, serving through the campaign (Medal); returned to his home in Johannesburg on the termination of the revolt; joined the British Navy Aug. 1908; took part in the actions in the Persian Gulf 1909 and 1910, and while serving on HMS *Arrogant* was complimented by Prince Louis of Battenberg on being the only many in the Navy wearing the Medal of the Zulu Rebellion.

On completing his term with the Navy, took up a position in the Municipal Offices at Johannesburg; but on the outbreak of the European War in Aug. 1914, relinquished his post, and joined the 1st Imperial Light Horse; took part in the fighting from Prisca to Groofontein; came to England when that campaign ended and the forces demobilized, and obtained a commission as 2nd Lieut.

In the Cheshire Regt. In Oct. 1915; served with the Expeditionary Force in France and Flanders from July, 1916, where he was given charge of a bombing squadron; took part in many bombing attacks, in which he taught his men to blacken their faces, and instructed them to lie flat among the dead after having thrown the bombs, and so escape the terrific fusillade of reply to which they were exposed, this being one of the manoeuvres of the Zulu Rebellion; was personally complimented by his Commanding Officer on his bravery and resource in Oct. 1916, and was killed in action at Thiépval on the 21st, while leading a bombing attack. He was an exceptionally fine horseman; unm.

Grave or Memorial Reference: Pier and Face 3 C and 4 A. Memorial: Thiepval Memorial in France.

O'CONNELL, Benjamin: Rank: Private. Regiment or Service: Irish Guards. Unit: 1st Bn. Age at death: 23. Date of death: 8 August 1918. Service No: 10686.

Supplementary information: Son of James and Mary O'Connell of Tinnarath, Foulksmills, Wexford. This man is not recorded in Ireland's Memorial records nor is he in Soldiers died in the Great War. From *Shot at Dawn* by Julian Putkowski and Julian Sykes(Wharncliffe Publishing Limited, 1989. Page 253):

> The 8th of August was later described as General Ludendorff's 'Black Day'. The tables were turned and henceforth the German armies fell back in retreat. Private Benjamin O'Connell,

who was serving in 1 Irish Guards, had already been convicted of two offences involving absence. Initially he had been sentenced to two years, and for a second offence ten years. Following his further offence the 23 year old was shot at Bailleumont.

Grave or Memorial Reference: C. 7. Cemetery: Bailleulmont Communal Cemetery in France.

O'CONNOR, Denis: Also see **CONNORS/CONNERS, Denis:** Rank: Rifleman. Regiment or Service: Royal Irish Rifles. Unit: 1st Bn. Age at death: 19. Date of death: 16 August 1917. Service No: 3/5926 and 5926. Born in Enniscorthy, Co. Wexford. Enlisted in Enniscorthy. Died of wounds.

Supplementary information: Son of William Thomas and Bridget Connors of 24, Ross Road, Enniscorthy, Co. Wexford. From an article in the *Enniscorthy Guardian* in 1917:

> News was received in Enniscorthy during the week of the death of Private Denis O'Connor, Royal Irish Rifles. Private O'Connor had been in the army for the past two years and had been through several engagements escaping without injury. He was the eldest son of Mr Wm, O'Connor, foreman in Messrs Buttle Bros' victualling establishment, with whom much sympathy will be felt in his bereavement.

Grave or Memorial Reference: XVII. AA.10A. Cemetery: Lijssenthoek Military Cemetery in Belgium.

O'CONNOR, James: Rank: Private. Regiment or Service: Irish Guards. Unit: 2nd Bn. Age at death: 26. Date of death: 15 September 1916. Service No: 6845. Born in Wexford, Co. Wexford. Enlisted in Wexford. Killed in action.

Supplementary information: Son of Martin and Mary O'Connor of 6 Upper King Street, Wexford. Husband of Mary O'Connor of Killeens, Wexford. From an article in the *Enniscorthy Guardian* in April, 1915:

A WEXFORD VOLUNTEER AND HIS SONS

Three sons in the Irish Guards and their father an active member of the National Volunteers, the phrase refers to the members of a Wexford family- the O'Connors of King Street.

Mr Martin O'Connor since the Volunteer movement was started locally has been one of the most consistant and active members of the Wexford Battalion. He has three sons in the Irish Guards. His son, Martin, who was promoted to the rank of Corporal some time ago has been connected with the service for a number of years. In the early stages of the war he fought in some of the most fierce encounters with the enemy and had the forefinger of his right hand blown off by a piece of shrapnel at the battle of the Aisne. His brothers, James and Edward, have joined the Irish Guards since the outbreak of hostilities.

From an article in the *People*, 1916:

News has been received by his wife that Private Jas. O'Connor, Killeens, of the Irish Guards, son of Mr Martin O'Connor, King Street, has been killed in action in France on the 15th September. He joined the colours about 18 months ago and two of his brothers are serving in the same regiment. Much sympathy is felt for his widow, parents and relatives in their affliction. Mrs O'Connor has received the following from the Catholic Chaplain of the Irish Guards – Dear Mrs O'Connor – It is with great sorrow that I have to tell you your dear husband who was reported missing is now known to have been killed on 15th September, his body having been found and buried. I am afraid I can say nothing to soothe your sorrow, but at least you must not be anxious about the welfare of his soul; he was well prepared to go.

He had Holy Communion and Confession only a few days before, and I gave them all absolution and the Holy Fathers Blessing and Plenary Indulgence when we were going on the march to the trenches. He gave his life to God, in the fulfilment of his duty "obedient" like his "Divine Mster unto death".

Grave or Memorial Reference: Pier and Face 7 D. Memorial: Thiepval Memorial in France.

O'CONNOR, James: Rank: Corporal. Regiment or Service: Royal Irish Regiment. Unit: 2nd Bn. Date of death: 21 October 1915. Service No: 10858. Born in Montreal, Canada. Enlisted in York while living in Dublin. Died of wounds. From another article in a Wexford newspaper:

Corporal James O'Connor of the 2nd Battalion, Royal Irish Regiment, who has died from wounds received on 22nd October.

The deceased soldier, who was but 18½ years of age, was son of Sergeant Roderick and Mrs O'Connor, of Redmondstown, Rathaspeck, and grandson of the late Mr James O'Connor, Clerk of the Wexford Union and of Mr John Fenlon, Herd, Johnstown Castle. He joined the army about two years ago and served all through the present campaign in France, being wounded at La Basse early in the present year. He was allowed home then on short leave and subsequently rejoined his regiment, taking part in many engagements until he was fatally wounded. His father, Sergeant O'Connor, is also serving with the Colours in France. Corporal O'Connor was a very popular young man in his native district, and the news of his death was learned with sincere regret.

The deceased leaves a wife and child to mourn his loss. Much sympathy is felt for her, his parents, brother and sister in their bereavement.

Grave or Memorial Reference: C.23. Cemetery: Beauval Communal Cemetery in France.

O'CONNOR, James: Rank: Private. Regiment or Service: Irish Guards. Unit: 2nd Bn. Date of death: 3 September 1915. Service No: 4424. Born in Ferns, Co. Wexford. Enlisted in Dublin, Co Dublin while living in Arklow, Co. Wicklow. Killed in action. He has no known grave but is commemorated on Panel 9 and 10. Memorial; Loos Memorial in France.

O'CONNOR, Lawrence Raymond: Rank: Trooper. Regiment or Service: Australian Light Horse. Unit: 2nd. Date of death: 16 July 1918. Age at death 38. Wounded in action and died the same day of the gunshot wound. Service No: 3250. Born in Ballygarret, Wexford. Next of Kin: Father, Mr Edward O'Connor, Ferns, Wexford. Age on enlistment: 36 years and three months. Height: 5 feet 8 inches. Hair: brown. Eyes: brown. Complexion: fair. Weight: 10 stone. Previous to enlistment he was apprenticed to J Bolger and Co, General Drapers, Enniscorthy for three years. Occupation on enlistment: station hand. Sworn in at Longreach, Queensland on 5 December 1916. Buried by Chaplain H. J. Clarke the day after he died. In his will he wanted his effects given to Miss Laura Ethel Drinkwell, c/o Mrs Barber Kalbar, via Ipswich.

Supplementary information: Son of Edward and Mary Anne O'Connor (*née* Sinnah). Born at Newtown, Gorey. Grave or Memorial Reference: H. 42. Cemetery: Jeruslaem War Cemetery, Israel.

O'CONNOR, Michael: Rank: Private. Regiment or Service: Irish Guards. Unit: 1st Bn. Date of death: 15 September 1916. Service No: 4839. Born in Monageer, Co. Wexford. Enlisted in Dublin. Killed in action. Grave or Memorial Reference: XVI. D. 2. Cemetery: Delville Wood Cemetery, Longueval in France.

O'CONNOR, Michael James: Rank: Private. Regiment or Service: Welsh Guards. Unit: 1st Bn. Age at death: 38. Date of death: 7 August 1918. Service No: 1833. Born in Tondu, Glamorgan. Enlisted in Bridgend, Glamorgan. Killed in action.

Supplementary information: Son of Michael O'Connor of Johnstown, Duncormick, Wexford. Grave or Memorial Reference: III.E.2. Cemetery: Berles New Military Cemetery in France.

O'CONNOR, Patrick: Rank: Private. Regiment or Service: Royal Irish Regiment. Unit: 2ⁿᵈ Bn. Age at death: 28. Date of death: 26 August 1914. Service No: 8281. Born in Rathangan, Co. Wexford. Enlisted in Clonmel, Co Tipperary while living in Rathangan. Killed in action. Also down in the records as **CONNORS, Patrick.**

Supplementary information: Son of Michael O'Connor of Johnstown, Duncormick, Wexford. Grave or Memorial Reference: I.D3. Cemetery: Belgrade Cemetery in Belgium.

O'CONNOR, Thomas/Tom: Rank: Private. Regiment or Service: Welsh Regiment. Unit: 15ᵗʰ Bn. Age at death: 23. Date of death: 6 September 1918. Service No: 241768. Born in Rathangan, Co. Wexford. Enlisted in Port Talbot. Died of wounds.

Supplementary information: Son of Thomas and Ellen Murphy O'Connor of Duncormick, Co. Wexford. Grave or Memorial Reference: D. 18. Cemetery: Fienvillers British Cemetery in France.

O'DONOVAN, Patrick Francis: Rank: Lance Corporal. Regiment or Service: King's Own (Royal Lancaster Regiment). Unit: 1ˢᵗ Bn. Age at death: 22. Date of death: 2 April 1918. Service No: 28374. Born in Cushinstown, Co. Wexford. Enlisted in Enniscorthy. Killed in action.

Supplementary information: Son of Edward and Kate Donovan of Begerin Loftus, New Ross, Co. Wexford. Grave or Memorial Reference: Sp. Mem. V. C. 11. Buried near this spot. Cemetery: Bailleul Road East Cemetery, ST. Laurent-Blangy in France.

O'FARRELL, Patrick: See; **FARRELL, Patrick.**

O'HANLON, Henry: Rank: Acting Company Sergeant Major. See **HANLON, Henry.**

O'HANLOW/O'HANLON, Richard: Rank: Corporal. Regiment or Service: Royal Irish Regiment. Unit: 'A' Coy. 6ᵗʰ Bn. Age at death: 20. Date of death: 12 August 1916. Service No: 11044. Born in Capetown, Cape Colony. Enlisted in Clonmel, Co. Tipperary while living in Duncormack, Co. Wexford. Killed in action.

Supplementary information: Son of John and Bridget O'Hanlow of Ballyfrory, Ballymitty, Co. Wexford. From an article in the *People*, 1916:

> Corporal Richard O'Hanlon, 4th Batt, Royal Irish Regiment was killed in action in France on the 12th August last. He was son of Mr and Mrs John O'Hanlon, Ballyfrory, Carrig-on-Bannow. He served two years in the Loco department, G. S& W. Railway at Waterford and Wexford. He volunteered for Kitcheners Army in February, 1915.

Grave or Memorial Reference: I.A.16. Cemetery: St. Patrick's Cemetery, Loos in France.

O'KEEFE, Thomas: Rank: Rifleman. Regiment or Service: Royal Irish Rifles. Unit: 2nd Bn. Date of death: 24 October 1914. Service No: 9087. Born in Wexford, Co. Wexford. Enlisted in Dublin while living in Wexford. Killed in action. From an article in the *Enniscorthy Guardian*:

Private Thomas O'Keefe of the Royal Irish Rifles, a native of Abbey Street, Wexford, has been killed in an engagement in France. Official confirmation of his death has been received by his mother and brothers for whom much sympathy is felt. One of his brothers was killed in the South African War. Extract from the war diary for this day; 26th Oct 14. Neuve Chapelle. Major Daunt having gone sick. Captain CS Dixon took over command of the Batt. B Coy in trenches, D Coy in support, A & C were ordered back to Billets at Richebourg St.Vaast. Enemy ... in the vicinity of B & D Coys (commanded by Lieut Finlay & Lieut Innes-Cross). No further trace of these Coys or the officers commanding them could be attained.

He has no known grave but is commemorated on Panel 42 and 43. Memorial: Le Touret Memorial in France.

O'KEEFE, William Henry: Rank: Lieutenant. Regiment or Service: Royal Field Artillery. Unit: 40th Bde. Age at death: 20. Date of death: 19 May 1917. Killed in action.

Supplementary information: Son of William and Matilda O'Keefe of Faythe House, Wexford. From another article in a Wexford newspaper:

Sec. Lieut. O'Keefe's Death; In our issue last week we recorded the death of Lieut Wm. H. O'Keefe, Royal Horse Artillery, son of Mr W. J. O'Keefe, Faythe House, Wexford, and the manner in which he met his death is described in the following letter to his father from Col. G. T. Mair, dated the 20th inst – 'It is with the greatest grief that I have to confirm what I expect you have already heard from the War Office, that your son Lieut, Wm. H. O'Keefe, was killed in action yesterday. It occurred 9. 30am yesterday, just after he had finished breakfast, the Battery Officer's Mess, in which he was sitting, getting a direct hit from a German shell. The Battery position was not being shelled at the time, and it was just an unlucky chance shell as no others came anywhere near. It may relieve any anxiety you may have as regards any suffering he may have had, to know that your son was killed instantaneously.

His death is a terrible loss to his battery and to me as Colonel of the Brigade, I have to mourn the loss of not only a very capable officer, but also a personal friend, who had endeared himself to me and others in a variety of ways, but especially by his charm and manner. But out great grief, great as it is, can be nothing compared with the irreparable loss of a son which you have sustained, and on behalf of all the officers of the Brigade, the N.C.O's, and men of his Battery may I be allowed to offer our sincerest sympathies? The funeral is to take place this afternoon in the Cemetery of the large town close to where we are in action, the position of which the Military Authorities at home will doubtless aquaint you with.

Any personal belongings which are not too much damaged by the effects of the shell will be forwarded to you in due course, and anything further which you wish to know, I shall esteem it a privilege to be allowed to furnish you with. Assuring you of my deepest sympathy. Yours Truly, G. T. Mair.'

Grave or Memorial Reference: V.F. 10. Cemetery: Faubourg D'Amiens Cemetery, Arras in France.

O'LEARY, Edward: Rank: Stoker. Regiment or Service: Royal Naval Reserve. Unit: HMS *Black Prince*. Age at death: 24. Date of death: 31 May 1916. Service No: 4487S. From an article in a Wexford newspaper, 'Edward O'Leary of Michael Street, Wexford, was a stoker on HMS *Black Prince*, which was sunk during the battle. When the news came to hand of the loss of that vessel his mother communicated with the Admiralty, but was notified on Thursday that his name did not appear on the list of survivors.'

Supplementary information: Son of Michael and Mary O'Leary of 9 Michael Street, Wexford. Grave or Memorial Reference: 19. Memorial: Plymouth Naval Memorial UK.

O'LEARY, James. See **LEARY, James**.

O'LEARY, John: Rank: Private. Regiment or Service: Royal Inniskilling Fusiliers. Unit: 7th Bn. Formerly he was with the Royal Irish Regiment where his number was 14391. Age at death: 20.

Date of death: 9 September 1916. Service No: 27717. Born in Castlebridge, Co. Wexford. Enlisted in Wexford while living in Cornaclos.

Supplementary information: Son of James and Bridget O'Leary of Galbally, Curracloe Road, Castlebridge, Wexford. Grave or Memorial Reference: Pier and Face 4 D and 5 B. Memorial: Thiepval Memorial in France.

O'LEARY, Michael James: Rank: Private. Regiment or Service: Middlesex Regiment. Unit: 3rd Bn. Age at death: 26. Date of death: 5 October 1918. Service No: 1684 and F/1684. Born in Wexford, Co. Wexford. Enlisted in Hammersmith, Middlesex. Died in Salonika.

Supplementary information: Son of John and Ellen O'Leary of Spring Hill, Enniscorthy, Co. Wexford. Grave or Memorial Reference: 246. Cemetery: Kirechkoi-Hortakoi Military Cemetery in Greece.

O'LEARY, Patrick: Rank: Chief Stoker. Regiment or Service: Royal Navy. Unit: HMS *Black Prince*. Date of death: 31 May 1916. Service No: 293649.

Supplementary information: Husband of Teresa O'Leary, of 538 Commercial Road, Portsmouth. From an article in the *Enniscorthy Guardian*:

Chief Stoker Patk, O'Leary, Kilmacoe, Curracloe, second son of Mr and Mrs James O'Leary, Kilmacoe was lost in the Black Prince in the recent naval battle in the North Sea. He was 16 years in the navy and was in the Gladiator when she was sunk about six years ago, and was two hours in the water before he was rescued.

He also served in China at the time of the Boxer rising, when he was wounded.

Grave or Memorial Reference: 15 on the Portsmouth Memorial. UK.

O'LEARY, P.: (O'Leary on the headstone, Leary in the records) Rank: Private. Regiment or Service: Leinster Regiment. Unit: 2nd Bn. Age at death: 32. Date of death: 10 January 1920. Service No: 7904.

Supplementary information: Son of John Leary, of Shannon Hill, Enniscorthy. He won the Military Medal and is listed in the *London Gazette*. Grave or Memorial Reference: D. 25. Cemetery: Enniscorthy New Catholic Cemetery, Wexford.

O'LEARY, Thomas: (also known as **LEARY**) Rank: Stoker 1st Class. Regiment or Service: Royal Navy. Unit: (RFR/PO/B/3391). HMS *Good Hope.* Age at death: 31. Date of death: 1 November 1914. Service No: SS/101169.

Supplementary information: Son of John and Margaret Leary of Shannon, Enniscorthy. Husband of Bridget Leary of 15 Duffey Gate, Enniscorthy, Co. Wexford. From an article in the *Enniscorthy Guardian*:

He was for years a member of the Catholic Workingmans Club and of the brass band attached to that institution with which he played the first cornet. He was a member of AOH, Enniscorthy up to the time of his departure to join the Navy as a reservist at the outbreak of the war. When called on to join the Navy he was engaged as a porter in the Munster and Leinster Bank. Since

the engagement in question with the German Squadron on the 1st of November hopes were entertained that he might have escaped but the official news received this week has dashed them to the ground. Much sympathy is felt with the wife and family of the dead sailor who is son-in-law to Mr P Hendrick of the Town tenants Association. He leaves a wife and one child to mourn the loss of a kind father and good husband. It is hoped that the naval authorities will make ample provision for the widow and child. RIP.

Grave or Memorial Reference: 4. Memorial: Portsmouth Naval Memorial UK.

OLLERENSHAW, Joseph Robert: Rank: Lance Corporal. Regiment or Service: Grenadier Guards. Unit: 2nd Bn. Date of death: 6 August 1915. Service No: 17011. Born in Wexford, Co. Wexford. Enlisted in Kilmuckridge, Co. Wexford. Killed in action. He has no known grave but is commemorated on Panel 158 and 170. Memorial: Helles Memorial in Turkey.

O'LOUCHLIN/O'LOUGHLIN, James: Rank: Private. Regiment or Service: Irish Guards. Unit: 1st Bn. Date of death: 6 September 1914. Service No: 3123. Born in New Ross, Co. Wexford. Enlisted in Tipperary. Died of wounds. Age at death: 25.

Supplementary information: Son of James O'Louchlin of Cordangan, Tipperary. Grave or Memorial Reference: Sp. Mem. Cemetery: Vaudoy Communal Cemetery in France.

O'NEILL, Aidan: Rank: Private. Regiment or Service: Royal Irish Regiment. Unit: 1st Bn. Age at death: 22. Date of death: 20 December 1918. Service No: 10849.

Supplementary information: Son of Aidan O'Neill of Shannon Hill, Enniscorthy, Co. Wexford. Grave or Memorial Reference: C. 139. Cemetery: Alexandria (Hadra) War Memorial Cemetery in Egypt.

O'NEILL/O'NEIL, James. Rank: Private. Regiment or Service: Irish Guards. Unit: 1st Bn. Date of death: 10 October 1918. Service No: 12192. Born in Adamstown, Co. Wexford. Enlisted in Cardiff, Glamorganshire while living in Adamstown. Killed in action. Grave or Memorial Reference: A. 5. Cemetery: St Hilaire 1st Cemetery, Frevent in France.

O'NEILL, John: Rank: Private. Regiment or Service: Royal Irish Regiment. Unit: 2nd Bn. Age at death: 20. Date of death: 19 October 1914. Service No: 10824. Born in Rosbercon, Co. Wexford. Enlisted in Waterford while living in Rosbercon. Killed in action.

Supplementary information: Son of Mary Meyler (formerly O'Neill) of 3 Abbey View, New Ross, Co. Wexford and the late John O'Neill. From an article in the *Enniscorthy Guardian*, 'The family of Private John O'Neill of the High Hill, New Ross, has received official intimation that he was killed in the war. He was a stepson of Mr Myler, tailor, High Hill, and was prayed for as being killed some months ago. He was through several battles since the outbreak of the war.' Grave or Memorial Reference: VI.D.11. Cemetery: Vielle-Chapelle New Military Cemetery, Lacouture in France.

O'NEILL, Michael: Rank: Fireman. Regiment or Service: Mercantile Marine. Unit: SS *Lusitania* (Liverpool). The Lusitania was sunk by German Submarine U-20. Age at death: 44. Date of death: 7 May 1915. From an article in the *Enniscorthy Guardian:*

One of the victims of the stupendous German crime which caused the destruction of the *Lusitania* and the murder of 1,500 men women and children, was Michael O'Neill, brother of Mr John O'Neill, William Street, New Ross, a baker in the employment of Mr John Murphy U. C. John Street. Michael was one of the *Lusitania's* stokers and the anxious enquiries of his brother elicited the sad tidings that the was not one of the survivors.

Prayers were offered up at all the Masses in both churches on Sunday last for the repose of the soul of the deceased. He was a man of about 42 years of age and a native of Wexford where another brother of his resides.

Supplementary information: Son of the late Michael and Mary O'Neill. Born at Wexford. Memorial: Tower Hill Memorial UK.

O'NEILL, Michael: Rank: Stoker. Regiment or Service: Royal Naval Reserve. Unit: HMS *Inflexible*. Age at death: 41. Date of death: 18 March 1915. Service No: 669V.

Supplementary information: Son of Patrick and Elizabeth O'Neill of Wexford. Grave or Memorial Reference: 8. Memorial: Plymouth Naval Memorial UK.

O'NEILL, Patrick: See **NEILL, Patrick**:

O'NEILL, Peter: Rank: Driver. Regiment or Service: Army Service Corps. Unit: 208th Coy. Age at death: 38. Date of death: 6 January 1918. Service No: T4/057358. Born in Ballymurn, Co. Wexford. Enlisted in Carlow while living in Carlow. Died in the Balkans.

Supplementary information: Son of Owen and Mary O'Neill of Ballyboy, Enniscorthy, Co. Wexford. Husband of Kate O'Neill of Newtownforbes, Co. Longford. Grave or Memorial Reference: 1338. Cemetery: Salonika (Lembet Road) Military Cemetery in Greece.

ORMSBY, George: Rank: Pioneer. Regiment or Service: Corps of Royal Engineers. Unit: 8th Signal Company, R. E. Date of death: 27 May 1918. Service No: 210867. Born in Wexford, Co. Wexford. Enlisted in Shepherdsbush, Middlesex while living in Hammersmith, Middlesex. Killed in action. He has no known grave but is listed on the Soissons Memorial in France.

O'REILLY, Edward: See **REILLY, Edward.**

O'REILLY, John: See **REILLY, John**.

O'ROCHE, Joseph: Rank: Gunner. Regiment or Service: Royal Horse Artillery and Royal Field Artillery. Unit: A Battery, 110th Brigade. Date of death: 21 July 1917. Service No: 66841. Born in Kilmore, Wexford. Enlisted in Neath, Glam. Killed in action. Grave or Memorial Reference: II. G. 24. Cemetery: Poperinghe New Military Cemetery Belgium.

O'ROURKE, Francis: Rank: Sergeant. Regiment or Service: Irish Guards. Unit: Reserve Battalion. Date of death: 8 June 1916. Service No: 1339. Born in Wexford, Co. Wexford. Enlisted in Dublin while living in Cavan, Co. Cavan. Died at home. Grave or Memorial Reference: L. 56. Cemetery: Great Warley (Christ Church) Cemetery, UK.

O'ROURKE, John: Rank: Rifleman. Regiment or Service: Rifle Brigade. Unit: 1st Bn. Date of death: 12 April 1917. Service No: S/6702. Born in Gorey, Co. Wexford. Enlisted in St Paul's Churchyard, Middlesex while living in Kildare. Killed in action. He has no known grave but is listed in Bay 9 on the Arras Memorial in France.

O'ROURKE, John: Rank: Fireman. Regiment or Service: Mercantile Marine. Unit: SS *Solway Queen* (Aberdeen). Age at death: 21. Date of death: 2 April 1918.

Supplementary information: (Served as **ROURKE**). Son of James and Kate O'Rourke of Raheen, Adamstown, Co. Wexford. The Steamship *Solway Queen* was sunk by a German submarine 7 miles west of Black Head, Wigtownshire carrying a cargo of coal. The Captain and ten of her crew died. The Submarine U-101 was commanded by Carl Siegfried Ritter Von Georg. 10 days after the war ended the Submarine surrendered and was broken up in Morcombe in 1920. Memorial: Tower Hill Memorial UK.

ORTON, Thomas Edward (Eddie): Rank: Company Sergeant Major. Regiment or Service: Welsh Guards. Unit: 1st Bn. Formerly he was with the Grenadier Guards where his number was 14366. Date of death: 20 July 1918. Service No: 8. Born in New Ross, Co. Wexford. Enlisted in Dublin. Died of wounds. Age at death: 27.

Supplementary information: Awarded the Meritorious Service Medal. Grave or Memorial Reference; I.O.2. Cemetery: Gezaincourt Communal Cemetery Extension in France.

O'SHEA, John: Rank: Private. Regiment or Service: Argyll and Southern Highlanders. Unit: 1/7th Bn. Date of death: 12 October 1918. Service No: S/23146. Born in Enniscorthy and enlisted in Stirling while living in Falkirk, Stirlings. Killed in action. Age at death: 19.

Supplementary information: Son of Bernard and Elizabeth O'Shea of 11 Patrick's Place, Enniscorthy. Grave or Memorial Reference: Has no known grave but is commemorated on Panel 10. Vis-En-Artois Memorial in France.

P

PARSLOW, Samuel: Rank: Stoker 1st Class. Regiment or Service: Royal Navy. Unit: HMS *Amphion*. Age at death: 24. Date of death: 6 August 1914. Service No: K/324. HMS *Amphion* (an active class scout cruiser) was the first Naval ship to be sunk during the First World War.

Supplementary information: Son of Elizabeth Parslow of Grange, Fethard, Co. Wexford. Grave or Memorial Reference: 3. Memorial: Plymouth Naval Memorial UK.

PAYNE, Henry: Rank: Able Seaman. Regiment or Service: Mercantile Marine. Unit: SS *Emlyndene* (Cardiff). Age at death: 40. Date of death: 10 December 1917.

Supplementary information: Husband of Elizabeth Payne of 19 Bullawn, New Ross, Co. Wexford. SS *Emlyndene* disappeared without trace while transporting coal from Cardiff. It is supposed she was sunk by German Submarine UC-50. Memorial: Tower Hill Memorial UK.

PEARE, Hilda Florence Letitia Anna: From an article in a Wexford newspaper:

The announcement in our issue of last week of the death of Miss Hilda Florence Letitia Anna Peare, only daughter of Mr R. H. and Mrs Peare, Kilmallock House, Enniscorthy was learned with feelings of profound sorrow by her many friends in the County. The sad event, which took place at the Military Hospital, Seymour Park, Manchester, on March 13th, was the outcome of a severe attack of Scarlatina [name Scarlet Fever] contracted while she was engaged nursing the sick and wounded of the fighting forces, and that her devotion to duty was fully appreciated was evident from the remarkable demonstration of regret on the occasion of her internment.

She was buried with full military honours, the gun-carriage and the firing party being supplied by the Commanding Officer of Heaton Park Depot. The sergeants of the local detachment of the Royal Army Medical Corps acted as pall bearers, and the band of St Joseph's School played the Dead March in Saul along the route. Beautiful wreaths and floral tributes were sent by the officers and men of the Royal Army Medical Corps, the Matron, Sisters, and Nurses of the vari-

Hilda Florence Letitia Anna Peare.

ous military hospitals in the locality, the ladies of the V.A. D., and the patients of the branch hospital where Nurse Peare worked. According to a document titled 'Summary of Work for March, 1917' published by the BRC and the Order of St John–Miss Peare was a member of the V. A. D. (Voluntary Aid Detachment), estimated year of birth, 1894, year of registration, 1917, age at death, 23, Prestwick, Lancashire. She was a member of Dublin Detachment, No 24.

PEMBERTON Pigott, Eric John Keefe: Rank, Lt. Regiment or Service: Royal Irish Regiment. Unit: 1ˢᵗ Bn. Date of death: 24 June 1916. Age at death: 21. He was a Grandson of Captain Pemberton Pigott of Slevoy Castle. Son of Surg. Col. F. K. Pigott, of Belmont House, Shrewsbury. Killed in action. From an article in a Wexford newspaper:

LIEUT PEMBERTON PIGOTT KILLED.

The casualty lists this week contained the name of Lieut Eric Pemberton Pigott as being killed in action.

The deceased young officer was a member of one of the oldest County Wexford families, and the sad announcement was learned with deep regret by a host of friends in Wexford. He was the son of Dr Frederick Pemberton Pigott, of Shrewsbury, Shropshire, grandson of the late Capt Pemberton Pigott, of Slevoy Castle, Wexford, and nephew of Mrs John E Barry and Mrs Charles Barry, of Rocklands, Wexford. Little more than a year ago Lieut Pigott, who was only 19 years of age, obtained a commission in the army, and was gazetted to the Royal Irish Regiment. Prior to the outbreak of war he served in

India and was drafted to the front last Autumn. During the terrible campaign in the opening stages of the war Lieut Pigott took part in many engagements until he was invalided home suffering from frost bite.

Whilst on leave he participated in the recruiting campaign being conducted in Ireland and delivered stirring appeals at Kilkenny and Cork. About a month ago he was sent out on active service again and rejoined his Regiment. In a gallant effort to save his guns Lieut Pigott was killed instantaneously. The Catholic Chaplain of the Regiment and the Commanding Officer wrote to the deceased's parents giving a graphic description of Lieut Pigott's bravery and telling how he died a hero's death.

Grave or Memorial Reference: Plot 3. Row A. Grave 27. Cemetery, Houplines Communal Cemetery Extension in France.

PHELAN, Lawrence: Rank: Private. Regiment or Service: Irish Guards. Unit: 2ⁿᵈ Bn. Date of death: 30 September 1915. Service No: 6676. Born in Adamstown, Co. Wexford. Enlisted in Whitehall in Middlesex while living in Adamstown, Co. Wexford. Killed in action. He has no known grave but is listed on Panel 9 and 10 on the Loos Memorial in France.

PHILLIPS, James: Rank: Private. Regiment or Service: Leinster Regiment. Unit: 2ⁿᵈ Bn. Formerly he was with the Royal Irish Regiment where his number was 5356. Age at death: 20. Date of death: 26 September 1916. Service No: 15043. Born in Gorey, Co. Wexford. Enlisted in

Gorey, Co. Wexford. Killed in action.

Supplementary information: Son of James and Eliza Phillips of Gorey, Co. Wexford. Grave or Memorial Reference: III.A.19. Cemetery: Villers Station Cemetery, Villers-Au-Bois in France.

PIERCE, James: Rank: Private. Regiment or Service: Royal Irish Regiment. Unit: 2nd Bn. Age at death: 21. Date of death: 21 October 1914. Service No: 4326. Born in Ballymore, Co. Wexford. Enlisted in Wexford while living in Ballymore. Killed in action

Supplementary information: Son of Walter and Elizabeth Pierce (*née* Merriman) of Grageen, Ballycogley, Co. Wexford. Grave or Memorial Reference: Panel 11 and 12. Memorial: Le Touret Memorial in France.

PIERCE, John: Rank: Rifleman. Regiment or Service: New Zealand Rifle Brigade. Unit: A Company, 4th Bn. 10th Reinforcements, NZEF. Age at death: 27. Date of death: 19 July 1916. Service No: 24/2074. Died of wounds received in action on the Somme.

Supplementary information: Son of William and Elizabeth Pierce, of Ballycale, Gorey. From an article in the *Enniscorthy Guardian*:

John Pierce, son of Mrs Wm Pierce, Ballykale, Gorey, who emigrated to New Zealand some three years ago, joined the New Zealand Rifle Brigade at Wellington in April of last year. He sailed on the 4th of March with the 10th Reinforced New Zealand Expeditionary Force, and was sent straight to the front, where

John Pierce.

he went through several engagements.

On the 11th April he was wounded in the right thigh by shrapnel, and having spent a while in the base hospital he was then taken to the second London General Hospital, Chelsea, where he succumbed to blood poisoning, as the result of the wound on the 17th July. The remains arrived at Gorey railway station on the 23rd July, where an exceedingly large number of sympathisers were in waiting and the funeral then left for the family burial ground, Tubberneering. The cortage was of exceedingly large dimensions, being representitive of every class and creed, and all were anxious to pay the last tribute of respect to the memory of the deceased who, before going foreign was a great favourite in the locality, and most exemplary in every way.

The deepest sympathy of all is tendered to his bereaved parents and family in the great loss sustained by the death of their son, who died in a noble cause. The chief mourners were; Wm Pierce (father) Ernest Pierce (son) John Hill, Ballydanie (uncle), John Hill, Plasnew, Thomas Hill, Ballydaniel, R. Poole, Dublin, George Hanstock, Ballykale, John Hill, Tubberneering, Thomas Hill, D. Hanstock and Wm Hanstock (cousins). The High Commissioner for New Zealand, writing from London and sending a beautiful wreath, tendered his personal sympathy to the parents of the deceased in the loss of their son, whom he said, was a brave soldier, and died in a noble cause for the honour of his country.

The officers of the New Zealand War Contingent, London, also sent a handsome wreath, and also by the following; With deepest sympathy, from the Hanstock family, Loving remembrance from John, Willie, Emma and Lillie Hall. With Sympathy from W Foley; Affectionate remembrance, from Daisy; To honour a brave soldier, with deepest sympathy, from the Godkin family, Banogue; In affectionate remembrance from his cousins at Tubberneering; With deepest sympathy, from Ethel; With tearful sorrow from Alice and Agnes; With deepest sympathy from Midlred, Hilda and H.T. Gray. In loving memory, from N. Cooke and family; With sincere sympathy, from J. and L. Cooke, With heartfelt sorrow, from his loving mother and sister.

Grave or Memorial Reference: Buried in the family plot, middle of the cemetery. Cemetery, Toberanierin Protestant Cemetery, 4 miles south of Gorey.

PIERCE, Peter: Rank: Private. Regiment or Service: Royal Irish Regiment. Unit: 2nd Bn. Age at death: 20. Date of death: 3 September 1916. Service No: 7185. Born in Lady's Island, Co. Wexford. Enlisted in Carlow while living in Carlow. Killed in action.

Supplementary information: Son of Mr J. Pierce of Murrintown, Wexford. Grave or Memorial Reference: R.35. Cemetery: Carnoy Military Cemetery in France.

PINNIONS, Thomas: Rank: Private. Regiment or Service: Royal Inniskilling Fusiliers. Unit: 2nd Bn. Age at death: 29. Date of death: 2 October 1918. Service No: 27176. Born in Killinahue, Co. Wexford. Enlisted in Gorey. Died of wounds.

Supplementary information: Son of Thomas and the late Jane Pinnions of Hollyfort, Gorey, Co. Wexford. Grave or Memorial Reference: I.D.1. Cemetery: Dadizeele New British Cemetery in Belgium.

PORTER, William James: Rank: Lieutenant. Regiment or Service: Leinster Regiment. Unit: 2nd Bn. Age at death: 21. Date of death: 3 August 1917. Died of wounds.

William James Porter.

Supplementary information: Son of William and Anne Elizabeth Porter of 'Elmfield' Wexford. Grave or Memorial Reference: XV.A.4. Cemetery: Lijssenthoek Military Cemetery in Belgium.

POTTS, Edward: Rank: Private. Regiment or Service: The King's (Liverpool Regiment). Unit: 'B' Coy. 4th Bn. Age at death: 22. Date of death: 20 May 1917. Born in Wexford. Enlisted in Liverpool while living in Wexford. Killed in action.

Supplementary information: Son of John and Catherine Potts of 33 Upper John Street, Wexford. From an article in the *People*, 1915, 'Private John Potts, John Street, Wexford of the 1st Royal Irish Regiment is a prisoner of war for the past twelve months in Germany. He is third son of Mr John Potts, John Street. His youngest brother, Richard Potts is also serving with the colours.' Grave or Memorial Reference: Bay 3. Memorial: Arras Memorial in France.

POTTS, John: Rank: Private. Regiment or Service: Royal Irish Regiment. Unit: 'B' Coy. 2nd Bn. Age at death: 21. Date of death: 29 July 1918. Service No: 3881. Born in Barntown, Co. Wexford. Enlisted in Wexford. Died.

Supplementary information: Son of John and Catherine Potts of 33, John St, Wexford. From an article in the *People*, 1915, 'Private John Potts, John Street, Wexford of the 1st Royal Irish Regiment is a prisoner of war for the past twelve months in Germany. He is third son of Mr John Potts, John Street.' Grave or Memorial Reference: V.M.9. Cemetery: Niederzwhren Cemetery in Germany.

POTTS, James: Rank: Boatswain (Bosun). Regiment or Service: Mercantile Marine. Unit: SS *Woolston* (London). Age at death: 33. Date of death: 14 May 1918.

Supplementary information: Son of John Potts of 33 John Street, Wexford and the late Catherine Potts. Torpedoed and sunk by German Submarine UC-52 while on voyage from Syracuse to Messina with a cargo of sulphur. There were 19 casualties including the Captain. From an article in the *People*, 1915, 'Private John Potts, John Street, Wexford of the 1st Royal Irish Regiment is a prisoner of war for the past twelve months in Germany. He is third son of Mr John Potts, John Street. His youngest brother, Richard Potts is also serving with the colours.' Memorial: Tower Hill Memorial UK.

POWELL, Peter: Rank: Private. Regiment or Service: East Surrey Regiment. Unit: 1st Bn. Date of death: 20 April 1915. Service No: 3525. Born in Newtown Barry, Co. Wexford. Enlisted in Hendon in Middlesex. Killed in action. From an article in the *Enniscorthy Guardian*:

> Private Peter Powell, Brady's Cross, Bunclody, and attached to the 1st Batt, S. [sic] Surrey Regiment, was killed at the battle of Hill 60 on the 20th April last. Yound Powell ws formerly an employee with Mr R.W. Hall-Dare, Netwonbarry House, – He emigrated to England a few years ago and was in the employment of Captain Walker, brother-in-law to Mr Hall-Dare.
>
> He volunteered at the outbreak of the war and was through all the big

battles along the French Frontier until he lost his life. He sleeps today, the sleep of the brave on the battlefield of France. May his soul rest in peace.

He has no known grave but is listed on Panel 34 on the Ypres (Menin Gate) Memorial in Belgium.

POWER, Henry: Rank: Fireman and Trimmer. Regiment or Service: Mercantile Marine. Unit: SS *Mirlo* (London). Age at death: 18. Date of death: 16 August 1918.

Supplementary information: Son of Robert and Kate Power, (*née* Woodroofe) of Dennistown, Murrintown, Wexford. Born at Wexford. SS *Mirlo* was torpedoed, set on fire and sunk by German Submarine U-117. Nine crew died. Memorial: Tower Hill Memorial UK.

POWER, John: Rank: Private. Regiment or Service: Royal Munster Fusiliers. Unit: 1st Bn. Age at death: 23. Date of death: 2 September 1918. Service No: 10259. Born in Waterford. Enlisted in Cork. Killed in action.

Supplementary information: Son of Patrick and Bridget Power of Ballykerogue, Co. Wexford. Grave or Memorial Reference: E. 23. Cemetery: Upton Wood Cemetery, Hendecourt-Les-Cagnicourt in France.

POWER, Lawrence/Laurence: Rank: Private. Regiment or Service: Manchester Regiment. Unit: 16th Bn. Date of death: 23 April 1917. Service No: 34101. Born in Rensgrave, Co. Wexford. Enlisted in Manchester while living in Arthurstown, Co. Wexford. Killed in action. From an article in a Wexford newspaper:

Mr Edward Power, Nook, Arthurstown, has been officially notified that his son, Laurence, who was serving with the Manchester Regiment, has been killed in France. The deceased had been through many engagements since the spring of 1915, and escaped unscathed until the 23rd ult., when he met his death. He has a brother at the front who has also seen much active service.

From an article in the *Enniscorthy Guardian*, June 1915:

Arthurstown Man a prisoner in Germany. Writing home to his mother at Nuke, Arthurstown, Thomas Power, a young farmer, who went to the front some months ago, and who is a prisoner of war in Germany, asks her to send him some tea, chocolate and tobacco, a s well as some home-made Irish bread. During the past few weeks the mother has forwarded the articles, the receipt of which he has acknowledged.

He has no known grave but is listed in Bay 7 on the Arras Memorial in France.

POWER, Walter: Rank: Able Seaman. Regiment or Service: Mercantile Marine. Unit: SS *Lough Fisher* (Barrow). Age at death: 66. Date of death: 30 March 1918.

Supplementary information: Son of the late Martin and Mary Power. Husband of the late Catherine Power (*née* Tubbit). Born at Wexford. Memorial: Tower Hill Memorial UK.

POWER, William: Rank: Private. Regiment or Service: Irish Guards. Unit: 1st Bn. Age at death: 19. Date of death: 17 June 1916. Service No: 6043. Born in Wexford, Co. Wexford. Enlisted in Wexford. Died of wounds.

Supplementary information: Son of Robert and Kate Power of Dennistown, Murrintown, Co. Wexford. Grave or Memorial Reference: I. P. 24. Cemetery: Essex Farm Cemetery in Belgium.

PRENDERGAST, Aiden: Rank: Private. Regiment or Service: Northamptonshire Regiment. Unit: 6th Bn. Formerly he was with the Yorks and Lancs Regiment where his number was 23378. Date of death: 18 September 1918. Service No: 41304. Born in Enniscorthy and enlisted in Mexborough, Yorks. Killed in action. Age at death: 28. He has no known grave but is commemorated on Panel 7. Vis-En-Artois Memorial in France.

PRENDERGAST, John: Rank: Private. Regiment or Service: Royal Irish Regiment. Unit: 2nd Bn. Age at death: 20. Date of death: 3 September 1916. Service No: 11462. Born in Mulrankin, Co. Wexford. Enlisted in Wexford while living in Mulrankin, Co. Wexford Killed in action.

Supplementary information: Son of Patrick and Bridget Prendergast of Mulrankin Bridgetown, Wexford. From an article in a Wexford newspaper:

Last week notification was received from the war office that Private John Prendergast, had been killed in action while serving with the 2nd Battalion, Royal Irish. The deceased

who was only twenty years of age was son of Mr Patrick Prendergast of Mulrankin.

With his brother, Michael, who is at present serving in Egypt, the deceased answered the call to arms shortly after the outbreak of war. He was a decent, hard working, industrious young man, and his early demise is deeply deplored by his many friends. Much sympathy is felt with his bereaved parents.

Grave or Memorial Reference: XVII. A. 12. Cemetery: Serre Road Cemetery No. 2 in France.

PURCELL, Andrew: Rank: Private. Regiment or Service: Royal Irish Fusiliers. Unit: 7th Bn. Formerly he was with the Royal Irish Regiment where his number was 383. Age at death: 37. Date of death: 9 September 1916. Service No: 16219. Born in Gorey, Co. Wexford. Enlisted in Waterford while living in Gorey. Killed in action.

Supplementary information: Son of Laurence and Margaret Purcell of Barnadown, Gorey. Grave or Memorial Reference: Pier and Face 15 A. Memorial: Thiepval Memorial in France.

PURCELL, Simon: Rank: Able Seaman. Regiment or Service: Mercantile Marine. Unit: SS *Lough Fisher* (Barrow). Age at death: 45. Date of death: 30 March 1918.

Supplementary information: Son of Michael and Mary Purcell. Husband of Lucy Purcell (*née* Byrne) of 5 Jail Street, Waterford, Co. Waterford. Born at Bannon, Co. Wexford. Memorial: Tower Hill Memorial UK.

Q

QUINLISK, Michael: Rank: Private. Regiment or Service: Royal Irish Regiment. Unit: 2nd Bn. Date of death: 15 October 1914. Service No: 10747. Born in St Bridget's Co. Wexford. Enlisted in Wexford. Killed in action. Age at death: 17.

Supplementary information: Son of Denis Joseph and Alice Quinlisk of 15 Lombard Street, Waterford. From an article in a Wexford newspaper:

A FAMILY OF FIGHTERS: WEXFORD YOUTH KILLED IN ACTION

His brother held a prisoner of war. Mr Denis Quinlisk, of Ram Street, Wexford, and ex-Sgt of the R.I.C. (mounted section) was notified by the War Office during the week that his son, Michael, who was a Private in the 2nd Battalion, 18th [*sic*] Royal Irish Regiment, had been killed in action on the 15th October. Mr Quinlisk received correspondance expressing the sympathy of the King, Queen and Lord Kitchener.

The deceased youth, who had been only about 18 months with the colours, was very popular in Wexford, and his end will be learned with sincere regret by a wide circle of friends. His elder brother, Timmy, of the same Regiment, who was promoted in ther field to the rank of Corporal for personal bravery, was taken prisoner on the day prior to that on which he was to receive his promotion. Writing to his father from Hamelin, Hannover, Timothy says; "I do not know if I can write to you in my usual coherent strain, for I don't know whether I am a prisoner of war or

not, as I am bewildered by the sudden train of events. Anyhow I am now settled down fairly well, and am certainly in Germany. Mr Dear father, I have a most unwelcome and sad piece of news for you, for which I find very hard in committing to paper. Poor Michael was killed on the 16th October. Poor lad, he died a soldiers death.

I am heartbroken now, as I think of him lying alone on the battlefield. I was by his side as he breathed his last; he died very peacefully, with a prayer on his lips. May God have mercy on his soul. My God, it was terrible that day! Nearly all the chaps that left Davenport with me are now buried in France. Dear Dad do not grieve too much over Michael's death, for someone had to go, and at last one of us is safe, but I would have been quite content to have been killed if I thought that Michael would be saved. We are well treated here and get enough to eat and drink, but I miss the cigarette very much. I was to be promoted still further the day after my capture, but when I return to Ireland after the war, I hope with God's help to wear the Sergeant's sash.

Don't fret too much on my account, and try not to think of poor Michael. The Germans are very good shots with the rifle, although people may say they are not." Another son of Mr Quinlisk's, a boy of 11 years, is a worthy chip off the old block, and as will be seen elsewhere in our columns, pluckily jumped over the quay to rescue a drowning child during the week. It may be of interest to learn that on the outbreak of war Mr Quinlisk wrote offering his services to the War Office, and was thanked by Sir Neville Chamberlain for his patriotic action.

From another article in the *People*, 1915:

Lance Corporal, T. A. Quinlisk, Son of ex-Sergeant Denis Quinlisk, Wexford, is at present a prisoner of war in Gefangenlagers, Germany. Writing to his father this week he states; – "We got shifted from Lemburg, In any case it was rather crowded there. How are you all getting on in dear old Wexford? Well I hope. We are still having very jolly weather here, but the nights are cold. What a difference in my daily life this September.

Last September I was in the trenches, the cold, miserable trenches. I have become quite reconciled in my captivity, though as I look out over the barricade and see the vista of green fields studded here and there with peaceful-looking farm houses. I find it hard to think that a horrible war is raging over the world. When do you think this war is going to end?" Lance Corporal Quinlisk, who is about 30 years of age, was in action for nearly a year in France. His brother, a Corporal, was killed in France some months ago.

From a snippet in the *People*:

In a letter to his father, Ex-Sergeant Quinlisk, Ram Street, Wexford, Corporal Timothy Quinlisk, of the 8th Royal Irish Regiment, now at the front, states that his brother, Michael, who was killed a short time ago, went back to aid a comrade after the order to retreat had been given, and before he was able to get away he was fatally wounded.

He has no known grave but is commemorated on Panel 11 and 12. Memorial: Le Touret Memorial in France.

QUINN, John: Rank: Private. Regiment or Service: Connaught Rangers. Unit: 6th Bn. Formerly he was with the Leinster Regiment where his number was 3356. Date of death: 7 May 1918. Service No: 18143. Born in Gorey, Co. Wexford. Enlisted in Longford while living in Edgeworthstown. Died. Grave or Memorial Reference: V.M.26. Cemetery: Peronne Communal Cemetery Extension in France.

QUINSEY, Henry: Rank: S/S. Regiment or Service: Household Cavalry and Cavalry of the line including the Yeomanry and Imperial Camel Corps. Unit: South Irish Horse. Date of death: 10 October 1918. Service No: 73120. Born in Ballyhuskard. Enlisted in Enniscorthy while living in Wexford. Died at Sea. Age at death: 37. Grave or Memorial Reference: Sperical New Plot, 701. Cemetery: Grangegorman Military Cemetery.

QUIRK, Myles: Rank: Private. Regiment or Service: East Yorkshire Regiment. Unit: 7th Bn. Formerly he was with the Royal Army Medical Corps where his number was 54653. Age at death: 36. Date of death: 27 August 1918. Service No: 29384. Born in Enniscorthy. Enlisted in Liverpool. Killed in action.
Supplementary information: Son of Myles and Johanna Quirk of 25 Shannon Hill,

Enniscorthy, Co. Wexford. Grave or Memorial Reference: III. K. 2. Cemetery: A. I. F. Burial Ground Flers in France.

QUIRKE, Michael: Rank: Private. Regiment or Service: Irish Guards. Unit: 2nd Bn. Age at death: 30. Date of death: 12 September 1917. Service No: 11530. Born in Oulart, Co. Wexford. Enlisted in Gorey. Killed in action.

Supplementary information: Son of John Quirke. Husband of Sarah Quirke of Clonganny, Clonevan, Gorey, Co. Wexford. Grave or Memorial Reference: Panel 10 to 11. Memorial: Tyne Cot Memorial in Belgium.

QUIRKE, Patrick: Rank: Bombardier. Regiment or Service: Royal Field Artillery. Unit: 5th Bty. 45th Bde. Age at death: 25. Date of death: 27 June 1916. Service No: 76755. Born in Wexford, Co. Wexford. Enlisted in Wexford. Killed in action.

Supplementary information: Son of James and Ellen Quirke of Coollycarney, Ballindaggin, Enniscorthy, Co. Wexford. Grave or Memorial Reference: II.C.1. Cemetery: Bouzincourt Communal Cemetery Extension in France.

QUIRKE, Thomas: Rank: Private. Regiment or Service: Royal Irish Regiment. Unit: 1st Bn. Age at death: 25. Date of death: 4 April 1915. Service No: 9822. Born in Blackwater, Co. Wexford. Enlisted in Wexford while living in Blackwater. Killed in action at the battle of Ypres on Easter Sunday.

Supplementary information: Son of Dora Quirke of Ballinahask, Kilmuckridge, Gorey, Co. Wexford. From an article in

Thomas Quirke.

a Wexford newspaper. 'Intimation has recently been conveyed to Mrs Dora Quirke, Blackwater, that her son, Private Thomas Qurike, R. I. R. was killed in action at the battle of Hodge-Ypres [*sic*] on Easter Sunday. Much sympathy is felt with his sorrowing mother in her bereavement. Prayers were offered up for the repose of his soul at Blackwater on Sunday week.' From an article in the *Enniscorthy Guardian:*

> Private Tommy Quirke. Tommy who served with the Royal Irish Regiment, enlisted six years ago and after serving in India arrived with a draft from that country about Christmas and was killed at Hooge, Ypres, on Easter Sunday.
>
> He was a great favourite with everyone in Blackwater being of an exceptionally amiable manner, and great regret has been expressed at his death.

Grave or Memorial Reference: Panel 33. Memorial: Ypres (Menin Gate) Memorial in Belgium.

R

RECK, David J.: Rank: Pioneer. Regiment or Service: Corps of Royal Engineers. Unit: 'M' Coy. 3rd Spec. Bn. Formerly he was with the Royal Irish Regiment (3rd Special Battalion, R. E.) where his number was 5456. Date of death: 1 March 1917. Service No: 129410. Born in Crossabeg, Co. Wexford. Enlisted in Gorey, Co. Wexford while living in Enniscorthy. Died of wounds. Age at death: 20.

Supplementary information: Son of Laurence and Bridget Reck of Killisk, The Ballagh, Enniscorthy. Grave or Memorial Reference: V. E. 8. Cemetery: Ecoivres Military Cemetery, Mont-St-Eloi in France.

REDMOND, Nicholas: Rank: Private. Regiment or Service: Irish Guards. Unit: 2nd Bn. Age at death: 21. Date of death: 19 August 1917. Service No: 10648. Born in Wexford. Enlisted in Wexford. Died of wounds.

Supplementary information: Son of Nicholas and Elizabeth Redmond of Wygram Place, Wexford. Grave or Memorial Reference: IV.M.8A. Cemetery: Mont Huon Military Cemetery, Le Treport in France.

REDMOND, James: Rank: Gunner. Regiment or Service: Royal Field Artillery and Royal Horse Artillery. Unit: 72nd Bty. 38th Bde. Date of death: 1 December 1917. Service No: 46850. Born in Wexford, Co. Wexford. Enlisted in Wicklow. Died of wounds at home.

Supplementary information: Brother of Mr M. Redmond of Kilmuckridge, Gorey, Co. Wexford. Grave or Memorial Reference: XII.D.16. Cemetery: Brookwood Military Cemetery UK.

REDMOND, James: Rank: Rifleman. Regiment or Service: King's Royal Rifle Corps. Date of death: 26 March 1916. Service No: 8375. Born in Faith, Co. Wexford. Enlisted in Liverpool. Killed in action. Grave or Memorial Reference: I.F.45. Cemetery: Maroc British Cemetery, Grenay in France.

REDMOND, James: Rank: Private. Regiment or Service: Canadian Infantry (Central Ontario Regiment). Unit: 5th Bn. Age at death: 32. Date of death: 1 October 1918. Service No: 3107077.

Supplementary information: Son of Michael and Bridget Redmond of Garryhaslin, Co. Wexford. Information from his enlistment documents: Eyes: grey. Hair: dark, Complexion: dark. Height: 5 feet 10½ inches. Address on enlistment: North Broadway Street, St Louis. Date of birth: 26 June 1889. Age on enlistment: 28 years 7 months. Place of birth: Newtownbarry, Co. Wexford. Marital status: single. Name and address of next of kin: Miss Mary Redmond, 142 Trobridge Street, Buffalo, New York. Date of attestation: 4 February 1918. Location of attestation: Toronto. Occupation on enlistment: Labourer. Grave or Memorial Reference: II.C.14. Cemetery: Canada Cemetery, Tilloy-Les-Cambrai in France.

REDMOND, John: Rank: Private. Regiment or Service: Royal Irish Regiment. Unit: 2nd Bn. Date of death: 28 October 1914. Service No: 4422. Born in Duncormick, Co. Wexford. Enlisted in Wexford while living in Rathaspick, Co. Wexford. Killed in action. Grave or Memorial Reference: 16. Cemetery: Sainghin-En-Weppes Communal Cemetery in France.

REDMOND, Matthew: Rank: Private. Regiment or Service: Argyll and Sutherland Highlanders. Unit: 2nd Bn. Age at death: 19. Date of death: 20 June 1916. Service No: 7005 and 3/7005. Born in Enniscorthy and enlisted in Glasgow, Lanarks. Died of wounds.

Supplementary information: Son of Patrick and Catherine Roberts Redmond of 124 Adelphi Street, Bridgeton, Glasgow. Native of Clohamon, Ferns, Co. Wexford. Grave or Memorial Reference: V.E. 50. Cemetery: Bethune Town Cemetery in France.

REDMOND, Nicholas: Rank: Private. Regiment or Service: Irish Guards. Unit: 2nd Bn. Date of death: 19 August 1917. Service No: 10648. Born in Wexford, Co. Wexford. Enlisted in Wexford. Died of wounds. Age at death: 21.

Supplementary information: Son of Nicholas and Elizabeth Redmond of Wygram Place, Wexford. From an article in the *People,* 1915, 'Nicholas Redmond, John Gorman and Thomas O'Brien from John Street, have volunteered for service in the Irish Guards.' From an article in the *Enniscorthy Guardian* in 1917:

The parents of Private Nicholas Redmond (Irish Guards) Wygram

Nicholas Redmond.

Place, Wexford have been notified of the death in hospital of their son.

Private Redmond's mother has received a letter from Father O'Sullivan, Army Chaplain, stating he was sorry to inform her that her son was pretty seriously wounded in the head by shrapnel. He was doing well at first, but he took a turn for the worst. Father O'Sullivan administered the last sacraments to him. Private redmonds mother had left to visit her son in hospital, and while on her journey the news of his death was given.

Grave or Memorial Reference: IV.M.2A. Cemetery: Mont Huon Military Cemetery, Le-Treport in France.

REDMOND, Philip: Rank: Private. Regiment or Service: Royal Irish Regiment. Unit: 1st Bn. Age at death: 21. Date of death: 2 May 1915. Service No: 4387. Born in Enniscorthy and enlisted in Enniscorthy. Killed in action.

Supplementary information: Son of James and Mary Redmond of Milehouse, Enniscorthy, Co. Wexford. Grave or Memorial Reference: Panel 33. Memorial: Ypres (Menin Gate) Memorial in Belgium.

REDMOND, Terence: Rank: Lance Corporal. Regiment or Service: Royal Irish Regiment. Unit: 2nd Bn. Date of death: 24 May 1915. Service No: 250. Born in Ferns, Co. Wexford. Enlisted in Kilkenny while living in Graiguenamanagh, Co. Wexford. Killed in action. He has no known grave but is listed on Panel 33 on the Ypres (Menin Gate) Memorial in Belgium.

REDMOND, William Hoey Kearnay: Rank: Major. Regiment or Service: Royal Irish Regiment. Unit: 6th Bn. Age at death: 56. Date of death: 7 June 1917. Died of wounds received in an attack at Wytschaete Wood in Belgium after being injured by a shell. Awards: Mentioned in Despatches.

Supplementary information: Husband of Eleanor Redmond. Nationalist Member of Parliament for Wexford since 1884. Awarded the Legion of Honour (France). Information taken from his records (WO339/19182) by Jimmy Taylor:

Served as an officer in the Wexford Militia and the 3rd (Militia) Battalion, Royal Irish regiment from 24 December 1879 till 11 January 1882. Temporary commission as captain in 6th (Service) Battalion, Royal Irish Regiment 22 February 1915. Home address Glenbrook, delgany, Co. Wicklow and Palace Manshions,

Kensington, London. Wife was Eleanor Mary. War Office telegram to wife 8 June 1917 reports Died of wounds 7 June 1917 and expresses sympathy. Death report dated 10 June 1917 shows died of wounds, 7 June 1917, 6th Royal Irish Regiment attached 16th Divisional Company.

Undated War Office memo reports burial "at the south end of the garden of the hospice, Locre, SW of Ypres". Letter to HQ Horse Guards Whitehall 21 June 1917 requests buglers of one Battlion Brigade of Guards to attend St Mary's Catholic Church, Clapham (London SW) 23rd June at 10am to sound Last Post at requiem Mass for Major Redmond. "All expenses incurred will be refunded privately. " (Irish Guards preffered). Estate valued at £4018.2. 9., against which there were debts of £1885.3.2 Whole estate to widow. Personal effects were taken directly to Mrs Redmond by the reverend M. O'Connell, S.C.F. 16th Division, whilst on leave. Mentioned in Despatches, London Gazette, 4 January 1917. French legion d'Honeur (Chevalier) London Gazette 14 July 1917. 1914-15 Star, British War Medal and Victory Medals, with oak leaf (MID). Willie was one of the rare people to be buried abroad during WW1 in a coffin.

Grave or Memorial Reference: Close to Path leading to the Cemetery. Cemetery: Locre Hospice Cemetery in Belgium.

REDMOND, William: Rank: Private. Regiment or Service: Royal Dublin Fusiliers. Unit: 1st Bn. Date of death: 13 August 1915. Service No: 19860. Born in Castlebridge, Co. Wexford. Enlisted in Wexford. Died of wounds in Gallipoli.

Age at death: 41.

Supplementary information: Son of Morgan and Elizabeth Redmond of 14 Lyme Street, Haydock, St Helen's. Grave or Memorial Reference: V.A.4. Cemetery: Hill 10 Cemetery in Turkey.

REEVES, Andrew: Rank: Private. Regiment or Service: Royal Irish Regiment. Unit: 'C' Company, 2nd Bn. Date of death: 19 October 1914. Service No: 2796. Born in New Ross, Co. Wexford. Enlisted in Wexford while living in Mallow Co Cork. Killed in action. Age at death: 40.

Supplementary information: Husband of Nora Reeves (*née* Callaghan) of Hume's Lane, Mallow, Co. Cork. Twenty-five years of service. He has no known grave but is commemorated on Panel 11 and 12. Memorial: Le Touret Memorial in France.

REGAN, Thomas: Rank: Private. Regiment or Service: Army Service Corps. Unit: Remount Depot. Age at death: 40. Date of death: 9 August 1917. Service No: R/359234. Born in Davistown, Co. Wexford. Epsom while living in Epsom. Died at home.

Supplementary information: Son of Laurence and Mary Regan of Clonroache, Co. Wexford. Husband of Edith Regan of Vicarage Cottage, 1 Downs Side, Epsom, Surrey. Grave or Memorial Reference: R.C.905. Cemetery: Netley Military Cemetery UK.

REID, Edgar: Rank: Private. Regiment or Service: Irish Guards. Unit: 2nd Bn. Date of death: 8 October 1915. Service No: 7111. Died of wounds.

Edgar Reid.

Born in Mullingar, Co Westmeath Enlisted in Wexford. From an article in the *Enniscorthy Guardian:*

Mr Wm Reid, Abbey Street, has received notification from the War Office, that his son, Samuel Edgar Reid, had died from wounds received in action 10th inst. Deceased, who was only 17 years of age, worked with the late Col Lonzy, Glasnevin House. When the colonel died he returned to Wexford and joined the Irish Guards last March.

Private Reid's Mother has received the following letter from Captain Witts of the Irish Guards; Dear Mrs Reid, In reply to your letter of the 20th inst, I regret to say that the information you have regarding the death of your son is only too true. He was killed on the morning of the 3rd by a shell which burst in the trench where he was standing at the time. It may be some consolation to you to know that he could have known nothing about it, and therefore suffered no pain at all, for he never recovered consiousness. Please accept my deepest sympathy with you in your irreparable loss, but you will, I hope, feel some pride that your son died a soldier's death and set an undying example to many young men at home who still shut their ears to the urgent call of King and country.

Your son is buried in the British cemetery close here at Vermelles, and his grave, I know, wil be well tended. Yours truly, Frank Witts, Captain Commanding No1 Coy.

Grave or Memorial Reference: I.L.33. Cemetery: Vermelles British Cemetery in France.

REILLY, Edward: Rank: Sergeant. Regiment or Service: Bedfordshire Regiment. Unit: 1st Bn. Date of death: 13 October 1914. Service No: 6985. Born in Shorncliffe, in Kent. Enlisted in Dublin while living Gorey, Co. Wexford. Killed in action. Age at death: 32.

Supplementary information: Husband of Mary Reilly of 28 St Albans Road, South Circular Road, Dublin. From an article in the *People*:

Universal regret was expressed in Gorey and district when it became known through a communication received from the War Office on Sunday the 8th inst; that Sergeant O'Reilly, who was married to Miss Mary Stokes, second eldest daughter of Mr James Stokes, church decorator, Lower Main Street, Gorey had been killed in action.

Sergeant O'Reilly who helt an important appointment in Dublin

was on the reserve of the Bedfordshire Regiment, and at the early stages of the war he was called to the colours – he having gone out with the second draft of Lord Kitcheners Expeditionary Force. The sympathy of all goes forth to his sorrowing widow and two young children and her relatives in their bereavement.

He has no known grave but is listed on Panels 10 and 11 on the Le Touret Memorial in France.

REILLY, John: Rank: Private. Regiment or Service: Royal Irish Regiment. Unit: 1st Bn. Age at death: 22. Date of death: 15 March 1915. Service No: 3975. Born in Marshalstown, Co. Wexford. Enlisted in Enniscorthy, Co. Wexford. Killed in action. In the *Enniscorthy Guardian* as **O'REILLY**.

Supplementary information: Son of Patrick and Mary Reilly of Kiltrea, Enniscorthy, Co. Wexford. From an article in the *Enniscorthy Guardian*:

The parents of Private John O'Reilly, Kiltrea, Enniscorthy, have received official information of the death of their son at the front. He joined the Royal Irish Regiment some months ago, and was only one week in the firing line when he fell by a German bullet. Much sympathy is felt for the parents and relatives of the young soldier. RIP.

Grave or Memorial Reference: J. 28. Cemetery: Bailleul Communal Cemetery (Nord) in France.

REILLY, John: Rank: Sergeant. Regiment or Service: Royal Garrison

Artillery. Unit: 59th Bty. Age at death: 31. Date of death: 5 January 1916. Service No: 14102. Born in Boolacreen, Co. Wexford. Enlisted in Enniscorthy while living in Boolacreen, Co. Wexford.

Supplementary information: Native of Ballyduff, Ferns, Co. Wexford. Son of John and Anne Reilly of Boolacreen, Boolavogue, Ferns. Grave or Memorial Reference: IV.G.86. Cemetery: Bethune Town Cemetery in France.

RENNISON, Walter Martyn: Rank: Lieutenant. Regiment or Service: Royal Irish Regiment. Unit: 3rd Bn, attached to the 5th Bn. Age at death: 23. Date of death: 30 December 1916. Killed in action.

Supplementary information: Son of the Revd Chancellor Henry Rennison and Mrs Kate Louisa Rennison of The Rectory, Wexford. From an article in a Wexford newspaper:

Walter Martyn Rennison.

> Sec Lieut Walter Martyn Rennison of the 3rd (Battalion Royal Irish Regiment), is the youngest son of the Rev, Canon Rennison, M.A. Kilpatrick Rectory, and Mrs Rennison. The young officer is now stationed at the Richmond Barracks, Dublin. He had been a medical student in Trinity College, Dublin, when in January last, he obtained his Majesty's Commission. The Rev, Canon Rennison is Secretary of the Ferns Diocesan Synod, and one of the most popular clergymen in the Church of Ireland, and his many friends hope that his gallant son will win distinction and renown in the defence of his country.

Grave or Memorial Reference: Panel 33. Memorial: Ypres (Menin Gate) Memorial in Belgium.

REVILLE, Patrick: Rank: Private. Regiment or Service: Royal Naval reserve. Unit: HMS *Laurentic*. Date of death: 25 January 1917. Service No: 2410B. From an article in a Wexford newspaper:

LOST ON THE 'LAURENTIC'
Mrs Teresa Reville, of Maudlinstown, Wexford, who has six sons serving in the Navy, was notified during the week that her Patrick, who was board the ill-fated ship "Laurentic", which was sunk off the Irish coast on the 25 January, was not amongst the survivors and had been given up as lost. Much sympathy is locally with Mrs Reville on the loss she has sustained.

The vessel sank in 1917 with the loss of 354 of its crew when it hit a mine at Fanad Head en route to Halifax, Nova Scotia. Some 121 crew members survived. The Laurentic was carrying the 1917 equivalent of £5 million in gold and a reported £3 million in silver coins to pay for arms for the British war effort.

Hehas no known grave but is commemorated on the Plymouth Naval Memorial, UK.

REYNOLDS, James: Rank: Private. Regiment or Service: Royal Dublin Fusiliers. Unit: 2nd Bn. Date of death: 21 March 1918. Service No: 26065. Enlisted in Sligo. Killed in action. From a Wexford Newspaper article, 'Ballyfad Soldier Killed. Private James Reynolds, a native of Ballyfad, and who was attached to the Royal Dublin Fusiliers, was sometime ago reported in these columns as being missing. His parents have now received information that he is dead'. He has no known grave but is listed on panel 79 and 80 on the Pozieres Memorial in France.

REYNOLDS, Michael: Rank: Private. Regiment or Service: Royal Inniskilling Fusiliers. Date of death: 21 August 1915. Service No: 7495. Born in Killashea, Wexford. Enlisted in Mullingar. Killed in action in Gallipoli. He has no known grave but is listed on Panel 97 to 101 on the Helles Memorial in Turkey.

RIGLEY, James: Rank: Donkeyman. Regiment or Service: Mercantile Marine. Unit: SS *Missanabie* (London). Age at death: 32. Date of death: 9 September 1918.
Supplementary information: (Served as **O'BRIEN**). Son of James and Jane Rigley of Clondaw Ferns, Co. Wexford. Born at Wexford. Torpedoed and sunk by German Submarine UB-87, 52 miles of Daunts Rock, Co Cork. Memorial: Tower Hill Memorial UK.

RITCHIE, Alexander: Rank: Deckhand. Regiment or Service: Royal Naval Reserve. nit: HMS Drifter *Barbara Cowie* (London). Date of death: 4 October 1916
Supplementary information: Husband of Jessie Ritchie, of 39 West End, Whitehills, Banffshire. Grave or Memorial Reference: In the southwest. Cemetery, Blackwater (Killila) Graveyard, Wexford.

RIVILL/REVILL/REVILLE, Patrick: Rank: Private. Regiment or Service: Irish Guards. Unit: 2nd Bn. Date of death: 15 September 1916. Service No: 6736. Born in Wexford, Co. Wexford. Enlisted in Wexford. Killed in action. Age at death: 29.
Supplementary information: Son of John and Mary Reville of Mary Street, Wexford. From an article in a Wexford newspaper:

Notification was received during the week from the war office that Private Patrick Reville, of Hill Street, Wexford, was killed in action on 15 September during an engagemnt on the Somme while serving with the Irish Guards. Deceased, who volunteered for active service in February 1915, was thirteen months in France when he received his death blow. His wife, Mrs Mary Reville, who resides at Patrick Square, Wexford, subsequently received a letter from his officer telling her of his gallantry while serving with the Guards, and also a letter from

Alexander Ritchie.

Patrick Reville.

Supplementary information: Son of John and Ellen Roberts of Ballyhaddock, Ferns, Co. Wexford. Grave or Memorial Reference: III.K.10. Cemetery: Vermelles British Cemetery in France.

ROBERTS, Joseph: Rank: Corporal. Regiment or Service: South Lancashire Regiment. Unit: 2nd Bn. Age at death: 22. Date of death: 14 April 1918. Service No: 31442. Enlisted in Birkenhead, Cheshire while living in Wexford. Killed in action.

Supplementary information: Son of Robert and Margaret Roberts of South Main Street, Wexford. Husband of Annie Roberts of 9 Bride Place, Wexford. Grave or Memorial Reference: Panel 6 and 7. Memorial: Ploegsteert Memorial in Belgium.

the Chaplain, Fr Knapp consoling her in her great sorrow. Much sympathy is felt for her and also for his widowed mother. Private Reville, has two brothers serving with the colours, one undergoing training at Warley, with the Irish Guards, and the other who is serving with the Dublins, and who had a very trying experience for 10 months in France.

He has no known grave but is commemorated on Pier and Face 7 D. Memorial: Thiepval Memorial in France.

ROBERTS, John: Rank: Private. Regiment or Service: Royal Dublin Fusiliers. Unit: 8th Bn. Age at death: 16. Date of death: 31 July 1916. Service No: 20352. Born in Ferns, Co. Wexford. Enlisted in Wicklow while living in Ferns. Killed in action

ROBERTS, William: Rank: Corporal. Regiment or Service: Royal Irish Regiment. Unit: B Company, 2nd Bn. Date of death: 24 May 1915. Service No: 10532. Born in Kilnamanagh, Co. Wexford. Enlisted in Kilkenny while living in Gorey, Co. Wexford. Killed in action. Age at death: 21.

Supplementary information: Mentioned in Dispatches. Son of John and Anne Roberts of Wells, Gorey. One of three brothers who served. He has no known grave but is commemorated on Panel 33. Memorial: Ypres (Menin Gate) Memorial in Belgium.

ROCHE, Edward: Rank: Private. Regiment or Service: Royal Irish Regiment. Unit: 1st Bn. Age at death: 20. Date of death: 24 April 1915. Service No: 4033. Born in Enniscorthy and enlisted in Enniscorthy, Co. Wexford. Killed in action.

Supplementary information: Son of Myles and Bridget Roche of Shannon Hill, Enniscorthy, Co. Wexford. Grave or Memorial Reference: Panel 33. Memorial: Ypres (Menin Gate) Memorial in Belgium.

ROCHE, James: Rank: Private. Regiment or Service: York and Lancaster Regiment. Unit: 2nd Bn. Date of death: 10 May 1916. Service No: 6701. Born in Wexford, Co. Wexford. Enlisted in Doncaster while living in Bootle, Liverpool. Killed in action. From an article in a Wexford newspaper:

> Private James Roche of the York and Lancashire Regiment, was as reported in a recent issue, killed in action recently in France. He was son of Mr James Roche, Ballycogley, and both he and his brother, Mr Walter Roche, Ballycogley, were well known and deservedly popular in commercial circles in Wexford.

James Roche.

Grave or Memorial Reference: II.P.8. Cemetery: Essex Farm Cemetery in Belgium.

ROCHE, Joseph: Rank: Private. Regiment or Service: Royal Dublin Fusiliers. Unit: 2nd Bn. Date of death: 21 March 1918. Service No: 19236. Born in Moudlan Town, Co. Wexford. Enlisted in Bridgend while living in Wexford. Killed in action. He has no known grave but is listed on Panel 79 and 80 on the Pozieres Memorial in France.

ROCHE, Laurence: Rank: Leading Seaman. Regiment or Service: Royal Naval Reserve. Unit: SS *Garmoyle*. Age at death: 31. Date of death: 10 July 1917. Service No: 4313A and 4313A/(DEV).
Supplementary information: Husband of Mary Roche, of Ballyask, Kilmore. SS *Garmoyle* was sunk by German Submarine U–57, 20k southeast of Mine Head, Cork. Grave or Memorial Reference: About two yards north of the ruin. Cemetery: Kilmore, (Grange) Graveyard, Wexford.

ROCHE, Michael Joseph: Rank: Rifleman. Regiment or Service: Royal Irish Rifles. Unit: 'B' Coy. 1st Bn. Age at death: 18. Date of death: 10 March 1915. Service No: 10309. Born in New Ross, Co. Wexford. Enlisted in Waterford while living in New Ross, Co. Wexford. Killed in action.
Supplementary information: Son of Mrs Stasia Roche of Mount Garrett Lane, New Ross, Co. Wexford. Under an unusable photograph in the *Enniscothy Guardian* it states that Michael was

L. ROCHE
LEADING SEAMAN RNR 4313 A
S.S. "GARMOYLE"
10TH JULY 1917 AGE 31

O COMPASSIONATE LORD JESUS
GRANT HIS SOUL ETERNAL REST
MY JESUS MERCY

Laurence
Roche.

Patrick Roche.

from Cockpit Lane, New Ross. He is seated beside a William Ryan who is supposed to have died also. No reference to the death of this William Ryan can be found in any of the databases available to me. Grave or Memorial Reference: Panel 42 and 43. Memorial: Le Touret Memorial in France.

ROCHE, Patrick: Rank: Corporal. Regiment or Service: Royal Irish Regiment. Unit: 1st Bn. Age at death: 23. Date of death: 21 November 1916. Service No: 10144. Born in Rowe Street, Wexford. Enlisted in Wexford while living in Cockpit-Lane. Killed in action in Salonika.

Supplementary information: Son of John and Mary Roche of Gibson Street, Wexford. From an article in the *Echo*:

Patrick Roche, Cockpit Lane, of the 18th Royal Irish Regiment was killed in the fight for the brow of the Hill 60. Weford soldiers death; details as to the manner in which Corporal Patrick Roche, 1st Batt, Royal Irish, met his death have been supplied to his family, which resides at Gibson Street, Wexford, by Rev Dominic O'Connor, Army Chaplain.

Father O'Connor, writing to the deceased soldier's mother, says "Dear Mrs Roche – I have the sad duty of telling you of the death in action of Lance-Corporal Roche (10144), 1st R. I. Regiment, on 21st November. I am, however, happy to say I attended him before he went into action, and when I heard of his being seriously wounded I went out myself and found him and attended him again before he died. He died peacefully after falling into unconsciousness, as I was having him brought in on a stretcher. He was wounded in the head and never spoke after. His comrades spoke in the highest terms of him and deeply regret him. The Commanding Officer and the other Officers and men who were not on duty or in the trenches attended his funeral. It will be some comfort to you to know he had the Priest and he lies in a blessed grave.

I said Mass for him the first opportunity I got, and many of his comrades attended and went to Holy Communion, offering it up for the repose of his soul. Praying God and Our Lady of Dolours to bless and comfort you in your sorrow and asking a small remembrance in your prayers. – I am, dear, Mrs Roche, yours very sincerely, Dominic O'Connor, Chaplain to the Forces".

Grave or Memorial Reference: VI.H.7. Cemetery: Struma Military Cemetery in Greece.

ROCHE, Patrick: Rank: Private. Regiment or Service: Leinster Regiment. Unit: 2nd Bn. Age at death: 22. Date of death: 27 August 1916. Service No: 4779. Born in Ballymittey, Co. Wexford. Enlisted in Wexford while living in Ballymittey, Co. Wexford. Died.

Supplementary information: Son of Patrick and Mary Roche of Oldhall, Bridgetown, Wexford. Grave or Memorial Reference: A.6. Cemetery: Allonville Communal Cemetery in France.

ROCHE, Richard: Rank: Private. Regiment or Service: Royal Irish Fusiliers. Unit: 5th Bn. Date of death: 28 August 1915. Service No: 16490. Born in Wexford, Co. Wexford. Enlisted in Wexford. Killed in action in Gallipoli.

Richard Roche.

Supplementary information: Son of John Roche of Francis Street, Wexford. Brother of William Roche below. From an article in a Wexford newspaper:

Private Richard Roche, Royal Irish Regiment. Mr John Roche, of Francis Street, Wexford, is mourning the loss of his two sons, who have given their all in defence of civilisation. His son, Richard, who enlisted in the 6th Batt, Royal Irish (Pioneer) last October, went out to Gallipoli a short time ago with the 10th Division, and participated in the memorable landing at Suvla Bay. During the fierce engagement on August 28th, when the Royal Irish suffered severe losses, Private Roche was killed.

Grave or Memorial Reference: Special Memorial H. 25. Cemetery: Green Hill Cemetery in Turkey.

ROCHE, William: Rank: Private. Regiment or Service: Royal Irish Regiment. Unit: 2nd Bn. Age at death: 26. Date of death: 24 May 1915. Service No: 5767. Born in Rowe Street, Wexford. Enlisted in Wexford. Killed in action.

Supplementary information: Son of John and Mary Ann Roche of 4 Francis Street, Wexford. Brother of Richard Roche above. From an article in a Wexford newspaper:

Private William Roche, Royal Irish Regiment is another son of Mr John Roche. He was reported missing on 24th May last but the circumstances under which he was last seen leaves little likelihood of his being still alive.

It appears that when the Germans resorted to the poisonous fumes to drive

William Roche.

back the Royal Irish Private Roche was amongst those gassed. When the Royal Irish were compelled by the deadly fumes to retire, some of Private Roche's comrades carried him to a "dug out" for safety from flying shrapnel. It appears that when they regained the ground lost the "dug out" was observed to have been blown to pieces, and there was no trace of Private Roche. Much sympathy is felt with Mr Roche in his double bereavement.

Grave or Memorial Reference: Panel 33. Memorial: Ypres (Menin Gate) Memorial in Belgium.

ROCHFORD, Andrew: Rank: Private. Regiment or Service: Royal Dublin Fusiliers. Unit: 2nd Bn. Age at death: 23. Date of death: 23 October 1916. Service No: 21661. Born in Wexford, Co. Wexford. Enlisted in New Ross, Co. Wexford. Killed in action.
Supplementary information: Son of Andrew and Bridget Rochford of 7 William Street, New Ross. Grave or Memorial Reference: Panel 44 and 46. Memorial: Ypres (Menin Gate) Memorial in Belgium.

ROCHFORD, John: Rank: Private. Regiment or Service: Royal Irish Regiment. Unit: 2nd Bn. Date of death: 19 October 1914. Service No: 6493. Born in St Mary's, New Ross, Co. Wexford. Enlisted in Enniscorthy, Co. Wexford. Killed in action. Grave or Memorial Reference: Panels 11 and 12. Memorial: Le Touret Memorial in France.

ROCHFORD, Patrick: Rank: Private. Regiment or Service: Royal Dublin Fusiliers. Unit: 2nd Bn. Date of death: 1 July 1916 (first day of the battle of the Somme). Service No: 22431. Born in Wexford, Co. Wexford. Enlisted in New Ross, Co. Wexford. Killed in action. He has no known grave but is listed

Bartholomew Rogers.

on Pier and Face 16C on the Thiepval
Memorial in France

ROGERS, Bartholomew: Rank:
Stoker. Regiment or Service: Royal
Naval Reserve. Unit: HMS *Indefatigable*.
Age at death: 43. Date of death: 31 May
1916. Service No: 2449T.

Supplementary information: Son of
Patrick and Mary Rogers of Emmet Place,
Wexford. Husband of Kate Rogers of 6
Emmet Place, Wexford. From an article
in a Wexford newspaper, 'He was well
known in Gaelic football circles and was
home on leave only a short time ago. His
wife was informed on Monday last that he
was not amongst those saved. There is still
some hope that he may have been picked
up as he was a powerful swimmer.' Grave
or Memorial Reference: 19. Memorial:
Plymouth Naval Memorial UK.

ROSSITER, E.: Rank: Able Seaman.
Regiment or Service: Mercantile
Marine. Unit: SS *Calliope* (London). Age
at death: 29. Date of death: 9 July 1917.
Born at Wexford. Memorial: Tower Hill
Memorial UK.

ROSSITER, James. Rank: Lance
Corporal. Regiment or Service: Irish
Guards. Unit: 2nd Bn. Date of death: 21
October 1915. Service No: 6846. Born
in Castlebridge, Co. Wexford Enlisted in
Wexford. Died of wounds.

Supplementary information: Brother
of Mr. J. Rossiter of Mary St, Wexford.
From an article in the *Enniscorthy
Guardian*:

Much regret was expressed in Wexford
amongst his numerous friends and

James Rossiter.

comrades when the sad news of the
death of Private Jas Rossiter, of Mary
Street was received. The announcement, communicated by a comrade
in a letter to his family, was afterwards
confirmed by a telegram from the War
Office. Private Rossiter, who enlisted
in the Irish Guards about seven months
ago was well known in Gaelic sporting
circles, not only in his native county
but far beyoned the borders of it.

He was a member of the County
Wexford football team and played
twice in the all Ireland final between
Wexford and Kerry, and was regarded
as one of the best right wing forwards
in Ireland. According to the meagre
particulars to hand he was in a fierce
engagement on October 21st, when he
was struck in the head with a bullet.
He was quickly removed to a field
hospital, where he died shortly after
admission. The greatest sympathy is
felt for his Father and relatives in their
great affliction. It may be mentioned
that another brother of the deceased,
Simon Rossiter, who was also well
known in ... football circles, joined the
Royal Garrison Artillery last week.

Private Thomas Foley. An Irish Guardsman, Thomas Foley, Mary Street, Wexford, writes home this week from France. He describes some serious enemy bombardments in which he had many narrow escapes. He was repeatedly struck by shell splinters but his injuries were slight, and he has not been knocked out of action. At present, he adds, they are giving the Germans all they want. He mentions how young Reid of Abbey Street was killed.

A shell burst on the parapet of the trench and he was buried alive. "It is terrible" he says, "the way these shells burst. One burst on the parapet of our trench a short time ago and buried six men." Private Foley deplores the death of a faithful Wexford comrade, Private James Ennis of King Street who was killed at his side by the gunfire of a German sniper. In a fierce bombardment he also states that Private James Rossiter, Mary Street, was fatally wounded, and died at the field hospital. He further mentions that he was convenient to Private Turner of Wexford when he was wounded, and he just learned before writing that Private Billy Armstrong was in hospital suffering from wounds. Private Foley joined the Irish Guards in the end of December last, and has been in action since August last. He is 22 years old.

Grave or Memorial Reference: M. 3. Cemetery: Sailly-Labourse Communal Cemetery in France.

ROSSITER, John: Rank: Private. Regiment or Service: Labour Corps. Regiment. Unit: 361st Company Base Depot. Date of death: 27 March 1918. Service No: 390341. Formerly he was with the Royal Irish Regiment where his number was 6786. Born in Taghmon, Co. Wexford. Enlisted in Wexford. Died. He has no known grave but is listed on Panel 94 on the Pozieres Memorial in France.

ROSSITER, Laurence: Fireman and Trimmer. Regiment or Service: Mercantile Marine. Unit: SS *Oslo* (Hull). Age at death: 33. Date of death: 21 August 1917. Laurence Rossiter is said to have survived the sinking of the *Lusitania*. Oslo was torpedoed and sunk by German Submarine U-87. Three lives lost.

Supplementary information: Son of Mary and the late Nicholas Rossiter. Husband of Elizabeth Rossiter (*née* Kavanagh) of 20 Hook Street, Liverpool. Born at Wexford. From an article in a Wexford newspaper:

The sad intelligence reached Wexford during the week that Mr Laurence Rossiter, son of Mr Nicholas Rossiter. John Street, Wexford, had been lost at sea.

No particulars as to actual manner in which the deceased came by his end are available, beyond the statement that he was killed in an explosion on board ship. For many years the deceased, who was well and popularly known in Wexford, had been in the Mercantile Marine. Sine the outbreak of war he had several narrow escapes from falling victim to piracy. He was one of the crew of the ill-fated *Lusitania*, and when that gigantic liner was sent to her doom by an unscrupulous enemy, carrying with her hundreds of non-combatants, Mr Rossiter was one of the survivors. On that occasion he was in the water for over two hours before being rescued by one of the patrol boats. Since then he has been almost constantly at sea braving the perils with which the path of the mariner are so thickly bestrewn in these terrible times.

The sad news of his untimely end caused a painful impression in his native town, where he was held in such his esteem, and much sympathy is felt with his sorrowing relatives.

From a snippet in the *Echo*, 1915:

Wexford Lusitania Survivor. Mr Joseph Rossiter, Linotype operator in The News Office, Waterford, has received a letter from his brother, Mr Laurence Rossiter, who was a fireman on board the Lusitania, and is one of the fortunate survivors.

Memorial: Tower Hill Memorial UK.

ROSSITTER/ROSSITER, Michael:
Rank: Private. Regiment or Service: Royal Dublin Fusiliers. Unit: 10th Bn. Date of death: 22 March 1918. Service No: 26672. Born in Knott, Co. Wexford. Enlisted in Manchester while living in Wexford. Killed in action.

Supplementary information: Son of Simon of 27 Emmett Square, Blackrock, Co. Dublin. He has no known grave but is listed on Panel 79 and 80 on the Pozieres Memorial in France.

Thomas Rossiter.

ROSSITER, Thomas:
Rank: Seaman. Regiment or Service: Royal Naval Reserve. Unit: HMS *Hampshire*. Age at death: 24. Date of death: 5 June 1916. Service No: 3095A. Son of Thomas Rossiter of William Street Wexford. From an article in a Wexford newspaper:

Lost with the 'Hampshire'. Seaman Thomas Rossiter, son of the late Mr Thomas Rossiter, of William Street, Wexford, who was on board HMS 'Hampshire' when that ill-fated vessel met her doom when conveying Kitchener and his staff on their mission to Russia. Prior to the outbreak of war Seaman Rossiter was engaged in the Mercantile Marine, and when hostilities were declared he rejoined the Naval Reserve.

He was only 22 years of age and

was well known in boxing circles in and about Wexford and more than once proved himself to be more than a novice at the manly art. He had two brothers with the Colours (one of whom has been discharged medically unfit and the other presently serving on an hospital ship), and with them and his sister's deep sympathy is felt.

Grave or Memorial Reference: 19. Memorial: Plymouth Naval Memorial UK.

ROTHWELL, John Francis: Rank: Private. Regiment or Service: Royal Irish Regiment. Unit: 7th (South Irish Horse) Bn. Age at death: 24. Date of death: 21 March 1918. Service No: 5624. Born in Taghmon, Co. Wexford. Enlisted in Wexford while living in Taghmon. Killed in action.

Supplementary information: Son of Matthias and Sarah Rothwell of Growtown, Taghmon, Co. Wexford. Grave or Memorial Reference: Panel 30 and 31. Memorial: Pozieres Memorial in France.

ROURKE, James: Rank: Company Sergeant Major. Regiment or Service: South African Infantry. Unit: 9th Regiment. Date of death: 27 July 1916. Service No: 5630. Age at death, 38.

Supplementary information: Mentioned in Dispatches. Son of Thomas and Rosanna Rourke, of 19, Cross Lane, New Ross, Co. Wexford. From an article in the *Enniscorthy Guardian*, 1916:

New Ross Officer Killed. Official information has reached New Ross of the death of Company Sergeant Major, Thomas Rourke, of the Sportsmen Battalion, South Africa, and son of Mr Thomas Rourke, ex Sergeant of the R.I.C., Cross Lane, New Ross. He was killed in action during a recent engagement.

During the time, extending over 12 months, that he had been in the fighting line, he had distinguished himself on several occasions, and was mentioned in dispatches by the superior officers. On one occasion during a hot fight he captured a German flag, which he sent home to his parents. He was a member of the R. I. C. for some years before going to South Africa, where he joined the force, and was promoted in a short time. After the outbreak of the war he volunteered and was soon promoted to Company Sergeant Major. He had intended making a trip home to Ireland at the end of the present month.

Grave or memorial Reference: II.F.6. Cemetery: Dodoma Cemetery in Tanzania.

ROWE, John: Rank: Private. Regiment or Service: Irish Guards. Unit: 3rd Bn. Age at death: 25. Date of death: 1 September 1917. Service No: 3668. Born in Clongeen, Co. Wexford. Enlisted in Wexford. Died at home.

Supplementary information: Son of Esther Rowe of Clougeen Foulksmills, Wexford and the late Nicholas Rowe. From an article in a Wexford newspaper:

Much regret is felt at the death of Private John Rowe, machine gun section, 1st Batt, Irish Guards, which took place at the hospital in Warley, Essex, on 1st September. Private Rowe, who was only 23 years of age, had seen two years of active service on the western front and had been twice wounded-once at Aix-la-Chapelle and again at the battle of the Somme.

Private Rowe was a son of the late Nicholas Rowe, Clongeen, who had seen much service abroad with the Royal Artillery. He was a very popular young man, and great sympathy is expressed with his mother, a well-known resident of Clongeen, in her sad bereavement. During the week Miss Rowe, a sister of Private Rowe, received a letter from Father Adkin, Chaplain to the Irish Guards, in the course of which he paid a glowing tribute to the dead soldier's memory, who, he said, was beloved by his comrades and well liked by his officers.

Grave or Memorial Reference: L.19. Cemetery: Great Warley (Christ Church) Cemetery UK.

RUTH, Patrick Joseph: Rank: Lance Corporal. Regiment or Service: Middlesex Regiment. Unit: 13th Bn. Date of death: 7 April 1917. Service No: G/41968. Formerly he was with the Lancers where his number was 29907. Enlisted in Waterford while living in Bristol, Glos. Killed in action. From an article in a Wexford newspaper:

Killed in action; Mrs E Ruth, Cathedral Street, Enniscorthy, has been officially informed that her husband, Lance Corporal Patrick Joseph Ruth, aged 24, Middlesex Regiment, was killed in action on April 7th last. The deceased, who was a son of Mr Wm Ruth, Ross Road, Enniscorthy, had been in France and other war

centres almost from the beginning of the war. Up to June of last year, when he was called to the colours, he had been attached to Central News staff at the front in the capacity of dispatch carrier. Not only did he discharge the duties of that position with fidelity and success which won the praise of his employers, but he displayed much originality in availing of opportunities which came his way to secure war news, happenings for the agency with which he was connected.

For his services for discovering subjects, which, in the hands of the correspondents under whom he served, were made the medium of interesting war messages, the deceased was handsomely rewarded, and thanked personally by the manager of the Central News. A well educated, intelligent young Irish soldier, the death of Lance Corporal Ruth at the age of 24 is deeply deplored. The greatest sympathy is felt for his wife and two children, and for his father and brothers who are respected residents of Enniscorthy. R.I.P.

Grave or Memorial Reference: 5.A.15. Cemetery: Canadian Cemetery No. 2, Neuville-St.Vaast in France.

RYAN, E.: Rank: Private. Regiment or Service: Army Service Corps. Date of death: 20 May 1917. Service No: S2/SR/04369. Born in Poona in India. Enlisted in Gorey while living in Monamolin, Co. Wexford. Died at home.

Supplementary information: Son of James and Ellen Ryan (*née* Clarke) of Clone, Monamolin, Gorey. Husband of Ellen Ryan of Ballyedmond, Gorey,

Co. Wexford. Grave or Memorial Reference: A.C.E.3. Cemetery: Southport (Duke Street) Cemetery UK.

RYAN, James: Rank: Second Lieutenant. Regiment or Service: Leinster Regiment. Unit: 7th. Bn. Age at death: 31. Date of death: 13 January 1918. Killed.

Supplementary information: Son of James and Catherine Ryan of Raheen Strahart, Ferns, Co. Wexford. Grave or Memorial Reference: Officers, B.7.13. Cemetery: St. Sever Cemetery, Rouen in France.

RYAN, James: Rank: Private. Regiment or Service: Irish Guards. Unit: 1st Bn. Date of death: 26 November 1917. Service No: 12129. Born in Oulart, Co. Wexford. Enlisted in Liverpool while living in Oulart. Killed in action. He has no known grave but is listed on Panel 2 and 3 on the Cambrai Memorial in Louveral in France

RYAN, John: Rank: Private. Regiment or Service: Loyal North Lancashire Regiment. Unit: 6th Bn. Date of death: 9 March 1917. Service No: 18345. Born in Wexford, Co. Wexford. Enlisted in Liverpool. Killed in action in Mesopotamia. No burial information can be found at this time.

RYAN, John: Rank: Gunner. Regiment or Service: Royal Garrison Artillery. Unit: 336th Siege Bty. Secondary Regiment: Royal Dublin Fusiliers. Secondary. Unit: formerly (Private. 17633) 3rd Bn. Age at death: 23. Date of death: 14 January 1919. Service No: 130898.

Supplementary information: Served

as **SULLIVAN**. Son of Patrick and Margaret Ryan of Priesthaggart, Co. Wexford. Memorial: Hollybrook Memorial, Southampton UK.

RYAN, Patrick: Rank: Gunner. Regiment or Service: Royal Garrison Artillery. Unit: Experimental Department, School of Gunnery. Date of death: 17 April 1916. Service No: 23997. Born in Bride Street, Wexford. Enlisted in Armagh while living in Fyth, Co. Wexford. Died at home. Cemetery: Shoebury (or south Shoebury) (St Andrew) Churchyard. UK.

RYAN, Peter Joseph: Rank: Private. Regiment or Service: Australian Infantry, A.I.F. Unit: 57th Bn. Age at death: 32. Date of death: 1 October 1918. Service No: 3775

Supplementary information: Born at Oilgate, Co. Wexford. Son of John and Cathrine McCarthy Ryan of Killoughtemane Corries, Bagenalstown, Co. Carlow. Date of birth: 2 January 1893. Age on enlistment: 25. Height: 5 feet 8½ inches. Eyes: blue. Hair: dark brown. Complexion: dark. Weight: 138lbs. Occupation on enlistment: labourer. Next of kin: Mrs McCarthy (remarried), Corries, Bagelnalstown, Co Carlow. Went to school in Carlow town. Personal effects were to be sent to his brother, John Ryan, 32 Hobson Street, Victoria. Peter was gassed on 29 September 1918 after only being on the battlefields for four weeks and died of gas poisoning on 1 October 1918 in the 50th Casualty Clearing Station based in Tincourt, Boucly in France. Grave or Memorial Reference: V.F.34. Cemetery: Tincourt New British Cemetery in France.

S

SAMPSON, Hugh: Rank: Private. Regiment or Service: King's Liverpool Regiment. Unit: 17th Bn. Date of death: 30 July 1917. Service No: 27579. Enlisted in Liverpool while living in Duncannon Fort, Co. Wexford. Killed in action. Grave or Memorial Reference: IX.L.3. Cemetery: Serre Road Cemetery No 1 in France.

SANE, Nicholas: Rank: Private. Regiment or Service: Royal Irish Regiment. Unit: 2nd Bn. Age at death: 22. Date of death: 10 December 1918. Service No: 4958. Born in Rowe Street, Wexford. Enlisted in Wexford. Killed in action. Son of William and Margaret Sane of Allen Street, Wexford. Grave or Memorial Reference: In the south-east part. Cemetery: Spinnes Communal Cemetery in Belgium.

SAUNDERS, John: Rank: Gunner. Regiment or Service: Royal Garrison Artillery. Unit: 118th Heavy Battery. Date of death: 12 March 1915. Service No: 1441. Born in Wexford, Co. Wexford. Enlisted in Liverpool. Killed in action. Brother of Mr R. Saunders of 6 Lunt Road, Bootle, Liverpool. Grave or Memorial Reference: III.G.4. Cemetery: Royal Irish Rifles Graveyard Laventie in France.

SCALLAN, Edward: Rank: Private. Regiment or Service: Royal Dublin Fusiliers. Unit: 1st Bn. Date of death: 3 May 1918. Service No: 29986. Born in Barringtown, Wexford. Enlisted in Dublin while living in Barringtown. Died of wounds. Grave or Memorial Reference: I.E.II. Cemetery: Ebblinghem Military Cemetery in France.

SCULLY, Henry: Rank: Lance Corporal. Regiment or Service: Royal Irish Rifles. Unit: 1st Garrison Bn. Age at death: 45. Date of death: 17 June 1919. Service No: 21189.

Supplementary information: Son of Thomas and Harriet Scully. Husband of Mary Jane Scully of Leskinfere, Gorey, Co. Wexford. Buried in Cawnpore Cantonment New Cemetery. Grave or Memorial Reference: Face 23. Memorial: Madras 1914-1918 War Memorial, Chennai in India.

SERGENT, William John: Rank: Fitter. Regiment or Service: Australian Field Artillery. Unit: 3rd A. F. A. Brigade and 3rd Brigade Ammunition Column. Date of death: 7 May 1915. Service No: 2262. Born in Rasslair, Wexford. Age on enlistment: 22 years 9 months. Height 5 feet 8¼ inches. Hair: brown. Eyes: blue. Enlisted in Brisbane in Queensland while living in. Previous to enlistment was apprenticed to Wilsons of Bristol for three years. Next of kin: (widowed) mother, Mrs Martha Mahala. Sergent, 288 North Street, Bedminster, Bristol and later changed to 54 Russell Terrace, Newtown, Wellington, New Zealand. Pension of £26 *per annum* granted to his Mother from 8 May 1915.

Supplementary information: Son of Henry and Mahala Sergent, of Plinburne, Hurworth, New Plymouth, New Zealand. Born in Ireland. Died of wounds received in action in the Dardanelles. Died in Malta. Buried by Chaplain M Tobias on the day of his death in the Government Hospital in Malta. Death was reported in the Brisbane papers, Sunday, 13 June 1915. His medals were sent to his mother after his death but she had left England at that time to go to Australia. She was eventually located in New Zealand and the medals were then sent to her. Grave or Memorial Reference: A.II.1. Cemetery: Pieta Military Cemetery in Malta.

SHALLOW, J.: Rank: Seaman. Regiment or Service: Mercantile Marine. Unit: SS *Ionian* Age at death: 36. Date of death: 20 October 1917. Sunk by a mine off Milford Haven laid by German Submarine UC-51. Seven lives were lost. Son of James Shallow of Fisherstown Campile, Co. Wexford. Cemetery: Castlemartin (St Michael) Churchyard UK.

SHANNON, John: Rank: Private. Regiment or Service: Sherwood Foresters. Unit: 2/8th Bn. Date of death: 7 June 1917. Service No: 306781. Born in Cloneven, Co. Wexford. Enlisted in Eastwood in Nottinghamshire while living in Jacksdale, Notts. Killed in action. Son of the late John Shannon. Grave or Memorial Reference: I.C.5. Cemetery: Metz-En-Couture Communal Cemetery British Extension in France.

SHANNON, Peter: Rank: Private. Regiment or Service: Australian Infantry. A.I.F. Unit: 53rd Bn. Date of

death: 19 July 1916. Service No: 3433. Born in Newross, Co. Wexford. Enlisted in Liverpool aged 34 years 4 months. Height: 5 feet 6¼ inches. Eyes: dark brown. Hair: black. Complexion: dark. Weight: 150lbs. Occupation on enlistment: shearer. Next of kin: Brother, John Joseph Shannon, c/o Mr Marshall, Farm No 732 Leeton, Via Yanco, NSW. Sister Miss Agnes Shannon, 186 Jersey Street, Paddington. Served six months with the Australian Commonwealth Horse and discharged at the end of the war (Boer war). Reported missing in action 19 July 1916. His identification disc was received from Germany and reported as Killed in action at Fleur Baix (on 20 July 1916). He has no known grave but is listed on the V.C. Corner Australian Cemetery Memorial in Fromelles in France.

SHANNON, William: Rank: Private. Regiment or Service: Royal Dublin Fusiliers. Unit: 'C' Coy. 1st Bn. Age at death: 24. Date of death: 22 December 1915. Service No: 21819. Born in Wexford, Co. Wexford. Enlisted in New Ross. Killed in action in Gallipoli.

Supplementary information: Son of James and Margaret Shannon of 22 Michael Street, New Ross, Co. Wexford. From an article in the *Enniscorthy Guardian*:

Official information has reached New Ross that Private William Shannon, Michael Street, was recently killed at the front.

It appears he received the fatal wound in the exciting engagement where the Irish Regiments kept at bay for some days a vastly superior force of Bulgars and Germans. He was working at the frim of Messrs, Graves and Co., New Ross, when he volunteered, and was at the front about two months. His officer paid a high tribute to his courage and bravery, and the official notice of his death to his widowed mother contained expressions of sincere sympathy. She has two other sons in the Amy and one in the Navy.

Grave or Memorial Reference: II.E.9. Cemetery:Twelve Tree Copse Cemetery in Turkey.

SHEA, Richard: Rank: Private. Regiment or Service: Canadian Infantry (Manitoba Regiment). Unit: 27th Bn. Age at death: 29. Date of death: 2 October 1918. Service No: 187695.

Supplementary information: Son of Michael John and Mary Shea of Kiltennell, Gorey, Co. Wexford. Information from his enlistment documents: Eyes: blue. Hair: dark brown. Complexion: fair. Height: 5 Feet 6 Inches. Address on enlistment: no fixed address. Date of birth: 8 April 1892. Place of birth: Gorey, Co. Wexford. Marital status: single. Name and address of next of kin: Sister, Mrs Margrette ?, Shea, Ballinapottage, Auger, Co. Tyrone. Date of attestation: 13 November 1915. Location of attestation Winnipeg. Occupation on enlistment: Electrician. Grave or Memorial Reference: I.A.18. Cemetery: Canada Cemetery, Tilloy-Les-Cambrai in France.

SHEEHAN, Patrick: Rank; Private. Regiment or Service: Royal Army Medical Corps. Unit: 16th Field Ambulance. Service No; 7385. Age at death: 18. Date of death: 9 August 1915.

Born in Rosbercan, Kilkenny and enlisted in New Ross. Killed in action. Supplementary Information, son of Mary Sheehan. From an article in the *People*:

> Official information has reached New Ross that two New Ross soldiers were killed at the front last week. One is Private Patrick Sheehan, who's parents are dead, but who has an Aunt living in Michael Street. He was about 21 [*sic*] years of age and was attached to the Royal Army Medical Corps.

Grave or Memorial Reference: I.G.5. Cemetery: Poperinghe New Military Cemetery in Belgium.

SHEEHAN, William: Rank: Sergeant. Regiment or Service: Royal Irish Regiment. Unit: 2nd Bn. Date of death: 22 July 1916. Service No: 4378. Born in New Ross, Co.Wexford. Enlisted in New Ross, Co.Wexford. Died of wounds.

Supplementary information: Husband of Ellen Sheehan of 6 Upper William Street, New Ross, Co. Wexford. Grave or Memorial Reference: IV.G.12. Cemetery: Abbeville Communal Cemetery in France.

SHERIDAN, Patrick: Rank: Lance Corporal. Regiment or Service: Royal Irish Regiment. Unit: 2nd Bn. Date of death: 24 May 1915. Age at death: 29. Killed in action. Service No: 7185. Born in St Mary's, Dublin. Enlisted in Gorey while living in Ballyrorey, Co.Wexford.

Supplementary information: Son of Mr and Mrs Sheridan, of Coolboy,Tinahely, Co. Wicklow. He has no known grave but is listed on Panel 33 on the Ypres (Menin Gate) Memorial in Belgium.

John Christopher Sherwood.

SHERWOOD, John Christopher:

Rank: Private. Regiment or Service: New Zealand Expeditionary Force, Wellington Regiment. Age at death: 28. Date of death: 17 December 1915. Service No: 10/1014.

Supplementary information: Son of John and Esther Victoria Sarah Sherwood, of 7 Parnell Street, Wexford. From an article in the *Enniscorthy Guardian*:

> Private John Christopher Sherwood who died in an Hospital Ship on December 17th from wounds received during and engagement at Gallipoli in which he participated with the New Zealand contingent. The deceased, who had only attained his 25th year, was son of Mr John Sherwood (Ex-Sergeant R.I.C.) of Parnell Street, Wexford. His elder brother, Richard, who was a Sergeant in the Royal Irish Regiment, was killed in action on the 17th March last, and the two surviving brothers, Albert and James are also serving with the colours. He

emigrated to New Zealand some years ago, where he held a lucrative position, but on the outbreak of the war he joined the New Zealand contingent of fighters whose deeds at Anzac have stirred the admiration of the whole world.

> Prior to his departure for the Antipodes, the late Private Sherwood had been employed at Messrs Thompson Bros, Wexford, and he was an exceedingly popular young man. The news of his death was learnt with deep regret by his many friends in Wexford, and the sympathies of all are extended to his sorrowing parents in their bereavement.

Grave or Memorial Reference: 76. Memorial, Lone Pine Memorial in Turkey.

SHERWOOD, Richard Atwell:

Rank: Sergeant. Regiment or Service: Royal Irish Regiment. Unit: 2nd Bn. Age at death: 31. Date of death: 17 March 1915. Service No: 9220. Born in Ardcolm, Co. Wexford. Enlisted in Wexford. Died of wounds. From an article in a Wexford newspaper:

> It was reported during the week that Sergeant Richard Sherwood, of the Royal Irish Regiment, a son of Mr John Sherwood, ex-R.I.C. Sergeant, Parnell Street, Wexford, has been killed in action. Sergeant Sherwood has been at the front almost since the commencement of hostilities. Three of his brothers are also serving with the colours. The announcement has been received with much regret in the town, where Sergeant Sherwood was very popular. With the official notification was a letter from the King and Lord Kitchener, expressing their sympathy.

Richard Sherwood.

Supplementary information: Son of John and Esther Sherwood of 7 Parnell Street, Wexford. Grave or Memorial Reference: J. 28. Cemetery: Bailleul Communal Cemetery (Nord) in France.

SHORE, J.: Rank: Private. Regiment or Service: Royal Irish Regiment. Age at death: 31. Date of death: 3 November 1920. Service Number; 1770.

Supplementary information: Husband of Mary Shore of Courtnacuddy. Grave or Memorial Reference: About 6 yards north-west of the entrance. Cemetery: Courtnacuddy Catholic Cemetery, 8 miles outside Enniscorthy.

SINGLETON, William: Rank: Lance Corporal. Regiment or Service: Royal Irish Regiment. Unit: 2nd Bn. Age at death: 35. Date of death: 22 October 1914. Service No: 7556. Born in Wexford, Co. Wexford. Enlisted in Wexford. Died of wounds.

Supplementary information: Son of Richard and Sarah Singleton of 5 Back Street, Wexford. Grave or Memorial Reference: I.C.16. Cemetery: Bethune Town Cemetery in France.

SINNOTT, Michael Peter: Rank: Wireless Operator. Regiment or Service: Mercantile Marine. Unit: HMS *Glenart Castle*. Torpedoed by German Submarine. 38 of the 206 on board survived. She was heading for Brest to load wounded. Age at death: 23. Date of death: 26 February 1918

Supplementary information: Son of Julia Anne Sinnott of Cahore, Gorey, Co. Wexford and the late Peter Sinnott. Born at Morriscastle, Co. Wexford. Grave or Memorial Reference: 6.RC. Cemetery: Penzance Cemetery UK.

SINNOTT, Stephen: Rank: Private. Regiment or Service: Royal Irish Regiment. Unit: 2nd Bn. Date of death: 19 October 1914. Service No: 6259. Born in St Bridget's, Co. Wexford. Enlisted in Wexford. Killed in action. Age at death: 28.

Supplementary information: Son of Anthony and Anne Sinnott. He has no known grave but is commemorated on Panel 11 and 12. Memorial: Le Touret Memorial in France.

SINNOTT, Thomas: Rank: Private. Regiment or Service: Worcestershire Regiment. Unit: 4th Bn. Date of death: 9 October 1917. Service No: 39765. Born in Enniscorthy, Co. Wexford. Enlisted in Worcester while living in Strokwell in London. Killed in action. Age at death: 36.

Supplementary information: Husband

J. Shore.

of Ella Gertrude Sinnott of 72 Atherfold Road, Clapham, London. He has no known grave but is commemorated on Panel 75 to 77. Memorial: Tyne Cot Memorial in Belgium.

SINNOTT, Thomas: Rank: Private. Regiment or Service: Royal Dublin Fusiliers. Unit: 10th Bn. Age at death: 32. Date of death: 2 February 1917. Service No: 26230. Born in Bannow. Enlisted in Wexford. Killed in action.

Supplementary information: Son of Patrick and Mary Sinnott of Brandane, Bannow, Co. Wexford. Grave or Memorial Reference: Pier and Face 16C. Memorial: Thiepval Memorial in France.

SINNOTT, Thomas: Rank: Seaman. Regiment or Service: Royal Naval Reserve. Unit: HMS *Laurentic*. Date of death: 25 January 1917. Service No: 2455A. Killed by a mine explosion off the Irish Coast.

Supplementary information: Son of John and Mary Sinnott of Ballyreilly, Co. Wexford. The vessel sank in 1917 with the loss of 354 of its crew when it hit a mine at Fanad Head en route to Halifax, Nova Scotia. Some 121 crew members survived. The *Laurentic* was carrying the 1917 equivalent of £5 million in gold and a reported £3 million in silver coins to pay for arms for the British war effort. Grave or Memorial Reference: 24. Memorial: Plymouth Naval Memorial UK.

SINNOTT, William: Rank: Seaman. Regiment or Service: Royal Naval Reserve. Unit: HMS *Louvain*. Age at death: 29. Date of death: 20 January

1918. Service No: 2479A.

Supplementary information: Son of Richard and Ellen Sinnott of Hardyglass, Co. Wexford. Grave or Memorial Reference: 29. Memorial: Plymouth Naval Memorial UK.

SINNOTT, William: Rank: Private. Regiment or Service: Royal Irish Regiment. Unit: 1st Bn. Date of death: 15 March 1915. Service No: 8846. Born in Enniscorthy, Co. Wexford. Enlisted in Wexford while living in Ennisbury. Killed in action. Age at death: 26.

Supplementary information: Son of Myles and Katie Sinnott of Pembroke Cottages, Donnybrook, Dublin. He has no known grave but is listed on Panel 33 on the Ypres (Menin Gate) Memorial in Belgium.

SMITH, George Joseph: Rank: Lance Corporal. Regiment or Service: Australian Infantry, A.I.F. Unit: 45th Bn. Age at death: 29. Date of death: 6 April 1918. Service No: 2534.

Supplementary information: Son of Michael and Johanna Smith of Maudlintown, Wexford. From an article in the *People*, 1918:

The news of the death of Sergt Geo. J. Smith, Maudlintown, Wexford, who was killed in action on the 5th April, will be received with genuine feelings of regret. He was son of Mr Michael Smith, joined the Australian Imperial Forces in the early stages of the war, and left for Gallipoli with the first Expeditionary Forces. Here he was wounded and was sent back to Australia, soon returning to Gallipoli, and after the evacuation was posted to Egypt, proceeding from thence to

France where he was killed on the date mentioned.

It is only a couple of weeks ago since he was home in Wexford on furlough when he renewed acquaintances with many of his old friends. He was very popular in his regiment, as the sub-joined letter indicates, and he died fortified by the rites of the Holy Church. Capt. T.D. Ferguson writes; Dear Mrs Smith, – No doubt you have by this time been informed of the death of your son, G.J.Smith. We, the officers, N.C.O's and men of his company, all deeply deplore his death, and wish to express our very deep sympathy with you in your bereavement. We all feel his loss here, as his cheerful disposition and good nature made him a general favourite. As a soldier, he was admired throughout the Battalion, and readily ranked as one of our very best front line men. We sincerely trust it will be some consolation to you to know that his end was sudden and painless, that he was prepared, and died facing the enemy like the true soldier that he was. Again expressing sincerest sympathy with yourself and all relatives and friends- Yours sincerely, T.D. Ferguson, Captain.

Memorial: Villers-Bretonneux Memorial in France.

SMITH, Patrick: Rank: Private. Regiment or Service: Royal Irish Regiment. Unit: 2nd Bn. Date of death: 9 May 1915. Service No: 7241. Born in Ballygarret, Co. Wexford. Enlisted in Gorey, Co.Wexford. Killed in action. From an article in the *Enniscorthy Guardian*:

News reached Balygarret district this week of the reported death of Patrick Smith, who was a private in the Royal Irish Regiment. Deceased joined the army since the outbreak of the war, and was for some time in training in Beggar's Bush Barracks. Only a short time ago he was ordered to the front, and went through some of the fiercest fighting in the war, being fatally wounded in one of the engagements which centred around Hill 60.

He has no known grave but is listed on Panel 33 on the Ypres (Menin Gate) Memorial in Belgium.

SMITH, William George: Rank: Lance Corporal. Regiment or Service: Australian Infantry. Unit: 45th Bn. Date of death: 6 April 1918. Age at death, 29. Service No: 2534. Born in Wexford. Age on enlistment: 28 years 5 months. Weight:140lbs. Height: 5 feet 7 ½ inches. Complexion: dark. Eyes: blue. Hair: black. Enlisted in Sydney (also listed as Liverpool, NSW) on 10 July 1915. Occupation on enlistment: bushman. Previous military experience: five years Naval Reserve. His last will states 'In the event of my death. I give the whole of my property and effects to my Mother. Mrs. Capt. Smith No 6 Maudlin Down, Wexford, Ireland.' Killed in action.He has no known grave but is listed on the Villers-Bretonneux Memorial in France.

SMYTH, Michael: Rank:Able Seaman. Regiment or Service:Mercantile Marine Reserve. Unit: H.M.Yacht *Jason II*.Age at death: 34. Date of death: 4 December 1917.

Supplementary information: Son of James and Anastasia Smyth of Wexford. Husband of Mary Elizabeth Smyth of 73 New Hedley Street, Boundary Street, Liverpool. Grave or Memorial Reference: H.340. Cemetery: Liverpool (Ford) Roman Catholic Cemetery UK.

SMYTH/SMYTHE, Robert Richard: Rank: Private. Regiment or Service: Irish Guards. Unit: 2nd Bn. Age at death: 19. Date of death: 13 April 1918. Service No: 10501. Born in Drumcondra, Co. Dublin. Enlisted in Enniscorthy, Co. Wexford. Killed in action

Supplementary information: Son of Frank and Sarah Smyth of Munfin, Ballycarney, Ferns, Co. Wexford. From De Ruvigny's Roll of Honour:

SMYTH, ROBERT RICHARD, Private, No. (---), Irish Guards, eldest s. of Frank Smyth, of Munfin, Ballycarney, by his wife, Sarah, dau. Of John Pratt; b. Dublin, 8 May, 1899; educ. Wexford, and Ballycarney; was a Garden Boy; volunteered for active service, and enlisted in the Irish

Robert Richard Smyth.

Guards 27 Nov. 1915; served with the Expeditionary Force in France and Flanders from 3 April to 13 April, 1918, when he was reported wounded and missing and is now reported to have been killed in action at Aral Wood 13 April, 1918. Buried where he fell; unm.

Grave or Memorial Reference: I.BB.38. Cemetery: Aval Wood Military Cemetery, Vieux-Berquin in France.

SOMERS, Albert J.: Rank: Sergeant. Regiment or Service: Royal Irish Regiment. Unit: 2nd Bn. Age at death: 20. Date of death: 2 October 1918. Service No: 3-7984 and 7984. Awarded the Military Medal and Bar and listed in the *London Gazette*. Born in Wexford and enlisted in Cloughjordan. Died of wounds.

Supplementary information: Son of Robert Wilson Somers and Charlotte Somers of Cloughjordan, Co. Tipperary. Grave or Memorial Reference: III.F.10. Cemetery: Sunken Road Cemetery, Boiusleux-St. Marc in France.

SOMERS, Patrick: Rank: Private. Regiment or Service: Irish Guards. Unit: 2nd Bn. Date of death: 26 September 1916. Service No: 10426. Born in Tintern, Co. Wexford. Enlisted in New Ross, Co. Wexford. Killed in action. Grave or Memorial Reference: Has no known grave but is commemorated on Pier and Face 7D on the Thiepval Memorial in France.

SPENCER, Charles: Rank: Private. Regiment or Service: Connaught

Rangers. Unit: 2nd Bn. Date of death: 14 September 1914. Service No: 7610. Born in Gorey, Co. Wexford. Enlisted in Gorey, Co. Wexford while living in Gorey. Killed in action.

Supplementary information: Husband of Annie Spencer of Ballygarron, Kilmuckridge, Gorey, Co. Wexford. From an article in the *Echo* newspaper:

> Victims of the War. Much sympathy is felt for Mrs Spencer, Gorey Bridge, whose young husband, Charles Spencer, was killed at Dixmude on Sept 14th. The eldest son of Mr Thomas Spencer, saddler, Gorey, he enlisted as a youth in the Connaught Rangers, and was summoned up with the reserve. He had a presentiment of what was to happen, for he sadly but emphatically stated at Gorey Railway Station when leaving that he was doomed never to see it again. A decent, respectable man, against whom no person ever had a word to say, his death in the continental shambles has caused much regret in Gorey, and his young wife, left with two little children, is heartbroken.

Memorial: La Ferte-Sous-Jouarre Memorial in France.

STAFFORD, Francis: Rank: Rifleman. Regiment or Service: Royal Irish Rifles. Unit: 6th Bn. Date of death: 11 August 1915. Service No: 14896. Born in Gorey, Co. Wexford. Enlisted in Dublin. Killed in action in Gallipoli. Age at death: 41.

Supplementary information: Husband of Gertrude Stafford of 161 Iveagh Building, 25, New Bride Street, Dublin. He has no known grave but is listed on Panel 177 to 178 on the Helles Memorial in Turkey.

STAFFORD, George: Rank: Leading Seaman. Regiment or Service: Royal Naval Reserve. Unit: SS *Intent*. Date of death: 26 December 1917. Service No: 4651/B.

Supplementary information: Son of Katherine Stafford of St Helen's, Kilrane, Co. Wexford. Grave or Memorial Reference: Div. 62.L.8. Cemetery: Ste. Marie Cemetery, Le Havre in France.

STEPHENS, Francis: Rank: Boatswain. Regiment or Service: Mercantile Marine. Unit: SS *Memphian* (Liverpool). Age at death: 48. Date of death: 8 October 1917.

Supplementary information: Son of James and Mary Stephens. Husband of Mrs Margaret O'Flaherty (formerly Stephens) of 88 Old Hall Street, Liverpool. Born at Wexford. Sailing from Liverpool to Boston she was sunk by German Submarine U-96 7 miles East South East of the North Arklow Lighship. Grave or Memorial Reference: In south-east corner. Cemetery: Llanllwchaiarn (St Llwchaiarn) (or New Quay) Churchyard UK.

SULLIVAN, Michael: Rank: Sergeant. Regiment or Service: Royal Irish Regiment. Unit: 1st Bn. Age at death: 40. Date of death: 9 May 1915. Service No: 5320. Born in Gorey, Co. Wexford. Enlisted in Wexford while living in Gorey, Co. Wexford. Killed in action.

Supplementary information: Son of William and Mary Sullivan of 13

Michael Sullivan.

Grattan Street, Gorey, Co. Wexford. Husband of Bridget Sullivan of 16 Robert Street South, Dublin. From an article in the *Enniscorthy Guardian*, 1915:

News has just been received in Gorey, that Michael Sullivan, a Sergeant attached to the Royal Irish Regiment, and late of William Street Gorey, has died at the front. Sergeant Sullivan who went through the South African War left for the front about three months ago and came out of several engagements unscathed, but at hill 60 he was struck by a shell and death shortly afterwards took place. Two Gorey men John Walker and Patrick Howard, who were in the same Regiment as the deceased, were close by when he was wounded and assisted in his burial subsequently.

Grave or Memorial Reference: Panel 33. Memorial: Ypres (Menin Gate) Memorial in Belgium.

SUNDERLAND, John: Rank: Private. Regiment or Service: Royal Dublin Fusiliers. Unit: 1st Bn. Date of death: 18 August 1917. Service No: 29236. Born in Enniscorthy and enlisted in Enniscorthy, Co. Wexford. Killed in action. Grave or Memorial Reference: VIII.D.12. Cemetery: Artillery Wood Cemetery in Belgium.

SUNDERLAND, John: Rank: Stoker. Regiment or Service: Royal Naval Reserve. Unit: HMS *Defence*. Age at death: 27. Date of death: 31 May 1916. Service No: 2793T.

Supplementary information: Son of Michael and Anne Sunderland of Ballywoodrane, Blackwater, Enniscorthy, Co. Wexford. Husband of Elizabeth Mary Roche (formerly Sunderland) of Ballywoodrane, Blackwater, Co. Wexford. Grave or Memorial Reference: 19. Memorial: Plymouth Naval Memorial UK.

SWIFT, Patrick: Rank: Private. Regiment or Service: Royal Irish Regiment. Unit: 2nd Bn. Date of death: 14 September 1914. Service No: 7026. Born in Wexford, Co. Wexford. Enlisted in Wexford. Killed in action. He has no known grave but is listed on the La-Ferte-Sous-Jouarre-Memorial in France.

SYMES, Thomas Arthur: Rank: Private. Regiment or Service: Royal Dublin Fusiliers. Unit: 7th Bn. Date of death: 18 August 1915. Age at death: 29. Died in Gallipoli. Service No: 14228. Born in Cross Patrick, Tinehely, Co. Wicklow. Enlisted in Boyle Co

Thomas Arthur Symes.

Roscommon while living in Tinehely.

Supplementary information: Son of Sandham John and Catherine Chamney Symes, of 'Hill View', Tinahely, Co. Wicklow. Educated privately. Occupation on enlistment: Clerk, Bank of Ireland. Disembarker at Mudros Bay, July 30. In August he developed dysentery which eventually killed him at the 2nd Australian Hospital in Mudros.

From an article in the *People* and the *Enniscorthy Guardian*, 'Announcement has been received from Alexandria of the death in hospital of Thomas A Symes, of D Company, 7th Battalion, Royal Dublin Fusiliers. Deceased was the seventh son of Mr Sandman J Symes, Hill View, Co. Wexford.' Grave or Memorial Reference: I.B.37. Cemetery: Portianos Military Cemetery in Greece.

T

TACKABERRY, John Barry: Rank: Captain. Regiment or Service: Indian Medical Service Unit: 83rd Combined Stationary Hospital. Age at death: 35. Date of death: 25 March 1917.

Supplementary information: Son of Thomas and Mary Tackaberry, of Co. Tyrone. Husband of Alice Tackaberry, of 6 Grafton Mansions, Brighton, England. From an article in a Wexford newspaper:

DEATH OF CAPT TACKABERRY.

Captain John Bailey Tackaberry, M.B., B.S. (Lond.), Indian Medical Service, Indian Army, whose death from cerebro-spinal meningitis on the Mesopotamian front on March 25th has lately been announced by the India Office, was the second surviving son of the late Thomas Tackaberry Esq, of Tomagaddy, Ballycanew, Co. Wexford, and of Dungannon, Co Tyrone.

He was closely related to many well known families of North County Wexford, and by his numerous friends in Wexford his untimely death is universally lamented. The late Captain Tackaberry was born in the year 1883 at Drumglass, Dungannon, County Tyrone. Educated at the Royal School, Dungannon, and Trinity College, Dublin, he migrated to London University and entered Middlesex Hospital Medical School. After a brilliant and distuinguished career at the Middlesex, where he held the position of House Surgeon – and on the conclusion of an equally brilliant career at London University, he graduated M. B, B. S. – first man of his year – with full marks in anatomy and physiology. This performance he repeated soon after at the competitive examination for Commissions in the Indian Medical Service, when he headed the list of successful candidates.

He married, in 1911, Miss Alice Hanby, of Rogerstone Park, Newport, Monmouth, who with a little son of five years survives him. He served successfully at Lucknow, Fyzbad, Hong Konh, and Fort Sandeman (British Beluchistan), where he was stationed at the outbreak of war and for some time afterwards. Captain Tackaberry was chief medical officer of the 129th Baluchis – a Regiment which by its gallantry won three Victoria Crosses and undying glory on the French front and was attached to the 6th Native Cavalry and the 66th Sikhs, and saw service with the Gurkhas and Pathans, In 1915 he joined the Mesopotamian Relief Force, and served under General Maude throughout the stiff fighting that led to the recapture of Kut and the fall of Baghdad.

Under the rigours of that campaign he became a victim to that dread malady cerebro-spinal meningitis, familiarly known as "Spotted fever", and his death on the 25th March last, at the early age of 34 years, brought a splendid career, successful in the highest sense of the term, to an untimely termination.

Grave or Memorial Reference: V.U.17. Cemetery: Basra War Cemetery in Iraq.

TAPLEY, Thomas: Rank: Private. Regiment or Service: Queen's Own (Royal West Kent Regiment). Unit: 10th Bn. Age at death: 43. Date of death: 25 September 1916. Service No: 10163 and G/10163. Born in Gorey. Enlisted in Maidstone in Kent. Died of wounds.

Supplementary information: Son of Henry and Hannah Tapley of Ballingarry, Gorey, Co. Wexford. Grave or Memorial Reference: EB. 35. Cemetery: Cardiff (Cathays) Cemetery UK.

TAYLOR, Charles: Rank: Major. Regiment or Service: Royal Irish Regiment. Unit: 3rd Bn. Date of death: 5 August 1917. Killed in action. From an article in a *Enniscorthy Guardian:*

> Major Charles Taylor, Royal Irish Regiment, who was killed in action in France on the 6th inst, was the youngest son of Godfrey Lovelace Taylor, of Grangeville, Fethard, Co. Wexford. Major Taylor, who as 35 years of age, had been formerly attached to the 3rd Batt, R. I. Regiment (Wexford Militia), and had served for several years in the Royal North West Mounted and Victoria Police. He returned to this country to join a service Battalion of his old Regiment shortly after the outbreak of the hostilities.
>
> He had been at the front two and a half years and was mentioned in dispatches. His eldest brother, Fleet Surgeon Godfrey Taylor was lost in the disaster to HMS *Formidable* in January 1915. While another, Lieut O. C. Taylor, RFSA was badly wounded on the Somme. The late Major taylor was one of the last to speak to the late Major William Redmond befire the latters death. He leaves a widow and one son to mourn his loss and with them as well as his respected father and other relatives much sympathy is felt.

Grave or Memorial Reference: Panel 33. Memorial: Ypres (Menin Gate) Memorial in Belgium.

TAYLOR, Godfrey: Rank: Fleet Surgeon. Regiment or Service: Royal Navy. Unit: HMS *Formidable*. Age at death: 42. Date of death: 1 January 1915. HMS *Formidable* was sunk by two German torpedoes fired by Submarine U-24 on New Year's Day 38 miles off the devon Coast. 551 men went down with her. There were only 199 survivors.

Supplementary information: Son of Godfrey Lovelace Taylor and Dorothea Marie Taylor of Grangeville, Fethard, Co. Wexford. M.B, M.A. From an article in a Wexford newspaper:

Godfrey Taylor.

The late Fleet Surgeon Godfrey L Taylor, son of Mr Godfrey L Taylor, of Fethard, who was on HMS "Formidable" when she was torpedoed off the Portland Coast of England on News Years morning. About two hundred of the crew were saved, and six hundred lost, of whom the young gentleman, whose picture we give above, was one. The deceased had a distinguished career in the Navy, and the utmost sympathy is felt for his respected family in their great sorrow.

Grave or Memorial Reference: 9. Memorial: Chatham Naval Memorial UK.

THOMAS, James: Rank: Private. Regiment or Service: Royal Irish Regiment. Unit: 7th (South Irish Horse) Bn. Date of death: 21 March 1918. Service No: 1981. Born in Barntown, Co. Wexford. Enlisted in Wexford. Killed in action. He has no known grave but is listed on Panel 30 and 31 on the Pozieres Memorial in France.

THORPE, Samuel: Rank: Private. Regiment or Service: Machine Gun Corps (Infantry). Unit: 45th Coy. Formerly he was with the Royal Irish Regiment where his number was 4919. Age at death: 30. Date of death: 9 August 1916. Service No: 11390. Born in Enniscorthy and enlisted in Enniscorthy, Co. Wexford. Killed in action.

Supplementary information: Husband of Catherine Thorpe of Drumfold, Enniscorthy, From an article in the *Enniscorthy Guardian*, 1915:

Samuel Thorpe.

Mrs W. Thorpe, Irish Street Bunclody, has two sons and a grandson on active service. Her two sons are Gunner Richard Thorpe, Royal Garrison Artillery, and Sergeant [sic] Samuel Thorpe, 18th Royal Irish Regiment, and her grandson in Private F. Sutton, Gunner, Royal Field Artillery, who belong to the Bunclody Corps of the National Volunteers.

The former was the organiser of this Corps and held supreme command. Sergeant S. Thorpe has been through all the sever fighting in Flanders without receiving a scar. Gunner R. Thorpe is stationed on one of the forts on the south east coast of England, and Private F. Sutton is with the Mediterranean Expeditonary Force. Gunner R. Thorpe belonged to the army reserve and was called up at the outbreak of the war. Samuel Thorpe volunteered shorthy after the outbreak of the war, and was through skill and efficiency, promoted to the rank of Sergeant. Frank Sutton volunteered the same time. Co. Wexford.

Grave or Memorial Reference: Pier and Face 5.C and 12.C. Memorial: Thiepval Memorial in France.

THORPE, Thomas: Rank: Lance Corporal. Regiment or Service: Royal Irish Regiment. Unit: 2nd Bn. Date of death: 21 March 1918. Service No: 5217. Born in Enniscorthy, Co. Wexford. Enlisted in Enniscorthy. Died of wounds. Killed in action. He has no known grave but is listed on Panel 30 and 31 on the Pozieres Memorial in France.

TIERNEY, Andrew: Rank: Private. Regiment or Service: Royal Irish Regiment. Unit: 4th Bn. Age at death: 18. Date of death: 27 August 1916. Service No: 11520. Born in St Mary's, New Ross, Co. Wexford. Enlisted in New Ross. Died at home.

Supplementary information: Son of Mrs Susan Tierney of 11 Bewley Street, New Ross. From an article in the *People*, 1916:

A soldier named Andrew Tierney, aged about 17, and a native of Bewley Street, New Ross, was drowned whilst bathing in the Barrow at New Ross on Sunday evening.

It appears that about five o'clock with some boys he went for a swim at the old quay, about 300 yards north of the bridge. After getting in, he swam about and the boys who were on the bank saw him throw up his hands whilst in comparatively shallow water and then stagger back into the deep water where he sank and did not rise again. The boys raised the alarm and a number of other boys and girls ran to the place, shouting for help. Mr James Hogan, South Street, was on the oppo-

site side of the river and hearing the alarm jumped into a boat and quickly pulled across. He divested himself of his clothes whilst going over and dived at the spot where the youth sank. Mr Hogan, who is a powerful swimmer and diver, went down no less than a dozen times and searched along the bed of the river but could not find any trance of a body. On that evening and during Monday the river was being dragged but up to the time of writing the body was not recovered.

Private Tierney belonged to the Royal Irish Regiment stationed at Queenstown where he was trained and was home on furlough. He was to return on Monday to his regiment. On Sunday morning he received Holy Communion. When his body is recovered an inquest will be heard.

Grave or Memorial Reference: On the north border of the main path. See Patrick Tierney (4729) below. Cemetery: New Ross (St Stephen) Catholic Churchyard, Co. Wexford.

TIERNEY, Patrick: Rank: Private. Regiment or Service: Royal Irish Regiment. Unit: 6th Bn. Date of death: 14 September 1916. Service No: 4729. Born in New Ross, Co. Wexford. Enlisted in Waterford while living in New Ross. Died of wounds From an article in a Wexford newspaper, 'Private Patrick Tierney, Bewley Street, New Ross has died from wounds. He was a brother to Andrew Tierney, a soldier, who was recently drowned in New Ross.' See **TIERNEY Andrew** above. Grave or Memorial Reference: II.D.61. Cemetery: La-Neuville British Cemetery, Corbie in France.

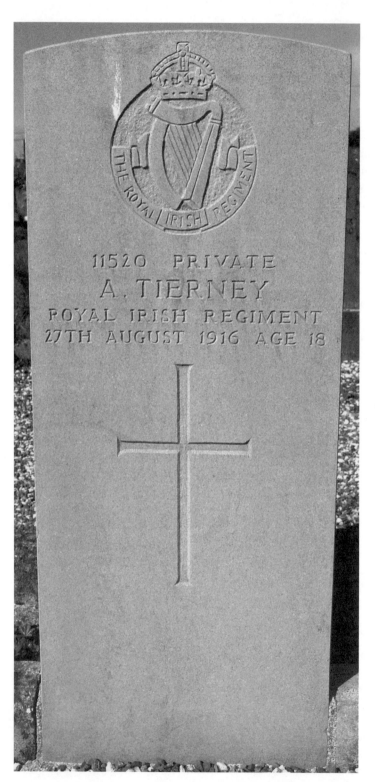

THE ROYAL IRISH REGIMENT

11520   PRIVATE
A. TIERNEY
ROYAL IRISH REGIMENT
27TH AUGUST 1916 AGE 18

Andrew
Tierney.

TIERNEY, Patrick: Rank: Private. Regiment or Service: Royal Irish Regiment. Unit: 1st Bn. Age at death: 21. Date of death: 22 October 1914. Service No: 10310. Born in Kilmore, Wexford. Enlisted in Wexford while living in Kilmore, Co. Wexford. Died at Sea.

Supplementary information: Son of Thomas and Johanna Tierney of Ballask, Kilmore, Co. Wexford. Memorial: Hollybrook Memorial, Southampton UK.

TOMPKINS, John: Rank: Private. Regiment or Service: The King's (Liverpool Regiment). Unit: 13th Bn. Formerly he was with the Royal Irish Regiment where his number was 6808. Age at death: 19. Date of death: 1 September 1918. Service No: 95072. Enlisted in Wexford while living in Wexford. Killed in action.

Supplementary information: Son of James Tompkins of Back Street, Wexford. Grave or Memorial Reference: D.23. Cemetery: Ecoust Mein British Cemetery in France.

TOOLE, David Federick Jack: Rank: Captain. Regiment or Service: Canadian Infantry (Alberta Regiment). Unit: 49th Bn. Age at death: 32. Date of death: 29 September 1918. Awards: M C and Bar.

Supplementary information: Son of William John and Magdalene Toole of Curracloe House, Curracloe, Wexford. Information from his enlistment documents: Eyes: brown. Hair: brown. Complexion: dark. Height: 5 Feet 11 Inches. 15th Light Horse, Calgary. Date of birth: 4 September 4 1886. Age on enlistment: 28 years 8 Months. Marital status: single. Name and address of next of kin: William J. Toole, Curracloe House, Wexford. Date of attestation: 6 May 1915. Location of attestation: Calgary. Occupation on enlistment: secretary. From an article in a Wexford newspaper:

Captain Toole, M. C. Killed; We deeply regret to announce the death of Capt. David Frederick Jack Toole, M. C. Canadian Infantry, who was killed in action on the 29th September, 1918. The deceased officer who was the youngest son of Mr Wm I Toole, of Curracloe House, Wexford, had been the local manager of the Canada Life Insurance Co at Calgary, Alberta, until early in 1915, when he volunteered for active service. He joined the Canadian Expeditionary Force and in the early part of 1916 he proceeded to join his Battalion, which was then in France. With the gallant Canadians Capt Toole went through much fighting, including the battle of the Somme where he won the Military Cross for gallantry in action and devotion to duty.

He was severely wounded in November 1916, and was in hospital in England for a considerable time. Subsequently he was musketry instructor at the Canadian training School, but he rejoined his Battalion at the front and served with them as Captain until his death. Capt. Toole was one of the officers selected to represent the Canadian Forces in Paris on "France's Day". Another of Mr Toole's sons, Lieut. E. T. Toole, was killed on the Somme in September, 1916, and two other sons are still serving with the Canadian forces, while a fourth son is Registrar of Recruiting for one of the Candian Districts. Much sympathy is felt with Mr Toole in his great bereavement, and the regret at the loss of his son. Who was well and popularly known in his native Country, is deep and unaffected.

Grave or Memorial Reference: I.D.4. Cemetery: Ontario Cemetery, Sains-Les-Marquion in France.

TOOLE, Edward Thomas: Rank: Lieutenant. Regiment or Service: Canadian Infantry (Alberta Regiment). Unit: 31st Bn. Age at death: 31. Date of death: 15 September 1916.

Supplementary information: Son of William John and Magdalene Toole of Curracloe House, Curracloe, Co. Wexford. Information from his enlistment documents: Eyes: hazel. Hair: black. Complexion: dark. Height: 5 Feet 10½ inches. Date of birth: 1 April 1885. Age on enlistment: 29 years, 5 months. Place of birth: Curracloe, Wexford. Marital status: single. Name and address of next of kin: William John Toole, Curracloe, Wexford. Date of attestation, 23 September 1914. Location of attestation: Valcartier. Occupation on enlistment: Civil Engineer. From an article in the *Enniscorthy Guardian*:

Lieut Edwd T Toole, Canadian Infantry, killed in action on the 25th September, was the fifth son of of Mr William I Toole of Curracloe House, Wexford. At the outbreak of the war he was in Canada and joined the Alberta Dragoons as a Trooper. He came to England with the First Canadian Contingent, and after a period of training went to France in February, 1915, and served with the cavalry there up to the following December, when he was recommended for a commission in the Canadian Infantry, with which he had been serving ever since, and had seen some heavy fighting including Neuve Chapelle, St Eloi and Ypres. He has three other brothers serving with the Canadians in France at the present.

From De Ruvigny's Roll of Honour:

TOOLE, EDWARD THOMAS, Lieut., 31st Infantry Battn., Canadian Expeditionary Force, s. of William J. Toole, of Curracloe, co. Wexford; Land Agent and Owner, by his wife, Magdalene, dau. Of William Thompson, Surgeon in Army Hospital, Madras, India; and gdson. Of Col. W. Toole, who served in the Peninsular War; b. Wexford, 1 April. 1885; educ. Liverpool College; went to Canada in 1903, where he was employed in the Engineering Department Staff of Western Canadian Power Company, and later with the Topographical Surveys Branch of the Department of Interior Office, Calgary, Alberta; volunteered for Imperial Service, and joined the 19th Alberta Dragoons as a Trooper 8 Aug. 1914, after the outbreak of the European War; came over with the 1st Contingent in Oct. ; served with the Expeditionary Force in France and Flanders from Dec. 1915; took part in many engagements, including fighting at Neuve Chapelle, St. Eloi and Ypres; obtained a commission as Lieut. In the 31st Infantry Battn. 16 Jan. 1916, and was killed in action at Courevlette, during the fighting on the Somme. 15 Sept. following. Buried there; unm.

From another article in the *People*, 1915:

It is interesting to note that Mr Toole, Curracloe House Wexford, has four sons serving in the army since the outbreak of the war. One, Trooper, E, Toole, has been in France since February with the 19th Alberta Dragoons and has done a lot of despatch and observation work out there. He joined in August 1914 and came over with the 1st contingent from Canada, and spent last winter on Salisbury Plains. Mr Archer Toole and Mr Jack Toole are Lieutenants in the 51st and 53rd Battalions, respectively and have both arrived at Shorncliffe from Canada awaiting orders to proceed to the front. Mr Archer Toole was married in May and his bride has just come over from Calgary to be with her husband till he leaves England. The last son to join is Mr Larry Toole who is still in Canada with the 96th (?) Battalion at Edmonton. These four young men gave up lucrative positions in Canada to serve with the colours.

He has no known grave but is listed on the Vimy Memorial in France.

TOOLE, Richard: Rank: Private. Regiment or Service: Royal Irish Regiment. Unit: 2nd Bn. Date of death: 14 July 1916. Service No: 3930. Born in St Mary's, Enniscorthy, Co. Wexford. Enlisted in Wexford while living in Enniscorthy. Landed in France on 7 October 1914. Information on the back of his Medal Index Card 'Pres. Died. 14 July 16'. Listed as 'Killed in action' in 'Soldiers Died in the Great War'. From an article in the *People*, 1915:

Private R Toole, R.I.R. Shannon, Enniscorthy, arrived home on Thursday for a few days rest preparatory to proceeding to the Dardanelles. He was 'gassed' some time ago in France, and after recovering from this he was buried alive by a trench falling in and covering him completely.

This caused an injury to his back, from which he has just recovered. He was rescued from his living tomb by an officer, who pulled him from beneath the bank of clay. Just as Toole was rescued a passing shell swept away the unfortunate officers head.

He has no known grave but is listed on Pier and Face 3A on the Thiepval Memorial in France.

TOOLE, William: Rank: Private. Regiment or Service: Royal Irish Regiment. Unit: 2nd Bn. Date of death: 19 October 1914. Service No: 6579. Born in St Mary's, Enniscorthy. Enlisted in Enniscorthy. Killed in action.

Supplementary information: Son of Patrick and Mary Toole. Husband of Matilda Toole of 53 St John's Street, Enniscorthy, Co. Wexford. Grave or Memorial Reference: Panel 11 and 12. Memorial: Le Touret Memorial in France.

TRAVERS, Francis: Rank: Able Seaman. Regiment or Service: Mercantile Marine. Unit: SS *Dowlais* (Cardiff). Age at death: 38. Date of death: 3 December 1917

Supplementary information: Son of Andrew and Mary Travers. Husband of Mary Travers (*née* Maher) of Duncannon, Co. Wexford. Born in Duncannon. Torpedoed by a German Submarine of Cap De Fer. There were no survivors. Memorial: Tower Hill Memorial UK.

TUMPTON, John: Rank: Private. 2nd Class. Regiment or Service: Royal Air Force. Unit: Reinforcements Wing (Blandford). Age at death: 18. Date of death: 5 December 1918. Service No: 308920.

Supplementary information: Son of Mrs Sarah Kavanagh of Fairfield, Enniscorthy, Co. Wexford. Grave or Memorial Reference: 72. Cemetery: Blandford Cemetery UK.

TWEEDY, George: Rank: Private. Regiment or Service: The King's (Liverpool Regiment). Unit: 20th Bn. Age at death: 26. Date of death: 4 August 1917. Service No: 42688. Born in Liverpool. Enlisted in Liverpool while living in Liverpool. Died of wounds.

Supplementary information: Son of John and Mary Tweedy of 11 Flinders Street Stanley Road, Liverpool. Grave or Memorial Reference: XVII. E. 16. Cemetery: Lijssenthoek Military Cemetery in Belgium.

TWEEDY, Thomas: Rank: Second Mate. Regiment or Service: Mercantile Marine. Unit: SS *Northfield* (London). Age at death: 48. Date of death: 3 March 1919.

Supplementary information: Son of the late George and Ellen Tweedy. Husband of Kate Tweedy of Portersgate, Fethard, Wexford. Born at Templetown, Wexford.

Memorial: Tower Hill Memorial UK.

TYGHE-KIRWAN, J. See **KIRWAN, JOHN T.**

V

VENEY, William Joseph: Rank: Private. Regiment or Service: Australian Infantry, AIF. Unit: D Company, 24th Bn. Age at death, 28. Date of death: 5 August 1916. Service No: 967. Born in Gorey, Co. Wicklow. Served his apprenticship with Mr Bates of Gorey. Age on arrival in Australia: 26. Enlisted in Victoria on 21 March 1916. Address on enlistment: Kongwak, Victoria. Religious Denomination: Roman Catholic. Weight: 171lbs, Complexion: browned. Eyes: brown. Hair: brown. Occupation on enlistment: Bodymaker and Mechanic. Address: North Parade, Gorey. Marital Status: Single. Parents: Frederick and Margaret Veney, North Parade, Gorey. Killed in action.

Supplementary information: Unit embarked from Melbourne, Victoria, on board HMAT A14 *Euripides* on 10 May 1915. A letter from his mother dated 12 July 1917 to the Commanding Officer of records:

'Could you let me have any information concerning Private W Veney No 967, D Coy, 24th Bn, 6th Inf Brigade, AIF Egypt. He joined the Army in Australia and I got word of his being killed in France on the 5th of August 1916. I never got any word on his belongings since I never got any separation allowance from him or money since he joined the army. I am his Mother and I would be thankful if you could let me have any information concerning him. Yours Faithfully, Mrs Margaret Varey, North Parade, Gorey, Co. Wexford.' The officer in charge of records replied stating that a search of Private Vereys Kit bag found nothing of his personal belongings. She applied for his pension but she was rejected. A note in the refusal states, 'Rejected, Unable to prove dependance on late son, your husband could earn adequate means of support if he so wished.' Also 'Rejected; Not dependant on the late M. F. for 12 months prior to enlistment.'

From an article in the *Enniscorthy Guardian*:

News has just been received that Private William Veney, son of Mr and Mrs Veney. North Parade, Gorey, has been killed in action at the front on 5th August last. The deceased left this country for Melbourne over two years ago and shortly after the outbreak of hostilities he joined the Australian Imperial Force, sailing for Egypt a few months later. He subsequently took part in the landing at Gallipoli and Suvla Bay and after the withdrawl of the troops from there he and his regiment were sent straight to France where he went through several engagements. He had been at the front over a year and escaped without a scratch till in one of the big engagements recently in which the British took the offensive where he met his death from shrapnel. Private Veney before leaving this country spent nine years with the firm Messrs Bates and Son, Gorey, as a cartmaker and subsequently motor mechanic and where he was held in the highest respect by his employed and fellow workmen.

He sent a postcard home to his people from the front on the 4th August last in which he stated he was in the best of spirits and they had not got any further account from him till the official notification from the War Office that he had been killed on the following day, the 5th August. He was a fine type of soldier and he died in a noble cause. The deepest sympathy is expended to his relatives in their great sorrow.

He has no known grave but is listed on the Australian National Memorial, Villers-Bretonneux in France.

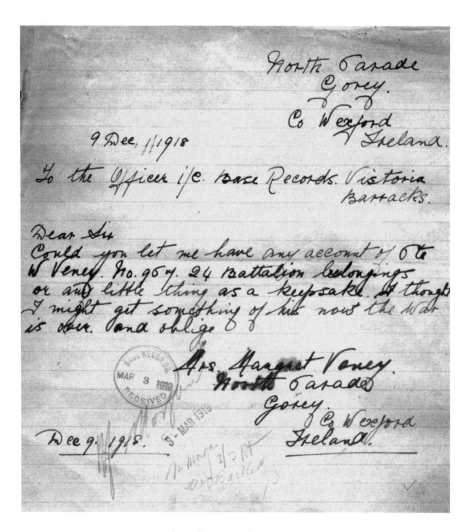

Letter by William Joseph Veney's mother.

W

WAFER, John: Rank: Able Seaman. Regiment or Service: Mercantile Marine. Unit: SS *Bandon* (Cork). Age at death: 24. Date of death: 13 April 1917.

Supplementary information: Husband of Hannah Wafer of 6 St Dominick's Terrace, Crosses Green, Cork. Born at Wexford. He has no known grave but is listed on the Tower Hill Memorial UK.

WALKER, Edward: Rank: Private. Regiment or Service: Royal Dublin Fusiliers. Unit: 10th Bn. Age at death: 24. Date of death: 20 April 1917. Service No: 27552, Born in Ballygarret, Co. Wexford. Enlisted in Gorey, Co. Wexford. Killed in action. From an article in a Wexford newspaper, 'News has been received of the death in action of Private Edward Walker, of the Royal Dublin Fusiliers. He was the son of the late Mr John Walker, of Courtown Harbour, and he lived and worked in Gorey. He had seen a great deal of active service and was home in Gorey on a short furlough about last Christmas.'

Supplementary information: Son of John and Mary Walker of 'Seaview', Courtown Harbour, Gorey, Co. Wexford. From De Ruvigny's Roll of Honour:

> son of the late John Walker, by his wife, Mary (Seamount, Courtown, Gorey), dau, of John Redmond, of Ballymoney; b, Courtown Harbour, Co. Wexford, 1 May, 1893; educ, Riverchapel; was a Seaman in the Naval Reserve; joined the Dublin Fusiliers 31 Aug, 1916; served with the Expeditionary Force in France and Flanders from jan, 1917, and was killed in action there 10 April following. Buried where he fell.

Grave or Memorial Reference: Bay 9. Memorial: Arras Memorial in France.

WALKER, John: Rank: Lance Corporal. Regiment or Service: Kings Own Yorkshire Light Infantry. Unit: 2/4th Bn. Date of death: 28 August 1918. Service No: 63380. Born in Gorey, Co. Wexford. Enlisted in Gorey, Jersey. Died of wounds. Age at death: 28. From an article in the *People*, 1915:

> Gorey man's letter – R.I.R. Gallantry. Private Patrick Howard. C Company, Royal Irish Regiment, writing from the front to his step-mother, Mrs Canavan, Thomas Street, Gorey, states; "We are having a big battle and we gained the day. The Germans had gas and turpentine fumes, and lost very heavily.
>
> We made a big capture of men and guns. It is a pity that all the Gorey boys are not here. There was only myself and J Walker in it. Our Captain got wounded. I am writing this in the trenches under heavy shell fire. I am sending you the telegram that the Commander-in-Chief sent to our Adjutant on our great victory and about the R. I. Regiment and the gallant stand they made. Get the letter published in the newspapers." Copy message received by Adjutant, Royal Irish, from Commander-in-

Chief, dated April; "Please convey my congratulations to the 12th Brigade on their gallant and brilliant repulse of the enemy last night in spite of of gas fumes and poisoned shells, and I think the artillery which supported them also deserve great praise."

Grave or Memorial Reference: A. 28. Cemetery: Ligny-Sur-Canche British Cemetery in France.

WALKER, Thomas Kynston: Rank: Lt. Regiment or Service: Irish Guards. Unit: 1st Company, 1st Bn. Date of death: 24 April 1916. Age at death, 19. Born in Tykillen, Co. Wexford. Killed in action.
Supplementary information: Son of Capt. T.J. and B.L. Walker of Tykillen, Wexlord. From an article in a Wexford newspaper:

The sad news reached Wexford on Friday that Lieut T.K. Walker, son of the late Captain T.J. Walker and Mrs Walker, Tykillen, had been killed in action. The gallant young fellow who, like every member of his family, is exceedingly popular in Wexford town and district, pluckily volunteered for active service shortly after the outbreak of war. His high qualifications speedily secured him a commission, and he was gazetted to the Irish Guards, with which his brother was already serving.

Having completed his training he was drafted out with the Guards to France, where he took part in many big engagements in which the Irish Guards upheld their reputation as the crack regiment of the army. Amongst other big engagements in which he figured was the Battle of Loos, in which his regiment shed further

lustre on the glorious traditions of the fighting race. On Friday evening the sad announcement came that he had been killed in action. No details concerning the unfortunate event, save that it occurred on the 24th April, are forthcoming, but we may be sure that the gallant young Lieutenant, who was scarcely out of his teens when he went into the firing line died as only a brave man could. The intelligence of his death was contained in the following notification from the war office, 'Deeply regret to inform you that Lieut T.K. Walker, Irish Guards, was killed in action on April 24th. Lord Kitchener expresses his sympathy'.

The paragraph below this continues:

A PATHETIC INCIDENT.

A very pathetic incident was witnessed on Saturday morning outside the offices of Messrs M. J. O'Connor and Co, Solicitors, Georges Street, Wexford. Mrs Walker of Tykillen, who had just received the sad intelligence that her son had been killed in action, came into Mr O'Connor in order that the tidings might be conveyed to her other son, Captain Charles Walker, who had been in England recuperating from the effects of gas. As Mrs Walker was about to dispatch the wire Capt, Walker met him and a moment later a touching scene took place when the Mother confronted her only surviving son. Their meeting was a sad one and Capt Walker, having sympathised with his Mother went straight to his hotel, donned his uniform and tendered his services to Col French.

One would have thought that Captain Walker would have spent some time at home with his widowed Mother and Sister; but noblesse oblege; duty called him. The sympathy of all the citizens are extended to the family in their sad bereavement.

From De Ruvigny's Roll of Honour:

WALKER, THOMAS KYNASTON, Lieut., 2nd, attd. 1st Battn. The Irish Guards, 2nd s. of the late Thomas Joseph Walker, 1st Royal Dragoons, for nine years Master of the County Wexford Foxhounds, by his wife, Blanche Louisa (Tykillen, Wexford), yst. Dau. Of Lieut. -Col. S. H. Smith; b. Wexford, 4 Nov. 1896; educ. Dublin, and abroad; entered the Royal Military College in April, 1915; was gazetted 2nd Lieut, 2nd Battn. The Irish Guards in July, and promoted Lieut. 28 Oct. 1915; served with the Expeditionary Force in France and Flanders from Aug. 1915, when he joined the 1st Battn. ; took part in the fighting at Hill 60, the Hohenzollern Redoubt, Loos and Poperinghe, and was killed in action near Ypres 24 April, 1916, by an aerial torpedo. . Buried in the cemetery on the Ypres-Menin Road; unm.

Grave or Memorial Reference: I.L.1. Cemetery: Menin Road South Military Cemetery in Belgium. Also on the Walker Memorial in Killurin Church of Ireland, Co. Wexford.

WALLACE, Mark: Rank: Private. Regiment or Service: Irish Guards. Unit: No. 3 Coy. 1st Bn. Age at death: 34. Date of death: 31 March 1918. Service No: 10425. Born in Bannow, Co. Wexford. Enlisted in Wexford. Died of wounds.
Supplementary information: Son of Bernard and Annie Wallace of Cullenstown, Bannow, Co. Wexford. Grave or Memorial Reference: II.A. 2. Cemetery: Bac-Ac-Du-Sud British Cemetery, Bailleulval in France.

WALSH, James: Rank: Lance Corporal. Regiment or Service: Royal Irish Rifles. Unit: 2nd Bn. Age at death: 27. Date of death: 19 January 1916. Service No: 8631. Born in New Ross, Co. Wexford, Enlisted in Bathgate Linlithgow while living in Curraghmore, Co. Wexford. Killed in action. From an article in the *Enniscorthy Guardian*, June 1915:

Arthurstown Mans letter. James Walsh of Curraghmore, Arthurstown, writing home to Sergeant Fitzgerald, R.I.C., Arthurstown, from the front, thanking the Sergeant for the nice pipe which he sent him, and which he appreciated so highly, states that he gets a chance of hearing Mass nearly every Sunday, and that they have a very nice and brave Priest as Chaplain-Father Gill, from Dublin. This Priest is so brave that he only laughs at the bullets, and saw him celebrating Mass with the shells flying around and did not take any notice of them. He hears confessions everywhere, and you could see the soldiers walk up to him, kneel down, and he hears their confessions.

Continuing, the writer says that in fact it is easier to get prepared for death there than at home. The Priest encourages them all the time, and tells the soldiers of his Regiment to keep their hearts up, and their heads down, so as to avoid the bullets. Such encouragement would keep up the heart of any soldier. Mass is celebrated in all kinds of places. One time in an old house, another time in a hut or in a brick hill, in fact, any place that is convenient. This priest got wounded on the leg some time ago, but it did not terrify him. Even the soldiers of different religion admire his pluck. Concluding, the writer states he is well and will not lose that pipe from Arthurstown at any cost.

Supplementary information: Brother of Mrs Annie Lacey of Curraghmore, Ramsgrange, Co. Wexford. Grave or Memorial Reference: Panel 9. Memorial: Ploegsteert Memorial in Belgium.

WALSH, Michael: Rank: Stoker 1ˢᵗ Class. Regiment or Service: Royal Navy. Unit: HMS *Lobelia*. Age at death: 28. Date of death: 18 January 1919. Service No: K/31017.

Supplementary information: Son of Matthew and Mary Anne Walsh of Rochestown, Taghmon, Co. Wexford. Grave or Memorial Reference: 36. Cemetery: Piraeus Naval and Air Consular Cemetery in Greece.

WALSH, Nicholas: Rank: Private. Regiment or Service: Irish Guards. Unit: No. 2 Coy. 1ˢᵗ Bn. Age at death: 28. Date of death: 2 August 1917. Service No: 10775. Born in Duncannon, Co Waterford. Enlisted in Whitehall in Middlesex. Killed in action.

Supplementary information: Son of Michael and Caroline Walsh of 13 Ponton Street, Nine Elms Lane, Battersea, London. Native of Duncannon, Co. Wexford. From an article in a Wexford newspaper:

Duncannon Soldier Killed; Private

Nicholas Walsh, of Duncannon, has been officially reported killed in action at the front, and the announcement has caused profound regret amongst a wide circle of friends. He joined the R. I. Regiment at the outbreak of the war and had since been on active service. In notifying his death to his relatives, his Captain paid a glowing tribute to the deceased's gallantry.

Grave or Memorial Reference: Panel 11. Memorial: Ypres (Menin Gate) Memorial in Belgium.

WALSH, Patrick: Rank: Sergeant. Regiment or Service: Grenadier Guards. Unit: 3ʳᵈ Bn. Age at death: 26. Date of death: 23 August 1918. Service No: 19488. Born in Pearces Town, Co. Wexford. Enlisted in Maesteg. Killed in action. He won the Military Medal and is listed in the *London Gazette*.

Supplementary information: Son of Mr and Mrs John Walsh of Killinick, Co. Wexford. Grave or Memorial Reference: I.H.3. Cemetery: Douchy-Les-Ayette British Cemetery in France.

WALSH, Patrick: Rank: Private. Regiment or Service: Royal Irish Regiment. Unit: 2ⁿᵈ Bn. Date of death: 19 October 1914. Service No: 5427. Born in St Mary's, Enniscorthy, Co. Wexford. Enlisted in Wexford while living in Enniscorthy. Killed in action. He has no known grave but is listed on Panels 11 and 12 on the Le Touret Memorial in France.

WALSH, Thomas: Rank: Private. Regiment or Service: Leinster Regiment.

Unit: 2nd Bn. Age at death: 35. Date of death: 1 October 1918. Service No: 5373. Born in New Ross, Co. Wexford. Enlisted in Dublin while living in Castleknock, Co Dublin. Killed in action.

Supplementary information: Son of Michael Walsh of New Ross, Go. Wexford. Husband of Bridgid Walsh of Church View, Castleknock, Co. Dublin. Grave or Memorial Reference: XIV.E.13. Cemetery: Hooge Crater Cemetery in Belgium.

WESTROPP-DAWSON, Walter Henry Mountiford: Rank: 2 Lt. Regiment or Service: Cheshire Regiment. Unit: 2nd Battalion. Age at death: 22. Date of death: 24 May 1915. Enlisted in Waterford. Killed in action. His medals and death plaque were sold in an English auction house in 2004. From an article in The *Enniscorthy Guardian*, 'County Wexford Officer reported killed. Second-Lieutenant W.H.M. Westropp-Dawson, 15th Hussars, who is unofficially reported killed in France on 25th ult, was the eldest son of Mr F Westropp-Dawson, Charlesfort, County Wexford.'

Supplementary information: Son of Frank and L.C. Westropp-Dawson, of 'Frondeg' Holyhead. He has no known grave but is listed on Panel 19-22 on the Ypres (Menin Gate) Memorial in Belgium.

WHELAN, C.P.: (Also listed as **WHELAN, Patrick:**) Rank: Lance Corporal. Regiment or Service: Leinster Regiment. Unit: 2nd Bn. Date of death: 27 August 1917. Service No: 5652. Born in Wexford. Enlisted in Tullamore, Kings County while living in Enniscorthy.

Died of wounds. Grave or Memorial Reference: IV.B.6. Cemetery: The Huts Cemetery in Belgium.

WHELAN, Edward: Rank: Private. Regiment or Service: Irish Guards. Unit: 1st Bn. Date of death: 8 May 1918. Service No: 12309. Born in Gorey, Co. Wexford. Enlisted in Cardiff, Glam while living in Killen, Co. Wexford. Killed in action. Grave or Memorial Reference: A. 9. Cemetery: Ayette British Cemetery in France.

WHELAN, John: Rank: Stoker. Regiment or Service: Royal Naval Reserve. Unit: HMS *Diana*. Age at death: 27. Date of death: 10 July 1918. Service No: 7034S.

Supplementary information: Son of John and Margaret Whelan of Upper King Street, Wexford. Grave or Memorial Reference: 29. Memorial: Plymouth Naval Memorial UK.

WHELAN, John: Rank: Private. Regiment or Service: Royal Irish Rifles. Unit: 1st Bn. Date of death: 5 July 1918. Service No: 10514. Born in Wexford, Co. Wexford. Enlisted in Wexford. Died. Grave or Memorial Reference: I.D.48. Cemetery: Terlincthun British Cemetery, Wimille in France.

WHELAN, Matthew: Rank: Private. Regiment or Service: Royal Dublin Fusiliers. Unit: 6th Bn. Age at death: 38. Date of death: 9 March 1917. Service No: 3/24672 and 24672. Born in Ballindaggin, Co. Wexford. Enlisted in Enniscorthy, Co. Wexford. Died in the

Balkans.

Supplementary information: Son of Thomas and Annie Whelan of Kiltealy, Emniscorthy, Co. Wexford. Grave or Memorial Reference: E.EA.A.700. Cemetery: Addolorata Cemetery in Malta.

WHELAN, Michael: Rank: Private. Regiment or Service: Royal Irish Regiment. Unit: 2nd Bn. Date of death: 19 October 1914. Service No: 8917. Born in Piercestown, Co. Wexford (Rathaspick, Co. Wexford). Enlisted in Wexford. Killed in action. He has no known grave but is listed on Panels 11 and 12 on the Le Touret Memorial in France.

WHELAN, Michael: Rank: Private. Regiment or Service: Royal Irish Regiment. Unit: 2nd Bn. Age at death: 30. Date of death: 19 October 1914. Service No: 7389. Born in St Mary's, New Ross, Co. Wexford. Enlisted in New Ross. Killed in action.

Supplementary information: Son of the late James and Catherine Whelan of 28 Neville Street, New Ross, Co. Wexford. From an article in the *People* and the *Enniscorthy Guardian:*

Private Michael Whelan, Neville Street, New Ross was killed at the front recently. He was missing for a good while back and at first it was thought he was a prisoner of war, but it transpired it was another man of the same name had been captured. He was amongst the first batch that left Ross after the outbreak of the war. He was an army reserve man.

Grave or Memorial Reference: Panel 11

and 12. Memorial: Le Touret Memorial in France.

WHELAN, Patrick: (Also listed as **WHELAN, C. P.)** Rank: Lance Corporal. Regiment or Service: Leinster Regiment. Unit: 2nd Bn. Date of death: 27 August 1917. Service No: 5652. Born in Wexford. Enlisted in Tullamore, King's County while living in Enniscorthy. Died of wounds. Grave or Memorial Reference: IV. B. 6. Cemetery: The Huts Cemetery in Belgium.

WHELAN, Peter: Rank: Private. Regiment or Service: Irish Guards. Unit: 2nd Bn. Age at death: 22. Date of death: 15 September 1916. Service No: 6965. Born in Rathdrum, Co. Wexford. Enlisted in Wexford. Killed in action.

Supplementary information: Son of Mr. J. and Mrs M.R. Whelan of 38 Parnell Street, Wexford. Grave or Memorial Reference: Pier and Face 7 D. Memorial: Thiepval Memorial in France.

WHELAN, Richard: Rank: Private. Regiment or Service: Irish Guards. Unit: 1st Bn. Age at death: 23. Date of death: 28 June 1916. Service No: 6094. Born in Wexford, Co. Wexford. Enlisted in Liverpool. Killed in action.

Supplementary information: Son of Richard and Catherine Whelan of 108A, Tatlock Street, Liverpool. Grave or Memorial Reference: I.Q.11. Cemetery: Essex Farm Cemetery in Belgium.

WHELAN, Thomas: Rank: Private. Regiment or Service: Royal Munster

Fusiliers. Unit: 1st Bn and Depot. Date of death: 23 November 1917. Service No: 4089. Born in Enniscorthy. Enlisted in Temple-More, Co Tipperary while living in Limerick. Died at home. Grave or Memorial Reference: W. U. 359. Cemetery: Newcastle-Upon-Tyne (St Andrews and Jesmond) Cemetery, UK.

James White.

WHITBY, Patrick: (also listed as **WHITTY, Patrick**) Rank: Private. Regiment or Service: Connaught Rangers. Unit: 6th Bn. Formerly he was with the Leinster Regiment where his number was 4619. Date of death: 21 March 1918. Service No: 18199. Born in Wexford, Co. Wexford. Enlisted in Wexford while living in Wexford. Killed in action. Grave or Memorial Reference: Special Memorial 2. Cemetery: Villiers-Faucon Communal Cemetery Extension in France.

WHITE, Edward: Rank: Able Seaman. Regiment or Service: Mercantile Marine. Unit: SS *Main* (Cardiff). Age at death: 38. Date of death: 9 October 1917.

Supplementary information: Son of the late Patrick and Margaret White. Born at Kilrane, Wexford. Memorial: Tower Hill Memorial UK.

WHITE, James: Rank: Able Seaman. Regiment or Service: Mercantile Marine. Unit: SS *Diomed* (Liverpool). Sunk by a Germa Submarine torpedo. Age at death: 25. Date of death: 22 August 1915.

Supplementary information: Born at Wexford. Memorial: Tower Hill Memorial UK.

WHITE, John: Rank: Sapper. Regiment or Service: Corps of Royal Engineers. Unit: Railways (118th Railway Company). Date of death: 16 November 1918. Age at death: 31. Service No: WR/215423, WR/215433. Born in Rainsgringe, Co. Wexford. Enlisted in Glasgow. Died of wounds at home. Grave or Memorial Reference: T. 3. Cemetery: Bathgate Cemetery, West Lothian, UK.

WHITE, John: Rank: Lance Corporal. Regiment or Service: Irish Guards. Unit: 1st Bn. He won the Military Medal and is listed in the *London Gazette*. Date of death: 10 October 1917. Service No: 2695. Born in Wexford, Co. Wexford. Enlisted in Whitehall, Middlesex while living in Johnstown, Co Kilkenny. Killed in action. Grave or Memorial Reference: VII.F.17. Cemetery: Artillery Wood Cemetery in Belgium.

WHITE, Patrick: Rank: Rifleman. Regiment or Service: Royal Irish Rifles. Unit: 1st Bn. Date of death: 16 August 1917. Service No: 9511. Born in Wexford, Co. Wexford. Enlisted in Wexford. Killed in action. Has no known grave but is commemorated on Panel 138 to 140 and 162 to 162A and 163A. Memorial; Tyne Cot Memorial in Belgium.

WHITE, Patrick Foley: Rank: Sergeant. Regiment or Service: Royal Horse Artillery. Unit: 'D' Bty. 14th Bde. Age at death: 26. Date of death: 5 September 1916. Service No: 35685. Born in Clonmel and enlisted there also. Killed in action.

Supplementary information: Son of Alexander White (R.Q.M.S, Royal Artillery), and Margaret White, of 18 Dillon Street, Clonmel, Co. Tipperary. From an article in the *Enniscorthy Guardian*:

Sergeant of R. F. A. Killed in action; News has just been received of the death in action of Sergeant Patrick White, R. F.A., brother of Messrs E.V. White and Alexander White, Rosslare Harbour.

The deceased enlisted in his native town of Clonmel in 1905, and had been in France since the beginning of the war. He had been in practically every engagement and was in the retreat from Mons. Mrs White, mother of the deceased, has received the following letter from Lieutenant Roger C Reynold, R. F.A., relative to the death of her son on September 5th—"Dear Mrs White. I regret to have to inform you of the death of your son. He was hit by a bursting shell at about 8pm, on the evening of September 5th. He was immediately carried by Gunner Hood, of his detachment, to a dressing station nearby, but died shortly after reaching it. I know how you will feel this loss as he was universally popular throughout the Battery.

He has been in my section for nearly two years and came with me from the 35th Battery when throughout the whole time I have found him absolutely trustworthy and willing, and always ready to do any work that was wanted, so you can guess how I miss him from my section. The Battery has had a very bad time in this position and our casualties have been big, but throughout the time No1 Sub-section, of which your son was in charge, has been very cheerful chiefly owing to your sons presence. Whenever I saw them I always found him cheering them up and heartening the men in their work. I am sending out a parcel containing various little things that he always carried with him.

He seemed to have no money with him. He has been buried beside five of his comrades of this Battery in Caterpiller Valley near Montauban, and I have had a small cross erected in his memory. Please accept my sincere regrets and let me know if there is anything further I can do to help you bear your loss. Believe me, yours very truly. Lieutenant Roger C Reynold, R. F.A.'

Grave or Memorial Reference: VI.A.6. Cemetery: Quarry Cemetery, Montauban in France.

WHITEHEAD, William: Rank: Private. Regiment or Service: Welsh Guards. Unit: 1st Bn. Date of death: 13

April 1917. Service No: 2097. Born in Kilscorran, Wexford. Enlisted in Carmarthen. Died. Grave or Memorial Reference: O.XIII.F.7. Cemetery: St Sever Cemetery Extension, Rouen in France.

WHITFORD, Myles: Rank: Second Lieutenant. Regiment or Service: Royal Irish Rifles. Unit: 7th Bn. Age at death: 29. Date of death: 28 April 1916. Killed in action.

Supplementary information: Son of John and Mary E. Whitford of Enniscorthy, Co. Wexford. From an article in the *Enniscorthy Guardian* in 1916:

Mr Thomas Whitford, Templeshannon, Enniscorthy, has received official intimation that his brother, Lieutenant Myles Whitford, Royal Irish Rifles, has been killed in France. The young officer fell on April 30th. In conveying the sad news, Lord Kitchener expressed his deep regret and sympathy with Lieutenant Whitford's family. Mr Whitford, who held the rank of Second Lieutenant in the Royal Irish Refles, joined the colours on March 23rd 1915, proceeding to Fermoy, where he was attached to the Cadet Corps. He was gazetted Second Lieutenant in the autumn of the same year, and went to the front a few days before last Christmas. He spent a weeks holiday in Enniscorthy about six weeks ago, after which, he again returned to the trenches. Previous to joining the colours, Mr Whitford belonged to the Enniscorthy National Volunteers, Vinegar Hill Rangers. Much sympathy is felt with his brother, Mr Myles Whitford [*sic*] and the other members of his family. He was nephew to Mr

Myles Whitford.

James Donohoe, J. P. Enniscorthy.

He was a most popular member of the Enniscorthy Musical Society, taking part in several operas. He also appeared with distinction as a member of the Pioneers Dramatic Class. His death is universally regretted by all classes in the town. R. I. P.

Grave or Memorial Reference: II.F.20. Cemetery: Vermelles British Cemetery in France.

WHITTY, John: Rank: Private. Regiment or Service: Irish Guards. Unit: 1st Bn. Age at death: 31. Date of death: 9 October 1917. Service No: 10942. Born in Sutton, Co. Wexford. Enlisted in Waterford. Killed in action.

Supplementary information: Son of Mrs Mary Whitty of Ballybrazil, Campile, Co. Wexford. Grave or Memorial Reference: Panel 10 to 11. Memorial: Tyne Cot Memorial in Belgium.

WHITTY, Patrick: (also listed as **WHITBY, Patrick**) Rank: Private. Regiment or Service: Connaught Rangers. Unit: 6th Bn. Formerly he was with the Leinster Regiment where his number was 4619. Date of death: 21 March 1918. Service No: 18199. Born in Wexford Enlisted in Wexford while living in Wexford. Killed in action. Grave or Memorial Reference: Special Memorial 2. Cemetery: Villiers-Faucon Communal Cemetery Extension in France.

WHITTY, Stephen: Rank: Able Seaman. Regiment or Service: Mercantile Marine. Unit: SS *Coningbeg* (Glasgow). Torpedoed by German Submarine U-62. There were no survivors. Age at death: 44. Date of death: 18 December 1917.

Supplementary information: Son of Thomas and the late Anastatia Whitty. Husband of Margaret Whitty (*née* Hayes) of 31 Roanmore Road, Ballybricke, Waterford. Born at Ballyhack, Co. Wexford. Memorial: Tower Hill Memorial UK.

WHITTY, Valentine (**Val**): Rank: Rifleman. Regiment or Service: Royal Irish Rifles. Unit: 'B' Coy. 1st Bn. Age at death: 23. Date of death: 19 April 1916. Service No: 4629. Born in New Ross,. Enlisted in New Ross while living in Irishtown, New Ross. Killed in action. There is a photograph in the *Enniscorthy Guardian* of Private Whitty but it is not clear enough to add.

Supplementary information: Son of John and Mary Ellen Whitty of Church Street, New Ross, Co. Wexford. Grave or Memorial Reference: I.J.4. Cemetery: Becourt Military Cemetery, Becordel-Becourt in France.

WILLIS, John Henry: Rank: Company Quartermaster Sergeant. Regiment or Service: London Regiment (London Irish Rifles). Unit: 18th Bn. Date of death: 25 September 1915. Service No: 219. Born in Gorey, Co. Wexford. Enlisted in London while living in North London. Killed in action. He has no known grave but is listed on Panel 133 on the Loos Memorial in France.

Y

YOUNG, William: Rank: Engineman. Regiment or Service: Royal Naval Reserve Unit: HMS Drifter *Speedwell V*. Date of death: 28 October 1916. Service No: 2031/ES. Grave or Memorial Reference: South East of the Church. Cemetery, Kilscoran Church of Irelaland Cemetery in Tagoat.

William Young.

Z

ZIMBER, Richard Frederick: Rank: Rifleman. Regiment or Service: King's Royal Rifle Corps. Unit: 4ᵗʰ Bn. Age at death: 28. Date of death: 8 May 1915. Service No: R/10201. Born in New Ross, Co. Wexford. Enlisted in Liverpool while living in Wexford. Killed in action in Ypres.

Supplementary information: (Served as **CAIRNS**), Son of Aaron and Elizabeth Zimber of New Ross,. Grave or Memorial Reference: Panel 51 and 53. Memorial: Ypres (Menin Gate) Memorial in Belgium.

The final word we will leave to Poet Laurence Binyon.
From the poem 'For The Fallen'

They shall grow not old, as we that are left grow old:
Age shall not weary them, nor the years condemn.
At the going down of the sun and in the morning
We will remember them.